Controversial Issues in Human Behavior in the Social Environment

Edited by

Martin Bloom
University of Connecticut

Waldo C. Klein
University of Connecticut

Series Editors

Eileen Gambrill

Robert Pruger

University of California, Berkeley

ALLYN AND BACON

Boston • London • Toronto • Sydney • Tokyo • Singapore

Series Editor, Social Work: Judy Fifer
Editor-in-Chief, Social Sciences: Karen Hanson
Editorial Assistant: Mary Visco
Marketing Manager: Quinn Perkson
Sr. Editorial Production Administrator: Susan McIntyre
Editorial Production Service: Ruttle, Shaw & Wetherill, Inc.
Composition Buyer: Linda Cox
Manufacturing Buyer: Suzanne Lareau
Cover Administrator: Suzanne Harbison

Library of Congress Cataloging-in-Publication Data
Controversial issues in human behavior in the social environment /
    edited by Martin Bloom, Waldo C. Klein.
        p.   cm.
    Includes bibliographical references.
    ISBN 0-205-19339-0
    1. Social psychology.   I. Bloom, Martin.   II. Klein,
Waldo C.
HM251.C76   1997
302–dc20   96-20610
                                                                 CIP

Printed in the United States of America
10 9 8 7 6 5 4 3 2 1   01 00 99 98 97 96

Contents

Preface

Democracy itself is founded on the belief that out of vigorous debate there can emerge vital new ideas, or old ideas presented in clearer form. So too, we have established a forum for debate of perennial controversies in that broad territory called Human Behavior in the Social Environment (HBSE). Consider these key ideas and their alternatives: neo-positivism, stage theories of development, a strengths perspective, critical thinking, empirical support for conceptual models, obsolete information, minority issues, the place of ethics in a world of facts and ideas, and political correctness, among others. These have been the rock on which some instructors build their courses, whereas for others, these have been the rocky shoals on which old ideas have collided with new. We follow a classical debate format—first the defenders of a debate topic make their statement in its support, followed by a brief rebuttal of the opposition; then, the opposition makes its main statement against the debate topic, followed by a brief rebuttal of the defenders. If we stimulate readers to face these challenges so as to decide more clearly how they themselves think, then we will have succeeded in this volume.

Our debaters include some of the foremost contributors in HBSE, and some new contributors who we have no doubt will continue to provide challenges in the future. It is to all of these contributors that we dedicate this book. Faced with sharp page limitations, yet directed to challenge the imagination as they provided information for the mind, this group of social work scholars has performed marvelously. We note in sadness that one contributor, Carel Germain, died shortly after completing her initial statement. Once again she has taught us that life is short, and art, and the artful presentation of great ideas, is long.

Is Neo-Positivism a Suitable Epistemological Framework for HBSE Courses?

EDITOR'S NOTE: One of the most far-reaching controversies of our time concerns the philosophy of science framework that guides of our theorizing, research, and practice. The current dominant framework, some version of logical positivism, has been under widespread attack for the past half-century or more. The social work variation of this epistemological discussion is here termed neopositivism or postpositivism, and yet they lead to the same fundamental questions of what can we know and what do we know?

William J. Reid, Ph.D., is Professor, School of Social Welfare, Rockefeller College of Public Policy and Affairs, University at Albany, State University of New York. His most recent books are *Qualitative Research in Social Work* (co-edited with Edmund Sherman) and *Generalist Practice: A Task-Centered Approach* (with Eleanor Tolson and Charles Garvin), both published by Columbia University Press.

Mary K. Rodwell, Ph.D., associate professor at the School of Social Work, Virginia Commonwealth University (VCU), is a major contributor to the new alternative epistemology in social work, and co-author of *Evaluating Social Programs* as well as publications on child welfare, philosophy of science, and international social work. Her most recent article is one product of her Fulbright research with street children in El Salvador, Bahia, and Brazil.

John Bricout, M.S.W., is a doctoral student at VCU working on natural supports and coworker relations in supported employment.

YES

WILLIAM J. REID

I shall begin the development of my "yes" position by clarifying what I mean by "postpositivism," one of the many philosophical movements that has emerged in the wake of logical positivism. Logical positivism, a dominant school of thought in the philosophy of science in the earlier part of this century but largely abandoned by the 1960s, was an unsuccessful attempt to ground science in the bedrock of sensory observation.

Postpositivism

In a sense, postpositivist epistemology could be thought of as embracing the entire gamut of points of view in philosophy of science since the fall of logical positivism, and sometimes the term is used that way. Following Phillips (1987, 1990); Guba (1990); Fraser, Taylor, Jackson, and O'Jack (1991), and others, I use the term to refer to epistemologies that share certain features. They tend to be realist in orientation; that is, they hold that "the external world exists independently of our sense experience, ideation, and volition, and that it can be known" (Bunge, 1993). Although the nature of this world, which includes human behavior, may be difficult to discern exactly, it is possible to obtain knowledge about it that is at least approximately true. Truth is viewed as a "regulative ideal" (Phillips, 1990, p. 43). Inquiry is aimed at determining what the truth is, even though one may fall short of revealing it completely. The position that phenomena exist independently of human perceptions makes it possible to obtain knowledge about them that is reasonably objective, that is relatively free from human bias. Even though our perceptions of reality may be filtered through our theories (Hanson, 1958) and may not always be based on observational data, it is possible to achieve close approximations to what is real through rules of logic and inference (Erwin, 1992). It is further recognized that phenomena can be construed in many different ways by different actors, but these constructions are regarded as differing viewpoints, not "multiple truths." Although what is true can be extraordinarily complex it should be contrasted with what is false rather than with "alternative truths." Truth or valid knowledge must ultimately be backed by evidence that can be appraised through such standards as corroboration and freedom from error (Reid, 1994). Although scientific knowledge can be built in many ways, incrementally or through paradigm shifts (Kuhn, 1970), its building over the long term is progressive (Kitcher, 1993). That is, we know more about the world and its human inhabitants now than a century ago, and we will know much more than we do now a century hence. However, progress about knowledge of human behavior and its social environments must necessarily be slow. The phenomena in question are difficult to study and in constant flux; much of the knowledge gained may be outdated by the march of events. Moreover, the main vehicles for advancing this kind of knowledge—behavioral and social theories—are difficult to put to definitive tests. It is recognized that theories are "underdetermined" by the evidence (Hesse, 1980); that is, they can be endlessly adjusted to avoid disconfirmation in the face of negative findings. Still in continual testing over the long term, some theories will prove to be superior to their rivals with respect to their predictive and explanatory powers; as various examples in the history of science have demonstrated, these superior theories will survive, and their rivals will be discarded (Brekke, 1986; Lakatos, 1972; Reid, 1994).

The kind of postpositivist epistemology I have described is not watered-down logical positivism. It is rather an epistemology that has its roots in philosophical movements that antedated logical positivism, such as realism (which, by the way, the logical positivists opposed), or that were never apart of logical positivism, such as pragmatism. In addition, postpositivist epistemology has incorporated many of the insights of philosophers of science that have emerged since the heyday of logical positivism. Indeed the works of some of these philosophers—Phillips, Hanson, Kuhn, Kitcher, Hesse, and Lakatos—were cited in my discussion of postpositivism.

Finally it is important to stress that practicing researchers have never depended on logical positivism or, for that matter, any philosophy of science, to guide their work. The basic ideas that researchers use have evolved from the rational, problem-solving capabilities of the human mind. As Dewey (1938) once put it, "Scientific subject-matter and procedures grow out of the direct problems and methods of common sense—but enormously refine, expand, and liberate the contents and the agencies at the disposal of common sense" (p. 66). That philosophers are needed to provide foundations or rationales for the practice of research is, as Rorty (1979) has said, an invention of the philosophers themselves.

In brief, postpositivism does not attempt to lay the foundations of science in sense experience or other presumed certainties. It holds that scientific knowledge, as well as the means of obtaining it, are fallible and open to correction. It recognizes that some of its key assumption, for example, those supporting a realist epistemology, are, in the final analysis, unprovable.

Although most research that relates to this epistemology is quantitative, the epistemology itself is by no means limited to quantitative methods. Indeed, much qualitative research has been conducted in accordance with the principles and assumptions of the kind of postpositivist epistemology that I have described. The point merits some comment because a counter-position to the one I have taken might stress the insufficiency of quantitative methods in studying human behavior.

In my view, a new epistemology is not needed to rationalize qualitative methodology. Such methodology can be seen as an essential tool of inquiry available to all researchers. If so, issues of whether to use qualitative methods and how to use them become largely methodological. As I have argued elsewhere (Reid, 1974; 1994), qualitative methods have much to contribute to social work knowledge, and there is much to be gained from their greater use, including their use in combination with quantitative methods.

However, the contributions of each need to be examined in relation to a single set of standards to evaluate their relative knowledge yields and to facilitate their differential use. Thus, the measures obtained from an objective test may be distorted by the respondent's social desirability bias. Participant observation may be able to avoid this form of bias but may be susceptible to observer bias. The shortcomings of a study using either quantitative or qualitative methods need to be made clear, not as a basis for discarding its findings but to know how much confidence to place in the knowledge produced.

An Epistemology for a Human Development Course

For purposes of discussion, I shall take a human development course to mean a course in a school of social work covering basic aspects of human behavior and the social environment (HBSE). In my view, an HBSE course need not be limited to any particular epistemological framework. Here, as elsewhere in social work education, it is possible to be pluralistic in use of frameworks (Reamer, 1993). It is also quite possible to teach an HBSE course without *explicit* reference to *any* epistemological framework, and my guess would be that that is how such courses are usually taught. It is also reasonable to assume that most HBSE courses make *implicit* use of one kind of epistemological framework or another, if only through the point of view the instructor conveys about the knowledge being taught.

Whether it is used implicitly or explicitly, as the sole framework, or one of several, the postpostivist paradigm, I would argue, makes an appropriate fit to the purposes and content of the usual HBSE course. (To justify my "yes" position, I need not deny that other paradigms might also make appropriate fits.) Support for this argument has several facets.

To begin with, a major purpose of the typical HBSE course is to familiarize students with basic knowledge about human behavior and the social environment. Much of this knowledge is based on research conducted within the kind of epistemological framework I have described. Moreover, critiques and reviews of this research, which may occur within HBSE texts, customarily draw on the assumptions of this framework. Studies may be criticized for making use of measures that lack objectivity or for design flaws that result in erroneous findings, that is, findings that lack truth. That a postpositivist epistemology fits well to the research base of HBSE courses is certainly an argument for the appropriateness of its use as an organizing paradigm.

However, advocates of alternative epistemologies may argue that much of the existing research relating to human behavior is severely limited *because* it is the product of a flawed "positivist" paradigm. Such research, they may say, needs to be critically examined in the light of a different paradigm, one that hopefully will produce knowledge that better captures the complexities of human phenomena. From my perspective, much of the criticism directed at "positivistic" research is actually criticism of a parody of that form of research, or at least of egregious expressions of it that are no longer characteristic of the contemporary research scene. For example, Lincoln and Guba (1985), writing from the point of view of their "naturalist paradigm," assert that "the aim of [positivist] inquiry is to develop a nomothetic body of knowledge in the form generalizations that are truth statements free from both time and context (they will hold anywhere and at any time)" (p. 38). I doubt if that aim characterizes much social work research within the postpositivist tradition. Most studies aim to produce a few tentative generalizations more or less restricted to the kind of population studied. It is hoped that an accumulation of studies may broaden the base of generalization, but it is generally recognized that the best that can be achieved are generalizations that have a certain probability of truth when applied to particular situations. As Cronbach (1975), a researcher within the postpositivist tradition, has put it, "When we give proper weight to local conditions any generalization is a working hypothesis, not a conclusion" (p. 125). To come full circle, Lincoln and Guba (1985) view the aim of research conducted under *their* paradigm as producing the self-same "working hypotheses" (p. 38)!

For a practice profession like social work, perhaps the acid test of an epistemological framework and the scientific methodology related to it lies in the potential usefulness of the research produced to the profession. As noted, almost all of the research base on which HBSE courses draw has been generated within the kind of epistemological framework I am defending. I would argue that this research-based knowledge has proved useful to social work and that its usefulness should increase as the knowledge base expands and methods of inquiry improve. A few illustrations may be in order. In their work with parents and children, social workers make use of research-based knowledge on norms and variations in human development and behavior, such as when infants and children on the average reach developmental milestones (Bloom, 1985) as well as knowledge of the effects on children of different kinds of trauma, such as divorce (Wiehe, 1985; Zaslow, 1988, 1989). Although research has produced few fully developed explanations of problems of psychosocial functioning, it has identified risk and protective factors for many problems. Examples of problems in which such factors have been particularly well delineated and of direct value to practitioners include schizophrenic relapse (Hogarty, 1993) and suicide in special populations (Clark & Fawcett, 1992; Ivanoff & Riedel, 1995). For numerous problems there is credible and useful scientific knowledge concerning onset, prevalence, natural course, and variation according to class, gender, and other factors.

As suggested earlier, such knowledge takes the form of probabilistic generalizations. Given the risk factors for a client with certain characteristics, how likely is it the problem will occur? Although the probabilities can seldom be quantified, they can be used as a basis for preventive or other action.

By contrast, the body of research generated by alternative paradigms is still quite modest, although increasing. Until alternative paradigms have been tested and developed through the production of a significant body of research and until that research has been in turn tested through criticism and utilization, it would be unwise to abandon the prevailing paradigm, which, despite its shortcomings, has brought us quite far. This position by no means precludes an approach to HBSE, such as the one developed in a recent text by Schriver (1995), in which traditional and alternative paradigms and related research are presented in a balanced manner.

REFERENCES

Bloom, M. (Ed.). (1985). *Life span development* (2nd ed.). New York: Macmillan.

Brekke, J. S. (1986). Scientific imperatives in social work research: Pluralism is not skepticism. *Social Service Review, 50,* 538–555.

Bunge, M. (1993). Realism and antirealism in social science. *Theory and Decision, 35,* 207–235.

Clark, D. C., & Fawcett, J. (1992). Review of empirical risk factors for evaluation of the suicidal patient. In B. Bongar (Ed.), *Suicide: Guidelines for assessment, management, and treatment.* New York: Oxford University Press.

Cronbach, L. (1975). Beyond the two disciplines of scientific psychology. *American Psychologist, 30,* 116–127.

Dewey, J. (1938). *Logic: The theory of inquiry.* New York: Holt, Rinehart & Winston.

Erwin, E. (1992). Current philosophical issues in the scientific evaluation of behavior therapy theory and outcome. *Behavior Therapy, 23;* 151–171.

Fraser, M., Taylor, M. J., Jackson, R., & O'Jack, J. (1991). Social work and science: Many ways of knowing? *Social Work Research & Abstracts, 27*(4).

Guba, E. C. (Ed.). (1990). *The paradigm dialog.* Newbury Park, CA: Sage.

Hanson, N. (1958). *Patterns of discovery.* Cambridge: Cambridge University Press.

Hesse, M. (1980). *Revolutions and reconstructions in the philosophy of science.* Bloomington, IN: Indiana University Press.

Hogarty, G. E. (1993). Prevention of relapse in chronic schizophrenic patients. *Clinical Psychiatry, 54,* 3.

Ivanoff, A., & Riedel, M. (1995.) Suicide. In R. Edwards & others (Eds.), *Encyclopedia of social work* (19th ed.). Washington, D.C.: NASW Press.

Kitcher, P. (1993). *The advancement of science.* New York: Oxford Press.

Kuhn, T. S. (1970). *The structure of scientific revolutions* (2nd ed.) Chicago: University of Chicago.

Lakatos, I. (1972). Falsification and the methodology of scientific research programs. In I. Lakatos & A. Musgrave (Eds.), *Criticisms and the growth of knowledge.* Cambridge: Cambridge University Press.

Lincoln, Y. S., & Guba, E. G. (1985). *Naturalistic inquiry.* Beverly Hill: Sage Publications.

Phillips, D. C. (1987). *Philosophy, science and social inquiry.* Elmsford, NY: Pergamon.

Phillips, D. C. (1990). Postpositivistic science. In E. G. Guba (Ed.), *The Paradigm Dialog.* Newbury Park, CA: Sage Publications.

Reamer, F. G. (1993). *The philosophical foundations of social work.* New York: Columbia University.

Reid, W. J. (1974). Developments in the use of organized data. *Social Work, 19,* 585–593.

Reid, W. J. (1994) Reframing the epistemological debate. In E. Sherman & W. J. Reid (Eds.), *Qualitative research in social work.* New York: Columbia University Press.

Rorty, R. (1979). *Philosophy and the mirror of nature.* Princeton, NJ: Princeton University Press.

Schriver, J. M. (1995). *Human behavior and the social environment: Shifting paradigms in essential knowledge for social work.* Boston: Allyn & Bacon.

Wiehe, V. R. (1985). Self-esteem, attitude toward parents, and locus of control in children of divorced and non-divorced families. *Journal of Social Service Research, 9*(1), 17–28.

Zaslow, M. J. (1988). Sex differences in children's response to parental divorce: 1. Research methodology and postdivorce family forms. *American Journal of Orthopsychiatry, 59,* 355–378.

Zaslow, M. J. (1989). Sex differences in children's response to parental divorce: 2. Samples, variables, ages, and sources. *American Journal of Orthopsychiatry, 59,* 118–140.

Rejoinder to Dr. Reid

Mary K. Rodwell
John Bricout

We agree with Dr. Reid that the "acid test of an epistemological framework lies in the potential usefulness . . . to the profession." Fundamentally, the social work profession seeks to put knowledge in the service of social change. Dr. Reid accurately notes some important change-oriented findings in postpositivist research. He subsequently points to the large and growing body of positivist research in social work, which he contrasts with the comparative paucity of results in alternative paradigm research. We could argue the political aspect of this lack of published research, but rather than deal with productivity, we emphasize the importance of the questions and the assumptions that drive research, regardless of paradigm. We advocate for whatever routes lead to an expansion in the number and kinds of social change relevant questions and assumptions, rather than for an expansion in the number of findings. As formerly disenfranchised groups develop a "group consciousness" and a voice, altogether new questions and assumptions are raised with respect to social change and to the larger topic of human development in the social environment.

The argument that the concerns and "realities" of "new" constituents to the knowledge-building and change process require new questions and assumptions that do not fit within the bounded world of postpositivist research has been made for some time now by feminist and other nonmajority researchers (Schriver, 1995). Dr. Reid's position that postpositivist research is sufficient for exploring and understanding all living and developmental concerns of all constituencies strikes us as rather like putting new wine into old bottles, bottles whose residue clouds the new content, and whose form creates the false impression of uniformity with previous cullings.

Other shortcomings are associated with using the postpositivist "lens" exclusively. The postpositivist paradigm contains certain self-limiting assumptions, like all paradigms. Dr. Reid's argument in favor of the post-positivist paradigm implicitly rests on two fundamental assumptions: (1) that social phenomena are universal, and are stable, or variable in a predictable way; (2) that all social phenomena can be understood within a framework of a single, bounded reality. Dr. Reid claims that postpositivist social science "progresses" as theories are developed that better fit or resemble known facts. This claim rests on assumptions about a single, comprehensive, and comprehensible social reality. In actuality, however, social science theories do not always progress in linear fashion, as instanced by the recent "rediscovery" of cognitive dissonance theory, which had been dismissed from active investigation for two decades (Aronson, 1992). We offer the notion that the dynamic, unpredictable nature of social phenomena and the resultant diverging social realities are important factors in the confounding of linear progress in scientific knowledge using the postpositivist frame alone. We readily acknowledge that other paradigms, by their very nature, also contain self-limiting assumptions. Moreover, postpositivist inquiry had indeed contributed much to what is known about human development. However, "progress" in knowledge about human development that relies solely of the postpositivist perspective will be lumpy and circuitous as it wends around patches of experience that do not meet its basic paradigmatic assumptions. The use of other, alternate paradigms will help assure that those "other" experiences are not lost for practical use in human behavior and social work practice.

REFERENCES

Aronson, E. (1992). The return of the repressed: Dissonance theory makes a comeback. *Psychological Inquiry, 3*(4), 303–311.

Schriver, J. (1995). *Human behavior and the social environment: Shifting paradigms in essential knowledge for social work practice.* Boston, MA: Allyn and Bacon.

NO

MARY K. RODWELL

JOHN BRICOUT

The overall purpose of teaching human development in social work is to introduce students to the complex interplay of biological, psychological, social, and spiritual factors that together find expression in marvels of humanity. With their emphasis on the person-in-environment, social work educators are sensitive to both the broad ecological factors involved in shaping all persons and the important ways in which every person is the unique expression of particular circumstances and potentialities (Saari, 1992; Scott, 1989). These educators seek to convey to their students an appreciation for the unique and the universal in their human development classes. This can prove a challenging task because there is a certain tension between universalizing and particularizing tendencies in social work practice and research. Although the two tendencies sometimes appear to exclude each other, both are necessary components of social work understanding and action (Haworth, 1991). Less useful is the notion that one or the other must be "true"; either human development is a normative series of stages and progressions or it is an idiosyncratic evolution comprehensible only in its own terms.

The quest for certainty has bedeviled investigators of human nature and development. Human development is a notion beset with scientific controversy and disagreement. Outside of some neurobiological stages for which there exists a good degree of consensus in the scientific community, there is discord around linguistic, moral, social, cognitive, and emotional development (Specht & Craig, 1987). The nature of human beings continues to be a puzzle to us. Is this a puzzle because we have not yet done enough research and amassed enough information about our behavior? Or is it, perhaps, because we have no given nature, no predetermined self, because we are self-determining and self-defining animals? Perhaps both of these questions are bounded inappropriately. Shotter (1975) suggests that what we need is to construct a human science,

> just as rigorous and disciplined as a natural science, but which is concerned not with discovering the order and structure of things "outside" us, but with the order and structure of things "inside" us, in the intersubjectively shared meanings and understandings by which we live our lives. (p. 14)

The ontological, epistemological, and methodological frameworks on which to structure a human development course, then, not only must provide what is possible in terms of prediction and control, but they also must seek understandings of what we are and the situation or positions we occupy. With rigor and discipline we must be able to describe these understandings explicitly. It is in this way that social work intervention can aid in the achievement of the possibilities available to us all, of what we might make of ourselves and our world. Information on human behavior must deal with the universal and idiosyncratic nature of the development of human beings. Students must be introduced to methods and modes of inquiry that allow the pursuit of multiple realities around human development. Knowledge must be available for knowledge's sake, but it must also be available for praxis or social action inspired by theory.

We propose an alternative, multiple paradigmatic approach to the study of human behavior. Taking the perspective that paradigms serve as lenses, not blinders, we suggest that, depending on the practice need, the human problem, or the human behavior question, different paradigmatic perspectives on knowledge, practice, and research will help the profession avoid over-simple conclusions regarding human development in the social environment.

Multiple Paradigms for Human Behavior Content

From our perspective, a paradigm is defined as the general organizing principles or framework governing perception and action. Paradigms include the beliefs, values, and techniques that describe what exists, what to look for, and what the scientist can expect to discover. To understand the possibilities of multiple paradigmatic perspectives in relation to structuring a human development course, it is first important to understand Burrell and Morgan's (1979) typology of sociological paradigms: functionalist, radical structuralist, radical humanist, and interpretive.

This scheme for the analysis of social theory is built on two dimensions of analysis. The subjective/objective dimension relates to assumptions about the nature of science—whether the reality to be investigated is external to the individual (imposing itself on the individual consciousness from without) or the product of individual consciousness (a product of one's mind). The regulation/radical change dimension relates to assumptions about the nature of society—explanations of society that emphasize its underlying unity and cohesiveness (equilibrium) in contrast to explanations that embrace radical change, deep-seated structural conflict, modes of domination, and structural contradiction (chaos, change, conflict, and coercion in social structures) as characteristic of social life. According to Burrell and Morgan, the four paradigms define fundamentally different frameworks for the analysis of social phenomena, generating different concepts and analytical tools. These mutually exclusive paradigms define four alternative views of the social world based on different metatheoretical assumptions regarding the nature of science and knowledge building. To understand the nature of all four is to understand four different views of society and human behavior.

The functionalist paradigm is a pragmatic, problem-oriented approach that applies the models and methods of the natural sciences to the study of human affairs, viewed within a consensus or social integration perspective. Neopositivism is one part of this paradigm, and it pursues universal "realities" or standards such as normative stages and causal determinations in human development.

The radical structuralist paradigm shares a similar approach to science as the functionalist paradigm, but is directed at different ends, viewing the social world as conflictual and oppressive, requiring change through political and economic crises. This approach values knowledge for change's sake. Postmodern and critical theories are part of this paradigm.

The radical humanist paradigm emphasizes the antihuman aspects of the social order, which depersonalizes people and prevents them from realizing their full potential. Self-actualization theories would fit this paradigm. The focus, like that of the radical structuralist paradigm, is knowledge for change, but in this case, the locus of change is individual consciousness.

The interpretive paradigm views the social world as an emergent process, which is created by the individuals concerned, who, as participants, seek to understand this subjective process. The constructivist approach with its hermeneutic dialectic, the process whereby insight and possible consensus is derived from inquiry, fits within the interpretive paradigm.

When approaching human behavior content from either the functionalist or radical structuralist perspective, factual data are produced that can summarize common characteristics of human development and behavior. Predications about the future are possible. Findings across time and geography are possible. But the range of human experience is sacrificed to obtain standardization and control of error. In-depth understanding is missing because of data aggregation and generalization.

For human behavior content, the interpretive and radical humanist perspectives provide in-depth understanding of individual development and behavior. Using these perspectives, the range in development and behavior can become clear; however, the idiographic information sacrifices the ability to generalize.

There are the same opportunities and challenges for content when comparing the two more radical paradigms with the two that are more accepting of existing order. The radical structuralist and radical humanist perspectives place the value of research on the amount of change produced as a result of the research/consciousness raising process. This process of valuation sacrifices the expansion of knowledge and the level of understanding by those outside the context, which are the shared goals of the interpretive and functionalist paradigms.

Each of the four paradigms has unique bounded assumptions, language, and possibilities. Despite the considerable advantages accruing from the use of any one paradigm, the greatest boon to understanding a human development question may lie with the sequential application of several paradigms to a single, broadly phrased question. Comparing the insights and uncertainties of different paradigms applied to the same "problem" of human development can provide a depth of understanding unobtainable from any one paradigm. This is an approach of comparative ignorance, as much as of comparative knowledge, inasmuch as the "blind spots" of each paradigm will actually add to what is known. We agree with Sardar and Ravetz (1994) when looking at what is needed to structure a human development course. A paradigmatic shift is required from neopositivist thinking, which stresses what is known, and increases certainty, to a science informed by uncertainty and error that can be provided multiparadigmatically.

Consequences for HBSE Content Given Alternative Paradigms

Just as generative theory "creates doubt and sheds light and normative theory promises certainty, and narrows its beam" (Saleebey, 1993, p. 17), a multiple paradigmatic framework provides gains and losses. Consideration of alternative paradigms in human behavior courses may force a reconceptualization of what constitutes knowledge. Instead of a building block hierarchy that will inevitably lead us to the pinnacle of truth, we may need to look at knowledge as circular, with different "clumps" of knowledge serving us at different points in time. What is certain is that certitude is lost. Certainty as to the role of theory, values, ethics, and the research process are gone. The language of the discourse changes as well.

Conversely, what is gained is worthy of consideration. There is a broader, more pluralistic conception of knowledge. With this comes a more critical consciousness of method and knowledge than would ordinarily be possible when guided by only one dominant paradigm. This means that clarification through clear articulation and examination of examined and unexamined assumptions becomes a part of both social work education and intervention based on human behavior information. All involved are required to present, defend, and perhaps, understand better what is being offered and learned.

Human behavior education, thus, becomes less parochial, and less dogmatic, allowing for cognitive and cultural pluralism, which may constitute more socially just education for practice. Alternative paradigms provide new resources for understanding and practice, thanks to multiple forms of acceptable representations of knowledge. Along with this will come new ways of conducting research with new potentials for discovery and understanding. These changes might in turn alter the form and content of curriculum, the practice that results, and even how schools of social work evaluate the effectiveness of human behavior research and education.

In sum, alternative frameworks allow the recognition of multiple ways of knowing and multiple uses of knowledge. By taking a multiple paradigmatic perspective, it is possible to structure a human development course that allows rigorous inclusion of all dimensions of human behavior and development. Finally, the multiple paradigmatic perspective puts the various ways of understanding human beings and their social environment in context.

REFERENCES

Burrell, G., & Morgan, G. (1979). *Four paradigms for the analysis of social theory.* London: Heinemann.

Haworth, G. O. (1991). My paradigm can beat your paradigm: Some reflections on knowledge conflicts. *Journal of Sociology and Social Welfare, 18*(3), 35–50.

Saari, C. S. (1992). The person-in-the-environment reconsidered: New theoretical bridges. *Child and Adolescent Social Work Journal, 9*(3), 205–219.

Saleebey, D. (1993). Theory and the generation and subversion of knowledge. *Journal of Sociology and Social Welfare, 20* (1), 2–26.

Sardar, Z., & Ravetz, J. (1994). Complexity: Fad or future. *Futures, 26*(6), 563–567.

Scott, D. (1989). Meaning construction and social work practice. *Social Service Review, 63*(1), 39–51.

Shotter, J. (1975). *Images of man in psychological research.* London: Metheun & Co.

Specht, R., & Craig, G. J. (1987). *Human development: A social work perspective.* Englewood Cliffs, NJ: Prentice-Hall.

Rejoinder to Dr. Rodwell and Mr. Bricout   WILLIAM J. REID

Despite Rodwell and Bricout's "NO!" I am not entirely opposed to their proposal for the use of multiple paradigms in an HBSE course, especially because two of the paradigms they propose (the functionalist and the radical structuralist) appear to share many of the tenets of postpositivism. Indeed, in presenting my "Yes!" position, I was willing to accept an approach to HBSE "in which traditional and alternative paradigms and related research are presented in a balanced manner." One finds such an approach in Burrell and Morgan (1979), developers of the framework that Rodwell and Bricout propose to use.

However, I would argue that the contributions of their four paradigms can all be realized within the postpositivist tradition. In support of this argument, I would like to cite three of the more important of these contributions, which supposedly are incompatible with postpositivist epistemology, and to show how indeed they can be realized within a postpositivist framework. If so, instructors can then concentrate on helping students learn about human behavior in the social environment, without the added burden of dealing with multiple epistemologies.

The first of these additions, emphasized by the radical structural paradigm, is "knowledge for change's sake" with respect to social action and reform. It is of course true that postpositivism is neutral on issues of how knowledge is to be used. But one does not need postpositivism or any other epistemology to use knowledge in striving to create change in the social order. What one needs are individuals committed to obtaining and using the knowledge for social action purposes. Social work has a long history of such use of knowledge within positivist traditions, from the survey movement to the present. Even when knowledge is not obtained with reform in mind, it can be used for that purpose. Among examples that come to mind is the use made of social science knowledge in the landmark Supreme Court decision, Brown *v.* Board of Education (1954), that led to the demise of segregation laws. In such contexts, the very neutrality of the postpositivist paradigm toward the use of knowledge can be an asset. Knowledge acquired in a dispassionate search for truth may have more credibility than knowledge obtained as a means of promoting reform.

A second contribution of nonpositivist paradigms relates to their presumed superiority in creating "generative" theory (Saleeby, 1993). According to Gergen (1983), a theory that has "generative capacity" is able to "challenge guiding assumptions of culture, to raise fundamental questions regarding contemporary social life, to foster reconsideration of that which is 'taken for granted,' and thereby generate fresh alternatives for social action" (p. 109).

It is certainly true that theories that would meet such criteria of "generativity," such as those of Marx or Gilligan (1982), have contributed much to social thought. But theories can also be generative by creating new ways of viewing phenomena, without necessarily "generating alternatives for social action." Any number of examples come to mind—learning theory, crisis theory, cognitive theories of depression, the opportunity theory of delinquency, and so on. A positivist viewpoint and revolutionary social theory are by no means mutually exclusive, as evident from the more visionary works of such scientists as Sigmund Freud (1963), B. F. Skinner (1978), and Edward Wilson (1978).

A third supposed contribution of alternative paradigms pertains to the presumed reductionistic tendencies of postpositivism. When human beings are thought of in terms of variables and numbers, so the argument goes, their complexity is diminished. Here it is important to distinguish between postpositivist epistemology and the kinds of research done within that framework. Certain kinds of quantitative research may be reductionistic in the sense described, but postpositivism also allows for qualitative research, as I pointed out in presenting my "Yes!" position. Certainly human complexity can be preserved in studies using ethnographic or grounded theory methods within a postpositivist framework. A postpositivist perspective would not deny the value of such studies but would call attention to limiting factors, such as the possible biases of the investigator or the atypicality of the sample. From the same perspective, one might fault large-scale quantitative studies for ignoring certain phenomena (the reductionist problem.)

Besides, little is gained in research from preserving human complexity unless we learn something about it in the process. Sometimes hard knowledge about human beings is best gained in bits and pieces, which are put together in mosaic fashion to understand larger patterns. To study a particular segment of human behavior does not necessarily diminish the complexity of the human being, as long as one is clear how the segment may relate to the whole and about the possible hazards of focusing only on the segment.

In conclusion, I would not deny the possible benefit in the kind of multiparadigmatic approach to HBSE that Rodwell and Bricout propose, especially because postpositivist thought would be much in evidence. However, as I have tried to show, a postpositivist epistemology is sufficiently versatile to accomplish what Rodwell and Bricout hope to gain by the introduction of other paradigms, such as emphasis on social change, generative theory, and respect for human complexity.

REFERENCES

Brown *v.* The Board of Education of Topeka, Kansas. (1954). 74 S. Ct. 686.

Burrell, G., & Morgan, G. (1979). *Sociological paradigms and organizational analysis*. London: Heinemann, Ltd.

Freud, S. (1963). *Character and culture*. New York: Collier.

Gergen, K. (1983). *The transformation of social knowledge*. Amsterdam: Springer-Verlag.

Gilligan, C. (1982). *In a different voice: Psychological theory and women's development*. Cambridge, MA: Harvard University Press.

Saleebey, D. (1993). Theory and the generation and subversion of knowledge. *Journal of Sociology and Social Welfare, 20*(1), 2–26.

Skinner, B. F. (1978) *Reflections on behaviorism and society*. Englewood Cliffs, N.J.: Prentice Hall

Wilson, E. O. (1978). *On human nature*. Cambridge: Harvard University Press.

Is It Feasible to Teach HBSE from a Strengths Perspective, in Contrast to One Emphasizing Limitations or Weaknesses?

EDITOR'S NOTE: The helping professions have long been identified by their work with problem situations, with pathology or abnormality, with social deviance of many types. Recently, an alternative "strengths" perspective has emerged that suggests that the helping professions should spend an equal effort studying normality and health—what do successful people have going for them that unsuccessful people in like circumstances do not have?—and using people's strengths as part of the helping process.

Dennis Saleebey, Ph.D., is professor and Chair, Ph.D. Program in Social Welfare at the School of Social Work, University of Kansas. He has recently completed a revision of his book, *Strength Perspective on Social Work Practice,* due to be published in 1996.

John Longres, Ph.D., is professor and Associate Dean at the School of Social Work, University of Washington. He is the current editor of the *Journal of Social Work Education,* and author of *Human Behavior in the Social Environment* (2nd ed., Peacock Publisher).

YES

DENNIS SALEEBEY

Not only is it feasible, it is imperative. The new CSWE (Council on Social Work Education) curriculum guidelines give faculty who teach HBSE considerable freedom to develop curriculum consonant with the best available knowledge about facets of human behavior. I argue that there are converging lines of development in several literatures about the nature of the human condition, human experience, and human development compatible with a strengths perspective. An HBSE curriculum founded on a strengths orientation and related approaches and knowledge departs in some important ways from the more standard curriculum. The strongest form of the argument for a strengths-based approach is that disease, disorder, and deficit are irrelevant to teaching and learning in HBSE, and, thus, social work practice. A milder form of the argument is presented here. Nonetheless, the proposals herein do mean significant changes in what is taught and how it is taught in the human behavior curriculum.

Let us begin with a brief review of some of the principles and concepts of the strengths perspective. It is important to remember here that the strengths perspective is just that—an orientation, a framework—and not a fully developed, robust theory. Whatever else it demands of practitioners, the strengths perspective requires them to adopt a different way of regarding their work, and the clients with whom they work, whether individuals, families, or communities. All must be understood and assessed in the light of their capacities, competencies, knowledge, survival skills, visions, possibilities, and hopes, however dashed and distorted these may have become because of oppression, discrimination, trauma, illness, or abuse. An essential, often early part of strengths-based practice requires an accounting of what people know, what they can do, what they want, and how they have managed to survive, given their circumstances. Practitioners must discover, name, and to help employ the resources within and around the individual or collectivity (Saleebey, 1992; Sullivan & Rapp, 1994; Weick, Rapp, Sullivan, & Kisthardt, 1989).

It takes some degree of rethinking and "re-visioning" to accommodate a strengths perspective in practice. Among other things, social workers are obliged to suspend initial disbelief in clients, especially those who have engaged in destructive, abusive, addictive, or "immoral" behavior. Practitioners, at the same time, have to adopt a somewhat different lexicon in addressing client needs and problems, a language of assets and possibilities, of capacity and transformation. In *Lord Jim,* Joseph Conrad (1900) wrote that "There is a weird power in a spoken word...And a word carries far—very far..." (p. 185). Words do have power, power to elevate or discourage; to ennoble or to debase. Too often professional discourse about clients is cluttered with metaphorical devices and phrases that frighten, isolate, and oppress. This is "totalizing discourse," an official language that is comprehensive in its description and definition, and a language that has the institutional power to preempt "native tongues" (Gergen, 1991). Whatever else the strengths perspective may yield in the way of tools, the language used is both ordinary and encouraging (Goldstein, 1992). Workers in human service organizations and bureaucracies often employ a vocabulary that overrides client words and narratives and turns individuals or families into a cases or labels, neatly tucked away in a category. The *Diagnostic and Statistical Manual of Mental Disorders IV* (DSM IV) (APA, 1994), although some improvement over its predecessors, is still basically an encyclopedia of totalizing discourse, a glossary of defect and disorder. To think that this sort of language has no effect on clients is to be naive. Many of the definitions in the lexicon have the power to infuse consciousness with images and symbols that, over time, capture the individual's sense of self. The ultimate referent for official language is institutionalized knowledge that gives us the power to name.

Pursuing a practice based on the ideas of resilience, rebound, possibility, and transformation is difficult because—oddly enough—it does not seem natural to the world of helping and service. This is so, to a degree, because practitioners are asked to eschew some of the conventions of professional knowledge and stance and to become more capable of entering, understanding, and honoring the clients' worlds of experience as well as the meanings they have created about those worlds. Such a shift is political, a realignment of the power relationships between clients and helpers.

An HBSE Curriculum Constructed on a Foundation of Strengths

Four themes underscore the curriculum: *context, construction, contingency,* and *competence. Context* means that, in all matters, whether considering individual resilience or family organization, we must always situate our concerns in the life world of those whom we would understand—culture and community, neighborhood and home. *Construction* directs us to the narratives, myths, and stories of individuals, families, and cultures because they underscore the centrality of meaning-making in human experience. Narrative immediately plunges us into the subjective world of others: the world of possibility, stories of triumph and fall, redemption and grace, migration and settlement, victory and victimization. *Contingency* refers to the recognition that time, place, sociohistorical situation, and luck have much to do with the character of the human experience and the course of development that, more often than not, is aleatory rather than stage-driven (Gergen, 1983). Finally, *competence* requires that we turn our curricular eye to individual and collective assets, capacities, resiliencies, and strengths. This should not order up a blithe ignoring of the real problems, the factual traumas, the serious pains that people(s) have endured. Nor should it encourage us to avert our gaze from the persistent fact of oppression in so many lives and communities. But it does require us, in our pursuit of a fuller understanding, to sift through the accumulated pains and trials of clients to discover what they know and the incontestable attributes they have plucked out of adversity (Benard, 1994; Garmezy, 1994; Wolin & Wolin, 1993). Selection of content for the curriculum, in addition to these notions, is guided by the search for knowledge having a genuinely biopsychosocial orientation, and knowledge that reflects principally but not exclusively on the generative, transformative powers of individuals and communities. What follows is a review of two very important bodies of knowledge in a strengths-based HBSE curriculum.

Resilience

The research and writing in the broad and varied field of resilience thrusts us conceptually in the midst of that elegant, complex, and mysterious interplay between person and environment. Likewise, it situates our concern immediately in the accounting of assets and capacities as well as risks and liabilities. This rapidly growing body of inquiry, theory, and method is elaborative, focused on process and person–environment transactions. It is a likely candidate to replace HBSE's continuing romance with stage theories of development, theories that, to a considerable degree, are focused on emergent pathology, and often ignore the antic and fortuitous interaction of political, social, and cultural factors. Furthermore, many of these theories are predicated on a simple equation that considerable inquiry (for example, Rutter, 1985) suggests is bankrupt: Childhood abuse, trauma, and stress of certain kinds *inevitably* leads to adult psychopathology. A preponderance of the resilience literature suggests the opposite. It focuses on those risk and protective factors that seem to propel children into adulthood with finely honed resiliencies, whether or not they confront persistent conflicts and struggles. However, it is recognized that *all* children, now become adults, have managed to put some assets into the bank of their character (Benard, 1994; Garmezy, 1994).

This rapidly expanding body of literature is not of one mind, but much of the writing, research, and inquiry here takes a step or two away from ideas that have dominated much of the HBSE curriculum over the years: (1) that there are fixed, immutable, and universal stages of development; (2) that childhood trauma inevitably leads to adult psychopathology; and (3) that there are social conditions, interpersonal relationships, and institutional arrangements that almost always lead to decrements or problems in the day-to-day functioning of children and adults (Masten, 1994; Vaillant, 1993; Werner & Smith, 1992).

Students of resilience and hardiness have identified two sets of factors that may be fateful in affecting the life chances and lifestyles: risk factors and protective factors (Garmezy, 1994). *Risk* factors apparently reduce the possibility of rebound and transformation in an individual's life or, at least, retard the development of certain competencies. More recently, these factors have been defined in terms of context and process. That is, one cannot make the case that a given stressor or risk factor invariably eventuates in poor adaptation. Instead, we must understand the evolution of the interaction between the individual and stressful life events, the individual's cognitive construction of these events, and the social, cultural, political, and physical environments in which these events occur. The idea of risk factors that accelerate disease processes comes from epidemiological research. From these factors—taken together—epidemiologists attempt to calculate the likelihood that particular vulnerabilities will appear. More recent research is somewhat less sanguine about the directness of the relationship among risk, vulnerability, and resilience, especially when they are viewed from a psychosocial, aleatory perspective (Mills, 1994).

Protective factors are thought to be those processes, events, and resources that reduce the probability that an individual or group will suffer decrements in functioning, competence, or health. Put more positively, protective factors invigorate resourcefulness and strength within individuals and groups (Wolin & Wolin, 1993). These factors are "quite heterogeneous" and probably include "genetic/ constitutional variables, personality dispositions, supportive milieus within the family and beyond, and the availability of some degree of societal supports" (Garmezy, 1994, p. 14). Researchers and clinicians have made much of risk factors but know far less about protective factors (Wolin & Wolin, 1993). Once these factors are better understood, they may become part of the foundation of practice methods designed to encourage the self-righting tendencies of individuals and groups. Some educators, as an example, have begun to put some of these ideas into practice—manipulating protective factors so that the competence and self-esteem of children at risk for failure or dropping out increase, thus prolonging their tenure in school (Consortium on School-based Promotion of Social Competence, 1994).

Another set of factors are critical to the development of strengths and capacities in individuals, especially those who confront adversity. These are *generative* factors, remarkable and revelatory experiences that, cumulatively, dramatically, and exponentially, increase learning, resourcefulness, hardiness, and rebound. These may be epiphanies, or sudden insights gained through struggles with hardship and misfortune. They might be lucky encounters with a caring adult affording some protection and inspiration. Perhaps they are unforeseen changes in a heretofore harsh environment now become more salubrious (Masten, 1994). In this regard, an exciting development in resilience research and inquiry is the increasing understanding of the important role of the community in fostering or forestalling resilience and adaptation.

In communities that seem to amplify resilience, acknowledgment and use of the assets of members of the community appear to be part of a widespread ethos. Formal and informal networks of individuals, families, and groups; social networks of peers; and intergenerational mentoring relationships offer succor, support, instruction, encouragement, and ethical/moral parameters and direction (Benard, 1994; Kretzmann & McKnight, 1993). Taylor (1993) defines such communities as "enabling niches." In such communities, neighborhoods, and social spaces, individuals are known for what they do and are encouraged and helped to become more competent and accomplished. In these communities, many ways exist for individuals and families to make contributions to the moral and civic life of the community, to take on the role of full-fledged citizen (McLaughlin, Irby, & Langman, 1994). High expectations of citizens are common. Youth, adults, elders, families, and individuals are all expected to do well and are given the opportunities and the tools for doing well and contributing to the vitality of communal life. Positive expectancies are related both to the durability of the community and to the developing aptitudes of the individual.

In sum, then, the resilience literature satisfies many of the tests of a strengths-based HBSE curriculum: it provides ways of thinking about individual and collective assets; it situates the focus of concern in the larger social context; and it traverses the range of experience and response from biological to psychological to social. The blooming literature on health, wellness, regeneration, and transformation does this as well (Adams, 1993; Cousins, 1989; Lerner, 1993; Murphy, 1993).

Conclusion

The argument here has been that the HBSE curriculum in social work education needs revamping and revision. Four principles and two areas of content have been offered as ways of the incipient rethinking of this curriculum. The proposal is obviously incomplete, and there remains to be more fully argued the serious concern about developing a more critical view of the relationship between people and their sociopolitical environment. Social work is a profession driven by allegiance to values that honor and promote social and distributive justice; that seek the light of dignity and recourse in the darkness of oppression and violation. We cannot ignore these, even though we may not know how to flesh them out in actual practice. To propose a curriculum based on acknowledging and articulating the strengths of clients and communities is not to propose that we ignore the obligations of political and social advocacy and outreach with our clients. It is, however, to intend, whatever the purpose of our work, that we help cultivate and put into use the considerable knowledge, wisdom, capabilities, and power of clients, regardless of their diagnoses, labels, troubles, problems, and pains. This requires of us, then, a model of professional knowing and doing more akin to liberation theology than to medicine or counseling.

References

Adams, P. (with Mylander, M.). (1993). *Gesundheit! Bringing good health to you, the medical system, and society through physician service, complementary therapies, humor, and joy.* Rochester, Vermont: Healing Arts Press.

American Psychiatric Association. (1994). *Diagnostic and statistical manual of mental disorders IV.* Washington, D.C.: American Psychiatric Association.

Benard, B. (1994). *Applications of resilience: Possibilities and promise.* Paper presented at a conference on the Role of Resilience in Drug Abuse, Alcohol Abuse, and Mental Illness. Washington, D.C.: National Institute on Drug Abuse.

Conrad, J. (1900). *Lord Jim.* Edinburgh & London: William Blackwood & Sons.

Consortium on the School-based Promotion of Social Competence. (1994). The school-based promotion of social competence: Theory, research, practice, and policy. In R. J. Haggerty, L. R. Sherrod, N. Garmezy, & M. Rutter (Eds.), *Stress, risk, and resilience in children and adolescents: Processes, mechanisms. and interventions.* New York: Cambridge University Press.

Cousins, N. (1989). *Head first: The biology of hope.* New York: E.P. Dutton.

Garmezy, N. (1994). Reflections and commentary on risk, resilience, and development. In R. J. Haggerty, L. R. Sherrod, N. Garmezy, & M. Rutter (Eds.), *Stress, risk, and resilience in children and adolescents: Processes, mechanisms, and interventions.* New York: Cambridge University Press.

Gergen, K. (1983). *The transformation of social knowledge.* Amsterdam: Springer-Verlag.

Gergen, K. (1991). *The saturated self.* New York: Basic Books.

Goldstein, H. (1992). Victors or victims: Contrasting views of clients in social work practice. In D. Saleebey (Ed.), *The strengths perspective in social work practice* (pp. 18–26). New York. Longman.

Kretzmann, J. P., & McKnight, J. L. (1993). *Building communities from the inside out.* Evanston, IL: Center for Urban Affairs and Policy Research, Northwestern University.

Lerner, M. (1993). Healing. In B. Moyers (Ed.), *Healing and the mind.* New York: Doubleday.

Masten, A. S. (1994) Resilience in individual development: Successful adaptation despite risk and adversity. In M. C. Wang, & E. W. Gordon (Eds.), *Educational resilience in inner-city America: Challenges and prospects.* Hillsdale, NJ: Lawrence Erlbaum.

McLaughlin, M., Irby, M., & Langman, J. (1994). *Urban sanctuaries: Neighborhood organizations in the lives and futures of inner city youth.* San Francisco: Jossey-Bass.

Mills, R. (1994). *Realizing mental health.* New York: Sulzberger & Graham.

Murphy, M. (1993). *The future of the body: Explorations into the further evolution of human nature.* New York: Tarcher/Perigee Books.

Rutter, M. (1985). Resilience in the face of adversity: Protective factors and resistance to psychiatric disorder. *British Journal of Psychiatry, 147,* 598–611.

Saleebey, D. (Ed.). (1992). *The strengths perspective in social work practice.* New York: Longman.

Sullivan, W. P., & Rapp, C. A. (1994). Breaking away: The potential and promise of a strengths-based approach to social work practice. In R. G. Meinert, J. T. Pardeck, & W. P. Sullivan (Eds.), *Issues in social work: A critical analysis.* Westport, CT: Auburn House.

Taylor, J. (1993). *Poverty and niches: A systems view.* Unpublished manuscript. Lawrence, Kansas: University of Kansas.

Vaillant, G. E. (1993). *The wisdom of the ego*. Cambridge, MA: Harvard University Press.

Weick, A., Rapp, C., Sullivan, W. P., & Kisthardt, W. (1989). A strengths perspective for social work practice. *Social Work, 34*(4), 350–354.

Werner, E., & Smith, R. S. (1992). *Overcoming the odds*. Ithaca, NY: Cornell University Press.

Wolin, S. J., & Wolin, S. (1993). *The resilient self: How survivors of troubled families rise above adversity*. New York: Villard.

Rejoinder to Dr. Saleeby John Longres

The strengths perspective is clearly a contribution to social work practice. It works best as a value statement, a reminder not to sell our clients or constituents short. As a framework for understanding human behavior, however, it is one-dimensional.

I believe Saleebey's description shows this and in so doing supports the correctness of my initial statement. There are very few of his particulars with which I disagree, largely because he is not presenting a new and divergent approach but merely using current thinking on human behavior. Looking at person-in-environment transactions, avoiding stage theories of development, and rejecting the DSM have nothing to do with strengths versus problems; either side may, and often do, take these positions. There are indeed "converging lines of development in several literatures about the nature of the human condition," but these literatures are holistic in that they teach us as much about problems as about strengths. We cannot talk of "context, construction, [and] contingency" without recognizing that "competence," if we can define it, exists in degrees. We need a complex view of human behavior, not a rose-colored, simplistic one. Life is about strengths and weaknesses, and much of the time these are so intertwined as to be inseparable.

Saleebey acknowledges that problems can not be ignored but he does not completely acknowledge how much he himself relies on problem identification and analysis. He comes to a strengths perspective by way of calling attention to the failures of social workers and their services. He ignores the civil and human rights advances of contemporary society. Instead, he chooses to assert that "few cultures have oppressed or ignored real bodily and organismic vitality the way western culture has." He calls attention to "risks" and acknowledges that "people do get sick, [and] do suffer seemingly irreparable trauma..." He qualifies just about every statement on resilience, wisdom, competence, and other strengths by acknowledging the need for "appropriate supports" or by noting that "[w]hether or not these [strength] potentials find expression depends mightily on the environment." He clearly recognizes that the role of social work is to transform people, that is, take them from a less desirable to a more desirable state. In sum, his perspective is as much problem as it is strength. He wants to argue that people are strong but repeatedly slides over to the argument that people need strengthening, which I do not believe is a hair different from saying clients need to overcome external or internal limitations.

In truth, a strengths perspective and a problem perspective need each other. The one without the other leads to incomplete knowledge of human behavior and the social environment. Dennis Saleebey errs in favor of strengths and I err in favor of problems. His, I believe, is the more serious error.

Perhaps we differ most in our starting points and in the directions we must travel to complete our understanding of human behavior. For Saleebey, "the strengths perspective begins with the body" and with a belief in "the inherent wisdom of the organism." The future, for Saleebey, is in the development of "a more critical view of the relationship between people and their sociopolitical environment." I do not believe he will ever reach that future using a perspective that by its emphasis on the positive limits critical analysis.

My perspective begins with the sociopolitical environment, and I do not see in it the expression of any inherent species-driven wisdom. Humans, I would argue, are as wise as we are stupid, as likely to fall into an evolutionary dead end as to survive the next million years. I see in my society the inequality emanating from a free market economy, and from systems of racial, ethnic, gender, and other forms of stratification. In such a society, some 20 percent will always experience serious problems, which, because the problems are rooted in flawed social arrangements, will not be easily erased by programs aimed at strengthening individuals. Social workers must indeed strengthen, that is, help people overcome private troubles, but unless we also generate progressive reform, we simply move one suffering individual out to make room for another. My gripe about social work practice is not that we engulf clients in a "totalizing discourse" but that, lacking a sociopolitical vision, we inevitably reinforce the authoritarian values that permeate our society. If strength is measured by the ability to survive, cope, or even excel in an unjust society, it is not the concept on which I wish to build my social work. The social work I wish to promote is one that emphasizes the problem of inequality and endeavors to find ways to bridge the personal with the political.

NO

JOHN LONGRES

The strengths perspective is, like motherhood and apple pie, impossible to be against. Those who are in favor easily sit on the high ground while anyone who would question it is, of necessity, on the defensive. Especially when talking about the individuals and families we hope to serve, there is no one, including myself, who will argue that we must see them as lumps of miserable deficits. My purpose in this debate, therefore, is not to dismiss the strengths perspective, for it makes an obvious contribution. My aim is to call attention to its limitations and by so doing indicate why it should not, indeed, cannot, replace a problems perspective in human behavior courses.

To situate the debate, I am construing the strengths perspective in a narrow way, drawing my issues from those relatively small number of books and articles that specifically attempt to define what I will call the "new" strengths perspective (Cowger, 1994; Saleebey, 1992; Weick, Rapp, Sullivan, & Kisthardt, 1989). As the framers of the new perspective recognize, social work theorists have long called attention to strengths. So too, those who teach human behavior and the social environment have always recognized strengths. These courses have historically been rooted in normal development (that is, healthy and positive) as distinguished from simple conformity to social expectations. Environmental strengths have also formed part of the content; social work students have long been taught that normal development can only take place in healthy and positive environments. Even the psychodynamic perspective, often treated as the antithesis of the new strengths, taught students to assess "ego strength" (the effective use of unconscious and conscious coping processes).

Those writing the new strengths perspective criticize what they believe is the limited attention to strengths in the past. They purport to develop a unique perspective that, while giving a nod to limitations and weakness, essentially writes off the study of problems as a legacy of an ineffective social work. My criticism, therefore, is not directed at the broader notion of strengths nor at those who have jumped on the bandwagon by making side allusions to "a strengths perspective."

Taking a narrow view is necessary because, without this new perspective, strengths versus limitations would not be under debate. Yet in taking the narrow view, my criticisms will of necessity have to talk to the contributions of specific authors. In so doing, it is not my intention to cause affront. I raise my issues in the spirit of intellectual inquiry and in the hope of improving courses in human behavior and the social environment.

Strengths versus Problems

The concept of strength is an enormously appealing metaphor but it is in need of substance. It works best within a "theory of caring," that is, a set of values guiding practice (Longres, 1995): social workers should not get mired in the deficits of people but should instead search out and build on the strengths of clients and their environments. These values are essential, and I have no quarrel with them. Yet the new strengths may prove a dead end because it is not rooted, as is the old, in a theory of human behavior. The new strengths wavers between a Pollyannaish attempt to see, hear, and speak no evil and a rugged individualist demand that people convert all problems into opportunities, all defeats into victories.

The major practice principle of the new strengths is that all negative thinking must be reframed. My students thrill to the strengths perspective and jump into reframing with complete abandon. They get so caught up in reframing that they soon begin to titter at the way important issues are swept under the rug. If people and their environments are so full of strengths and resources, why, they ask, are clients receiving services in the first place, and why is it so difficult to supply them with needed services? Are the problems of practice resolved by converting a "psychopathic child molester" into "a person who means well and wants to be loved"? Are the problems of practice resolved by focusing on the resources of a free market economy while soft-pedaling its role in producing poverty, unemployment, and homelessness? Although I sincerely hope not, history may show that the strengths perspective is merely a pep talk during a particularly difficult period in the history of social work practice. The new strengths fits in well with a "chin-up" approach to working in a downsized welfare state but ultimately may not prove of much use to our clients or to progressive social reform.

In this light, it is not clear to me why the concept of problem is seen in such a negative light. I believe it is an extremely useful concept. Knowing our own limitations and those of others can be liberating. Knowing the environmental obstacles we must address to achieve our goals seems a necessary step to overcoming them. Indeed, the framers of the new strengths actually use a problems perspective in outlining their ideas. They do not start by calling attention to the many strengths of past and present social work theorists. They do not emphasize the wonderfully creative ideas that emerged as each successive generation built on the strengths of those who went before them. Instead they use a problems perspective; they call attention to the weaknesses and limitations of other social work models as a preamble to touting their new and presumably better ideas. The new strengths, in spite of its desire to eliminate problems, is bathed in the very critical analysis that may well be the most important and distinguishing contribution of the problems approach.

My chief concern is that the new strengths does not yet constitute a "theory for practice" (Longres, 1995) and is not therefore rooted in a sound base of knowledge. In particular, the framers do not provide a useful definition of strength nor do they develop a theory of system in environment that can be taught in human behavior courses. When you go in search of a strengths theory of human behavior you keep bumping into the ideas of those in the problems tradition.

Defining Strengths

Goldstein (1992) makes the definition of strengths a nonissue. He considers the concept of strength "an unpretentious term" that exists in a world apart from it presumed opposite, "pathology." Strengths, he claims, "did not have to be invented," nor can it be "cataloged, compared or measured" (p. 35). Nonetheless, he notes that strengths refer to such complex ideas as "moral courage, fortitude, physical force, and vigor" (p. 30) as well as "virtue, willpower, [and] integrity" (p. 31).

I assert that the concept of strengths is as abstract as any and that its opposite, weakness, is not easily disentangled from it. Strengths are not self-evident, for their identification is itself a perception that always takes place in context. One person's "moral courage" may be another person's "foolhardiness." Is the woman who protects her child-abusing husband demonstrating "fortitude" and "integrity," or is she "identifying with the aggressor" and demonstrating "internalized sexism"? Are the husband and wife who stay together for the good of the children—in spite of a very destructive interpersonal relationship—expressing "virtue" or "folly"?

Strengths are not either/or but exist on a continuum. One can have more or less fortitude, more or less courage, more or less integrity. Once we admit a continuum, we must take the next step and acknowledge that someone whose courage needs to be strengthened has limited or weak courage. Furthermore, the continuum of strength and weakness does not run easily from a strong end to a weak end. All along the continuum, strengths and weaknesses may be one and the same. Too much willpower may in fact be stubbornness, and too little willpower may be flexibility. Someone who is relatively empowered is simultaneously relatively disempowered. Whether the glass is half-full or half-empty, the quantity of strength and weakness remains the same.

The lack of a clear definition of strengths enables practitioners to call anything a strength. We fall easily into double-speak and assume that because we are in favor of a strengths perspective everything we do automatically reflects it. When Weick et al. (1989) described the strengths perspective to working with chronically mentally ill clients, one got the sense that a breakthrough had been made. Yet doubts arose as they posed assessment questions such as the following: "What do [the chronically ill] need to develop into more creative and loving adults?" (p. 354). Although supposedly eschewing problems, this question clearly acknowledges deficiencies: clients or their environment are lacking something, because they are not as creative or as loving as they themselves may want to be.

By the time the perspective became popularly accepted, it was clear the breakthrough had not occurred. For instance, Rappaport, Reichl, and Zimmerman (1992) talk of a "strengths approach to problems in living." In so doing, they recognize that their clients suffer from "human helplessness" and that their "loss of power may play an etiologic role in the onset of depression." From this assessment of "powerlessness," they aim to effect "empowerment" by helping clients gain "access and control over needed resources." They do this by setting up support groups to teach clients to think of problems as opportunities, permit themselves to have flaws, disregard self-doubt and criticism by others, and take responsibility for "one's own recovery." There is considerable value in their social work practice, and I have no criticism of it. My question is: How is theirs a unique strengths approach? How is a program that starts with problem assessment and moves to problem solution doing something fundamentally different from a problems approach? Without a clear definition, anything—even a problems approach—can be called a strength approach.

We not only need a definition of strengths, we need to catalogue and develop a guide to identifying them. Those working in the new strengths perspective have supplied us with some incipient typologies, and these turn out to be the same as typologies in the problems perspective. Saleebey (1992) distinguishes between personal and environmental strengths and includes among these "cognitive, intentional, behavioral and political" (p. 170). Cowger (1992) suggests that we assess five types of personal strengths, each existing on a continuum from strength to deficit: cognitive, emotional, motivational, coping, and interpersonal. Again the issue here is not any disagreement with the ideas they are presenting, just confusion about why they are calling it a unique strengths approach. When the concept of strength is deconstructed, it seems to have as much to do with weakness as with strength.

Person in Environment

Not only is the perspective lacking a useful definition of strength, it also lacks a theory of person in environment. The strengths approach puts forth no systematic theory of psychology, no theory of environment, and no theory of the transactions between the two. It does present some incipient theories, but most of these are either not unique to a strengths perspective or simply inadequate.

How should we understand the behavior of individuals? Weick (1992) believes that traditional theories of human behavior have distorted and limited our understanding of normal development because they are rooted in a rational, scientific model. She suggests that a nonpositivist strengths approach leads us to recognize that universal and discrete stages of individual development do not exist, that a wide range of behaviors can be considered normal, and that humans have enormous transformational capacities. Although her dicta on human development are true, they have hardly emerged from a unique strengths theory of human behavior and development. Anyone reading and teaching the mainstream scientific research on child and adult development will reach these same conclusions. Packaging them as the insights gained from a special strengths perspective using alternative research methods is false advertising.

Similarly, when Saleebey (1992) and Cowger (1994) ask social workers to suspend their disbelief in clients or simply nudge them gently into telling the truth, they are promoting a very strange theory of psychology. Do they mean that personalities may be divided into liars and truth tellers? Do they mean that people always perceive accurately, have perfect memory and perfect recall, that people always understand themselves, know what they want, and do what is in their and other people's best interests? Is saying the truth and doing the right thing simply a matter of having a person believe everything you say at face value?

Social workers have never been taught to think of their clients as liars. They have been taught to begin where the client is, in his or her meanings and attributions. Saleebey (1992) appears to acknowledge this and contradicts himself when in a different context he writes, "Why is it that people do not look as though they have strengths? Why do they seem beaten, angry, depressed, rebellious?" and answers his questions with the very poignant reminder that "Dominated people are often alienated people" (p. 171). By acknowledging that people may not always be as they appear, he is suggesting a psychology that is much closer to beginning where the client is than suspending disbelief.

Mainstream psychological and sociological theories have a lot to offer and should not be easily discarded. Psychological theories of cognitive, emotional, and behavioral functioning have taught us a lot even though they call attention to limitations and weaknesses. Should we discard attribution theory because it has tuned us into perceptual biases, or cognitive dissonance theory because it has highlighted immobilizing states of ambivalence? Are cognitive development theories to be discarded because they are not universally applicable or because they instruct us as much on poor development as on healthy development? Should we discard motivational theories because they inform us that people act defensively, feel out of control, or hold unsavory drives for lust, oppression, and power? Should we toss out social learning theory because it reminds us that people learn many of their negative behaviors through negative family, peer, and media role models? Do we reject outright the thinking of those who see substance abuse as a disease and schizophrenia as a disorder?

I especially bemoan the threat to sociological theory that is evident in the strengths perspective. Sociological theory has provided us with a rich set of concepts geared to critical evaluation of society and social relations. Marxian and other conflict theorists have taught us about class, political, and culture wars. Equity theory has taught us about the anger and frustration that comes from inequity and unfairness. Functionalism has taught us that anomie results from normative breakdown and contradictions between socially desirable goals and the institutionalized opportunities for achieving them. Symbolic interactionism has taught us how the responses of others may result in self-defeating labels. Role theory has taught us to understand the strains generated from overburdening expectations, unclear expectations, mixed messages, and the like. All of these problem-oriented theories have shed light on the conditions under which alienated, exploited, anomic, negatively labeled, or conflicted people may or may not resist others and fight for their interests.

Yet all of these contributions appear shunted to the side as the new strengths proclaims that "[the] social environment is, among other things, a fund of resources..." (Sullivan, 1992) and urges us to avoid "blaming the community for lack of employment, housing, and recreation opportunities" (Rapp, 1992). The negative aspects of environments are swept under the rug of the strengths perspective. Yet the lump it makes is so large that it finally cannot be ignored. Saleebey (1992) is forced to make an impassioned series of statements calling attention to inequality, injustice, and the negative effects of marketplace values on the collective conscious (pp. 169–171). These acknowledgments, coming as they do at the end of his edited book, hit with such force that they put the pin in the balloon of the new strengths.

There is no doubt that the task of social workers is to find or create resources. Yet without any systematic attention to why resources are unequally distributed in society and without systematically preparing students to confront environmental limitations head on, we are in danger of not only ignoring the need for reform but blaming social workers for the inadequacies of our social institutions.

REFERENCES

Cowger, C. D. (1992). Assessment of client strengths. In D. Saleebey (Ed.), *The strengths perspective in social work practice* (pp. 139–147). New York: Longman.

Cowger, C. D. (1994). Assessing client strengths: Clinical assessment for client empowerment. *Social Work, 39*(3), 262–268.

Goldstein, H. (1992). Victors or victims: Contrasting views of clients in social work practice. In D. Saleebey (Ed.), *The strengths perspective in social work practice* (pp. 18–26). New York: Longman.

Longres, J. F. (1995). *Human behavior in the social environment* (2nd ed.). Itasca, IL: Peacock.

Rapp, C. A. (1992). The strengths perspective of case management with persons suffering from severe mental illness. In D. Saleebey (Ed.), *The strengths perspective in social work practice* (pp. 45–58). New York: Longman.

Rappaport, J., Reichl, T. M., & Zimmerman, M. A. (1992). Mutual help mechanisms in the empowerment of former mental patients. In D. Saleebey (Ed.), *The strengths perspective in social work practice* (pp. 84–97). New York: Longman.

Saleebey, D. (Ed.). (1992). *The strengths perspective in social work practice.* New York: Longman.

Sullivan, W. P. (1992). Reconsidering the environment as a helping resource. In D. Saleebey (Ed.), *The strengths perspective in social work practice* (pp. 48–159). New York: Longman.

Weick, A. (1992). In D. Saleebey (Ed.), *The strengths perspective in social work practice.* New York: Longman.

Weick, A., Rapp, C., Sullivan, W. P., & Kisthardt, W. (1989). A strengths perspective for social work practice. *Social Work, 34*(4), 350–354.

Rejoinder to Dr. Longres

DENNIS SALEEBEY

Professor Longres claims that a strengths perspective is little more than an "appealing metaphor" in need of more "substance." It is not, he argues, rooted in a theory of human behavior. Rather, it "wavers between a Pollyannaish attempt to see, hear, and speak no evil and a rugged individualist demand that people convert all problems into opportunities, all defeats into victories." Clearly, the strengths perspective is not a theory. Nonetheless, it has conceptual, contextual, and methodological ties to a variety of bodies of knowledge, both empirical and theoretical: the vast and rapidly increasing research on resilience and the surmounting of adversity; the extensive literature of wellness and healing; the developing literature and practice on community empowerment and development; the emergence of reflective practice as an orientation to professional methodology; the lengthy tradition of liberation theology and the "pedagogy of the oppressed," and by no means least, the recent rethinking of the idea of ego defense, adaptation, coping, and health. The central appreciation in all of these is that the strengths and resources of the afflicted and oppressed, the abused and alienated are not only remarkable, not only internal and external, but are the tools that might pave the road to a better life, the securing of a place to be, and the achievement of a vision.

Professor Longres calls us back to the essential traditions of social work thinking: theories of "normal" development, and the problem focus (and I assume the problem-solving tradition). Developmental theories, especially the stage variety, do describe normal achievements and outcomes, but inevitably counterpose those with their nether side (e.g., autonomy versus shame and doubt; symbiosis versus autism). In my experience, the fascination is with, and the practice focus is on, the inimical outcome. The normative achievement becomes a standard by which we assay how far short one has fallen during a particular point on the developmental trajectory. The stage theories have sustained, over the years, a pivotal interest in how failures and deficits in managing the normative tasks of childhood have their sequelae in adult psychopathology. This parable of eventual fall is a staple of many developmental theories from Freud to Erikson, from Mahler to Loevinger, from Klein to Kohlberg. The reality seems to be that, yes, some children are so hurt and damaged by people and institutions in their psychosocial journey that they bear serious scarring in adulthood. But to say this alone is to be silent about two other realities: most children who suffer and are traumatized eventually do rebound. They, too, bear scars, but the remarkable feature of their journey is how much they have gathered inner resources, outer support, and have avoided falling into various states of pathology, deficit, or abuse. Another reality is that those who do suffer from psychological and interpersonal troubles, signs, and symptoms of pathology still have a reservoir of personal and social resources, and hopes that can be summoned in the struggle toward a better life. Looking only backward and inward for the causes (and, thus, cures) of the pathology usually leads to dead ends.

One of Prof. Longres's concerns is that there is no viable definition of strength, nor any categorization of strengths that is substantially different than the lexicon of problems. It does seem difficult to conceive that there might be a way of thinking about strengths and of categorizing them. To imagine that there might even be a DSM of strengths and virtues seems to defy clinical acumen. But why not seriously think about cataloguing personal virtues such as loyalty, steadfastness, courage, or thoughtfulness? Why not create a roster of the kinds of knowledge and pride that people develop as they encounter and overcome adversity? Why not develop an inventory of the knowledge that people have gathered as they have lived life, what they have learned in school, in the family, in the workplace, even in poverty? Why not accumulate a register of the kinds of talents and skills that people possess? Why not come to understand, in a deliberate fashion, how cultural narratives and family stories offer succor and direction? Why not develop an index of the environment's nourishing resources? The fact is that people who practice under the aegis of a strengths perspective *do* all of the accounting just suggested.

In closing, I believe I understand most of Prof. Longres's concerns, and I would commend the following to him:

> We confide in our strength, without boasting of it; we respect that of others, without fearing it (Thomas Jefferson in a letter to William Carmichael and William Short, June 30, 1793).

Should HBSE Be Taught from a Stage Perspective?

EDITOR'S NOTE: Another persistent issue concerns the orderliness and regularity of human behavior over time and across cultures and circumstances. Some theorists postulate that there are clear psychosocial stages of development, in addition to the widely acknowledged bio-physiological ones, whereas other theorists find the idea of necessary and universal stages of human development to be an unnecessary assumption and a misleading idea.

Henry S. Maas, Ph.D., since 1984 professor emeritus, School of Social Work, the University of British Columbia, continues his professional publishing (see references to his chapter) as well as writing several volumes of poetry.

Carel B. Germain, D.S.W., professor emerita, School of Social Work, the University of Connecticut, was a world-renowned scholar, still actively writing at the time of her death in August 1995. She had just completed a revision of a prominent book, *The Life Model Approach to Social Work Practice* (with Alex Gitterman), and was in the process of revising her scholarly work, *Human Behavior in the Social Environment*.

YES

HENRY S. MAAS

In this chapter I describe how certain life experiences in different contexts in my career led me to formulate a Contextual-Developmental-Interactional (CDI) approach to developmental changes over the life course. I also outline the CDI's life course stages. Each stage concerns social *capacities* that develop in interaction with facilitative *contexts*. This idea is consonant with social work's focus on person-and-environment in interaction.

The CDI framework had its origins in professional experiences antecedent to my teaching HBSE. After my college education in the humanities and part-time volunteer group work with urban ghettoed youth in a neighborhood center, I entered Columbia University School of Social Work, where versions of psycho-analytic theory were the dominant if not the only cohesive set of ideas in the case-work program. I was then catapulted into the Signal Corps of the U.S. Army, where, after misclassification and misassignment to radio mechanic training [does a social work master's degree qualify one as a communications specialist?], I was transferred to a newly organized "mental hygiene unit" and thus became a "military psychiatric social worker" (Maas, 1951, 1953). I discovered how men who had coped adequately in civilian society "broke down" in a de-individualiz-ing culture of uniforms, authority's commands, and sanctioned physical stresses, mutilations, and violent deaths. The impact of macrosocietal and face-to-face contexts and catastrophic experiences and the context-specific nature of personal capacities hit me dramatically. There was much more to understanding how people coped than my introduction to psychosexual development showed.

After four years of military service, my doctoral education at the University of Chicago (with the interdisciplinary faculty of the Committee on Human Development) extended my knowledge about human development in environments or contexts. Here were educator Robert Havighurst, social scientists Allison Davis, Bernice Neugarten, and Lloyd Warner, psychologists Bruno Bettelheim, Bill Henry, and Carl Rogers, and many others studying collaboratively persons of all ages, social classes, ethnic groups, and genders as they changed over time. Unfortunately, social work was slow to pick up on this kind of interdisciplinary thinking in its HBSE courses. Later, as a member of a clinical research team studying patients in group therapy, I worked under the auspices of Harry Stack Sullivan's Washington School of Psychiatry, and with Jerome D. Frank as research director, a psychiatrist who had studied with social psychologist Kurt Lewin and who was deeply concerned about world peace and other social causes (Frank, 1968, 1978). The Washington School's publication, *Psychiatry,* included on its editorial board anthropologist Clyde Kluckhohn and sociologists Talcott Parsons and Erving Goffman. Social contexts were never forgotten in the central focus on personal development.

I joined the faculty of the University of California School of Social Welfare at Berkeley, ready to coordinate the teaching of the year-long HBSE sequence. My identification remained a joint or bridging one as both interdisciplinary human developmentalist and social worker. I remain convinced now as then that social work practitioners need to learn a body of knowledge bearing on how we all, interacting with conducive environments, become participating members of societies that foster and use persons' capacities for socially responsible involvements. After a year in England, where I studied the long-term effects of early childhood separation (Maas, 1963), I became associate director of Berkeley's interdepartmentally staffed Institute of Human Development (IHD). IHD's ongoing longitudinal studies provided us with wonderful opportunities to investigate antecedent and subsequent conditions over the course of many lives. I studied relationships between school-aged friendships and young-adult intimacy (Maas, 1968) and how young-adult parents changed when they reached old age (Maas & Kuypers, 1974).

This autobiographical sketch illustrates not only how one's contexts may influence the development of one's conceptualizations of behavior but also how one's life stage may affect one's choice of behavior. For I am writing this chapter in my mid-seventies, and my decision to write autobiographically reflects a highly functional process we often engage in old age, called by Robert Butler (1963) "the life review." Knowledge about stages helps us understand what people do.

The Contextual-Developmental-Interactional (CDI) Framework

I came to see social work as centrally concerned, in both its micro and its macro practices, with people's growing capacities to cope, ideally in increasingly responsive environments (Maas, 1986). My CDI proposals assume that a major aim of social work is to promote responsive environments through social development, both macro and micro. The purpose is to help develop capacities for *socially responsible behavior* that recognizes the needs of others *and contexts* that facilitate such behavior's development. "The greater the number of contexts with which people can cope, the fewer the situations in which they are overwhelmed by feelings of helplessness and stress. The more often they engage in socially responsive interaction, the more likely they are to help to generate or sustain a caring and sharing society" (Maas, 1984, pp. 3–4).

The central question (and the one to which this debate is directed) is: How do people arrive at a socially responsible approach to living? This question is more fully discussed in my book *People and Contexts* (Maas, 1984). Briefly, there are three fundamental phases in the development of children as responsible participants in their society. First, the infant strengthens innate capacities for attachment in its circle of caretakers. But infants' capacities for attachment can develop adequately only when caretakers are interactive in supportive social networks. Social work's fostering such networks can influence early attachment development. Second, out of this attachment grow the infant/toddler's curiosity and security to explore the world. Pursuing curiosity's manipulative investigations, one begins to develop competencies and an awareness of one's own efficacy—

that is, a sense of "I can do." But for such explorations and concomitant developments to occur, appropriate milieus must be accessible, sufficiently varied, and responsive to one's efforts to affect them. The third phase involves a maturing child who

> by about age seven or eight, if not before, is able to take the role of others so that genuine reciprocity (give-and-take and love . . .) become possible. But this kind of reciprocity is a capacity most likely to develop in a caring community, in which responsibility and caring behavior are modeled by others. Thus, again, the child's organismic potentials must be matched or complemented by contextually supportive structures and processes. . . . (Maas, 1980, p. 204)

I can only outline, within this chapter's space limits, some aspects of subsequent CDI life course stages. We have thus far discussed capacities for attachment, a sense of efficacy, and abilities to engage in reciprocity and collaboration. The last-named develop most fully in caring and sharing groups, communities, and subcultures. They offer experiences in team-play and peer group belonging, together with an expanding awareness of "the other" and mutuality. Capacities for collaborative play and work are developed in schools and workplaces that reward cooperation. Capacities for intimacy and love may grow in contexts supportive of—not, as in some groups, threatened by—twosome caring. Subsequent cohabiting (with or without coparenting) and the attendant abilities needed in a mature relationship flourish in contexts that foster partnership commitments and feelings of concern about our world's future. The latter concern arises especially when children are born. With such concern, capacities for social responsibility may be exercised in neighborhoods and societies that provide options for such kinds of social participation—informally in neighbor-to-neighbor interaction or, for example, in social work programs or other organizations dedicated to furthering human welfare. Familial and work contexts for both women and men allow for socially responsible involvements, especially in middle age (Maas, 1989). Finally, old age calls for abilities to cope with losses and legacies, developed in diverse, flexible social and physical spaces. Contexts must accommodate and complement the widely varying and often diminishing capacities of old people, leaving them still with some feelings of efficacy and other satisfactions.

Each capacity in the CDI stages of human social development leads under ideal or conducive contexts not only to the development of the next stage's capacities but also cumulatively to personal abilities for socially responsible behavior. The CDI approach is not, however, to be taken as a rigid or prescriptive sequence, but rather as a frequent pattern, offering environmental *and* personal–developmental guidance to *both* macro and micro social workers (Amacher & Maas, 1985; Maas, 1971, 1983, 1985, 1994). Nor is it a finished proposal, but one that further research should amplify and correct.

Many elements in each of the CDI stages have specific empirical research bases on which I have reported elsewhere (Maas, 1984). Moreover, the schema has several general theoretical antecedents, for example, Erikson's (1975, p. 102) observation that:

> an intricate relationship between inner (cognitive and emotional) development and a stimulating and encouraging environment exists from the beginning of life so that, in fact, no stage and no crisis could be formulated without a characterization of the mutual fit of individual and environment—that is, of the individual's capacity to relate to an ever expanding life space of people and institutions, on the one hand, and, on the other, the readiness of these people and institutions to make him part of an ongoing cultural concern.

Frequent criticisms of stage concepts do not seem relevant to the CDI's propositions. CDI capacities and contexts are formulated at levels of abstraction that permit them to have universal applicability. They do not deny cultural diversity or gender differences. Nor are the stages tightly tied to specific ages. The approximate timing of the beginning of a CDI stage is analogous to historians' "periodicization" of what they call the Middle Ages or the Renaissance, which cannot be precisely dated. Yet such imprecision does not vitiate the usefulness of these historical terms.

Finally, because social work's practice in "neighborhoods, organizations, communities and societies has been largely atheoretical or based in ad hoc midrange theories without ties to concepts at other systemic levels" (Mattaini, 1992, p. 420), I believe that the relevance of the CDI thinking to both micro and macro topics is one of its prime values (see Pijl, 1994). Throughout social work, but especially in preventive programs, the ability to anticipate and to avoid painful consequences and to attain desired goals requires knowledge of relationships both within and among stages. More generally, a unifying knowledge base for the many levels of social work's long-standing and innovative practices can be amplified by CDI understandings—and their further testing and development.

References

Amacher, K. A., & Maas, H. (1985). Children, youth and social work practice. In S. A. Yelaja (Ed.), *An introduction to social work practice in Canada* (pp. 217–233). Scarborough: Prentice-Hall Canada.

Butler, R. N. (1963). The life review: An interpretation of reminiscence in the aged. *Psychiatry, 26,* 65–76.

Erikson, E. (1975). *Life history and the historical moment.* New York: Norton.

Frank, J. D. (1968). *Sanity and survival: Psychological aspects of war and peace.* New York: Vintage.

Frank, J. D. (1978). Self-centeredness versus social action in contemporary American society. In P. E. Dietz (Ed.), *Psychotherapy and the human predicament: A psychosocial approach.* New York: Schocken.

Maas, H. (Ed.). (1951). *Adventure in mental health: Psychiatric social work with the armed forces in World War II.* New York: Columbia University Press.

Maas, H. (1953). Personal-social disequilibria in a bureaucratic system, *Psychiatry, 16,* 129–137.

Maas, H. (1963). The young adult adjustment of twenty wartime residential nursery children. *Child Welfare, 42,* 57–72.

Maas, H. (1968). Preadolescent peer relations and adult intimacy. *Psychiatry, 31,* 161–172.

Maas, H. (1971). Children's environments and child welfare. *Child Welfare, 50,* 132–142.

Maas, H. (1980). The child's responsibility to society. In D. S. Freeman (Ed.), *Perspectives on family therapy* (pp. 201–214). Toronto: Butterworth.

Maas, H. (1983). Social development, its contexts, and child welfare. In *Child welfare in Canada: Social work papers* (of the School of Social Work, University of Southern California) *17,* 1–9.

Maas, H. (1984). *People and contexts: Social development from birth to old age.* Englewood Cliffs, NJ: Prentice-Hall.

Maas, H. (1985). The development of adult development: Recollections and reflections. In J. A. Munnichs, et al. (Eds.), *Life-span and change in a gerontological perspective.* New York: Academic Press.

Maas, H. (1986). *From crib to crypt: Social development and responsive environments as professional focus* (2nd Werner and Bernice Boehm Distinguished Lectureship in Social Work). New Brunswick, NJ: Rutgers University School of Social Work.

Maas, H. (1989). Social responsibility in middle age: Prospects and preconditions. In S. Hunter & M. Sundel (Eds.), *Midlife myths: Issues, findings, and practice implications.* Newbury Park, CA: Sage.

Maas, H. (1994). Linking micro and macro in social policy: Some historical notes on relevant social science. *Social Policy and Administration, 28,* 174–183.

Maas, H., & Kuypers, J. A. (1974). *From thirty to seventy: A forty-year longitudinal study of adult life styles and personality.* San Francisco: Jossey-Bass.

Mattaini, M. A. (1992). Book review of P. A. Lamal, *Behavioral analyses of societies and cultural practices* (New York: Hemisphere, 1991). In *Reseach in Social Work Practice, 2,* 420–424.

Pijl, M. A. (1994). Social policies, from the individual to the world level by way of conclusions. In H. C. Rasmussen and M. A. Pijl (Eds.), *Some reflections on social development in Europe: A contribution to the UN social summit.* International Council on Social Welfare, European Region.

Rejoinder to Dr. Maas

CAREL B. GERMAIN

> EDITORS' NOTE: Carel Germain died in August 1995, shortly after she had completed a revision of her *Life Model* book (with Alex Gitterman), and the initial statement for this debate. The editors offer this rebuttal to Henry Maas's statement, attempting to reflect her thinking.

Professor Maas has it half right. Human development certainly is strongly influenced by the psychosocial and cultural contexts in which human development occurs. What a wonderful collection of professional experiences he had that led him to recognize the intricate interplay of personal, social, and cultural events that shape a life and are shaped by that life. (He spends more time telling us how he was shaped, but his many writings suggest that he did his share of shaping of others along the way.)

However, Professor Maas quotes with evident satisfaction the writings of Erikson, whose universal stage model does not leave as much room as the Contextual-Developmental-Interactional (CDI) model for unique themes and variations. Indeed, because Professor Maas claims Erikson as an antecedent, we must look more closely at the CDI model for its possible universal, necessary stage implications, which ecologists deny. He suggests that "there are three fundamental phases in the development of children as responsible participants in their society." The first includes "innate capacities for attachment." In claiming innateness for a social characteristic, Professor Maas comes very close to implying that this is a first universal crisis (in Erikson's sense), which may or may not be resolved successfully, similar to basic trust versus mistrust.

The second fundamental phase involves the development of competencies and self-efficacies. Again, this sounds very similar to Erikson's crisis of autonomy versus doubt, as Professor Maas's third phase sounds like Erikson's crisis of initiative versus guilt. What is very different between Professor Maas's phases and Erikson's stages is the context of social responsibility, which supplies the meaning for all of Maas's later phases. This has a good social work ring to it, a value context surrounding development in and through various sociocultural contexts. But even this value of social responsibility sounds as if it too was a necessary human crisis, for which some resolve and others fail. This sounds quite moralistic, like the elect and the damned, a value posture that most ecologists would prefer not to assume as part of their theoretical orientation.

In short, Professor Maas seems to be claiming the flexibility and sensitivity that a nonstage position offers (such as the ecological approach) while at the same time wanting the structure and certainty of a stage model. What he ends up with is a "frequent pattern," not an inevitable stage. What is the practical difference between this frequent pattern and a stage at which some resolve successfully, and others do not? What Professor Maas seems to be doing beyond the rigid stage theorists is to pay more attention to the transactions between the individual and his or her many environmental contexts that can lead to a greater variety of resultant personalities and behaviors. As the number of different personalities and behaviors grow, the need for "frequent patterns" or universal stages lessens. It makes more sense to Professor Germain to look directly at the unique patterns that emerge in that person–environment interchange than to assume any quasi-universal frequent pattern that may be used to impose common meanings on unique human transactions. This would be misinformation for social work practice, whether it is for micro or macro practice. Professor Maas is right to assert that guiding approaches should enable social workers to have this dual orientation. Professor Germain would claim that the ecological approach offered a better perspective in doing this.

NO

An informal historical review quickly shows our profession's long dependence on stage models in the absence, until recently, of another approach to understanding psychosocial development and human behavior. Social work has outgrown these limited models because they cannot incorporate new data. Gilligan (1982) asserted that human development must be reconceived to take into account the differing socialization and life experiences of women and men. She pointed out that women's socialization and life experiences are missing in the traditional stage models of development. When women are measured against criteria for developmental progression in stage models, they are found wanting because the models are based on the study of males and their life experiences.

Stage models also cannot take account of culture, historic contexts, variations in sexual orientation, new family forms, and the influence of poverty and oppression. Instead, they assume uniform pathways of development that ineluctably lead to universal, fixed, predictable end points without regard to these various powerful and differentiating influences. Additionally, concepts of universal, uniform stages ignore the fact that such models are rooted in the dominant culture's assumptions, values, and social norms at a particular time in history. Hence stage models are time bound as well as culture bound.

Such limitations call out for a new and realistic approach to conceiving human psychosocial growth and behavior. Education for effective professional practice demands date theory and knowledge in the foundation for practice. Social workers, cheer up! We are saved at the (im)passe by a train of thought carrying the needed approach. It is the "Life Course" conception, which can replace the outmoded stage models of human development and behavior. The result of the collaboration of historians (Hareven, 1982), two sociologists (Elder, 1978, 1984; Rossi, 1981), and a gerontologist (Riley, 1978, 1979, 1985), the new model reflects contemporary thought about the very real complexities of psychosocial development and its indeterminate nature. This multidisciplinary approach is augmented by the efforts of other individuals working in a similar vineyard, including a social psychologist (Neugarten, 1969, 1979), anthropologists (Myerhoff and Simic, 1978), psychiatrists (Chess, Fernandez & Korn, 1980; Rutter, 1979; Thomas, 1981), and social workers (Germain, 1990, 1994; Germain & Gitterman, 1995). The work of this unaffiliated group is congruent with the ideas of life course theorists, although the conception per se of the former is not explicit in their work. Common to both groups is the rejection of stage models in favor of concepts of diverse pathways of development shaped, in part, by the diversity of environments, cultures, and temperaments. Emphasis is on the self-regulating, self-determining nature of human beings and the indeterminate nature of psychosocial development. (Biological–maturational development within the human is uniform within certain limits, influenced by genetic and environmental factors.)

The life course conception is transactional in nature, thus exquisitely fitting the centrality of person(s)/environment relations in social work. The conception emphasizes life transitions, critical life events, and other life issues as outcomes of person(s)/environment processes rather than as separate segments of life confined to predetermined ages and stages of experience. The life course conception readily incorporates ongoing theory/knowledge development and new meanings about older theory/knowledge as they appear. For example, the life course notion that individual processes merge into collective processes in the family (described later) adds a new dimension to understanding family development.

A distinctive feature of the life course model is its time perspective: the notion that psychosocial development and functioning take place over historical, individual, and social time. For example, individual eras such as childhood, youth, adulthood, or old age are to be understood in the continuum of the entire life course, including (1) effects of societal changes on individual and collective life experience (historical time); (2) the timing of life transitions within both the cultural context and the chronology of family and community life (social time); and (3) people's life stories (individual time). Cohort theory aids our understanding of the effects of historical time. A birth cohort is defined as all persons who were born at a particular historical time and thereby exposed to the same sequence of social and historical change over their life course (Riley, 1978). Members of a birth cohort grow up and grow older differently from the members of every other birth cohort because they live through different historical and social processes or through the same processes but at a different point in life. For example, women and men born in 1900 were shaped emotionally, socially, and behaviorally, in part, by life experiences and historical forces (e.g., the Great Depression, World War II) different from those that have been shaping women and men who were born in 1970 (e.g., Vietnam, feminism, affirmative action).

Age and gender crossovers reflect changes in *social time,* again surpassing simplistic stage models. For example, traditional timetables of many life transitions are disappearing. No longer is there a fixed, age-connected time for going to school, marrying or remarrying, first-time parenting, changing careers, retiring, or moving into other new statuses and roles. Life transitions are becoming relatively independent of age (Neugarten, 1978).

Many people are transcending traditional gender roles formerly viewed as unalterable (Giele, 1980). Gender crossovers include the exchange of traditional male and female roles in some families, solo parenting by fathers, single career women having their own children by various means and raising them alone, and the entry of women into previously male occupations and of some men into previously female occupations.

Individual time across the life course is expressed through our life stories that both reflect and help shape how we experience our individual lives. Interest in reminiscence and life review in social work began some thirty years ago when Butler (1963) wrote of its helpfulness in practice with elderly persons. In postmodern thought, life stories appear in new garb in psychoanalytic theory (Spence, 1982; Stern, 1985), social constructivism (Laird, 1993), and social work practice theory (e.g., Goldstein, 1990; Laird, 1989; Middleman & Wood, 1993; Riessman, 1989). Stern, for example, suggests that storying our lives may be an innate characteristic of the human brain, because the development of life stories that we tell to ourselves and others begins at about age three in all cultures and continues over the life course. The empathic, active listening of the clinician allows clients to reinterpret and reconstruct their life stories to contain new concepts of the self and of relationships with others. As the life story is being reconstructed, it gains increased intelligibility, consistency, and continuity.

Still another serious shortcoming of stage models is their sole concern with individual psychosocial development. The only available constructions of family development until now had been limited to fixed stages related solely to the marital axis: marriage, birth of children, child-rearing, empty nest, retirement, and death of the spouse (e.g., Hill, 1958, who did include the impact of some environmental events; Pollack, 1960; Rhodes, 1977). These fixed, uniform stages never reflected real life experiences of most families in our multicultural society. From the social time perspective of the life course conception, family members develop simultaneously in ways that involve both generations and in which parents and offspring are active agents in their own and one another's development. That is, parents and children develop together—in tandem, as Bloom (1980) put it. Individual processes of development that merge into collective processes in social time lead to family development through transformations.

Here we move to the work of two family theorists that is remarkably congruent with the life course conception (Reiss, 1981; Terkelsen, 1980). Their complementary ideas suggest that family development arises from various common and unique life transitions and life events that confront a family over its life course and set family transformations in motion. Their theories are more dynamic and closer to the life experience of contemporary families than are constructions based on universal, fixed, sequential stages of family development, especially because these newer formulations incorporate family, individual, culture, and environmental diversity. Critical life issues that families may face include (1) those generated internally by difficult life transitions or painful family patterns such as marital and parent–child conflict, violence, and abuse; (2) those generated by the family's exchanges with school, workplace, health care system, and other societal institutions; (3) those generated externally, such as poverty, powerlessness, or lack of resources; and (4) those generated by traumatic life events such as a grievous loss eventually suffered in one form or another by all families.

In his extensive family studies, Reiss (1981) found that families construct unique world views or "family paradigms," defined as the members' assumptions about themselves and their social world. These implicit beliefs are shared by all members, despite existing disagreements and conflicts. They shape the family's basic patterns of living and its experiences in its physical and social environments, and in turn are shaped by those environments. A painful life issue, causing discontinuity in family life, requires a family to change its ways of functioning as embodied in its world view and to construct a new one if the life issue is to be managed well and if the developmental needs of all members are to be met under greatly changed conditions. These ideas supplant the outmoded notion of fixed, uniform, sequential family stages.

Further enlightenment is provided by Terkelsen's (1980) distinction between first- and second-order life issues that clarify the collective processes involved in family development. First-order life transitions occur very frequently and are expectable in average family experience, fitting into the continuous flow of family life through time. They include continuing biological–maturational and social transitions that present family members with new requirements and opportunities for mastery. They are usually perceived by members as challenges rather than stressors, and most families manage them more or less smoothly, without serious disruptions. First-order issues, then, lead to increments of mastery that yield pride and satisfaction to members despite the frustrations involved. The family paradigm does not change. Instead, it is enough that several new behaviors emerge as the family seeks a new structure to manage the transition. As the new behaviors appear, outmoded ones drop away.

Second-order life issues, which are much more prominent in social work practice than first-order ones, consist of severely painful transitions and life events. Except for losses, few are expectable in the average family's experience. When they do occur, they represent a severe discontinuity in the expected flow of family life. All such issues, however, threaten to put the family in harm's way. They also may include any first-order issue perceived by a family or threat of harm, either because of the meaning the issue has for the members or because of the absence of resources needed for moving through it.

Second-order issues could be thought to include grievous harms of poverty and oppression. But these wrongful societal conditions themselves generate multiple second-order transitions and life events, and they make all second-order issues, and even first-order ones, extremely difficult to manage. Successful first- and second-order changes, then, can be viewed as an engine that drives family development throughout the family's life course. Through incremental, first-order changes the family evolves continually, and through successful second-order changes the paradigm governing family life and development is transformed. A new paradigm must incorporate the painful new reality and integrate the family's revised goals and future plans, interpretation of its past, and beliefs about itself and the environment with the new reality. By so doing the family reduces or removes the threat of disorganization or dissolution.

Terkelsen points out that first-order issues usually require insertion of a new behavioral sequence to replace an outmoded sequence and thus lead to continued family development. First-order issues appear frequently, leading the family to experience its life course as being in a state of flux. Second-order life issues usually require new behavioral sequences and major changes in family structure (including rules, routines, roles, and tasks) and meanings (loyalties, affectional and communication patterns, and exchanges with the environment). When effective, second-order changes lead to transformation of the family and hence to its development. However, such changes occur infrequently, leading the family to experience its life course as being in a state of constancy. Terkelsen concluded that flux and constancy proceed together, transforming the family over its life course. Through incremental first-order changes, the family continually evolves and develops, whereas through second-order change, it develops through episodic transformations.

Contemporary realities of new and diverse family forms, multicultural diversity, and increasingly diverse social and physical environments can be readily assimilated in first-order and second-order family development. The ideas of Reiss and Terkelsen also appear to fit well with the social-time perspective of the life course conception, in its assumption that individual processes merge into collective processes in family development. My conclusions are twofold: (1) Stage models of individual and family development were never adequate to the tasks expected of them in social work practice. (2) The life course conception is more than adequate to meet the challenges of current practice and in the twenty-first century because of its openness to new conditions and new theory and knowledge as these promise to appear again and again.

Note: This position is adapted, in part, from Germain, C. B. (1990). Life forces and the anatomy of practice. *Smith College Studies in Social Work, 60*(2), 138–152; (1991). *Human behavior in the social environment, an ecological view.* New York: Columbia University Press; and (1994). Emerging conceptions of family development over the life course. *Families in Society, 75*(5), 259–268.

REFERENCES

Bloom, M. (Ed.). (1980). *Life span development*. New York: Macmillan.

Butler, R. N. (1963). The life review: An interpretation of reminiscence in the aged. *Psychiatry, 26,* 65–76.

Chess, S., Fernandez, P., & Korn, S. (1980). The handicapped child and his family: Consonance and dissonance. *Journal of the American Academy of Child Psychiatry, 19,* 56–67.

Elder, G. H., Jr. (1978). Family history and the life course. In T. K. Hareven (Ed.), *Transitions: The family and the life course in historical perspective.* New York: Academic Press.

Elder, G. H., Jr. (1984). Families, kin, and the life course. In Parke (Ed.), *Review of Child Development Research, 7* (pp. 80–136). Chicago: University of Chicago Press.

Germain, C. B. (1990). Life forces and the anatomy of practice. *Smith College Studies in Social Work, 60*(2), 138–152.

Germain, C. B. (1991). *Human behavior in the social environment: An ecological perspective.* New York: Columbia University Press.

Germain, C. B. (1994). Emerging conceptions of family development over the life course. *Families in Society, 75*(5), 259–268.

Germain, C. B., & Gitterman, A. (1980). *The life model of social work practice.* New York: Columbia University Press.

Germain, C. B., & Gitterman, A. (1995). Ecological perspective. In R. L. Edwards et al. (Eds.), *Encyclopedia of Social Work* (19th Edition). V. 1 (pp. 816–824). Silver Springs, MD: National Association of Social Workers.

Giele, J. Z. (1980). Adulthood as transcendence of age and sex. In N. J. Smelser & E. Erikson (Eds.), *Themes of work and love in adulthood* (pp. 151–173). Cambridge, MA: Harvard University Press.

Gilligan, C. (1982). *In a different voice: Psychological theory and women's development.* Cambridge, MA: Harvard University Press.

Goldstein, H. (1990). Strength or pathology: Ethical and rhetorical contrasts in approaches to practice. *Families in Society, 71,* 267–275.

Hareven, T. K. (1982). The life course and aging in historical perspective. Hareven & K. J. Adams (Eds.), *Aging and life course transitions: An interdisciplinary perspective* (pp. 1–25). New York: Guilford.

Hill, R. (1958). Generic features of families under stress. *Social Casework, 39,* 139–150.

Laird, J. (1989). Women and stories: Restorying women's self-constructions. In M. McGoldrick, C. Anderson, & F. Walsh, (Eds.), *Women in families: A framework for family therapy* (pp. 422–450). New York: Norton.

Laird, J. (Ed.). (1993), *Revisioning social work education: A social constructionist approach.* New York: Haworth Press.

Middleman, R. R., & Wood, G. (1993). So much for the bell curve: Constructionism, power/conflict, and the structural approach to direct practice in social work. In J. Laird (Ed.), *Revisioning social work education: A social constructionist approach* (pp. 129–146). New York: Haworth.

Myerhoff, B., & Simic, A. (Eds.). (1978). *Life's career—Aging: Cultural variations in growing old.* Beverly Hills, CA: Sage Publishers.

Neugarten, B. L. (1969). Continuities and discontinuities of psychological issues into adult life. *Human Development, 12,* 121–130.

Neugarten, B. L. (1978). The future and the young-old. In L. F. Jarvik (Ed.), *Aging into the 21st century* (pp. 137–152). New York: Gardner Press.

Pollack, O. (1960). A family diagnosis model. *Social Service Review, 34,* 1–50.

Reiss, D. (1981). *The family's construction of reality.* Cambridge, MA: Harvard University Press.

Rhodes, S. (1977). A developmental approach to the life cycle of the family. *Social Casework, 58,* 301–311.

Riessman, C. K. (1989). From victim to survivor: Woman's narrative reconstruction of marital sexual abuse. *Smith College Studies in Social Work, 59,* 232–251.

Riley, M. W. (1978). Aging, social change and the power of ideas. *Daedalus, 107,* 39–52.

Riley, M. W. (1979). *Aging from birth to death: Interdisciplinary perspectives.* Boulder, CO: Westview.

Riley, M. W. (1985). Women, men, and the lengthening of the life course. In A. S. Rossi (Ed.), *Aging and the life course* (p. 47). New York: Aldine Publishers.

Rossi, A. S. (1981). Life span theories and women's lives. *Signs: Journal of Women in Culture and Society, 6,* 4–32.

Rutter, M. (1979). Protective factors in children's responses to stress and disadvantage. In M. W. Kent & J. E. Rolf (Eds.), *Primary prevention of psychopathology* (pp. 49–74). Hanover, NH: University Press of New England.

Spence, D. P. (1982). *Narrative truth and historical truth.* New York: Norton.

Stern, D. (1985). *The interpersonal world of the infant.* New York: Basic Books.

Terkelsen, K. G. (1980). Toward a theory of the family life cycle. In E. A. Carter & M. McGoldrick (Eds.), *The family life cycle: A framework for family therapy* (pp. 21–52). New York: Gardner Press.

Thomas, A. (1981). Current trends in developmental theory. *American Journal of Orthopsychiatry, 51,* 580–609.

Rejoinder to Dr. Germain

Henry S. Maas

Carel Germain's chapter does two things. It very skillfully, within imposed space limits, sketches multiple interacting elements in a set of conceptual perspectives on human behavior. Whether the changes she refers to are "developmental"—in terms of the etymological meaning of development as "unfolding"—is not clear to me. Secondly, she criticizes and denigrates all "stage models" as "simplistic," "outmoded," and "limited models" that "social work has outgrown." In addition, she makes some more substantive observations, which I shall try briefly to address.

Developmental changes of human organisms are exceedingly complex and thus very complicated to study. Several developmental stage theories have been proposed and built on over the years, although Germain claims, without citing examples, that "stage models" are all fixed and "cannot incorporate new data." This despite the fact that since the 1920s continuing research has expanded such stage theories as Piaget's through, for example, studies by McCarthy (1930), Nielsen (1951), and countless others. A host of social developmental stage schema have been built on one another—for example, the CDI framework outlined in my chapter. It draws on Sullivan's interpersonal relations stages (Sullivan, 1936–37) as well as Erikson's "eight stages," which he generated from Freud's stages of psychosexual development—as far as the latter went. Erikson then himself expanded his "eight stages," especially identity formation, in his own writings of several decades beyond his 1950 *Childhood and Society* formulations. Stage theories have not been fixed or closed to new data.

Secondly, Germain maintains that "stage models" ignore cultural and gender diversity. She overlooks Erikson's reported field work with the Sioux and the Yurok, the latter with world-renowned anthropologist Alfred Kroeber by his side, and Erikson's consultations with other culture-scholars, Bateson, Ruth Benedict, and Margaret Mead. The diversity of social classes and comparable numbers of males and females in the Berkeley and Oakland longitudinal studies used in "mental growth" and "personality change" schema (Jones, Bayley, Macfarlane, & Honzig, 1971) are further examples of evidence contrary to "culture-bound" and only-male-subjects criticisms. My own experiences as a UNICEF consultant with staff and children at institutions in Karsiyaka and Ankara, Turkey, and outside Manila, as well as in villages where children played near their caretakers in Uganda, were illuminated by attachment theory (see Maier, 1994, for child care workers' uses of such ideas) as well as by knowledge about stages of exploratory, efficacy, and reciprocity development.

Critical of stage models' sequential age-linked changes, Germain writes approvingly of "life stories" development, which "begins at about age three in all cultures." Objecting to what is "predetermined," she nevertheless reports what "occur very frequently and are expectable in average family experience." Moreover, her Life Course "Emphasis is on the self-regulating, self-determining nature of human beings." Her concern that stage models ignore cultural and gender differences and at the same time her support for individual controls have a confusing postmodern p.c. (politically correct) ring to them, perspectives that Brewster Smith brilliantly criticizes with regard to the development of self theory (Smith, 1994).

The complexities of social work's responsibilities and of the fields into which we must intervene can use all the valid theoretical enlightenment available to us, including such studies as the Social Science Research Council's (SSRC) mission-oriented research (McDonnell & Ranis, 1995). This includes also understandings of stages of human development, which, like the Contextual-Developmental-Interactional framework, specify environments conducive to optimal growth.

REFERENCES

Erikson, E. (1965). *Childhood and society* (2nd ed.). London: Hogarth Press.

Jones, M. C., Bayley, N., Macfarlane, J., & Honzig, M. (Eds.). (1971). *The course of human developoment.* Waltham, MA, & Toronto: Xerox Publishing Co.

Maier, H. W. (1994). Attachment development is "In." *Journal of Child and Youth Care, 9,* 35–51.

McCarthy, D. (1930). Language development of the preschool child. *Institute of Child Welfare Monograph, 4.* Minneapolis: University of Minnesota Press.

McDonnell, M. B., & Ranis, S. H. (1995). Interaction, collaboration, and engagement. *Items, Social Science Research Council, 49,* 405–411.

Nielsen, R. F. (1951). *Le développement de la sociabilité chez l'enfant: Étude expérimentale.* Neuchatel: Delachaux & Niestelé.

Smith, M. B. (1994). Selfhood at risk: Postmodern perils and the perils of postmodernism. *American Psychologist, 49,* 405–411.

Sullivan, H. S. (1936–37). A note on the implications of psychiatry, the study of interpersonal relations, for investigations in the social sciences, *American Journal of Sociology, 42,* 848–861.

Should Human Behavior Theories with Limited Empirical Support Be Included in HBSE Classes?

EDITOR'S NOTE: Social work is an applied social science, and, as such, has some obligation to look for substantive research to document the validity of its practices. In selecting what knowledge to use, it is tempting to look only at those methods that have received positive confirmation through empirical research. Others resist this temptation and assert that we do not know enough to exclude any form of information, including the nonempirical.

Stanley Witkin, Ph.D., serves as professor and Director of the Department of Social Work, University of Vermont. His current papers include "Wither Social Work Research? An Essay Review" in *Social Work* (vol. 40) and "Making Social Work Scientific: Analysis and Recommendations" in Katherine Tyson's *New Foundations* for *Scientific Social and Behavioral Research: The Huristic Paradigm* (Allyn & Bacon). He would like to express his appreciation to Mary K. Rodwell for her helpful comments on an earlier draft of this paper.

Paula Nurius, Ph.D., is professor and Director of the social welfare doctoral program at the School of Social Work, University of Washington. Her current scholarship focuses on cognitive processes in stress and coping, particularly with respect to violence against women, self-concept change, and critical thinking in practice judgment. Recent publications include *Social Cognition and Individual Change* with A. Brower and *Controversial Issues in Social Work Research* with W. Hudson.

Susan Kemp, Ph.D., is assistant professor at the School of Social Work, University of Washington, where she teaches direct practice. Her scholarly interests include social work history and epistemology, women's issues, and community-based practice with low-income families. Recent projects include a historical study of the concept of environment in social casework theory.

YES

STANLEY WITKIN

Choose your favorite theories from the following list (or add your own): general systems theory, object relations theory, attachment theory, social learning theory, labeling theory, role theory, conflict theory, exchange theory, and psychodynamic theory. Question one: Which, if any, of these theories have limited empirical support? Answer: All of them. Question two: Name any theory that does not have limited empirical support? Answer: There are none. Question three: Should human behavior theories for which there is limited empirical support be included in course outlines for HBSE? Answer: Only if one wants to teach anything at all!

It is widely accepted that theories are underdetermined by data; that is, theories always attempt to explain more than is (or can be) empirically supported. Even individual concepts such as intelligence, love, and creativity are underdetermined. Their varied and complex meanings are not reducible to empirical data. Because theories consist of multiple concepts, they are even more likely to have "limited empirical support." Another implication of underdetermination is that new data can usually be accommodated by several theories (Phillips, 1987).

In addition to concepts, theories also contain background assumptions that are not amenable or subject to empirical testing. These assumptions are critical to understanding the meaning and scope of theories. The assumption that humans are rational decision makers, that marriage is a voluntary relationship, or that interpersonal relationships move toward equilibrium are examples of background assumptions of theories. Often these assumptions are implicit and only revealed when contrasted with another theory holding different assumptions. Assumptions about gender illustrate this situation.

Given that all theories have limited empirical support, rephrasing the above question in relative terms may be more useful. For instance: Should the selection of theories for inclusion in HBSE courses be based on their degree of empirical support? Unfortunately, even this "softer" version of the question runs into difficulties, particularly when considered within an instructional setting.

Deciphering Empirical Support

Comparing theories on their degree of empirical support is not a straightforward process. In part this is because "support" itself is theory determined. This can occur in at least three ways. First, what counts as supportive data can differ between theories. (The symbolic meaning of a dream may be supportive data to a psychodynamic theorist but mere anecdote to a behaviorist.) Second, there may be disagreement about the methodological basis for empirical support. If a research procedure is judged as faulty, inappropriate, or weak, the supporting data that were generated will also be diminished in value (at least by critics). Third, investigations may be restricted to areas that fit the theory, leading to a situation in which "everyone is right." The sometimes vehement debates among proponents of competing theories often reflect their differential assessments of empirical support. Moreover, the fact that even disconfirming data can be easily discounted suggests that theoretical allegiances go beyond empirical support and may influence the assessment of such support. Thus, both the meaning and the quality of empirical support will vary depending on who is doing the assessing.

Theory Assessment Is Further Complicated by Language

Theories are expressed in words; they are linguistic representations of some aspect of the world. The language used to express these representations is complex, dynamic, and culturally situated. Thus, the meanings of theoretical terms are equivocal and bounded by time and context. Moreover, because empirical data themselves are contextually and linguistically contingent, knowing the degree of "correspondence" (in any generalized way) between a theoretical term and the empirical data that appear to support it is difficult (or perhaps impossible). A theory about intimate relationships is a theory about a view of relationships within a particular culture at a particular time. Such a theory is tested, not against the "real world," but against other theory-laden conceptualizations (e.g., relationship satisfaction). There is no theory-absent world to compare with one's theory. Even "observation terms are themselves for the most part theoretical terms whose credentials we have come to accept at face value" (Rozeboom, 1962, cited in Diesing, 1991, p. 15).

The Meaning of Theory

One's view of the nature and purpose of theory also influences the interpretation and importance of empirical support. This in turn depends on the broader cognitive framework (i.e., "paradigm") to which one subscribes. (Interestingly, these broader frameworks are generally viewed as beyond the reach of empirical tests.) For instance, theories may be seen as maps of reality, as quasipolitical statements, or as expressions of cultural beliefs. Thus, a theory with strong empirical support may be considered a "mirror of nature" (to use Richard Rorty's [1979] term), a manifestation of the dominance of those holding that theory, or as simply a particular construction of social life among many potential constructions. Depending on one's metatheoretical perspective, the importance of empirical support may vary greatly. For example, a theory about adult intimacy may also be a statement about what is valued within the culture (e.g., relationships based on mutual affection). By helping to make social life intelligible and legitimate, the theory both creates and sustains the reality that it "discovers." These "sensemaking" and value expression functions of theories are important but not dependent on empirical support.

Finally, it is not always clear what qualifies as a theory. There are many explanatory conceptual systems within social work, for example, the strengths perspective, the ecological perspective, which do not label themselves as theories and yet are the mainstays of HBSE courses. Should these be subject to the same "empirical support" criterion? And if they should, then does "theory" encompass any conceptual system? Any concept? Without clear guidelines demarcating theory from nontheory, it is impossible to know how far this, or any other, criterion should extend.

The lack of consensus regarding assessments of empirical support and the nature of theory leaves individual instructors—even those who believe in the empirical support criterion—free to decide which theories to include in HBSE courses.

Criteria for Including Theories with Limited Empirical Support

If HBSE courses must include theories with limited empirical support and if deciding among those theories on the basis of that support is problematic, what criteria should be used to select theories? Obviously one cannot teach every theory, nor are all theories equally important.

Theories do not teach themselves, nor do they exist in isolation from other aspects of an educational program. Social work programs have various orientations to practice. Theory selection undoubtedly is influenced by these orientations. Thus, a clinical program may be more apt to teach theories focusing on individuals and individual change, whereas a program emphasizing community practice would consider theories that address issues at this level. Additional pragmatic criteria might include accreditation issues, the prior educational training and theoretical allegiances of course instructors, and the relationships among various stakeholder groups within the program. Although these criteria are not directly related to the value of theories, they have a direct impact on what will be taught.

One's "theory" of social work education also might influence the criteria for theory selection. For instance, if one views HBSE courses as places in which students are primarily taught "facts," then one might emphasize teaching "true" content over content not known to be true (sidestepping for the purposes of this part of the discussion all the problems involved in making that determination). In contrast, if one views the purpose of HBSE courses as teaching students how to critically analyze theories, then theories that help students develop these skills might be selected. In fact, a weakly supported theory might be included as a means of demonstrating and developing various analysis strategies.

Exposure to a plurality of views may be necessary for a sound understanding of theories. The advantages of not discarding untested, or even discredited, theories were recognized by John Stuart Mill in his famous essay "On Liberty." Mill argued that considering multiple perspectives was important because ejected views may still be true; because "problematic" views usually contain some truth whereas prevailing ones rarely contain the whole truth; and because views that are not contested or contrasted with other views can become "held in the manner of a prejudice" and become "a mere formal confession." To this list Feyerabend (1987) added another reason: "that decisive evidence against an opinion can often be articulated and found only with the help of an alternative. To forbid the use of alternatives until contrary evidence turns up while still demanding that theories be confronted with facts, therefore, means putting the cart before the horse" (p. 34). Social work education can ill afford to narrow its field of vision to only "approved" (empirically supported) theories.

Other criteria also are important for selecting theories. For example, Kuhn (1977) believes that theories should be simple, accurate, consistent, broad, and fruitful. Each of these criteria is subject to varying definitions and individual or collective judgments, and each may influence the importance and interpretation of empirical support.

Within social work, additional criteria for evaluating theories may be relevant (e.g., Witkin and Gottschalk, 1988). Examples include the extent to which a theory challenges taken-for-granted beliefs and assumptions (its "generative" dimension), is "grounded" in the lives of the people it attempts to explain, is consistent with and promotes a more just world, and promotes new approaches to social work practice. Thus, theories are assessed not only in relation to their empirical support or other cognitive criteria, but in terms of their congruence with the values and purposes of the profession. From this perspective, a theory that explains the plight of poor people as related to structural inequalities may be more relevant to social work education than one that attributes problems to internal pathology (although the latter may be used for other instructional goals).

Theories provide an important sense-making function (Kaplan, 1964). They help make situations and events intelligible and bring a sense of coherence and order to our lives. Theories that do this well (e.g., Erikson, 1965) are interesting and often influential. Understanding what makes theories interesting (e.g., Davis, 1980) or influential can have broad educational benefits for social work students. For instance, why one theory supplants another as a dominant explanation may have more to do with social and political factors than empirical support. Emphasizing importance would assure that students are familiar with the major explanatory concepts used in social work practice and that they have assessed the value of those explanations.

In conclusion, the inclusion of theories in HBSE courses is related to several factors. Empirical support may be one of these, but it is neither sufficient nor necessary. Claims of empirical support for a theory can have multiple meanings, for example, an assertion of a theory's truth value, the ability of its proponents to attract funding, or its support of mainstream ideology. The value of this support must be assessed in relation to these and other theory relevant criteria (e.g., Kuhn, 1977) and in relation to social work values. If an important goal of social work education is to generate informed, reflective, critical social work practitioners, then exposure to multiple and diverse theories that can be compared and contrasted on a variety of criteria is necessary.

REFERENCES

Davis, M. S. (1980). That's interesting. *Philosophy of Social Science, 1,* 309–344.
Diesing, P. (1991). *How does social science work?* Pittsburgh: University of Pittsburgh Press.
Erikson, E. (1965). *Childhood and society* (2nd ed.). London: Hogarth Press.
Feyerabend, P. (1987). *Farewell to reason.* London: Verso.
Kaplan, A. (1964). *The conduct of inquiry.* San Francisco: Chandler.
Kuhn, T. S. (1977). *The essential tension.* Chicago: University of Chicago Press.
Phillips, D. C. (1987). *Philosophy, science and social inquiry.* Elmsford, NY: Pergamon.
Rorty, R. (1979). *Philosophy and the mirror of nature.* Princeton, NJ: Princeton University Press.
Witkin, S. L. & Gottschalk, S. (1988). Alternative criteria for theory evaluation. *Social Service Review, 62,* 83–98.

Rejoinder to Dr. Witkin

PAULA NURIUS
SUSAN KEMP

Language is complex, people vary widely in their opinions and priorities, concepts and understandings are inherently colored and shaped by the times and contexts in which they are derived, nothing can ever absolutely be known for sure, time is limited and choices have to be made about what to include in any given course, answers seldom come in comfortingly simple or unambiguous form, and social work students need to recognize and be prepared to contend with all this. The good news is that we and almost all other social work educators are in complete agreement with Professor Witkin on these matters! Indeed, social workers have historically understood these to be the normal (and tremendously challenging) circumstances of everyday social work practice. Such multilayered professional issues and needs are reflected in the Council on Social Work's curriculum guidelines and stand as requisites for all educational programs—requisites that include thorough grounding in the best supported theory and knowledge *as well as* critical thinking skills *and* socialization into the fundamental values and purposes of the profession. Fortunately, we need not pit these learning objectives against one another but rather teach for an integrative whole.

More perplexing is what Professor Witkin is saying beyond reminding us of these complexities. It especially worries us that he may be seen as suggesting that, once conceived or printed, all notions or theories are equal, or should be treated as equal. This would be neither an ethical nor an accountable stance for social work professionals to adopt. Knowledge for practice can and should be generated in multiple ways and from a variety of perspectives, but we must also concern ourselves with evidence of its predictive and interventive value in the real world of social work practice. Effective and accountable practice requires both access to systematic, reliable, and valid information and the ability to interrogate—on multiple levels—the knowledge being applied to determine which is most useful in any particular situation.

We thoroughly concur with the importance of fostering critical thinking and analysis as part of effective practice reasoning and decision making. Our own experience is that development of a critical perspective, a commitment to social work values, and a durable capacity to "work in the gray" are key objectives not only of HBSE courses but of social work programs as a whole. But this is not the debate question we were asked to address. As we argued in our position, skills in critical analysis provide an intellectual framework within which professional knowledge can be presented, evaluated, and applied to fit unique lives and circumstances. Skills in such analysis build progressively and are linked closely to the ability to understand and appraise the evidence for or against particular theoretical positions or findings. Does not this capacity develop in tandem with rather than in opposition to instructional efforts to provide students with the most current and solidly supported theory and knowledge to draw on in current and future practice?

The issue of the link between professional knowledge and decision making bears additional emphasis. Substantive professional knowledge is both an essential component of professional inference and judgment and a primary basis of public sanction for professional practice (Rosen, Proctor, Morrow-Howell, & Staudt, in press.). If such knowledge is not available, workers typically seek guidance either from agency rules and regulations (with the result that practice becomes increasingly routine, bureaucratized, and vulnerable to groupthink) or from personal theories, experiences, and heuristics (risking practice that is more practitioner centered than client focused). This is not a risk unique to social workers but rather a function of how human thinking functions when insufficient information is available (Nurius & Gibson, 1990). Either outcome, however, threatens to dilute or distort the essential nature of professional practice.

Arguments such as those presented by Professor Witkin risk carrying us backward to an overreliance on agency mandates, practice wisdom, and personal experience, rather than forward to a more sophisticated epistemology based on many ways of knowing and multiple sources of evidence. Though perhaps not intentionally, Professor Witkin seems to be equating concern regarding degree of substantiation with a mindless, lockstep approach to thinking or instruction. Although an effective debate strategy, this paints more a caricature than a real-life portrait of the role of empirical evidence as one important basis for developing a rich, reliable, and predictive professional knowledge base. We would all agree that social work is not an intellectual hobby that one dabbles in. Our first obligation is to the people and communities in whose behalf we work, and in this work choices must be made about what information is most likely to inform professional decisions and interventions that are appropriate, reliable, and effective. In our view, our best efforts to provide students with a sturdy base of knowledge and theory for practice are an important part of our obligations to them and the people they serve.

REFERENCES

Nurius, P. S., & Gibson, J. (1990). Clinical observation, inference, reasoning and judgment in social work: An update. *Social Work Research and Abstracts,* 26(2), 18–25.

Rosen, A., Proctor, E. E., Morrow-Howell, N., & Staudt, M. (1995). Rationales for practice decisions: Variations in knowledge use by decision task and social work service. *Research in Social Work Practice,* 5, 501-523.

NO

PAULA NURIUS
SUSAN KEMP

We base our argument that theories of human behavior for which there is limited empirical support should *not* be included in HBSE courses on a discussion of two forms of responsibility; first, our responsibilities as educators; second, our responsibilities as professionals. Although in reality these are deeply intertwined, for the sake of clarity we focus first on issues of educational responsibility, and then relate these to broader issues of professionalism. As a frame for this discussion, we first attempt to clarify some of the definitional questions that typically complicate and derail discussions of social work knowledge.

Just What Do We Mean?

Discussions of the relative merits of different kinds of social work knowledge tend to be plagued by confusion deriving from the haphazard and inconsistent use of terms such as theory, approach, method, model, perspective, and framework.

Although tedious, the definitional issue is not trivial. Blurriness in how we use terms leads to blurriness regarding educational and professional objectives; what should or should not be included in the curriculum—and why. Students also need to understand the differences between different terms and to have the analytical skills to gauge when terms and claims are being applied inappropriately.

In summarizing some of these distinctions as well as the relevance of a strong theory base for social work practice, Francis Turner (1986) notes that the profession once had a very limited theory base and has gone through periods of overreliance on a particular theoretical perspective (e.g., psychodynamic theory). The contemporary social work, however, has access to a broad range of theories that provide a systematic and testable basis on which to build and refine practice interventions. This is not to say that current theories fully address all experiences, needs, or conditions. Life is not static, and neither is our knowledge base. Theory emerges through a process of ordering phenomena in a meaningful way. Relationships are posited among objects and events with expectations or predictions that certain outcomes will most likely result. As these hypotheses undergo repeated testing and are found through disciplined observation to yield dependable, predictable outcomes, principles emerge as statements about some aspect of reality. Indeed, the core utility of human behavior theory to practitioners is theextent to which it assists them to synthesize observations, to predict outcomes, and to explain the "why's" underlying relationships and outcomes (Levitan, 1989; Longres, 1995; Polansky, 1986).

Theory, then, refers not to a body of dogma or ideology but to an organized body of concepts that attempt to explain some phenomenon in a manner that has been, or is capable of being, systematically tested to determine the merits of evidence (Turner, 1995). Because the debate question is about human behavior theories (and not, for example, about values or philosophy), we interpret the question of empirical support to mean how fully any given formal theory has undergone various forms of testing and been found, across a range of both research and practice situations, to yield robust, coherent, and generalizable prediction of outcomes relevant to social work practice.

A commitment to action based on carefully gathered and multidimensional "evidence" has a long, sturdy, and bipartisan history in social work, including both the systematic case records of Mary Richmond and the early social caseworkers and the community surveys of the settlement workers. Only in more recent times has there been a tendency to assume some mutual incompatibility between "empirical" or evidence-based approaches and a commitment to social justice and client empowerment. As we see it, characteristics of an evidence-based approach include: (1) a style of constant questioning; (2) systematic observation; (3) efforts to obtain the strongest possible sources of evidence (e.g., regarding what factors in the natural environment and in helping efforts are most likely to contribute to positive or negative outcomes for clients, the specific nature of relationships among factors presumed to cause observed outcomes, and the outcomes themselves); (4) attention to inconsistencies and rival possibilities in interpreting observations; (5) an understanding that all findings are tentative and inherently bounded by the context of the inquiry; (6) a willingness to submit one's working theories and practice to scrutiny and to make adjustments on the basis of the best available evidence; and (7) an understanding that sturdy, systematic data enhances both personal and social change efforts.

This is not an either/or, forced-choice situation. That is, developing an understanding of theories of human behavior supported by empirical evidence can and should reside alongside the development of a critical perspective and skills in critical analysis (e.g., the capacity to analyze the merits of an argument; to search for and gauge strength of evidence of claims; to locate and assess the adequacy of the extant knowledge base; to judge the appropriateness of a course of action relevant to specific situations and individuals). There are a number of criteria that social workers must, in their work with clients, be capable of applying in assessing need and making considered judgments about the most effective means of helping. Metaphorically, social workers must become multilingual in their capacity to understand and apply concepts and criteria across multiple levels and referent sources (Bloom, Wood, & Chambon, 1991). Learning goals, and the content that supports their attainment, should thus be constructed in both/and rather than either/or terms. Such inclusiveness does not mean, however, that "anything goes" in course content.

Educational Responsibility

Given the lively debate in social work about the relative merits of empirical versus naturalistic forms of knowledge (Rodwell, 1987; Witkin, 1991), it is tempting to address the question of human behavior content in HBSE courses primarily from this perspective. At heart, however, this is an educational issue, and it should be considered from this standpoint. Although broader questions, such as what constitutes valid and appropriate knowledge for social work practice, are certainly relevant and important, our focus here is to weigh these in the particular context of HBSE as an educational sequence. From this perspective, epistemological and philosophical issues must be balanced with other educational and pedagogical concerns. These include, for example: accreditation requirements; the articulation of HBSE content with other courses in the required curriculum; including the need for HBSE courses to support learning in practice classes and in the practicum; and questions (ethical and professional) about what constitutes an adequate level of knowledge for practice (particularly considering the limited professional experience and preparation typical of students at this point in their training).

In considering the debate question, it is also important to remember that the HBSE curriculum does not consist solely, or even largely, of content on "human behavior." Our position that theories of human behavior taught in HBSE courses should be empirically based is not, therefore, an argument that all material taught in HBSE courses should be empirical in nature. The Council on Social Work Education (CSWE) Curriculum Policy Statement for both baccalaureate and master's degree programs indicates that "the professional foundation must provide content about theories and knowledge of human bio-psycho-social development, including theories and knowledge about the range of social systems in which individuals live (families, groups, organizations, institutions, and communities)" (CSWE Curriculum Policy Statement, 1995, p. 2652), as well as instruction on how to evaluate theory and apply theory to client situations. Council guidelines are, however, unambiguous about an educational commitment both to strengthen students' understanding and appreciation of a scientific, analytic approach to building knowledge for the delivery and evaluation of practice (including the ability to critically analyze and apply knowledge and to conduct empirical evaluations of their own practice interventions and those of relevant systems) *and* to recognize that these professional skills and obligations reside alongside those reflecting other aspects of professional values and perspectives.

The educational objectives contained within the CSWE guidelines for HBSE courses thus reflect a synthesis of (1) the current knowledge base with respect to theory and findings on human development and interactions among social systems as they affect and are affected by human behavior, (2) socialization regarding a professional perspective, set of values, and priorities, and (3) enhancement of critical thinking skills to evaluate and appropriately apply theory, findings, and a perspective regarding professional purpose to specific client situations. Perusal of current HBSE texts (Germain, 1991; Longres, 1995), as well as HBSE syllabi, indicates that pedagogically these objectives are deeply interrelated. Content on the impact of differential racial and ethnic experience on human development, for example, is presented along with material that encourages students to examine issues of race, class, and culture in American society as well as social work's commitment to social justice relative to these issues. An ecological, or ecological-systems perspective, typically provides the metatheoretical framework, or intellectual structure within which these various levels and forms of knowledge (substantive material, critical perspectives, and professional values) can be organized.

Content in HBSE is also shaped, to an increasing degree, by practice perspectives that have an explicit ideological or value bias. Such perspectives provide social workers not only with guidance about how to act (skills), but also with a set of principles and values. These, in effect, direct practitioners to act in some ways rather than others. Currently influential perspectives (in HBSE as in much of the rest of the curriculum) include empowerment practice, the strengths perspective, feminist practice, and multicultural practice. An important contribution of such perspectives is the way in which they frame practice in terms of the mission and purposes of the profession.

Many forms of knowledge thus have a place in the HBSE curriculum, and some of these appropriately are analytical or ideological in nature. Such materials have their own place, however, and are not a substitute for a solid grounding in formal theories of human behavior. A clear understanding of the ecosystems perspective does not, for example, obviate the need for practitioners to have a firm grasp of developmental theories and the ability to differentiate among them. Nor does an intellectual commitment to empowerment necessarily translate directly (or easily) into knowledge and skills for everyday practice. These intellectual frameworks and perspectives must, therefore, be supported by a substantial foundation of empirically tested substantive knowledge (Rosen, 1994).

Professional Responsibility

The question of educational responsibility both flows from and is informed by larger issues of professional responsibility and jurisdiction. Like other professionals, social workers claim professional status on the basis that they have mastered a distinctive body of knowledge and skill that has been tested and systematized so that it can be transmitted through professional education and applied reliably in practice. Indeed, the ability to apply substantive knowledge inferentially to complex and messy issues distinguishes professional practice (by which we mean practice that is effective, accountable, ethical, and responsive to the particular and "individual" needs of client systems) from technical competence. Without this ability, Aaron Rosen (1994) has argued, practice becomes "ritualistic," guided more by familiar methods and individual preferences than by the worker's ability to develop unique solutions derived from the connections between client system data and relevant substantive knowledge.

The use of evidence-based knowledge not only enables more effective and consistent practice, but also addresses the profession's need to meet external accountability expectations, for example, in the form of requirements by funders, underwriters, and legislative, judicial, and regulatory bodies to specify the conceptual and empirical bases for how needs and problems are defined, for which intervention plans are selected, for how intervention outcomes are evaluated. Ultimately, of course, social workers are also accountable to their clients. The ability to fully justify and explain our professional judgments and recommendations is central to ethical, client-centered and empowering practice, providing that professional knowledge is used, not as an instrument of hierarchy and control, but in ways that enhance client self-direction and participation. Where this does not occur, the problems lie not in the knowledge that we use, but in the ways that we use it.

An evidence-based approach to reasoning and decision making constitutes, in short, both a practical and an ethical obligation of social workers in their efforts to understand and intervene in their clients' lives. To support such an approach, social work educators must actively and intentionally incorporate empirical knowledge in course content, and reinforce the value of research-based knowledge in their teaching. This is particularly important in HBSE, given the centrality of this sequence to other educational objectives and the rich knowledge base it encompasses. Let us reiterate, however, that an emphasis on empirical content does not mean, *ipso facto*, that other content is not also important. Indeed, the teaching of values, analytical perspectives, and critical thinking skills provides an essential framework for substantive material, for it is these dimensions that enable students to situate, analyze, and differentiate between the multiple domains of knowledge available to them.

Conclusions

Should human behavior theories for which there is limited empirical support be included in the course outlines for HBSE? We have laid out key elements of the educational, professional, and ethical contexts within which this question must realistically be addressed. We would answer the question with questions. For what purpose would unsupported theories be included (e.g., what are the specific learning objectives)? What efforts have been made to assess the availability of better-supported theories in the existing knowledge base? To what extent are the substantive educational foundations of the HBSE sequence being risked or compromised (e.g., that better-supported substantive theories relevant to subsequent instruction or practice are being excluded to make room for the unsupported theory in question)? Given the lack of supportive evidence, what criteria are being applied to evaluate the merits of the proposed theory? Given the lack of supportive evidence, what safeguards or qualifications are being employed to minimize undue risk to students or clients in the application of untested theory? Is the theory in question truly a substantive theory about human behavior or is it more an expression of values, philosophy, or ideology (the latter having a legitimate role, yet one that should not supplant substantive theory content)? If there is little or no evidence base to support the theory in question, how is the instructor planning to assist students in applying critical thinking skills to evaluate for themselves the merits of the theory? Only through struggling with such questions can we move past the rhetoric of the empirical debate to address the core educational, professional, and ethical issues that lie within it.

REFERENCES

Bloom, M., Wood, K., & Chambon, A. (1991). The six languages of social work. *Social Work, 36,* 530–534.

Germain, C. B. (1991). *Human behavior in the social environment: An ecological perspective.* New York: Columbia University Press.

Levitan, L. C. (1989). Theoretical foundations of AIDS-prevention programs. In R. O. Valdiserri (Ed.), *Prevention AIDS: The design of effective programs.* New Brunswick, NJ: Rutgers University Press.

Longres, J. F. (1995). *Human behavior in the social environment* (2nd ed.). Itasca, IL: Peacock.

Polansky, N. (1986). There is nothing so practical as a good theory. *Child Welfare, 65,* 3–15.

Rodwell, M. K. (1987). Naturalistic enquiry: An alternative model for social work assessment. *Social Service Review, 61*(2), 231–246.

Rosen, A. (1994). Knowledge use in direct practice. *Social Service Review, 68,* 561–577.

Turner, F. J. (1986). *Social work treatment: Interlocking theoretical approaches* (3rd ed.). New York: Free Press.

Turner, F. J. (1995). Social work practice: Theoretical base. In R. L. Edwards and others (Eds.), *Encyclopedia of social work* (19th ed., pp. 2258–2265). Washington, DC: NASW Press.

Witkin, S. L. (1991). Empirical clinical practice: A critical analysis. *Social Work, 36,* 158–163.

Rejoinder to Drs. Nurius and Kemp Stanley Witkin

Kemp and Nurius's thoughtful paper left me feeling somewhat optimistic. Despite arguing different sides of the question, we still managed to agree on some significant matters. Particularly noteworthy, in my opinion, were our similar views about the need to expose students to multiple forms of knowing and knowledge and the importance of helping students to think critically about both. We also agreed that the selection of theories for HBSE courses is, in part, a pedagogical issue, not simple a philosophical one, and that many factors (not only empirical content) should be considered when selecting theories for course inclusion. These areas of concordance suggest that even when educators seem to be on opposite sides of an issue, there may be common ground on which they can collaborate and even enrich the curriculum.

Differences exist as well. Most salient is the meaning of empirical support and the evidentiary warrant it provides. As I have argued previously, claims of such support are often difficult to assess, and it is common for different groups to claim empirical support for their favorite theory while decrying the lack of support for rival conceptual schemes. Kemp and Nurius further complicate this issue by their particularly broad definition of empirical support: "how fully any given formal theory has undergone various forms of testing and been found, across a range of both research and practice situations, to yield robust, coherent, and generalizable prediction of outcomes relevant to social work practice." Although such a definition may be lauded for its comprehensiveness, its application remains a mystery. Perhaps this is why Kemp and Nurius fail to name even one theory that meets their criteria.

The ambiguity surrounding the assessment of empirical support reflects the equivocal relationship between observations and empirical data. Because all such relationships are mediated through language, research that supports one theory may be reinterpreted as support for an alternative theory (Gergen, 1994). I can only speculate that these difficulties partially explain Kemp and Nurius's shift in language from empirical support of theory to "evidence-based knowledge."

Kemp and Nurius distinguish between "formal theories of human behavior" and other forms of knowledge such as "practice perspectives" and "metatheoretical frameworks." They imply that these other knowledge forms are more value based and "analytical or ideological in nature" than formal theories. Therefore, practitioners need "...to have a firm grasp of developmental theories...." Although their conclusion may be correct, their reasoning is not. Analysis of formal theories shows that they too are value based and ideological: favoring certain conceptions of human functioning over others, using certain language terms to name actions, and supporting (or challenging) certain cultural and political beliefs.

Another justification for distinguishing formal theories from other forms of knowledge is the need for social work knowledge to be useful in practice. For example, Kemp and Nurius state that "intellectual commitments to empowerment [do not] necessarily translate directly (or easily) into knowledge and skills for everyday practice." Again, this may be true, but it does not establish that formal theory would translate any more easily. Instead, their argument confounds a theory's empirical content with its utility.

A critical understanding of theory and its relationship to practice is of vital importance to social work education. Despite our differences, I believe that Kemp and Nurius share these beliefs.

REFERENCES

Gergen, K. (1994). *Toward transformation in social knowledge* (2nd ed.). Thousand Oaks, CA: Sage.

Is It Possible to Know When Theories Are Obsolete?

EDITOR'S NOTE: Social history is rich in theories about human behavior, most of which have not been formally tested. Even today, there are literally hundreds of distinctive human behavioral theories, although they tend to share roots in some dozen families of theories. It is not possible to teach all of these distinctive theories, but is it possible to eliminate some from consideration, while concentrating on others? If so, how should these choices be made?

Bruce Thyer, Ph.D., L.C.S.W., is professor of social work at the University of Georgia. He has authored more than 130 journal articles and is the founding and current editor of the peer-reviewed journal *Research in Social Work Practice.* He is currently hard at work preparing an edited volume titled *Handbook of Empirical Social Work Practice.*

Teresa Morris, Ph.D., is an associate professor in the Department of Social Work, California State University at San Bernardino. The project currently consuming most of her time is chairing the faculty senate during a period of cutbacks in the California education budget, with debates about union agreements requiring "merit" systems so that large numbers of faculty can compete for small numbers of pay increases, and with attacks on affirmative action. She reports that she's learning about crisis leadership as fast as possible—the book will follow!

YES

BRUCE THYER

In a previous essay of this type, I have stated that "Most theories we teach in social work are wrong" (Thyer, 1994, p. 149). Thus it was no disagreeable task which Professors Bloom and Klein set before me, an opportunity to expand on this proposition, and it was with a pleasant sigh of anticipation that I located a new yellow pad, uncapped my Waterman, charged it with fresh ink, and set down to compose my thesis.

The first definition of obsolete that my dictionary provided was "1. no longer in use or practice, discarded." I suspect I would get little argument from Dr. Morris that some theories are no longer in use, so I shall rather reframe my comments to deal with whether it is possible to conclude if a theory has become obsolete in a scientific sense and hence, not to be taught in the core HBSE curriculum. My arguments shall be marshaled along three distinct lines: (1) appeals to authority, (2) appeals to logic, and (3) appeals to fact. These arguments may be seen to ascend from low to high in terms of their validity, culminating, I believe, in a strong position. I will conclude by outlining some proposed standards that can be used to judge when theories are obsolete.

Argument by Authority

In preparing for this essay, quite literally the first volume I took down from my office bookshelf is a widely used textbook called *Comparing Theories of Child Development* by R. Murray Thomas (1992), now in its third edition. In it the author begins by describing the usual features of a good theory, and prominent among these is the question of a theory being potentially falsifiable. Here is what he has to say on the matter:

> Researchers must test the validity of hypotheses derived from the theory in order to determine to what extent it does indeed explain the facts satisfactorily. Thus if a theory's hypotheses can be tested to determine whether they are true, then the reverse should also obtain—it should be possible to test that a hypothesis is false. . . . the validity of a theory should not only be confirmable through logic and the presentation of data, it should also be falsifiable or disconfirmable. (Thomas, 1992, p. 21)

The extent to which a theory is falsifiable has long been held to be an important characteristic of its potential usefulness. Indeed, Sir Karl Popper (deceased, but not obsolete) contended for quite some time that *disproving* theories is a more valuable (and feasible) contribution to science than is trying to confirm them as accurate (Popper, 1959, 1963).

Enough of secular authorities such as Thomas and Popper. Let us turn to spiritual ones, such as the Nobel Laureate for Peace and God Incarnate, the Dalai Lama, who says:

> There are many things we Buddhists should learn from the latest scientific findings. And scientists can learn from Buddhist explanation. We must conduct research, and accept the results. If they don't stand up to experimentation, Buddha's own words must be *rejected*. (cited from Iyer, 1988, p. 60, italics added)

Because leading philosophers of science, experts in human development, and religious leaders agree that the potential to reject or falsify a theory is of great import, we should accept the proposition that we can tell when to do so.

Argument by Logic

It has long been recognized that science typically proceeds incrementally, punctuated by periodic bursts of progress (e.g., evolution of species through natural selection, à la Darwin; evolution of behavior through reinforcement, à la Skinner, etc.). In general, the major tool by which scientific advances are attained is called the hypothetico-deductive process. With respect to human development, theories are often arrived at by one or more individuals gathering careful observations over time regarding how people grow up: Piaget watched his own children, as well as others; Freud listened to his adult patients' accounts of their childhood experiences; Gesell described various cohorts of children in cross-sectional studies; and Sheldon took thousands of systematic photographs of bodily somatotypes. Purported similarities and differences are noted and gradually a comprehensive accounting in terms of theoretical mechanisms is arrived at, in other words, a theory.

By definition a theory generates hypotheses, specific predictions of the results of as-yet-uncollected data. According to Piaget, children younger than a certain age (in this case, about age eleven years) are not usually capable of performing particular intellectual tasks he called formal operations. If it could be shown that with proper structured training, children far younger than those his theory predicted could perform formal operations, his theory would be weakened, because the behaviors indicating formal operations could be more parsimoniously ascribed to a child's learning history than to hypothetical cognitive developmental stages irrevocably linked to one's chronological age (This, by the way, is what has happened to Piaget's findings, and is one reason why his theory is no longer given much credence, i.e., is obsolete.)

Similarly, Freud's theory of psychosexual development hypothesized that gay men share certain common childhood experiences, such as having difficulty in resolving Oedipal conflicts and becoming fixated at the latency state of development (Thomas, 1992, p. 143). In fact, this is clearly not the case, and this psychoanalytic account of male homosexuality is no longer seen as valid (i.e., is obsolete). Through the accrual of such refutations of the predictions (hypotheses) derived from particular theories, eventually the theory can be completely discarded.

As articulated in a masterful essay by Platt (1964), the problem can be explained thusly. If one tests a hypothesis derived from theory A, and obtains results consistent with theory A, at best one may have said to "corroborate" that theory; never (or almost never) can one claim to have proved it to be true. The reason for this is that it is usually the case that theories B, C, D, and so forth can also account for the results of one's research. Conversely, if theory A clearly predicts finding X, the proper data are garnered, and the result is *not*-X, then theory A is weakened. If, over time, a sufficient number of *not*-Xs are obtained, using various methodologies, legitimate tests, and by independent investigators, then eventually theory A can be clearly said to have been disconfirmed, or to be obsolete. No matter how many hypotheses are corroborated, they can usually be collectively accounted for by a variety of theories, not just by theory A. Thus, rejecting the validity of a theory of human development is easier than confirming it. Science can be said to whisper "yes," but to shout "NO!"

Argument by Fact

Carel Germain (1987) has produced a very fine social work critique of stage theories of human development, noting that these theories share a number of questionable assumptions, tend to ignore larger societal forces, lack attention to changing gender roles, and are at variance with contemporary longitudinal research on development. Thomas (1992) also provides a number of examples of developmental theories that are obsolete. He quotes C. J. Brainerd (1983, p. vi), who states that the early 1980s witnessed: "a rapid decline in the influence of orthodox Piagetian theory, a fact that is now acknowledged by Piagetians and non-Piagetians alike... Empirical and conceptual objections to the theory have become so numerous that it can no longer be regarded as a positive force in mainstream cognitive developmental research..." (Thomas, 1992, p. 313). Thomas also notes that "... since the 1950s, adherents of traditional psychoanalytic theory have declined among psychotherapists, researchers, writers and teachers about child development... Social learning models and other cognitive theories founded on the study of normal children have come to dominate the field" (p. 479).

Similar conclusions can be drawn about selected practice theories. For example, neurolinguistic programming, which has been widely disseminated as one approach to social work intervention (e.g., Zastrow, 1995, pp. 471–485), is based on theoretical propositions that research has shown to be erroneous

(Einspruch & Forman, 1985; Sharpley, 1987), as well as not being helpful to clients (Krugman, Kirsch, Wickless, Milling, Golicz, & Toth, 1985). Similarly, the panacea of so-called facilitated communication aimed at helping persons with autism has been thoroughly tested and found wanting (Wheeler, Jacobson, Paglieri, & Schwartz, 1993).

Thus it would seem that the facts of the matter are in accord with affirming this chapter's proposition. Piagetian and Freudian views are no longer seen as viable theories of human development. Neurolinguistic programming and facilitated communication are obsolete therapies. These conclusions are based on the findings of empirical research, illustrating the usefulness of the hypothetico-deductive process as a major tool in developing social work knowledge. I now conclude this initial essay with some general principles that can guide us in determining when a theory is obsolescent (These are not listed in any particular order of primacy).

Criteria to Help Determine If a Theory is Obsolete

Criterion 1

If, after a fair amount of time, the theory has failed to garner appreciable empirical support, then it is obsolete.
Example: Contemporary science no longer supports the Hippocratic theory that the human personality is an amalgam of the four humors (black bile, yellow bile, blood, and phlegm). The failure of this developmental model to be supported has rendered it obsolete.

Criterion 2

If a theory has been shown, through credible scientific research, to be false, then it is obsolete.
Examples: Astrological theory claims that human development and personality are largely a function of the position of various heavenly bodies at the time and place of one's birth. Empirical research has clearly shown that astrology is false (e.g., Carlson, 1985) and thus is obsolete. More than seventy years ago, John B. Watson made the assertion:

> Give me a dozen healthy infants, well-formed, and my own specified world to bring them up in and I'll guarantee to take any one at random and train him to become any type of specialist I might select—doctor, lawyer, artist, merchant–chief, and yes, even beggar-man and thief, regardless of his talents,

penchants, tendencies, abilities, vocations and race of his ancestors." (Watson, 1924/1970, p. 104)

Watson's exaggerated environmentalist claims have been superseded by more temperate Skinnerian behavioral views, namely, that although learning factors (nurture) are important, they are not the *sole* determinant of human development and behavior (Skinner, 1966; see also Kagan, 1989; Thyer, 1992; Bijou, 1993).

Criterion 3

If the developmental phenomena accounted for by theory A can be better (i.e., empirically, comprehensively, parsimoniously) accounted for by theory B, then theory A is obsolete.

Example: Certain types of complex behavior have been labeled "novel," or "creative," and a variety of involved cognitive models have been invoked to account for them. If relatively simpler learning theory explanations that do not involve unobservable mentalistic mechanisms can be developed, tested, and corroborated, then the more parsimonious account renders the more complex theory obsolete. Some examples include "insight" (Epstein, Kirshnit, Lanza & Rubin, 1984), tool use (Epstein & Medalie, 1983), and self-awareness (Epstein, Lanza, & Skinner, 1981). See Epstein (1984) for an elaboration of this contention.

Criterion 4

When significant authorities agree that a theory is obsolete, then it is obsolete.

Example: This is offered only partially tongue in cheek, inasmuch as appeal to authority has never carried much weight in terms of scientific merit. Nevertheless, if the considered judgment of credible scientists points in a particular direction, such opinions should certainly be accorded weight similar to that of the venerated entities "clinical wisdom" and "traditional practice."

Criterion 5

If a theory promotes sexist, racist, or homophobic viewpoints, then it is obsolete.

Examples: Take for example Freud's views on the creativity of women:

It seems that women have made few contributions to the discoveries and inventions in the history of civilization; there is however, one technique which they may have invented—that of plaiting and weaving. If that is so, we should be tempted to guess the unconscious motive for the achievement. Nature herself would seem to have given the model which this achievement imitates by causing the growth at maturity of the pubic hair that conceals the genitals. The step that remained to be taken lay in making the threads adhere to one another, while on the body they stick to the skin and are only matted together (Freud, 1933, p. 132).

This ghastly notion that women have contributed little to creative discovery (except weaving!) during the course of human history could be seen as contributory to the continuing oppression of women in society. Similarly, Freud's views on the psychological development of male homosexuality and of lesbianism would no longer be given much credence today, partly because of strong scientific evidence of their invalidity, and also because they fail to promote social justice (see Witkin & Gottschalk, 1988, for an elaboration of this latter contention).

Summary

A major endeavor of the scientific enterprise is the determination of truth from falsehood, of the factual from the obsolete. Not every social work theory is "true" or has equal scientific merit. In fact, I suspect that in the fullness of time most social work theories will be proved to be false! This is good. As our field progresses, we shall continue to see a continuing winnowing out of the obsolete and the adoption of the effective and the true. This is called scientific progress and has been made possible by the intellectual tools of empirical research that have served social work well for decades.

REFERENCES

Bijou, S. W. (1993). *Behavior analysis of child development* (2nd ed.). Reno, NE: Context Press.
Carlson, S. (1985). A double-blind test of astrology. *Nature, 318,* 419–425.
Einspruch, E. L., & Forman, B. D. (1985). Observations concerning research literature on neurolinguistic programming. *Journal of Counseling Psychology, 32,* 589–596.
Epstein, R., & Medalie, S. (1983). The spontaneous use of a tool by a pigeon. *Behaviour Analysis Letters, 3,* 6251–6253.
Epstein, R. (1984). The principle of parsimony and some applications in psychology. *Journal of Mind and Behavior, 5,* 119–130.
Epstein, R., Kirshnit, C., Lanza, R. P., & Rubin, L. (1984). "Insight" in the pigeon: Antecedents and determinants of an intelligent performance. *Nature, 308,* 61–62.
Epstein, R., Lanza, R. P., & Skinner, B. F. (1981). "Self-awareness" in the pigeon. *Science, 212,* 695–696.
Freud, S. (1933). *New introductory lectures on psychoanalysis* (Vol. 22, standard edition). London: Hogarth.

Germain, C. B. (1987). Human development in contemporary environments. *Social Service Review, 61,* 565–579.

Iyer, P. (1988, April 11). Tibet's living Buddha. *Time,* pp. 58–60.

Kagan, J. (1989). Temperamental contributions to social behavior. *American Psychologist, 44,* 668–674.

Krugman, M., Kirsch, I., Wickless, C., Milling, L., Golicz, H., & Toth, A. (1985). Neurolinguistic programming treatments for anxiety: Myth or magic? *Journal of Consulting and Clinical Psychology, 53,* 526–530.

Platt, J. R. (1964). Strong inference. *Science, 146,* 347–353.

Popper, K. R. (1959). *The logic of scientific discovery.* London: Hutchinson.

Popper, K. R. (1963). *Conjectures and refutations.* London: Routledge & Kegan Paul.

Sharpley, C. F. (1987). Research findings on neurolinguistic programming: Nonsupportive data or an untestable theory? *Journal of Counseling Psychology, 34,* 103–107.

Skinner, B. F. (1966). The phylogeny and ontogeny of behavior. *Science, 153,* 1205–1213.

Thomas, R. M. (1992). *Comparing theories of child development* (3rd ed.). Belmont, CA: Wadsworth.

Thyer, B. A. (1992). A behavioral perspective on human development. In M. Bloom (Ed.), *Changing lives: Studies in human development and professional helping* (pp. 410–418). Columbia, SC: University of South Carolina Press.

Thyer, B. A. (1994). Are theories of practice necessary? No. *Journal of Social Work Education, 30,* 147–151.

Watson, J. B. (1924/1970). *Behaviorism* (rev. ed.). New York: Norton.

Wheeler, D. L., Jacobson, J. W., Paglieri, R. A., & Schwartz, A. A. (1993). An experimental assessment of facilitated communication. *Mental Retardation, 31,* 49–60.

Witkin, S. L., & Gottschalk, S. (1988). Alternative criteria for theory evaluation. *Social Service Review, 62,* 83–98.

Zastrow, C. (1995). *The practice of social work* (5th ed.). Belmont, CA: Brooks/Cole.

Rejoinder to Dr. Thyer

TERESA MORRIS

An Invitation to Dance

I have been invited to a boxing match but I intend to go to a dance. I can hear referees Bloom and Klein give instructions to Dr. Thyer and myself for a clean fight, but in the distance the band is striking up a Strauss waltz, or is it a cowboy cha-cha? Whatever it is, I am going to take Dr. Thyer's arm and join him in the dance. I would rather do this than sock him on the jaw!

Because this is my dance, I will lead. I would like to suggest that we listen to the music first and then decide which dance to do. However, Dr. Thyer has a different suggestion. He knows his dance theory. He knows what others have said about appropriate steps. He references Sir Karl Popper, a man with admirable footwork, who was able to get around the problem of induction by suggesting we falsify rather than prove theories. Of course the problem of induction remains. We cannot prove a theory by confirming a hypothesis in the same way that we cannot disprove a theory by rejecting a null. Dr. Thyer also quotes the words of the Dalai Lama, another graceful mover. Maybe the quote, though, is out of context, because I cannot believe that His Holiness would give up his religious beliefs on the basis of a falsified hypothesis.

Perhaps reading about the dance is not the same as doing the dance. If we relax and listen to the music, we will move together according to what we hear and feel. There are a number of rhythms and themes in the music, and we must respond to them all to dance well. Dr. Thyer is clearly skilled at one particular dance (positivist empiricism) and does that dance well. We can dance together as long as this is the music accompanying us. However, I get the feeling that he plans to do that same dance regardless of the music or the rhythm around him. No matter what the knowledge is needed, he will always call on "objective" logic and fact, stating that empirically supported, nonfalsified, nonimproved, authoritative, nondistasteful theory is the only theory we have. There might be a need for the postpositivists' discovery of theory, the critical theorists' study of power and diversity, and the constructivists' development of subjective knowledge through a hermeneutic dialectic process. However, these are not dance steps that Dr. Thyer entertains.

So we have a problem on the dance floor. I can only ask Dr. Thyer to mark his card for me when the music suggests positivist empiricism. Then we can enjoy each other's proficiency and sense of rhythm. If there is other music playing, though, I must look elsewhere for a partner. Perhaps Corbin and Strauss (1990), Roberts (1990), or Erlandson, Jarris, Skipper, & Allen (1993) will then take my arm.

References

Corbin J., & Strauss, A. (1990). Grounded theory research: procedures, canons, and evaluative criteria. *Qualitative Sociology. 13*(1), 3–21.

Erlandson, D. A., Jarris, E. L., Skipper, B. L., Allen, S. D. (1993). *Doing naturalistic inquiry.* Thousand Oaks: Sage.

Roberts, H. (1990). *Doing feminist research.* London: Routledge.

NO

TERESA MORRIS

In America with our short attention spans we quite frequently recycle: a book (*Gone with the Wind* returning as *Slow Waltz in Cedar Bend*); a musical (Andrew Lloyd Webber... over and over again); a movie ("An Affair to Remember" with Cary Grant and Deborah Kerr remade as Warren Beaty and Annette Benning's story); or a fashion (bell-bottom jeans and platform shoes, as ugly as ever, again). We pretend, each time, that something new has been invented. We think the recycled product is new because we forget. We have forgotten the headlines in yesterday's newspaper, let alone what happened five or ten years ago. Studs Terkle (1988) has called this America's "collective Alzheimer's" (p. 4). Goethe (Gaarder, 1994) once said, "Anyone who is not operating on 300 years of history is living from hand to mouth." (p. 126). We are clearly starving for knowledge.

Theory Is a Cloth That We Weave

A commitment to understanding theory is a commitment to history. We cannot understand the human experience today without tracing the historical context of that understanding. If we review a history of western philosophy, we see that the questions we tend to ask, such as, "Who are we?" "How did we get here?" "Why are we here?" "How should we live our lives here?" and " Is there life after death?" tend to be constant preoccupations. However, our answers to those questions at different times have lead us to new insights about the nature of existence.

While Plato and Aristotle (Adler, 1978; Plato, 1968) distinguished between the world of the senses and the world of ideas, others such as Plotinus (Mackenna, 1956) suggested that there was no such separation and that all of our experiences of the world around us are experiences of a God. In medieval times, Augustine and Aquinas (Crombie, 1961) also thought that human experience was a revelation of God. Renaissance and Enlightenment (Copleston, 1951) thinking rebelled against such deference to a supreme being and venerated the individual who is able to ask questions about existence. Empiricists such as Locke and Hume (Kolakowski, 1972) continued this individualist line of thought by suggesting that reality is known through the senses, whereas ideas are simply personal perceptions not necessarily related to anything real. By the time we get to the twentieth century, we are comfortable with philosophies suggesting multiple realities depending on context (Gutting, 1980). We are also returning to a more detailed and complex notion of combining science and spirituality (Friedman, 1994).

If we narrow our focus to a philosophy of science (Oldroyd, 1986), we again see a spiraling evolution of ideas. Ancient and medieval (Adler, 1978; Crombie, 1961) scientists rely on knowledge gained through the senses, whereas Galileo introduces the notion of mathematical models and Bacon and Hume (Kolakowski, 1972) narrow science down to a search for cause and effect. In this century with Einstein (Schwartz & McGuiness, 1979), Kuhn (1970), and Feyerabend (1988), we have explored cultural and metaphorical influences on science and have a current proposition that there is no scientific method, only counterintuitive thinking (Feyerabend, 1988).

These explorations of the nature of human existence do not tell us that Aristotle is obsolete or that current theories are "correct." Such a conclusion misses the point. We could also say that the American civil war is obsolete! However, that experience is a major ingredient of modern American consciousness. No, to understand current philosophies we need to know how and why the strands of those philosophies have been woven together. Our current notions of human existence are a result of another recycling process that has revisited ideas at different periods and woven together new strands of understanding. We need to know about this creative process to truly comprehend current thinking.

If we move on from theories of knowledge to theories of society, we can identify a similar process. We note that late nineteenth to mid-twentieth century writers such as Durkheim (1951), Merton (1968), and Parsons (1954) described society as a well-organized, equilibrium-seeking, system. They suggested that anything that upsets societal equilibrium is dysfunctional and anything that maintains equilibrium is functional. However, the critical theories (Horkheimer, 1972; Marcuse, 1964) of members of the Frankfurt school, living in a Germany experiencing fascism and the oppression of minority groups such as Jews, homosexuals, and gypsies, addressed ideology and the battle for power, wealth, and prestige in society. They suggested that we cannot understand society without ideological, or political, consciousness. The interactionists (Faules, 1978) who emerged during the sixties and seventies, challenged traditional institutions, switched from objective notions of society, and took a relativist perspective theorizing that subjective experience of "everyday" interactions define and redefine society as social symbols and labels are defined and redefined.

Each of these theories has sharpened our understanding of society. We needlessly limit ourselves by suggesting that one of these theories is correct and others might be obsolete. Rather, we can acknowledge that the aspect of society that we are interested in and value dictates the societal theory we adopt. If we want to describe differences in attributes and needs according to gender, ethnicity, or class, we might take the functionalist view. This would give us data on gender, cultural, and class sensitivity. However, if we are directing our interest to power relationships according to gender, ethnicity, and class, then clearly the critical theory of society is more useful. Furthermore, if we think that power relations are to be included in attributes and needs according to gender, ethnicity, and class, then we might take an interactional view and discover subjective experiences of society. Because sociology is a young discipline, these theories have evolved in a limited timeframe and have often been presented as competing views of society. However, each of these approaches gives us alternative strategies for researching our concerns. Awareness of these alternative theories and their domains gives us an intelligent grounding in current social theory.

When we survey theories of individual behavior, again we see a cloth of knowledge being woven together. Adams & Schvaneveldt (1991) outlined three major frameworks in contemporary psychology: mechanistic, organic, and interactional. The mechanistic frame of reference, in its ideal form, assumes that human behavior is simply a response to external physical and social stimulation. The environment is thought to cause individual behavior. Like a machine, the individual acts in response to external forces. Theories adopting this model include behavioral theory (Skinner, who suggests that everything we do has been learned and can be unlearned and that behavior is a response to a stimulus, whereas conditioning is the repetition of these patterns until the behavior has a permanent connection with that stimulus; social learning theory (Bandura, 1977), which includes cognition in the behavioral learning process: and radical theories (Bailey & Brake, 1975), which see behavior as a response to society's structural inequity.

The organic frame of reference also sees the individual as a reactor to the environment, but it assumes that individuals are active in selecting experiences from the environment that can be used to transform and mature the individual. The individual maintains a sense of direction and growth by deciding between relevant and irrelevant experiences. Psychodynamic theories (Pearson, Treseder, & Yelloly, 1988) that assume that behavior is determined by people's feelings and thoughts and that we have unconscious conflicts influencing conscious mental activities are examples of this model.

The interactional frame of reference accepts the above ideas but also assumes that certain individual traits interact with certain aspects of the environment to influence a person's behavior. Theories with an interactional foundation include systems theories (Hearn, 1969) embracing concepts of input, throughput, output, feedback loops, and entropy; communication theories (Bateson, 1975) stressing the role of our understanding of social reactions and labels in building our roles and personalities; and humanistic approaches (Rogers & Strauss, 1967), which suggest that each individual is making sense of the world in a unique way that should be honored.

We see here, not theories becoming obsolete, but a combination of ideas, each of which gives us a new insight into human behavior. The word *obsolete* means disused, discarded, antiquated. How could any theory be any of these things? Of course, the next question addresses theories that we do not know about. Are there theories that do not get into our textbooks? What is the difference between those theories and the theories we do know about? This question directs our attention to the particular theories being woven into our cloth of knowledge.

Each Theory Is a Strand to Be Woven into That Cloth

Theories are not products that are useful at one time and then later are thrown away. Theories are ideas that tell us about our current consciousness of the world around us. They are useful at different times because of our changing concerns and problems. For example, in the United States, we currently focus on economic problems, and so we use economic concepts and theories to define our reality. In social welfare policy, we now discuss clients' success in terms of potential for economic self-sufficiency (Gueron and Pauly, 1991) and advocate for clients by suggesting that they are a resource in which the nation should invest (Reich, 1983).

So why are certain problems defined as important, and why do certain theories become received wisdom? Euro-American education stresses Euro-American history and Euro-American thinkers: usually men. It has only been in recent times through the challenges of powerful and vocal groups that an awareness of societal plurality and diversity has confronted us with our limited schooling. We have now begun to explore the concerns and world views of women and various ethnic and cultural groups as well as international and indigenous philosophical traditions. Understanding of these perspectives is now part of our expanded consciousness. We can see that our previous philosophies, theories, and concerns were culturally and colonially defined. However, this does not make that previous education obsolete. We now know that the cloth of knowledge that we are continually weaving is larger and more complex than we previously thought.

There is a lesson here, however. Keeping learning alive and growing requires opportunities for new voices to be heard. So . . . whose theories get publicized? Even with our new consciousness of diversity, some people's ideas will be published and taught in schools of social work, and other people's ideas will remain a private fantasy. How is this decision made? This is where our progress as a profession is tested. How broad is our consciousness of knowledge and theory? How open are we to new ideas and new styles of expression? Is it safer to stay with received wisdom and gain a partial glimpse of the cloth of knowledge? Who is defining "good" theory right now, and what are the politics of these decisions? Frequently, prominent female philosophers' and theoreticians' (Hildegard of Bingen, 1994; Starhawk, 1990) work is compartmentalized into "women's studies," while such writers from minority ethnic groups (Black Elk & Lyon, 1991) are studied in "ethnic studies" classes. How are we including such thinking in mainstream HBSE theorizing? Are these theories integrated into life span perspectives or are they separately described in a session on diversity? How are we addressing our responsibilities as students of theory?

Students of Theory

Our role as students of theory is not to decide which theories are correct or which are obsolete, but to strive to understand the overall pattern of theoretical knowledge and the contribution that each theory is making to that pattern. In this way we expand our consciousness and perceptions to gain a deeper understanding and wisdom about human experience.

Theoretical knowledge is not something proved on a multiple choice test but an evolving understanding that requires constant intellectual attention. The morality and values that we apply to theories shift as this understanding evolves and so what was once acceptable theory can be, at a later date, rejected. However, even theories that have been discredited, such as social Darwinism (Spencer, 1904) and the racism of the nineteenth century still play a role in our acquisition of knowledge. Such theories not only illustrate the darker side of human nature, much like the "Pulp Fiction" movie explores numbing violence or a play like "Macbeth" explores power lust, but they also provide signposts to dead ends we do not want to revisit and give us a measure that gauges the evolution of our understanding. Because of their presence in the history of the development of theories on diversity, we now have a more sophisticated understanding of the requirements of diversity. If we simply dismiss these nineteenth-century racial theories as obsolete, we are doomed to revisit a racist intellectual life.

Theories are a congregation rather than an aggregation of ideas. Theories are frequently set up to compete against each other in the name of rigor. However, this is simply a manifestation of a competitive rather than a collaborative approach to knowledge generation. The real question is not whether a theory is obsolete, but what each theory and our evaluation of it tells us about our current consciousness of the universe and human experience. The most productive approach to theory development is to value each contribution and honor its role in giving us a better understanding of the fabric of theories that we are weaving. Obsolete means antiquated, which means old-fashioned. Theory is often about fashion, but it should not be. Theory is a changing interweaving of ideas, the esthetics of which we need to understand, appreciate, and admire.

REFERENCES

Adams, G., & Schvaneveldt, J. (1991). *Understanding research methods*. New York: Longman.

Adler, M. J. (1978). *Aristotle for everybody: A difficult thought made easy*. New York: Macmillan.

Bailey, R., & Brake, M. (Eds.). (1975). *Radical social work*. London: Edward Arnold.

Bandura, A. (1977). *Social learning theory*. Englewood Cliffs, NJ: Prentice-Hall.

Bateson, G. (1975). *Steps to an ecology of mind*. New York: Ballantine.

Black Elk, W., & Lyon, W. E. (1991). *Black Elk: The sacred ways of a Lakota*. New York: Harper Collins.

Copleston, F. (1951). *A history of philosophy*. Longon: Burns & Oates and Searach Press.

Crombie, A. (1961) *Augustine to Galileo*. London: Mercury Books.

Durkheim, E. (1951). *Suicide*. (trans. by John A. Spaulding and George Simpson). New York: Free Press.

Faules, D. (1978). *Communication and social behavior: A symbolic interaction perspective.* Reading, MA: Addison-Wesley.

Feyerabend, P. (1988). *Against method.* London: Verso.

Friedman, N. (1994). *Bridging science and spirit.* Sausalito: Living Lake Books.

Gaarder, J. (1994). *Sophie's world.* New York: Farrar, Straus and Giroux.

Gueron, J., & Pauly. E. (1991). *From welfare to work.* New York: Russell Sage Foundation.

Gutting, G. (Ed.). (1980). *Paradigms and revolutions: Appraisals and applications of Thomas Kuhn's philosophy of science.* Notre Dame: University of Notre Dame Press.

Haeberle, E. (1983). *The sex atlas.* New York: Cointinuum.

Hearn, G. (1969). *The general systems approach: Contributions toward a holistic conception of social work.* New York: Council on Social Work Education.

Hildegard of Bingen. (1994). *Hildegard of Bingen: The book of the rewards of life* (B. W. Hozeski, Trans.) New York: Garland Pub.

Hite, S. (1987a). *The Hite report.* New York: Dell.

Hite, S. (1987b). *The Hite report on male sexuality.* New York: Ballantine.

Horkheimer, M. (1972). *Critical theory.* New York: Seabury.

Kolakowski, L. (1972). *Positivist philosophy from Hume to the Vienna circle.* Harmondsworth: Penguin.

Kuhn, T. S. (1970). *The structure of scientific revolutions* (2nd ed.) Chicago: University of Chicago.

Marcuse, H. (1964). *One dimensional man.* Boston: South End.

Merton, R. (1968). *Social theory and social structure.* New York: Free Press.

Michael, R., Laumann, E., & Kolata, G. (1994). *Sex in America: A definitive survey.* Boston: Little Brown.

Oldroyd, D. (1986). *The arch of knowledge.* Kensington: New South Wales University Press.

Parsons, T. (1954). *Essays in sociological theory.* Glencoe, IL: Free Press.

Pearson, G., Treseder, J., & Yelloly, M. (1988). *Social work and the legacy of Freud.* London: McMillan.

Plato. (1968). *The republic of plato.* (A. Bloom, Trans.). New York: Basic Books.

Plotinus. (1956). *The Enneads.* (S. MacKenna, Trans.). London: Faber and Faber.

Reich, R. (1983). *The next American frontier.* New York: Times Books.

Rogers, C., & Strauss, M. (1967). *Person to person: The problem of being human.* London: Souvenir Press.

Schwartz, J., & McGuiness, M. (1979). *Einstein for beginners.* London: Writers & Readers.

Spencer, H. (1904). *The principles of ethics.* New York: D. Appleton & Co.

Starhawk. (1990) *Truth or dare.* San Francisco: Harper.

Terkle, S. (1988). *The great American divide: Second thoughts on the American dream.* New York: Pantheon.

Rejoinder to Dr. Morris

BRUCE THYER

"The great tragedy of science—
the slaying of a beautiful hypothesis by an ugly fact"
T. H. Huxley

Dr. Morris's contention that we cannot understand human experience today without tracing the historical context of that understanding has some truth to it. Certainly, knowing something of the origins and precursors to a given theory of human behavior is often useful. However, it does not follow that we cannot know when a given theory is obsolete. Indeed, such determinations are the very heart of the scientific enterprise. Perhaps graduate students in astronomy should know something of the history of astrology, and modern-day budding chemists be acquainted with the views of medieval alchemists, but it would be folly to devote all but the briefest amount of class time and readings to these intellectual antecedents of contemporary astronomy and chemistry. Similarly, I see no possible justification in teaching social work students content on Nazi eugenic theories of human racial development and behavior. The comfortable intellectual egalitarianism espoused by Morris, that all theories are equal and deserving of equal treatment, irrespective of the degree of "scientific" support they may enjoy, is a prescription to burden the profession with an exponentially expanding plethora of theories and views with no possibility of sorting truth from fiction, fact from folly.

Just as relativist views of cultural practices collapse in the face of the objective reality of concentration camps, involuntary female circumcision, and contemporary chattel slavery, Morris's perspective of theories of equal value, "each of which gives us a new insight into human behavior," spontaneously combusts when scientific research clearly shows that a given perspective is simply *wrong*. Morris's suggestion that "Our role as students of theory is not to decide which theories are correct or which are obsolete" is at odds with the Council on Social Work Education's *Curriculum Policy Statement*'s stress on the importance of "an understanding and appreciation of a scientific, analytic approach to building knowledge from practice..."(CSWE, 1991, p. 141). Before building knowledge, one is required to clear away accumulated theoretical rubble, to separate the relevant from the irrelevant, the current from the obsolete. Given the time constraints of the social work curriculum, shall we devote time to explicating Freud's views on lesbianism? Are these a valid perspective to understand the development of sexual orientation among women? Or, is it correct to say that such misogynist views have little relevance for contemporary social workers? To the extent we disseminate outmoded views, the latest empirically supported content is reduced in the curriculum.

In the early nineteenth century, a group of manual laborers known as the Luddites were briefly active. Fearing the consequences of mechanization, the

Luddites' tactic was to smash or otherwise sabotage weaving machinery and other primitive industrial equipment. We have a contemporary version of the Luddites today, except these are *intellectual* Luddites, seemingly dedicated to trashing the significant advances that have been made in social work theory and practice, advances largely brought about because of our profession's successful adoption of the hypothetico-deductive process and of the tools of systematic empirical research. Not content with advocating many ways of knowing (a useful endeavor, as outlined in Thyer, 1995), it seems that such postmodernist thinkers are bent on destroying the existing edifice of scientific training and research methodology. To contend, as does Morris, that we should not attempt to determine if a given theory of obsolete chucks the whole structure of conventional, quantitative, empirical research out the window.

Theories are constructed to account for natural phenomena: human behavior and its development. As accurate data accrue, it becomes increasingly evident that a given theory is either largely consistent with the facts or is inconsistent with them. In the former, the theory should be retained pending further testing by gathering new data. In the latter, the theory should be discarded. In the opinion of the writer, it is both scientifically unjustifiable and actually unethical to promulgate obsolete theories of human development among M.S.W. students as if these accounts possessed any particular validity. The NASW Code of Ethics mandates that "The social worker should base practice upon recognized knowledge relevant to social work" (NASW, 1990, p. 9). The term *recognized knowledge* implies its opposite, unrecognized or obsolete knowledge. To the extent we hold on and disseminate these latter views, the profession and the clients we serve will suffer. The M.S.W. curriculum is not a history or a philosophy program. We need to be teaching students theoretical content clearly and directly *relevant* to preparation for practice.

REFERENCES

Council on Social Work Education. (1991). *Handbook of accreditation standards and procedures.* Alexandria, VA: Author.

National Association of Social Workers. (1990). *NASW code of ethics.* Washington, DC: Author.

Thyer, B. A. (1995). Reflection and controversy on entering our fifth year (editorial). *Research on Social Work Practice, 5,* 3–9.

Can Critical Thinking and HBSE Course Content Be Taught Concurrently?

EDITOR'S NOTE: Not only must social workers have a good knowledge base for practice, they must also be able to add to it, or subtract
from it, from time to time, which requires a critical reading and thinking
about the current literature. How should a helping profession learn this
critical thinking skill? Some suggest that it should be taught (and modeled) at the same time one is teaching substantive content, whereas others suggest that a separate course is needed.

Leonard E. Gibbs, Ph.D., professor of social work at the School of Social
Work, University of Wisconsin—Eau Claire, teaches research methods, field
work, and other courses. He is author of *Scientific Reasoning for Social Workers:
Bridging the Gap Between Research and Practice* (1991, Merrill Publisher) and
the recent workbook, *Critical Thinking for Social Workers* with E. Gambrill
(1996).

Steve Tallant, Ph.D., is an assistant professor at the School of Social Work,
University of Wisconsin—Eau Claire, where he teaches HBSE at the undergraduate level. His current research interests include family separation and
social support.

EDITORS' NOTE: Drs. Gibbs and Tallant accepted our invitation to
participate in this debate with the agreement that "sides" would be assigned by the toss of a coin. They acknowledge help from Professor
Emeritus Michael Hakeem, Carol Modl, and the University of Wisconsin—Eau Claire Foundation.

YES

Leonard E. Gibbs

Critical thinking refers to "the careful and deliberate determination of whether to accept, reject, or suspend judgment about a claim." (Moore & Parker, 1986, p. 4). In social work, our claims concern vital inferences about clients and their care. Here is a definition of critical thinking for social workers:

> (1) a predisposition to question conclusions that concern client care and welfare; (2) asking "does it work?" and "how do you know?" when confronted with claims that a method helps clients, and also questioning generalizations about treatment methods; (3) weighing evidence for and against assertions in a logical, rational, systematic, data-based way; and, (4) analyzing arguments to see what is being argued, spotting and explaining common fallacies in reasoning, and applying basic methodological principles of scientific reasoning. (Gibbs et al., 1995, p. 196)

Measures to assess critical thinking among social workers have been developed, including a Professional Thinking Form that tests ability to think critically about written case material (Gibbs, 1991, pp. 54–59, 274–278) and a Principles of Reasoning, Inference, Decision Making, and Evaluation I (PRIDE1) that solicits reactions to audiovisual case material (Gibbs, 1992). The following three arguments favor teaching critical thinking in Human Behavior in the Social Environment (HBSE) courses.

Thinking in Social Work Is Not an Empty Intellectual Exercise

Social workers deal with complex problems that often require complex solutions. How social workers reason determines what actions social workers take, and our actions can profoundly affect human lives. Even medical researchers, who study complexities of decision making, give examples from social work to illustrate difficulties in decision making. For example, Pettit (1993) writes the following in *Controlled Clinical* Trials about reasoning among child welfare workers:

> Consider the context within which social workers operate. In making decisions about whether to take children into care ... we must expect social workers to be more and more cautious about leaving children with their parents. Even if they believe that that is for the best overall. Social workers get little credit for correct decisions, whether the decisions be cautious or liberal; the only relevant sanctions are the penalties that may follow on incorrect judgments. But the penalties for incorrect decisions are not evenhanded. Social workers get

little blame for any error they may make in taking a child into care; the child may be worse off than he or she would have been at home but who is to tell? On the other side, social workers are liable to attract great blame, even public humiliation and dismissal, for any error they make in leaving a child with the parents; if the child is abused then, short even of newspaper coverage, they will suffer the wrath of their superiors. (p. 262)

Pettit intended principally to discuss the implications of two particular types of reasoning errors called "false positive" (unnecessarily removing the child from its home) and "false negative" (not removing the child where the child is later abused), but his example underscores that those in other disciplines recognize how patterns of reasoning among social workers, who must make difficult decisions, can profoundly affect human lives.

To weigh risk, child welfare workers must consider factors that constitute the substance of all HBSE courses, including family systems, capabilities of children of various developmental ages, social stressors and their effects on individuals (including parents), theories of how persons cope with stresses, cultural differences regarding child-rearing practices, childhood disorders (e.g., autism) that can stress parents, patterns of bonding between parent and child, and so on. Truly, the thinking in an HBSE course has great implications for the manner by which students assess the vast amount of information taught in an HBSE course. How students learn to reason in HBSE courses is not merely an empty intellectual exercise—this course lays a groundwork for vital practice decisions later.

It Would Be Unethical Not to Teach Critical Thinking in an HBSE Course

If we accept the argument that HBSE content concerns vital issues, then the nature of critical thinking implies that, in the name of respect for clients and a genuine concern for helping them, one must teach critical thinking about vital issues in an HBSE class. To make this point, here are definitions for a few features of critical thinking.

Intellectual honesty implies that the instructor should teach students to revere the truth, let it fall where it may, not teach from a preconceived notion about what the truth "should" be. An instructor committed to intellectual honesty searches out and presents all vital information for students, even if that evidence contradicts the instructor's favored position. For example, the intellectually honest instructor may personally believe that human immunodeficiency virus (HIV) positive mothers should not be required to get AZT drug treatment that may prevent acquired immune deficiency syndrome (AIDS) in their unborn child, because forcing treatment on the mother might stigmatize her. In spite of the instructor's personal beliefs, this intellectually honest instructor would still present evidence to the HBSE class that AZT treatment for the mother during her pregnancy, and at the birth of her child, reduces the risk of the child's HIV infection from 25% to 8% (Center for Diseases Control and Prevention, 1995, p. 1). Similarly, an intellectually honest instructor would not downgrade students for drawing their own well-reasoned conclusions, even if their conclusions disagree with those of the instructor.

Objectivity implies that in the search for truth the critical thinker will try, as much as possible, to rule out bias. Objectivity implies looking just as diligently for evidence that supports one's hypothesis as one looks for evidence that refutes one's hypothesis (e.g., looking just as hard for evidence that supports a child development theory as for evidence that refutes the theory). Objectivity implies trying to apply principles of scientific reasoning that help to rule out bias (e.g. experimental designs, measurement, and appropriate statistical tests). Objectivity implies listening carefully to an opposing argument and restating it so an opponent can clarify it further before one tries to refute the argument.

Knowing how to weigh arguments implies that the instructor will teach students to understand that all evidence is not equally credible. That is, no conclusion is better than the method by which it was drawn. In HBSE, as with any course, there are controversial issues: all is not known definitively and finally; so teachers need to demonstrate criteria for evaluating arguments. For example, HBSE students might read in their textbook about the prevalence of drug abuse among persons in the United States. To augment their textbook's section on drug abuse, their instructor might have students read a summary of a National Household Survey on Drug Abuse (National Institute on Drug Abuse, 1990) that reports on a stratified random survey of approximately 9 thousand households in the United States. The survey supports the conclusion that marijuana and hashish use has declined significantly from 1972 to 1990. The students might also hear a guest speaker in the class who vividly describes her own experience to support the conclusion that marijuana use increased during that period. The guest speaker supports her conclusion with vivid personal details from her own life and those of her close friends. A responsible instructor would have to discuss how the study's credibility vastly outweighs the vivid case example and testimonial evidence that was presented by the speaker—of course not discussing this difference in a way that embarrasses the guest speaker.

Students must be taught to think critically in an HBSE course by learning to weigh the credibility of arguments, to protect themselves against those who would advocate ideas about their practice that are fraud, quackery, and nonsense. For example, one person tells students that encounter groups help people; another person tells them that encounter groups can harm or kill the group's vulnerable members. Whom should the students believe? Without an understanding of how to critically evaluate an argument, the students are helpless to decide whom to believe. The method by which the speaker drew his or her conclusion determines whether students should believe an argument. A conclusion without reasons that have been carefully weighed is nothing. One must be able to defend a position.

A reverence for data refers to the idea that careful observations, systematically recorded and honestly reported, far outweigh vague impressions and theoretical notions not based on observations. For example, a textbook's author may argue that a classical two-parent family produces adults who are better adjusted and more successful in life than those who grow up in single-parent families. This notion has great implications for students who become practitioners. If as practitioners students accept the former, they may make every effort to keep families intact. An instructor who models critical thinking would define what is meant by "better adjusted" and "more successful" and then would present data about how adults from single-parent and intact families fare relative to these criteria.

In summary for this second argument, principal earmarks of critical thinking imply intellectual honesty, objectivity, knowing how to weigh arguments, and a reverence for data. Instructors have an ethical obligation to teach critical thinking in HBSE courses, because future professionals need to learn what to believe and what to cast off as trash and nonsense so they make good decisions in their professional practice.

Critical Thinking Has Already Been Taught Successfully in an HBSE Course

Although it makes sense ethically and logically that we should teach students to think critically in HBSE courses, in fact we have no published literature about whether students can learn to think critically in HBSE courses. In March of 1995, I searched the *Social Work Abstracts* database for documents that concerned "HBSE" or "Human Behavior in the Social Environment" anywhere in the title, descriptors, or abstract. There were thirty-four documents, but only one of these contained the term "critical thinking" somewhere in the abstract. This one reference—an edited volume of several works—referred not to critical thinking in the objective, persistent, data-based, logical, scientific sense that I mean here, but instead stated a particular philosophical point of view that seems contrary to critical thinking as defined.

This philosophical point of view seems to argue that there is no objective truth to be found (Saleebey, 1993); all conclusions are relative to socially defined reality. There are only our socially determined perceptions of events that determine which events we define as being problems and potential solutions. Saleebey (1993) seems to argue for a particular philosophical and political point of view that is critical of the established social order, rather than addressing critical thinking as defined. Consequently, if the *Social Work Abstracts* database reflects the social work literature accurately, then it looks as though there is no published literature about teaching critical thinking that is specific to HBSE courses as defined here.

Fortunately, Linda Ryan (unpublished), an outstanding doctoral student at Arizona State University, will soon publish the results of her evaluation of a program to teach critical thinking to graduate students in an HBSE course. Ryan's six-week program uses group activity, lecture, and discussion regarding social work case scenarios to illustrate fallacious thinking regarding issues in practice. Scenarios reflect HBSE content. To evaluate the teaching program, Ryan conducted a quasi-experimental study involving 108 students. One HBSE class received her critical thinking teaching program, one class got partial exposure to her program, and one class served as a control group. All students were pretested regarding seven variables, including their professional thinking and the number of hypotheses that students generated regarding case scenarios; then students were posttested six weeks later, after the program ended. Ryan's results favor the critical thinking program with statistical significance on professional thinking and number of hypotheses generated.

General Conclusions

If we can agree that HBSE course content concerns thinking about vital practice issues, and we can agree that what we accept as the truth can affect our actions in practice, then it seems that we should also agree that teaching critical thinking in HBSE courses is essential to good teaching. Admittedly, we know little about how best to teach critical thinking in HBSE courses, but Linda Ryan's fine work helps to point the way.

REFERENCES

Center for Disease Control and Prevention. (1995, August 5). Recommendations of the U.S. Public Health Service Task Force on the use of zidovudine to reduce prenatal transmission of human immunodeficiency virus (RR-11). *Morbidity and Mortality Weekly Report,* Public Health Service, Centers for Disease Control and Prevention, Atlanta, GA 30333, pp. 1–20.

Gibbs, L. E. (1991). *Scientific reasoning for social workers: Bridging the gap between research and practice.* New York: Macmillan/Allyn & Bacon.

Gibbs, L. E. (1992). *Principles of reasoning, inference, decision making and evaluation I (PRIDE1),* Department of Social Work, University of Wisconsin-Eau Claire.

Gibbs, L. E., Gambrill, E., Blakemore, J., Begun, A., Keniston, A., Preden, B., & Lefcowitz, J. (1995). A measure of critical thinking about practice. *Research on Social Work Practice, 5*(2), 193–204.

Moore, N. M., & Parker, R. (1986). *Critical thinking: Evaluating claims and arguments in everyday life.* Palo Alto, CA: Mayfield.

National Institute of Drug Abuse. (1990). *National household survey on drug abuse.* (DHHS Pub. No. ADM90–1681). National Institute of Drug Abuse, Division of Epidemiology and Prevention Research, Rockville, MD.

Pettit, P. (1993). Suspended judgment: Instituting a research ethic. *Controlled Clinical Trials, 14,* 261–265.

Ryan, L. (unpublished). *Critical thinking in social work practice: A quasi-experimental evaluation.* Doctoral Dissertation, School of Social Work, Arizona State University, Tempe, Arizona.

Saleebey, D. (1993). Theory and the generation and subversion of knowledge. *Journal of Sociology and Social Welfare, 20*(1), 2–26.

Rejoinder to Dr. Gibbs   Steve Tallant

Dr. Gibbs presents three arguments in favor of teaching critical thinking in the Human Behavior in the Social Environment course. First, Dr. Gibbs states that social workers make important and vital decisions for their clients and the HBSE course lays a groundwork for vital practice decisions later. Second, because critical thinking skills are vital to social workers in their practice, it would be unethical not to teach critical thinking in an HBSE course. Finally, critical thinking has already been taught successfully in an HBSE course.

I fully agree with Dr. Gibbs with regard to the importance of critical thinking in the social work profession. Social workers do make important decisions on a daily basis that can effect their client's lives. As a result, critical thinking is a skill we should value and reward in both the academic and practice settings.

However, Dr. Gibbs's paper presents two important questions for social work educators. First, what set of skills constitute critical thinking (i.e., what is the content) and second, where do we teach these skills (i.e., what is the context)? In terms of content, I believe the model presented by Gibbs is inadequate for social workers and, furthermore, I believe the HBSE course is not the appropriate setting to teach these skills.

In his paper, Dr. Gibbs states that the "principle earmarks of critical thinking imply intellectual honesty, knowing how to weigh arguments, objectivity, and a reverence for data." In addition, Dr. Gibbs notes that "no conclusion is better than the method by which it was drawn." Does this imply that the process is more important than the truth? I hope not. It appears as if Dr. Gibbs' model of critical thinking is based solely on the principles and the philosophy of logical empiricism. As such, it is extremely limited in content.

As "critical thinkers," social workers need to be taught that there are many ways of knowing (Hartman, 1990), many ways to evaluate theory (Zastrow & Kirst-Ashman, 1994), and no one way of knowing is inherently superior to any other for generating scientific knowledge (Tyson, 1995, XIV). We should not rule out the "truth" of scientific knowledge solely because of the methodological process from which it was drawn. I believe critical thinking is synonymous with scientific reasoning, but as Gambrill notes, quantitative research is not synonymous with scientific reasoning (Gambrill, 1992, p. 25). Teaching critical thinking may imply intellectual honesty, but intellectual honesty implies teaching more than one definition of scientific reasoning.

Although I believe that social work educators should be teaching a pluralistic model of critical thinking, I do not believe the HBSE course is the appropriate setting for teaching and building critical thinking skills. My rationale is stated in my position paper. Without repeating myself, it is worth noting that a HBSE course is not a practice course nor do all social workers engage in clinical practice. In addition, the teaching of critical thinking is a labor intensive effort. As such, critical thinking skills should be taught in the research methods course and applied in practice courses and internship.

Finally, Gibbs notes that critical thinking has already been taught successfully in an HBSE course. Unfortunately, Gibbs was able to locate only one study to support this position. Interestingly, because the experiment was quasi-experimental (Ryan, unpublished), it is impossible to generalize these findings to other populations.

In summary, although I agree with Dr. Gibbs that critical thinking skills are vital to good social work practice, I do not believe the content of these skills should be limited to a quantitative epistemology. Furthermore, for pragmatic and educational reasons, the HBSE course is not an appropriate setting for the teaching of these skills. Finally, although the work of Linda Ryan can point us in the right direction, there is limited evidence to support the effectiveness of incorporating critical thinking skills into the HBSE sequence.

REFERENCES

Gambrill, E. (1992, October 1). *Social work research: Priorities and obstacles.* Keynote address, Group for the Advancement of Doctoral Education in Social Work Conference, University of Pittsburgh, PA.

Hartman, A. (1990). Editorial: Many ways of knowing. *Social Work, 35,* 3–4.

Tyson, K. (Ed.). (1995). *New foundations for scientific social and behavioral research: The heuristic paradigm.* Boston: Allyn & Bacon.

Zastrow, C., & Kirst-Ashman, K. (1994). *Understanding human behavior and the social environment* (3rd ed.) Chicago: Nelson-Hall.

NO

STEVE TALLANT

The question posed for this article is, "is it possible to teach HBSE students to think critically at the same time we teach information about human behavior"? "At the same time" implies during the same course. That is, can students be taught to think critically about the information being presented to them in an HBSE course? The obvious answer to this question is yes. We all desire to teach our students the ability to think critically about the issues being presented to them.

One would develop a framework and process to teach critical thinking skills and apply this process to the course content as it is presented. However, this is an oversimplistic question and does not get to the heart of the current debate.

More importantly, there appear to be two questions of equal or greater merit to be addressed: one pragmatic and the other philosophic. First, it is possible to teach HBSE students to think critically at the same time we teach information about human behavior without diluting the intent or purpose of the HBSE sequence? Second, *should* we teach critical thinking skills as a pedagogical goal at the same time we teach information about human behavior? To address these two questions, one must have an understanding of the content and purpose of the Human Behavior and the Social Environment sequence and an understanding of what is meant by the term critically thinking.

Human Behavior and the Social Environment Content

The Council on Social Work Education (CSWE, 1992), the national accrediting body, provides the following guidelines for HBSE content in its Curriculum Policy Statement:

> Programs of social work education must provide content about theories and knowledge of human bio-psycho-social development, including theories and knowledge about the range of social systems in which individuals live (families, groups, organizations, institutions, and communities). The human behavior and the social environment curriculum must provide an understanding of the interactions between and among human biological, social, psychological, and cultural systems as they affect and are affected by human behavior. The impact of social and economic forces on individuals and social systems must be presented. Content must be provided about the ways in which systems promote or deter people in the maintenance or attainment of optimal health and well-being. Content about values and ethical issues related to bio-psycho-social theories must be included. Students must be taught to evaluate theory and apply theory to client situations. (p. 7)

In addition, the following must also be incorporated throughout the curriculum: social work values and ethics, diversity, promotion of social and economic justice, and populations at risk (p. 6–7).

HBSE course is not a practice course. It is a knowledge-oriented course taught within the value base of social work. The information presented in the course enables the student to understand that behavior is not independent of the environment. Although the material presented in this course can be transferred into the practice setting, the course is not intended to be a social work practice course.

Operational Definition of Critical Thinking

As defined by Gibbs, et al. (1995) , critical thinking in social work involves:

1. A predisposition to question conclusions that concern clients and welfare
2. Asking "does it work?" and "how do you know?" when confronted with claims that a method helps clients, and also questioning generalizations about treatment methods and clients
3. Weighing evidence for and against assertions in a logical, rational, systematic, data-based way
4. Analyzing arguments to see what is being argued, spotting and explaining common fallacies in reasoning, and applying basic methodological principles of scientific reasoning (p.196)

From my understanding, there appear to be two separate, but related goals for teaching critical thinking. First, it is hoped that the student will apply newly required critical thinking skills in processing all new information. The final goal is to have the student transfer the critical thinking skills acquired in the academic setting to the real world on entering the social work profession.

These four arguments support the conclusion that critical thinking should not be taught as part of a Human Behavior in the Social Environment course.

Instructors Do Not Have Time to Teach Critical Thinking in an HBSE Course

As noted by Gibbs, students are taught to transfer basic methodological principles of scientific reasoning to the practice setting. Because most students are totally unfamiliar with these principles, the process of teaching critical thinking is a time-consuming and labor-intensive endeavor. The massive amount of material that must be covered in an HBSE course precludes teaching additional material. It is difficult to cover the required course content in depth during one semester. Students already voice their concerns regarding the large amount of material covered in the course. Trying to teach critical thinking skills and the massive amount of material already required may be possible, but would significantly dilute if not totally negate the intent and purpose of the course as stated by CSWE.

My experience in teaching HBSE may very well reflect the concerns that other instructors may have over the tension between covering the required material and trying to teach critical thinking skills. In a randomized controlled trial (n = 100) to test the effectiveness of a program to enhance critical thinking by faculty at the University of Wisconsin—Eau Claire (UWEC), Gibbs, Browne, and Kelley (1989) asked the experimental group participants what they thought of their efforts to teach critical thinking in a one-semester course of their own choosing. These authors concluded: "... another generalization we can draw from the UWEC project is the omnipresent tension between the desire of most instructors to cover content (usually implying that their lectures are the vehicle for coverage) and their reverence for critical thinking as a pedagogical goal" (p. 57). This tension between covering the material and teaching critical thinking skills in an HBSE course not only would frustrate the instructor, but it might put a program at risk for nonaccreditation by CSWE for not covering the required materials sufficiently.

Social Work Faculty Themselves Cannot Teach Critical Thinking Skills without Special Training

It was not until the 1992 standard that CSWE first mandated that critical thinking would be taught in practice courses; so it seems highly unlikely that social work faculty would have a very clear understanding of how to teach critical thinking. To emphasize this point, here is some evidence: In the randomized control trial of a faculty development program just described (Gibbs, et al, 1989), "program participants and control group faculty did not differ with statistical significance on the Watson-Glaser Measure of Critical Thinking Appraisal pretest. However, controls had statistically significant higher posttest scores on the Ennis-Weir Critical Thinking Test (independent t, $P < .03$)" (p. 53). These results suggest that the faculty enhancement program harmed the critical thinking abilities of participating faculty. The authors claimed that they hand picked experts in critical thinking to conduct the faculty development program; so these experts, if anyone could, should have been able to sharpen the critical thinking ability for faculty. In social work, a discipline that has only just recently listed critical thinking in its standards, the faculty training problem might be more formidable than in other disciplines that may have a longer tradition in this competency.

Critical Thinking Skills and a Quantitative Epistemology Model

The critical thinking model presented in the literature is drawn from the principles of positivism and quantitative methodology and does not embrace methodological diversity. For example, one of the major components of critical thinking is "weighing evidence for and against assertions in a logical, rational, systematic, data-based way and analyzing arguments to see what is being argued, spotting and explaining common fallacies in reasoning, and applying basic methodological principles of scientific reasoning" (Gibbs et al., 1995, p. 196).

Although the purpose of this article is not to rekindle the debate between quantitative and qualitative methodologies, the model presented by Gibbs has significant implications for the teaching of HBSE and the education of social work students. Why would we want to limit the scope of "critical thinking" to a quantitative epistemology? Contemporary social work problems require diverse modes of inquiry (Riesman, 1994), and there are many ways of knowing (Hartman, 1990). Our students need to be exposed to the different ways of knowing, and critical thinking should embrace a methodological diversity. The current critical thinking model does not expose the student to methodological diversity and as a result has implications for students as they enter the social work profession.

An example is in order. To help the student assess new forms of information, Gibbs has developed a list of "practitioners' fallacies" based on "fallacious thinking" (Gibbs, 1991, p. 24). An example of fallacious thinking is the propensity to accept testimonials as evidence of truth (Gibbs, 1991, p. 31). The critical thinking model teaches the student to reject any testimonial unless there are data to support the testimonial. What implications does this have for students as they engage in relationships with their clients? Does it imply that the client's experience is not "real" unless data are presented by the client? If so, does it further imply that information gathered from phenomenology/interpretive research methods are invalid and not useful to the knowledge base of social work?

I believe the answer to both of these questions is yes. If I am correct in this assumption, the critical thinking model teaches the student to reject all information and knowledge that is not supported by sound empirical data. As a result, teaching critical thinking skills in an HBSE course will limit the knowledge base available to students. For example, we will not be concerned with the meaning of isolation of the chronically ill or the meaning of abuse for women and girls as experienced by the client.

This is unfortunate because in the applied setting, social workers will need knowledge to address problems that do not lend themselves to quantification and computer manipulation (Riesman, 1994). In addressing these problems, "we must not turn our back on opportunities to enhance our knowledge, whether they be examinations of correlations or explications of myths" (Rein & White, 1981, p. 16). As Hartman notes, "we are concerned about the life stories and the inner experiences of the people we serve and about the meaning to them of their experiences. No one way of knowing can explore this vast and varied territory" (Hartman, 1990, p. 4). Critical thinking, as defined by Gibbs et al., limits our way of knowing and should not be taught at the same time we teach HBSE.

The Relation of Critical Thinking Skills to the Importance of Values in the Profession of Social Work

As Longres (1995) notes, social workers are reformers operating as much from values as from knowledge (p. xiii). As we conduct our daily business of teaching students about " human behavior in the social environment," we must not lose sight of this reality. This does not mean that students should not be taught to evaluate theory and apply theory to client situations. However, social workers assess problems and attempt to understand human behavior within the context of social work values and ethics (Zastrow & Kirst-Ashman, 1994, p.107). Therefore, evaluating a theory on the evidence of research alone is insufficient. In addition to the empirical data, we must evaluate the extent to which the theory coincides with social work values and ethics. "For example, consider a theory that one group of people is by nature more intelligent than another group. This theory obviously conflicts with professional values. Therefore, it should not be used or supported by social workers " (Zastrow & Kirst-Ashman, 1994, p. 107). Critical thinking does not incorporate the value base of social work and, therefore, should not be taught in an HBSE course.

In summary, critical thinking should not be taught at the same time we teach about human behavior and the social environment. Pragmatically, instructors have neither the training nor the time to adequately teach critical thinking skills at the same time they teach the required content of the HBSE sequence. Any attempt would dilute the purpose and intent of the course. Philosophically, the critical thinking model is drawn from the principles of positivism and quantitative methodology and, therefore, limits the knowledge base of social work. Social workers should not be limited to one way of knowing. Finally, the critical thinking model does not incorporate the value base of social work. Because the purpose of HBSE is to teach knowledge within the value base of the profession, critical thinking is not appropriate for the HBSE sequence.

REFERENCES

Council on Social Work Education. (1992). *Curriculum policy statement for master's degree programs in social work education.* Washington, DC: Author.

Gibbs, L. E. (1991). *Scientific reasoning for social workers: Bridging the gap between research and practice.* New York: Macmillan/Allyn & Bacon.

Gibbs, L. E., Browne, M. N., & Keeley, S. (1989). Critical thinking: A study's outcome. *The Journal of Professional Studies, 13*(1), 44–59.

Gibbs, L. E., Gambrill, E., Blakemore, J., Begun, A., Keniston, A., Preden, B., & Lefcowitz, J. (1995). A measure of critical thinking about practice. *Research on Social Work Practice, 5*(2), 193–204.

Hartman, A. (1990). Editorial: Many ways of knowing. *Social Work, 35,* 3–4.

Longres, J. F. (1995). *Human behavior in the social environment* (2nd ed.). Itasca, IL: Peacock.

Rein, M. & White, S. H. (1981). Knowledge for practice. *Social Service Review, 55,* 1–41.

Riesman, C. A. (1994). Preface: Making room for diversity in social work research. In A. Riesman (Ed.), *Qualitative studies in social work research* (pp. vii–xx). Thousand Oaks: Sage Publication.

Zastrow, C., & Kirst-Ashman, K. (1994). *Understanding human behavior and the social environment* (3rd ed.) Chicago: Nelson-Hall.

Rejoinder to Dr. Tallant   Leonard E. Gibbs

Dr. Tallant has argued that instructors simply do not have the time to teach critical thinking, given the massive amount of information that must be taught in an HBSE course, and he cites a study that reported how instructors think there is a tension between teaching critical thinking and teaching information. Well, there is a tension, but it does not follow that given this tension one should teach a mass of information that students will promptly forget. How many students could pass a multiple-choice midterm examination that covers the content of their HBSE course if they took the examination a year after completing the HBSE course? They would probably score low or not pass. Because students may forget what they do not immediately apply, they should be exposed to less material to memorize and more to locate and weigh evidence for themselves. For example, HBSE texts provide much information about developmental stages for children, but students who enter practice will have forgotten lists of age-appropriate developmental milestones by the time they must decide whether a child needs referral to preschool training because of developmental delays. Instead of memorizing age-appropriate milestones, students' time would be better spent learning how to locate developmental inventories, knowing how to critically evaluate their measurement qualities, and knowing about how normal variation can account for apparent developmental delays.

Second, Dr. Tallant argues that social work educators have not themselves been taught how to think critically, and that the University of Wisconsin—Eau Claire's faculty development program that was designed to enhance critical thinking failed to sharpen faculty's thinking; so how could we expect social work faculty to learn to teach critical thinking in an HBSE course? This is a powerful argument. We think that the apparent negative effect of our program for faculty resulted when controls, who had been denied admission into the program, became rivals of program participants and wrote longer Ennis-Weir essays in the final evaluation (Gibbs, Browne, & Keeley, 1989, p. 54). In other words, compensatory rivalry explains our discouraging results. Furthermore, I admit that surely there are obstacles to sharpening critical thinking among social work faculty, but it does not follow that such difficulties preclude those who do think critically from teaching it in HBSE courses.

Dr. Tallant argues that there is no hierarchy of evidence, that different ways of knowing are all relatively credible. I believe that there is a hierarchy of evidence. For example, direct observations made by oneself are more accurate than those reported by someone who says they made an observation. Direct observations based on measures are still more credible, and direct observations based on measures that are concurrently evaluated for interrater agreement are still more credible. Anyone who denies that there is a hierarchy of evidence should report equal satisfaction with a bacteriologist's microscopic oil immersion lens examination of Gram-stained streptococcal bacteria compared with Grandma's or Uncle Mike's judgment: "Nah, he ain't infected." I believe that sound measures applied to representatively chosen individuals can tell us more about the success of interventions than testimonials can.

REFERENCES

Gibbs, L. E., Browne, M. N., & Keeley, S. (1989). Critical thinking: A study's outcome. *The Journal of Professional Studies, 13*(1), 44–59.

Is It Possible to Generate Any Universal List of Basic HBSE Concepts and Principles That All Students Should Learn?

EDITOR'S NOTE: Large numbers of students are taking the equivalent of HBSE every semester, from many different instructors across the country. This raises the disturbing thought that what students are being taught may not be the same content, and thus may lead practitioners in different directions when dealing with the same kind of cases. One possible solution is to have a common set of concepts and principles that can be taught to all students everywhere as the basic knowledge of human behavior.

Harriette Johnson, Ph.D., is a professor at the School of Social Work, University of Connecticut. Her areas of specialization include child and adult mental health, developmental psychology, practice methods, parent/professional collaboration, and professional ethics.

Katherine Tyson, Ph. D., associate professor at the School of Social Work, Loyola University, has recently edited an important volume in the alternative epistemology debate, *New Foundations for Scientific Social and Behavioral Research: The Heuristic Paradigm* (1995, Allyn & Bacon).

YES

HARRIETTE JOHNSON

The U.S. Congress has convened the first-ever Joint Congressional/Executive Committee on the Study of Human Behavior in the Social Environment. The event that has occasioned this gathering was the news from major pollsters that all incumbents are about to be voted out of office. The reasons most frequently cited by respondents were that the politicians do not understand what the people want, feel, think, or do. Accordingly, the Committee has set as its agenda the discovery of what the American people want, feel, think, and are doing. Or in more academic terms, the topics to be studied are motivation, emotion, cognition, and behavior in relation to the social, cultural, economic, and political environment. Chairperson of the Committee, Vice President Al Bore, introduces the group's opening session.

Vice President Al Bore: Colleagues, we are all aware that there is growing unrest among the American electorate. Quite frankly, unless we quickly learn about people's motivations, emotions, cognitions, and behavior, we'll all be dead in the water next November. Our charge is to compile concepts and principles to include in a course for ourselves on human behavior in the social environment. One of our in-house social workers, Rep. Barbara McKlutzki, will then pull together our suggestions in a summary draft.

Senator Richard Cougar [smiling]: Mr. Vice President, members of my staff have identified nineteen academic disciplines that draw on HBSE content. In psychology alone there are 14,513 books and 137,410 published articles in professional journals on HBSE content (PsycLit, 1995). I propose we learn how to analyze *any* aspect of HBSE. Then no matter what the particular issue, we will have the skills to address it.

Representative Newt Getrich: With all due respect to Senator Cougar, I submit that there are a few simple motives that drive the American psyche. They're described in our Contract with America. The people want government off their backs. They want to send the foreigners back where they came from. They want to stop the people on welfare from living high-on-the-hog at taxpayer expense. They want the government to stop ripping off hard-working Americans by making them pay taxes. We know all this already. I see no reason why we have to learn anything else. Let's just do what the people want. If we do, we'll get reelected.

Representative Pat Shredder [former welfare mother]: Mr. Getrich, do you really believe a single parent with two children would prefer to live at taxpayer expense on $610 a month if she had a choice of working at a living wage? That is the highest benefit a family of three on AFDC gets in any state in the continental United States. In some states, it's as little as $120 a month for three people (Center for Social Welfare Policy and Law, 1995). If you can tell me with a straight face that this is high-on-the-hog living, I would have some serious doubts about your understanding of motivation. A course in HBSE might do you a world of good.

Representative Donald Rellums [former social worker]: My colleague's reference to the welfare system brings us to another issue: diversity. We are not only a nation of white middle-class two-parent families. We are a multicultural people with diverse wants, thoughts, feelings, and behaviors. In my view, we need specific content that illustrates diversity.

Senator Phil Grimm [clearing his throat, and speaking with a slow deliberate drawl]: Mr. Vice President, there is another important issue: normality. Some of our esteemed colleagues are overly preoccupied with the deviants, the misfits, the losers in our society. I believe our study should focus on normal American people. They are the ones who make this country the greatest in the world.

Senator Jesse Hell [nodding and smiling in an uncharacteristic show of cordiality]: An excellent suggestion. We already have a lot of information about what is normal. Why just look at television programs. In one day in 1994, ten Washington, D.C., channels showed 2,605 violent scenes (Center for Media and Public Affairs, 1994).

Former Vice President Dan Male: And the American family. We already know what the normal American family is—a husband, a wife, two biological children, two cars, a microwave, a dishwasher, two computers, and a hook-up to the Information Highway. Never poor, never out of work, seldom sick, never old, and still married for the first time.

Senator Ted Candy: With all respect to the previous speakers, many of us do not define normality the way you do. Poverty, unemployment, ill health, single parenthood, old age, even homosexuality, are normal for many Americans. In fact, at least one of these states is normal for much of the electorate. Normal development does not read like writings from Freud or Erikson or Mahler. Many needs and wants are culturally determined, not universal. Not everyone needs two parents. Not everyone needs two parents of the opposite sex. Some children do fine with a single parent or with a gay parent or with two gay parents. Not everyone needs a spouse. Not everyone even needs an intimate partner.

I do not believe we can say what normal development is. Normality is culturally defined. For example, in one of the cultures in New Guinea, starting at the age of seven boys regularly perform fellatio on older adolescent males for about six years as part of a sacred ritual. It is believed this is necessary for the boy to assume the adult male role and successfully impregnate a wife (Herdt, 1981). The Mehinaku Indians of central Brazil treat a disobedient older child by grabbing him by the wrists, sloshing a dipperful of water on his legs, and scratching his legs with a fish-tooth scraper. This despite the fact the Mehinaku are very indulgent with their infants. Yet the adults in the community who were punished in this way as children are not more aggressive or more conforming than children growing up in groups that do not follow this harsh practice (Gregor, 1977). In our culture, we would call these two examples child abuse. In other cultures, they are normal behavior.

Furthermore, people change through time in diverse ways (Kagan, 1994). People are born with temperaments that are genetically different and that influence not only how they respond to the environment but how the environment responds to them. And behavior is context specific (Kagan, 1994). It is not accurate to designate people with global concepts, such as "Rosa is repressed." People's characteristics are not present in every situation. Rosa may repress her angry feelings toward her mother but be a sexual live wire.

Mrs. Flipper Bore [wife of the Vice President]: Senator Candy has illustrated another concept for us, "biopsychosociocultural." Back in the 1960s, human service professionals called their assessments of motivation, emotion, cognition, and behavior "psychosocial diagnosis." In the 1970s, the word "assessment" was substituted for "diagnosis," reflecting a growing distaste for the medical model. In the 1980s and 1990s, attention has increasingly focused on the importance of cultural factors. During this same period, we have had a revolution in our knowledge about the importance of biological factors and their mechanisms of action (Johnson, Atkins, et al., 1990). As a result, the term "biopsychosociocultural" is now in vogue. New technologies such as the positron-emission tomography (PET) scan, magnetic resonance imaging (MRI), and methods of analyzing brain chemistry have changed our understanding so radically that President Geoge Bush responded by designating the 1990s the Decade of the Brain (Aldous, 1992). We now know that all motivation, emotion, cognition, and behavior have biological substrates that continually interact with the environment. What is more, the major mental illnesses are biological diseases of the brain that can be triggered by stress, just the way heart disease and diabetes and cancer are diseases that can be triggered by stress. There is no dichotomy between biology and environment—they influence each other. Let us learn how this amazing brain interacts with the world around us to create mental health or mental illness, sobriety or addiction.

Representative John Older [former psychology professor]: Your discussion of the biological underpinnings of behavior suggests two other principles: critical thinking and validity. Promoting critical thinking is a *sine qua non* of any HBSE curriculum. We should structure our self-education program so as to require ourselves to critically evaluate every axiom, every assertion. But critical thinking uninformed by evidence will not help us much. We need evidence as well. But *what kind* of evidence? Members of SCIP (Social Construction Independent Party) assert that in research, what questions are posed, how they are posed, how the data are collected, and how the data are analyzed, are determined by the investigators in pursuit of their personal, subjective, and biased agendas. We agree.

However, SCIP further contends that because of this influence of investigator bias, knowledge generated by so-called scientific data is no more objective, no more valid, than stories recounted by individuals. It is here that we scientists take issue with the constructivists. We contend that the very nature of scientifically acceptable methodology builds in a range of controls that *reduce but do not eliminate* effects of bias. Such controls are available in qualitative as well as quantitative research (Kazdin, 1981), but absent in individual stories, narratives, and case studies. Our HBSE curriculum should combine knowledge derived from quantitative and qualitative research using scientifically acceptable methodology. I think it is unethical for people who mess around with other people's lives to do otherwise. Consider the words of the psychologist Robyn Dawes (1994): "What was never envisioned was that a body of research and established principles would be available to inform practice, but that practice would ignore that research and those principles. Worse yet, far too much professional practice...has grown and achieved status by espousing principles that are known to be untrue and by employing techniques known to be invalid." The task I've proposed is not as overwhelming as it sounds. Computerized indices can pop up abstracts on most of the recent research on almost any topic—all in a half-hour or an hour.

Representative Getrich: We are all concerned with crime here. What about kids who get into trouble? Crime on the streets. Like a kid that mugs an old lady on her way home from the grocery store. We all have constituents who are concerned about that sort of thing. How would your proposal work on that one, John?

Representative Older: Good example. Say we have a thirteen-year-old boy who is brought into juvenile court for stealing a pocketbook from an old lady. We find out this kid has a history of being disruptive in the classroom, gets into fights with peers, does not listen to his mother or to his teachers, and never finishes anything he starts. His parents are divorced, and his father has a history of alcoholism and physically abused his mother. He has not seen his father for years. He lives with his mother, a brother, and a sister. Ah ha, we say. The boy comes from a dysfunctional family. Send him and his mother in for some therapy, maybe bring in his brother and sister—they have surely got problems too. Give the whole crew a little family therapy.

The scenario I have just presented is what we usually do. Take some fragments of information, make a case out of these fragments, prescribe a remedy. Suppose the family goes for family therapy, but the kid keeps getting into trouble. Pretty soon he has dropped out of school, and then he is doing time for armed robbery and aggravated assault. By now he is seventeen. So we shrug our shoulders and say, "Well, we did what we could. With a family like that, it was bound to end like this."

What might have happened if we'd done our homework? We go to the library's CD-ROM and run searches. We find out that he meets criteria for Attention Deficit Hyperactivity Disorder (ADHD). We find out that about 40 percent of ADHD kids engage in antisocial behavior, and that evidence indicates ADHD is a neurobiological disorder involving an underactive inhibitory system in the brain. And that 70 to 80 percent of children with the disorder improve significantly on medication, their parents like them better and praise them more, their teachers like them better, and they start having more friends (Amaya-Jackson, Mesco, McGough, & Cantwell, 1992; Johnson, 1988). Why? Because the medication has helped them change their behavior by remedying a biochemical deficiency in the brain. We also learn from social psychology research that attribution and scapegoating can escalate problems of self-esteem, depression, and aggressive behavior (Aronson, 1988). We learn that kids like this boy are prime candidates for negative attributions and scapegoating.

After we do this homework, we realize we need to find out if all this information we have gathered has any relevance for this particular unique individual. His history suggests that it does. So he gets some good treatment based on these research findings. The kid manages to stay in school and graduates. We cannot predict the future—but it sounds as though he is going to make it as a law-abiding citizen.

What made the difference between the two scenarios? Two factors were decisive: differences in the professional cultures (one valued research, the other did not) and the availability of appropriate services. What can research do that practice wisdom cannot? Here is the heart of the matter in my view. You acknowledge that a lot of people have already done a lot of work on a problem or in relation to a population. You do not want to reinvent the wheel and find out by trial and error what a lot of other people have already learned. Would you want a doctor working on *you* who had lots of practice wisdom and bedside charm, but who was twenty years behind the times in medical research? So you read about what people have already discovered, based on groups of individuals, not just single cases. Then you have got a much better chance of understanding the problem or situation and of choosing interventions that are going to work than if you rely solely on your own experience. Two heads are better than one, and many heads are better than two.

Representative Pat Shredder: But where do people's personal stories fit in? I have told my story about getting off welfare and getting elected to the House of Representatives to a lot of people, and I think my story has done a lot of good—it has made some voters more sympathetic to women in that predicament.

Representative Older: There is no conflict. Narratives and case studies are important too. They provide rich details and insights and they have an emotional impact in a way number crunching cannot. When we have dialogues with our constituents, we learn things about their motives, emotions, thoughts, and behavior that amplify or modify or refine what we learn about them from data.

Senator Daniel Patrick Benign-Neglect [the erstwhile Harvard professor peers over his spectacles at his colleagues.]: Gentlemen, or rather gentlepersons, we have omitted another important principle: political correctness. Our curriculum should raise questions that are not politically correct. Sweeping them under the rug does not further our knowledge; it simply obscures it. Should we not raise questions such as: is incest necessarily damaging psychologically? Or do we sometimes make it damaging by defining it that way? Do professional cultures have ideologies that oppress certain client groups (for instance, that dysfunctional parents cause mental illness)? There now are data that show that professional cultures do this (Dawes, 1994; Johnson, Cournoyer, & Fisher, 1994; Johnson, Cournoyer, & Bond, 1995). Is physical discipline always harmful? There is evidence that it is not (Kagan, 1994). Does one race have a higher native intelligence than another? What is the evidence for and against? What is intelligence anyway? The verbal sections of our so-called intelligence tests are acknowledged to be culture-bound tests of acquired information, not native ability. Let us not be afraid to raise these inflammatory questions. Let us hold them up to scrutiny in light of evidence. Is not a course on HBSE a proper context for such exploration?

Vice President Bore: Thank you, Senator. Now may we have a summary from the Recorder?

Representative Barbara McKlutzki: Mr. Vice President and colleagues: I have culled some general principles and concepts from your recommendations for inclusion in our curriculum:

Principles

1. Because content for HBSE is too vast to "cover" this subject area, we should learn a *method* for studying any instance of HBSE.
2. The specific content we select to include as a basis for learning this method of analysis should be *consistent with scientific evidence*. There is no room in our abbreviated course of study for interesting theories that have been discredited by research.
3. There are *different ways of knowing*. Knowledge derived from quantitative and qualitative research, and understanding gained through introspection, interpersonal experience, narrative, and intuition, all play a role in illuminating HBSE phenomena. However, inferences that run counter to research-based evidence require *taking cognizance of that evidence.*
4. The method for learning about human behavior is *first to review research-based knowledge on a topic*. Theories supported by research are appropriate for inclusion. The second step is to amplify, modify, or refine our knowledge of specific situations with narrative or intuition.
5. Politically incorrect views should be introduced and subjected to critical scrutiny.

Concepts

1. Human motivation, emotion, cognition, and behavior are *biopsychosociocultural* in origin. HBSE curricula must integrate content on *all* of these components and show how they *interact.*

2. HBSE phenomena are characterized by *diversity.*
3. *Individuals and their environments interact and mutually influence each other.*
4. *Behavior is context-specific.* Global concepts applied to complex person-in-environment transactions oversimplify and distort. Behavior can only be understood in the context in which it takes place.
5. *It is not meaningful to study "normal" development* because people vary so much. Normality is culturally defined.

Respectfully submitted, Representative Barbara McKlutzki, Recorder, 6/25/95

REFERENCES

Aldous, P. (1992). An uncertain start for a brain decade. *Science, 258:*23.
Amaya-Jackson, L., Mesco, R., McGough, J., & Cantwell, D. (1992). Attention deficit hyperactivity disorder. In E. Peschel, R. Peschel, C. W. Howe, J. W. Howe, (Eds.), *Neurobiological disorders in children and adolescents* (pp. 45–50). San Francisco: Jossey-Bass.
Aronson, E. (1988). *The social animal* (5th ed.). New York: W. H. Freeman.
Center for Media and Public Affairs, cited by the *New York Times,* August 30th, 1994, p C20. Beyond the body count: qualifying the quantity of on-screen violence.
Center for Social Welfare Policy and Law. (1995). Personal communication, June 12th. In addition to these cash benefits, recipients also get food stamps and Medicaid.
Dawes, R. (1994). *House of cards: Psychology and psychotherapy built on myth.* New York: Free Press.
Gregor, T. (1977). *Mehinaku.* Chicago: University of Chicago Press, cited in Kagan, n. 7.
Herdt, G. H. (1981). *Guardians of the flute.* New York: McGraw-Hill, cited in Kagan, n. 7.
Johnson, H. C. (1988). Drugs, dialogue, or diet: Diagnosing and treating the hyperactive child. *Social Work, 33,* 349–355.
Johnson, H. C., Atkins, S., Battle, S., Hernandez-Arata, L., Hesselbrock, M., Libassi, M. F., & Parish, M. (1990). Strengthening the 'bio' in the biopsychosocial paradigm. *Journal of Social Work Education, 26*(2), 109–123.
Johnson, H. C., Cournoyer, D. E., & Bond, B. M. (1995). Professional ethics and parents as consumers: How well are we doing? *Families in Society, 76,* 408–420.
Johnson, H. C., Cournoyer, D. E., & Fisher, G. A. (1994). Measuring worker cognitions about parents of children with mental and emotional disabilities. *Journal of Emotional and Behavioral Disorders, 2*(2), 99–108.
Kagan, J. (1994). *The Nature of the Child* (10th Anniv. ed.). Scranton, PA: HarperCollins.

Kazdin, A. E. (1981). Drawing valid inferences from case studies. *Journal of Consulting and Clinical Psychology, 2,* 183–192.

PsycLit, June 1995.

Rejoinder to Dr. Johnson KATHERINE TYSON

We can begin our consideration of Professor Johnson's argument by restating it. In arguing "yes," that it is possible to generate a list of universal HBSE concepts and principles that all students should learn, Professor Johnson proposes "a method for studying any instance of HBSE as the need arises." Her method assumes that research can straightforwardly yield evidence to conclusively test the veracity of a concept or principle. Let us take a closer look at her argument.

First, to look at Professor Johnson's logic, we need to consider the major elements that constitute a sound argument: defining one's terms, developing the premises and assertions, and formulating the logic that leads to the conclusions of the argument. Professor Johnson's argument lacks these crucial elements. To begin with, she does not offer definitions of either research or evidence. Undefined terms reflect unexamined assumptions. It follows that unexamined assumptions yield unreliable assertions and, in turn, unreliable assertions cannot be the basis for the sound reasoning of a valid argument. Therefore, let us look at her primary assumption because if it is untenable, then her argument falls of its own weight.

Professor Johnson's proposed "method" rests on the assumption that research can be used to demonstrate the truth of concepts and principles. Is this assumption tenable? To answer this question we need to consider the nature of the research process itself. Every aspect of the research process, from problem formulation through data collection and data analysis, rests on an ontology (beliefs about the "real" to be known) and an epistemology (beliefs about how that "real" can be known). For instance, one cannot study a star unless one begins with a definition of "starness" and uses a tool to know the star (e.g., one would not use a microscope). Furthermore, every method of collecting and analyzing data also rests on the researcher's choice of ontological and epistemological assumptions. For example, researchers developed the new Hubble telescope based on certain assumptions about galactic reality and how that reality could be known. The history of philosophy testifies to the fact that one cannot prove either an ontology or the epistemology that is assumed in and accompanies every ontology. Accordingly, the research process itself rests on assumptions that, although open to examination, are not, by their nature, open to proof. However, it is important to realize that the recognition that the research process cannot yield a conclusive type of truth is compatible with (that is, supports) a perspective of reality that is nonrelativistic. A strong body of literature cogently supports this case (Callebaut, 1993; Heineman {Pieper}, 1981; Tyson, 1995).

Let us return to Professor Johnson's assumption that research can be straightforwardly used to evaluate concepts and principles. I said in my paper that concepts and principles rest on ontological and epistemological assumptions. And I have said that the research process also rests on ontological and epistemological assumptions. Bias is inevitably part of the evaluation process because the relationship between the researcher's chosen assumptions and the assumptions underlying the concepts and principles predetermines the researcher's conclusions. To illustrate, behaviorists commonly choose the ontology of observable behavior rather than the subjective experience of purposiveness. When behaviorists use their own research standards to evaluate concepts and principles grounded in another ontology (e.g., the subjective experience of purposiveness), they regularly conclude that those concepts and principles have not been shown to be true. Yet, because the behaviorist has already ruled out alternative ontologies and epistemologies, the behaviorist's argument that concepts and principles based on those ontologies and epistemologies have not been demonstrated to be true is circular and therefore invalid. The behaviorist's evaluative process is "begging the question"—she or he is restating conclusions that are the same as where she or he started.

In sum, with regard to Professor Johnson's positivist argument, the "method" she proposes for evaluating concepts and principles is untenable because it rests on a foundation (her assumptions about research) that does not exist. Does this mean that we can never have good grounds for believing that some concepts and principles are closer to the truth than others? Contemporary postpositivist researchers have argued that it does not. In contrast to the impossible positivist effort to conclusively prove concepts and principles, a postpositivist understanding of research process makes the complexity of our social realities tractable for study and focuses on discovering relevant solutions to the important problems we face.

REFERENCES

Callebaut, W. (1993). *Taking the naturalistic turn, or how real philosophy of science is done.* Chicago: University of Chicago Press.

Heineman (Pieper), M. (1981). The obsolete scientific imperative in social work research. *Social Service Review, 55,* 371–397. See also Pieper, M. Heineman

Tyson, K. (Ed.). (1995). *New foundations for scientific social and behavioral research: The heuristic paradigm.* Boston: Allyn & Bacon.

NO

KATHERINE TYSON

To answer the question at hand, we need to understand what it would mean for the concepts and principles that might form a list to be "universal." Building on the many meanings "universal" has had in philosophy (see for example Reese, 1980), for our purpose we can assume that universality means that the potential list's concepts and principles *would hold true* for entire classes of HBSE phenomena across diverse contexts. What are the *criteria* used to ascertain whether the concepts and principles constituting the potential list are universals? I argue that if our criteria for evaluating the universality of concepts and principles are derived from a philosophy of research termed *logical positivism*—such as that the concepts and principles must be proved to be true, or verified, or guaranteed to hold up across diverse contexts (Hanfling, 1981)—the answer to the question at hand is "no." Then, I show how one can use more up-to-date, *postpositivist* criteria for evaluating scientific concepts and principles.

All components of theories, including concepts and principles, rest on assumptions. An *assumption* is an idea taken for granted for the sake of the argument that follows (Reese, 1980, p. 36). Following are examples of concepts, principles, and assumptions in contemporary HBSE theories:

Theories	Concepts	Principles	Assumptions
Behaviorism (Schwartz, 1983)	Stimulus Response	The frequency of a behavior increases when reinforced.	Many human behaviors can be understood without loss of important meaning by studying animal behavior.
Family systems (Hartman & Laird, 1983)	Identified patient Parental child	Symptomatic behavior develops to preserve the family system's homeostasis.	A system is more than the sum of its parts.
Psychoanalysis (Freud, S., *The ego and the id* in S. E.)	Impulse Affect	Drive frustration is a necessary stimulus to ego development.	The primary substrate of human consciousness is instinctual drives.
Intrapsychic humanism (Pieper & Pieper, 1990)	Motive Meaning structure Ideal	Without gratification of the intrapsychic motive an individual will not remain alive.	Humans are primarily motivated by relationship pleasure.

Any list of HBSE concepts and principles is generated by a research process that in turn is based on assumptions about scientific knowledge (a philosophy of research). Currently in the field of social work there are passionate debates about the two prevalent philosophies of scientific research—logical positivism and postpositivism (Falck, 1995; Grinnell et al., 1994; Heineman [Pieper] 1981; Mathews, 1995; Tyson, 1994; Witkin, 1995). Aspects of these philosophies that pertain directly to our question are summarized below.

Why "No" under Logical Positivist Criteria

The logical positivist philosophers sought to render scientific knowledge as certain as possible, primarily by prescribing that methodologically based criteria should be used to evaluate whether concepts and principles are scientifically meaningful (Hanfling, 1981). Thus, under logical positivism, the methodology that yields concepts and principles is a central criterion in evaluating their veracity. The logical positivist researcher holds that certain methodological preferences have universal applicability, in that the most valuable scientific knowledge is generated when research problems are tailored so that they can be studied using the methods she or he deems unconditionally privileged for testing theories (such as experimental design, Grinnell, 1993; Reid & Smith, 1989).

The problems with logical positivism and its applications in social work have been amply summarized elsewhere (Heineman [Pieper], 1981; Tyson, 1995). Four points most pertinent to our question follow. First, logical positivism is not an accurate description of actual scientific practice. For example, the restrictiveness of logical positivism, such as the claim that specific methodologies are unconditionally privileged, does not hold up in any field of science. Moreover, many contemporary historians of science, whose findings have been one basis for postpositivism, have shown that scientific methods and theories vary within periods and that, over time, methods and theories change considerably or are abandoned as untenable (Kuhn, 1970).

Second, the logical positivists were concerned that inductive reasoning can never produce universals and took pains to try to eliminate inductive reasoning from scientific theory-testing. However, they were inevitably unsuccessful, because any component of a scientific theory, including a concept or principle, relies to some extent on inductive reasoning. Given a particular observation, or even several observations, we cannot guarantee that a concept or principle induced from those instances will not be disconfirmed by subsequent observations. Consider Sir Karl Popper's example, "all swans are white" (1959/1934). Popper pointed out that we can never conclusively confirm this proposition because the possibility always continues to exist that we could find a black swan.

Third, given any one observation, we can always devise multiple explanations for it, and there may always be another, better explanation we have not yet discovered. No research methodology can rule out all alternative explanations. For example, even if we set up a matched control group to try to rule out some alternative explanations for our findings, there are always other explanations for which we have not controlled.

Fourth, every methodology sets up its own form of bias, and there is no basis for the logical positivist claim that some methods are unconditionally privileged for testing theories. For instance, although tape recording for data collection produces a form of accuracy, at the same time it also introduces biases, such as stimulating reactions to the tape-recording process (Heineman Pieper, 1994). No concept can be conclusively verified because every concept is based on induction and is developed using a bias-laden methodology. Principles are subject to the same constraints. In short, one reason one cannot generate a universal list of concepts or principles is because it is impossible to confirm that the components of any such list are true.

Under Postpositivist Criteria: Not an Absolute No

If we change the criteria for evaluating the universality of concepts and principles, will this change the response to the question at hand? Instead of turning to particular methodologies for universals, which occurs under logical positivism, one can develop higher-order principles of investigation. The postpositivist philosophy of research was developed from the study of how scientists in diverse fields actually generate knowledge. It offers alternative assumptions about knowledge that can be broadly applicable in part because they are also context-sensitive. Some pertinent postpositivist assumptions about scientific knowledge are: (1) there is no basis for the belief that specific methodological prescriptions or proscriptions will improve scientific knowledge; (2) every research method generates a form of bias, and no method is unconditionally privileged for testing scientific theories; (3) although bias cannot be eliminated, it can be regulated by bias recognition; (4) value-free knowledge is impossible, so (a) it is important that the scientist recognize and monitor her or his value commitments, and (b) advocacy can be compatible with a scientific stance (Heineman [Pieper], 1981; Simon, 1966; Tyson, 1995; Wimsatt, 1986).

From a postpositivist standpoint, the issue in our question at hand is not to prove, verify, or confirm the truth of concepts and principles, but instead to ascertain whether they are good *heuristics* (Heineman [Pieper], 1981). Following Herbert Simon (1966), a heuristic is a problem-solving strategy. Humans inevitably use heuristics to organize perceiving and knowing. Heuristics range in scope and, in knowledge generation, include concepts, theories, and research methods (Heineman [Pieper], 1981; Tyson, 1995; Wimsatt, 1986). Herbert Simon (1966) points out that a good heuristic is facilitative of ongoing scientific inquiry, well supported, and "satisficing," or good enough according to an explicit criterion. Being limited to heuristic grounds does not preclude a scientist *believing* that her or his concepts and principles are true, but refers to what the scientist claims she or he can *prove*. Postpositivist principles have been imported into social work research and termed the *heuristic paradigm* (Heineman [Pieper] 1981; Tyson, 1995). Although the heuristic paradigm embraces contemporary forms of relativism such as social constructionism, the heuristic paradigm also includes the qualified realist position that reality cannot be defined on the basis of what one can know, and that some theories are truer than others.

As I have said, logical positivists claim certain concepts and principles are universals on methodological grounds. From a postpositivist standpoint, in appraising concepts or principles, one asks whether they fit the characteristics of a good heuristic, including: whether they are consistent with other aspects of the theory, such as the ontological and epistemological assumptions; whether they explain insufficiently understood observations; and whether they facilitate further application and scientific inquiry (Callebaut, 1993; Heineman [Pieper], 1981; Tyson, 1995; Wimsatt, 1986). Following is a brief sketch of how one can use postpositivist principles to appraise concepts and principles as heuristics, using a concept and principle drawn from the new postpositivist psychology, intrapsychic humanism.

Intrapsychic humanism is the first comprehensive reformulation of human development, psychopathology, and treatment since Freud developed psychoanalytic theory (Pieper & Pieper, 1990). Intrapsychic humanism reflects postpositivist assumptions about science in many respects. Most importantly, although the authors of intrapsychic humanism, Martha Heineman Pieper and William Joseph Pieper, state that they believe the concepts, principles, and assumptions of intrapsychic humanism are true (fit reality), in fact they are arguing only that it is heuristic to understand human nature according to intrapsychic humanism (1990, p. 301, n. 6).

An initial consideration is that by definition a heuristic applies within a particular domain. To illustrate, the postpositivist metatheory of scientific knowledge is a very broad heuristic that applies to diverse fields of science, but it does not claim to apply to the domain of artistic expressions such as poetry. Among the most important ways that a scientist delineates her or his theory's domain of applicability are through her or his ontological assumptions (beliefs about the "real" under study) and epistemological assumptions (beliefs about how that "real" is known). For instance, an astronomer studies "reals" such as planets using a telescope as a way of knowing. Every psychology is built on explicit or implicit assumptions about human nature (ontological assumptions) and how the aspects of human nature identified in the ontology can be known (epistemological assumptions). A theory's concepts and principles should be consistent with its ontology and epistemology, so to appraise a concept and principle from intrapsychic humanism, first we need to understand the psychology's ontology and epistemology.

The authors of intrapsychic humanism take pains to explicate that for the purpose of understanding the subjective experience of personal existence (psychic reality), it is heuristic to assume that humans do not live by bread alone but rather hunt and gather meaning, especially significant personal meaning—the experience of one's life as meaningful and of oneself as having a sense of purpose (Pieper & Pieper, 1990). Although people commonly experience instability in their sense of purposiveness and self-worth, especially in response to the plentiful losses of everyday life, the Piepers explain how this instability occurs. Moreover, based on their applications of intrapsychic humanism for child care and psychological treatment, the Piepers observed that this instability is not inevitable. One of their most surprising observations is that a cared-for individual can develop significant and stable personal meaning through the relationship with a caregiver (parent or social worker), which occurs as the cared-for individual discovers that she or he can regulate her or his inner well-being by causing the caregiver's caregiving.

The Piepers also give the epistemology of intrapsychic humanism careful consideration, and present the underlying assumptions explicitly. The way in which the personal meaning structures of the cared-for individual can be known is a relationship based, mutual, nonsolipsistic form of introspection—the intrapsychic caregiving relationship (Pieper & Pieper, 1990, pp. 17–18). This relationship affords a unique vantage point because, first, the cared-for individual has a motive to be involved with the caregiver (parent or therapist) to acquire stable self-regulation. Second, caregivers have caregiving motives (motives to help the child or client acquire self-regulatory self-worth) and personal motives (all other motives, such as motives to talk about what one had for lunch). The caregiver aims to have her or his caregiving motives in charge when she or he relates with the cared-for individual. Just as a microscope affords a unique perspective, so the mutual commitment that forms the intrapsychic caregiving relationship also offers a unique perspective; it is the basis for the caregiver's accurate knowledge of the personal meaning structures of the cared-for individual.

The concept of the *intrapsychic motive* is a heuristic that follows from intrapsychic humanism's ontological and epistemological assumptions, in combination with the Piepers' clinical observations. The intrapsychic motive is the motive to acquire a stable, self-regulating self-worth, a sense of personal meaning that endures despite life's ups and downs. This heuristic offers new explanations for many human behaviors. For example, some theoreticians such as Freud and Stern overlooked the smile response; and other explanations for this behavior (such as Spitz's), have been unsatisfactory. Using the concept of the intrapsychic motive, one understands the infant's smile as a behavioral expression of this primary motive to experience self-worth by causing the caregiver's caregiving. One supporting observation for the heuristic notion that the intrapsychic motive is present in every human regardless of specifics of race, gender, or state of physiological challenge or disability is that if they are minimally cared for, by approximately three months of age, all infants in every culture will begin to develop a special or "differentiated" smile for their caregivers (Pieper & Pieper, 1990, pp. 37–44). Although the Piepers *believe* the intrapsychic motive exists in every person (is a type of universal), they *argue only* that the intrapsychic motive is the most useful heuristic for understanding human consciousness.

The logical extension of accepting the heuristic of a universal intrapsychic motive is to argue that all human development is powered by the *intrapsychic pleasure principle,* which is an innately determined set of ideals with the power to regulate an individual's subjective experience. The intrapsychic pleasure principle causes an individual, when given a choice, to prefer more genuine or veridical forms of care-getting pleasure (or personal meaning, Pieper & Pieper, 1990, p. 93). For example, clients may have developed a core personal meaning structure based on nonoptimal and even abusive caregetting experiences. In intrapsychic treatment, the client can develop a new, self-regulating experience of personal meaning based on the therapeutic caregiving relationship (Pieper & Pieper, 1990, 1995). Then, the client will have a choice between these two inner sources of personal meaning, and the intrapsychic pleasure principle explains how the client can, over time, prefer the more genuine and pleasurable personal meaning built by the therapeutic mutuality. The findings of social workers who have applied intrapsychic humanism to treat diverse populations and problems support the heuristic of the intrapsychic pleasure principle in particular and, more broadly, the promise of intrapsychic humanism's treatment principles. See for examples school social work practice with multicultural children (Ishibashi, 1991), residential care for treating previously "untreatable" homicidal and suicidal teenagers (Pieper & Pieper, 1995), outpatient treatment of out-of-control adolescents (Pieper & Pieper, 1992), and treatment of children with the symptom cluster commonly termed childhood hyperactivity (Tyson, 1991).

To gather the data for the studies just cited, the researchers followed postpositivist principles and selected research methods that would allow them access to the ontology they sought to study and that would be consistent with the epistemology of their chosen theory (intrapsychic humanism). The efficacy of intrapsychic caregiving depends on the therapist's or parent's ability to stably prefer caregiving to personal motives. But the motive to introduce research-driven interventions is a personal, not a caregiving motive. Therefore, to introduce such research-driven interventions as tape recorders, third-party observers, or videotapes would have a material negative effect on the subject under study, namely, the therapeutic relationship. Accordingly, if the therapist alters her or his caregiving process to gather data, she or he will destroy the very caregiving process she or he aims to study. However, the intrapsychic therapist can preserve the caregiving process and use naturalistic research methods—methods in which the researcher is a member of the system under study and does not alter the interactions in the system for research purposes (Heineman Pieper, 1994). To illustrate, the Piepers did not alter their interactions with clients to gather data, but instead systematically observed caregiving interactions as they occurred naturally and memorialized them in the form of process recordings completed after the treatment sessions ended (Pieper & Pieper, 1990, 1995).

In conclusion, I have argued that for several reasons, if to be considered universal a list of concepts and principles must be capable of conclusive proof, then such a universal list is not possible. However, from a postpositivist standpoint, the most important issue is not to prove that certain concepts and principles are universal, but to appraise whether they are valuable heuristics. We can use up-to-date, postpositivist criteria for appraising whether concepts and principles are worth learning, including conceptual consistency, explanatory power, applicability to diverse and changing conditions, and compatibility with humanistic values. The assumptions of postpositivism can facilitate the growth of our science, because they affirm openness to new discoveries, theoretical diversity, reflective analysis of heuristics and their biases, and the emancipatory potential of scientific knowledge.

REFERENCES

Callebaut, W. (1993). *Taking the naturalistic turn, or how real philosophy of science is done.* Chicago: University of Chicago Press.

Falck, H. (1995). Letter to the editor. *Social Work, 40*(1), 142.

Grinnell, R. (1993). *Social work research and evaluation* (4th ed.). Itasca, IL: F. E. Peacock.

Grinnell, R. et al. (1994). Social work researchers' quest for respectability. *Social Work, 39*, 469–470.

Hanfling, O. (1981). *Logical positivism.* New York: Columbia University Press.

Hartman, A., & Laird, J. (1983). *Family centered social work practice.* New York: Free Press.

Heineman (Pieper), M. (1981). The obsolete scientific imperative in social work research. *Social Service Review, 55*, 371–397. See also Pieper, M. Heineman

Ishibashi, N. (1991). Multicultural students: What do they want? *School Social Work Journal, 16*, 41–45.

Kuhn, T. S. (1970). *The structure of scientific revolutions* (2nd ed.) Chicago: University of Chicago.

Mathews, G. (1995). Letter to the editor. *Social Work, 40*(1), 142.

Pieper, M. Heineman, & Pieper, W. J. (1990). *Intrapsychic humanism: An introduction to a comprehensive psychology and philosophy of mind.* Chicago: Falcon II Press.

Pieper, M. Heineman, & Pieper, W. J. (1992). It's not tough, it's tender love. *Child Welfare, 71*, 369–377.

Pieper, M. Heineman, & Pieper, W. J. (1995). Treating violent, "untreatable" adolescents: Applications of intrapsychic humanism in a state-funded demonstration project. In K. Tyson (Ed.), *New foundations for scientific social and behavioral research: The heuristic paradigm.* Boston: Allyn & Bacon.

Pieper, M. Heineman. (1994). Science, not scientism: The robustness of naturalistic clinical research. In E. Sherman & W. J. Reid (Eds.), *Qualitative research in social work.* New York: Columbia University Press. See also Heineman (Pieper), M.

Popper, K. R. (1959) (1934). *The logic of scientific discovery.* New York: Basic Books.

Reese, W. L. (1980). *Dictionary of philosophy and religion: Eastern and Western thought.* New Jersey: Humanities Press.

Reid, W. J., & Smith, A. (1989). *Research in social work.* New York: Columbia University Press.

Schwartz, A. (1983). Behavioral principles and approaches. In D. Waldfogel & A. Rosenblatt (Eds.), *Handbook of clinical social work* (pp. 202–208). San Francisco: Jossey Bass.

Simon, H. (1966). Scientific discovery and the psychology of problem solving. In R. Colodny (Ed.), *Mind and cosmos: Essays in contemporary science and philosophy.* Pittsburgh: University of Pittsburgh Press.

Tyson, K. (1991). The understanding and treatment of childhood hyperactivity: Old problems and new approaches. *Smith College Studies in Social Work, 61,* 133–166.

Tyson, K. (1994). Author's reply: Response to "Social work researchers' quest for respectability." *Social Work, 39,* 737–741.

Tyson, K. (Ed.). (1995). *New foundations for scientific social and behavioral research: The heuristic paradigm.* Boston: Allyn & Bacon.

Wimsatt, W. (1986). Heuristics and the study of human behavior. In D. W. Fiske & R. A. Shweder (Eds.), *Metatheory in social science: Pluralisms and subjectivities* (pp. 293–314). Chicago: University of Chicago Press.

Witkin, S. (1995). Letter to the editor. *Social Work, 40*(1), 142.

Rejoinder to Dr. Tyson HARRIETTE JOHNSON

Senator Benign-Neglect: Good morning, colleagues. I have just read Professor Tyson's treatise. As a card-carrying intellectual, I must say I can't blame the American people for being fed up with eggheads. [Reading from the manuscript:] "The client will have a choice between these two inner sources of personal meaning, and the intrapsychic pleasure principle explains how the client can, over time, prefer the more genuine and pleasurable personal meaning built by the therapeutic mutuality." What, may I ask, does this have to do with the daily struggles of the American people?

Rep. Older: I agree with you, Pat. Tyson proposes that no list of concepts or principles can be generated because it is impossible to confirm that the components of any such list are true. I cannot help wondering if Ms. Tyson uses a telephone or television, or rides in automobiles or airplanes. Does she think the "bias-laden methodology" used to develop such devices is no more objective than the methodology used by a single individual to unearth his or her "core personal meaning structure"? If so, I admire her courage in riding in a car or an airplane, given the extreme likelihood of lethal mechanical failure.

Sen. Candy: It seems to me that Tyson is making rather extravagant claims when she asserts that "intrapsychic humanism is the first comprehensive reformulation of human development, psychopathology, and treatment since Freud developed psychoanalytic theory." Has she read any of the developmental psychology of the past ten years, such as the works of Jerome Kagan? Kagan (1994) incorporates biological, cultural, interpersonal, economic, and political forces and even the role of chance events in his formulation. He integrates knowledge from the subjective individual perspective with knowledge from quantitative studies. He illuminates the role of cultural differences in psychological states of being. That, indeed, is a comprehensive formulation. Where in intrapsychic humanism is there anything remotely resembling "comprehensive"?

Rep. Older: My greatest concerns about Tyson's position are ethical. First, while framing the infant/ caretaker relationship as the major determinant of later psychological well-being, she neglects the multiple forces that impinge on that caretaker and support or impede caretaking. Another variation on the mother-is-to-blame theme. Second, Tyson promotes psychotherapeutic exchanges to a preeminent role in people's lives. Although we may like to believe that we are emotionally indispensable to our clients, such a belief suggests professional narcissism if not arrogance. Third, Tyson barely acknowledges the need for a bona fide knowledge base—all that is required is a heuristic posture. Yet the vast majority of our constituents are not the middle-class worried well, seeking personal enrichment through psychotherapy. To provide competent services, we need knowledge provided by research in such diverse fields as medicine, social psychology, economics, and social welfare policy, the flaws in such research notwithstanding. To emphasize the heuristic paradigm or intrapsychic humanism at the expense of solid bodies of interdisciplinary knowledge seems to reflect a certain hubris with respect to the contributions of thousands of scholars and researchers to our existing knowledge base.

Should the HBSE Core Curriculum Include Major Value Theories in Addition to the Profession's Code of Ethics?

Editor's Note: Ethics and values (especially seeking desired goals while using appropriate means, and value conflict resolution) are an important part of every social work student's education, and are taught in many parts of the curriculum. The question posed here is whether HBSE is an appropriate place to teach value theories such as those of Rawls, Nozick, Gewirth, and the utilitarians, just as we teach other behavioral and social theories.

Frederic G. Reamer, Ph.D., professor, at the School of Social Work, Rhode Island College, is the author of many books, including his recent *Social Work Values and Ethics* (1995, Columbia University Press). He was past editor of the *Journal of Social Work Education*.

Kevin M. Marett, Ph.D., is assistant professor of Social Work in the School of Social Work at Brigham Young University. Dr. Marett teaches human behavior and the social environment at the undergraduate and graduate levels as well as marriage and family treatment at the graduate level. His current research interests include interdisciplinary collaboration and performance criteria in professional social work.

W. Eugene Gibbons, D.S.W., is professor of Social Work in the School of Social Work and founder of both the B.S.W. and M.S.W. programs at Brigham Young University. Dr. Gibbons is the Director of Field Placement and teaches groupwork, crisis intervention, and clinical practice. His research interests include aging, women in the military, and interdisciplinary collaboration.

YES

FREDERIC G. REAMER

The glib answer to this question is "of course." Of course social work students need to be acquainted with major value theories, and, for a variety of reasons, the HBSE curriculum is a very important place—albeit not the only place—to broach the subject.

But before we explore the reasons why the HBSE curriculum is a good home for content on value theories, let us make sure we understand what this topic entails. Not surprisingly, the term *value theories* means different things to different people. Let me clarify my understanding of the term. Value theories reflect various conceptualizations about what values are and how they evolve, not just in individuals, but in families, groups, organizations, and communities as well.

We recognize easily that individuals have values, for example, related to honesty, keeping promises, obeying the law, and so on. But families, groups, organizations, and communities also have values. Some families, for example, explicitly value charitable giving and organize family activities to carry out this commitment; other families value criminal activity and domestic violence. Furthermore, a support group of clients who are adult children of alcoholics may, as a group, embrace certain values concerning confidentiality and privacy; a delinquent gang may endorse certain values related to violence or drug use. A particular community may value organized efforts to help its low-income residents; another community may value racial intolerance and conflict. In addition, one social service organization may value parenting and, thus, promotes flexible work schedules for its employees; another organization may value profit above all else and, consequently, is stingy with worker benefits.

Value theories also concern conflicts among values. There are several possibilities here of which social workers need to be aware. One involves conflicts between social workers' and clients' values, for example, when a social worker who is personally opposed to abortion is approached by a pregnant client who wants advice about how to arrange an abortion, or when a social worker encounters a client who frequently makes racist comments. Value conflicts also can involve clashes between a social worker's values and those of his or her employer. For instance, a social worker may oppose her agency's policy to limit low-income clients' access to certain services and programs.

Yet another form of values conflict involves tension between a social worker's values and those of the social work profession or its principal organization, the National Association of Social Workers (NASW). Periodically, for example, the NASW adopts formal policies concerning a variety of controversial social issues, such as welfare and health care reform, end-of-life decisions, abortion, human immunodeficiency virus (HIV)/acquired immune deficiency syndrome (AIDS), and gay and lesbian rights. Although these policies may be endorsed by most social workers, there may be a minority who disagree with NASW's position on particular issues. These social workers must wrestle with the conflict between their personal values and those of the profession.

This phenomenon leads to another aspect of value theories—conceptual frameworks for analyzing and understanding conflicts among values. It is one thing for social workers to grasp the nature of values and values-related conflicts. It is quite another to have conceptual tools to help social workers analyze and resolve these conflicts. These are typically known as ethical theories (Reamer & Abramson, 1982).

So why should all of this values-related content be part of the HBSE curriculum? At least one part of the answer seems obvious. According to the Council on Social Work Education *Curriculum Policy Statement* (1994), the primary goal of the HBSE curriculum is to convey content "about theories and knowledge of human bio-psycho-social development, including theories and knowledge about the range of social systems in which individuals live (families, groups, organizations, institutions, and communities).... *Content about values and ethical issues related to bio-psycho-social theories must be included*" (standards B6.7 and M6.9; emphasis added). Apparently CSWE has taken this stance because it recognizes that values are linked inextricably to theories and knowledge of biopsychosocial development.

HBSE sequences typically address some combination of theories related to human development (usually called life cycle or life course issues), personality, physical and mental disability, organizational and community dynamics, oppression, and cultural and ethnic diversity. There is no question that serious exploration of these topics must lead, inevitably, to some complex values-related issues. These include questions and debates about how individuals develop and are taught values, the impact of values on individual development, value biases embedded within some well-known human development theories, value conflicts that emerge in organizations and communities, variation in values embraced by different cultural and ethnic groups, and conflicts between social workers' and clients' values. To omit this content would strip this portion of the social work curriculum of one of its essential ingredients.

This is not to say that value theories can or should be addressed *only* in the HBSE sequence. This would be remarkably shortsighted. In fact, the CSWE *Curriculum Policy Statement* states clearly that content on values and ethics should permeate the social work curriculum—and with good reason. No reasonable person would question the need for social work educators to address this content in, as well, practice, policy, and research and evaluation courses. Value theories are relevant to all of them.

What, then, belongs in the HBSE curriculum? Four major questions should be addressed:

1. What are values?
2. How are values relevant to human behavior in the social environment?

3. In what ways do values related to HBSE-content conflict?
4. What theoretical perspectives can be used to understand and analyze conflicts among values?

What are Values?

Put succinctly, a value is an enduring belief concerning what is right, worthwhile, or desirable. Many discussions of values distinguish among ultimate, proximate, and instrumental values (Rokeach, 1973). Ultimate values are those beliefs that shape people's goals and aims. In social work, commonly cited ultimate values are social justice, social change, and mental health. For clients, ultimate values might include marital stability, mental health, and financial security. In contrast, proximate values are more immediate and specific. In social work, examples are enhanced access to social services and high-quality assurance standards in social service programs. For clients, proximate values might include adequate health care services, heat for one's home, or some kind of behavior change. Finally, instrumental values include specific desirable means to valued ends. In social work, instrumental values focus on the ways in which practitioners conduct their work, as opposed to their ultimate or shorter-term aims. Examples include engaging clients as partners in goal-setting, handling confidential information properly, and obtaining clients' informed consent appropriately. For clients, instrumental values might include having good social skills and adequate transportation. The social work literature includes several valuable typologies of social work values that can be usefully introduced in the HBSE curriculum (Abbott, 1988; Levy, 1973, 1984; Pumphrey, 1959, pp. 79–80; Reamer, 1994, 1995a, 1995b).

How Are Values Relevant to Human Behavior in the Social Environment?

Social workers need to understand the ways in which clients' values evolve during the life course and their influence on human behavior. Understanding clients' ultimate, proximate, and instrumental values, for instance, can help social workers address the significant issues and concerns in their lives. A social worker who finds herself dealing with a racist client or a client who is distressed about participating in an extramarital affair needs to know about values and how to deal with conflicts among them. The same goes for social workers who provide services to families, for example, when a family's values concerning boundaries or behavior management clash with the practitioner's values.

Similarly, social workers involved in work with organizations and communities need to understand the key role values can play in these settings. In addition to being exposed in HBSE courses to theories on organizational and community dynamics, social workers need to be able to recognize and deal with complicated values issues that may have an important bearing on their attempts to intervene effectively based on these theories. Examples include social workers who find themselves embroiled in a community-based controversy about the opening of a residential facility for people who are HIV+ or who are consulting with a social service agency where morale suffers because of disagreement among staff concerning the fairness of affirmative action guidelines for promotion. Social workers who do not understand the relevance of values to the organizational and community theories taught in the HBSE curriculum are likely to miss the boat in such situations.

Another critically important way in which values are relevant to the HBSE curriculum concerns the biases embedded in a number of theories typically taught in these courses, particularly related to individual development. By now social work educators are well aware of the ways in which time-honored theories associated with Freud, Erikson, Kohlberg, and others have been critiqued because of their apparent gender or class bias and their lack of attention to the ways in which values vary across culturally diverse groups.

In What Ways Do Values Conflict?

Among the most persistent challenges for social workers are those involving conflicts among values, whether they involve their clients' values, their own, the social work profession's, or the broader society's. In direct practice, for example, social workers may find themselves caught between their clients' values and their own. Imagine, for example, a social worker who is providing counseling services to a thirty-four-year-old woman who is having serious marital problems. The client feels as if the marriage is hopeless. Because of the client's values, however, inculcated by her deeply religious family, the client feels guilty about contemplating divorce. For her, divorce is contrary to the religious teachings and values with which she was raised. At the same time, the social worker believes that the client must escape her abusive husband. For the social worker, divorce is an important option for the client to consider.

To be helpful to this client, the social worker must understand various life course issues that are often addressed in HBSE courses, related, for example, to marriage, domestic violence, young adulthood, stress, coping, and adaptation. But the social worker would be terribly shortsighted if she did not recognize the need to address the role of values in this case, with respect to not only the client's efforts to wrestle with her own values, but also the tension between the client's values and the social worker's values.

Equally difficult value choices arise in indirect practice, too, when social workers are involved in community- or organizationally based activities. Consider a social worker who is a community organizer. A group of neighborhood residents, who have been working with a prominent developer, asks the social worker to work on a proposal that would seize through eminent domain a group of small apartment buildings for low-income people, who are mostly people of color and recent immigrants, to create an "upscale" residential and shopping district. The community group's proposal provides compelling data suggesting that this development project is likely to produce a significant net gain to the neighborhood's economy and strengthen its deteriorating tax base. In this instance, the social worker must decide whether to join forces with the community group, which clearly enjoys broad-based community support, or oppose the popular proposal in an effort to ensure that low-income residents of the community are not displaced.

To address this dilemma, the social worker needs to understand commonly taught HBSE theory and knowledge related to community dynamics. But the social worker's understanding must also include recognition of the influence of values in the case, particularly the clash between the community group's values and the social worker's values.

What Theoretical Perspectives Can Be Used to Understand and Analyze Conflicts among Values?

Several key examples of value theories and concepts can help social workers grapple with conflicts among values and can incorporated nicely in HBSE courses (see, for example, Frankena, 1973; Gewirth 1978; Rawls, 1971; Reamer, 1990, 1995a; and Ross, 1930). One common perspective involves different ways of examining competing values: Is a proposed action inherently right or wrong (known as a deontological view), or which action is likely to result in the most favorable or least favorable consequences (known as a teleological or consequentialist view)? These contrasting perspectives, which are based on radically different assumptions about how people should make value choices, can lead to very different actions. Consider the situation involving the proposed opening of a residential facility for people who are HIV+. Should the social worker support this course of action because people as human beings have an inherent right to be helped (a deontological view), or should the social worker act on the proposal based on her calculation of the consequences—good or bad—that are likely to result (a teleological or consequentialist view)?

Students should wrestle with such value questions in many places in the social work curriculum, but particularly when these issues involve theories of human behavior that guide practice. Social work educators would be remiss if they did not address these values-related issues within the context of HBSE courses. The emphasis here should not be on practice or policy principles per se, but in recognizing how values are keenly relevant to social workers' understanding of how people, families, groups, communities, and organizations develop and function, and how this understanding has important implications for social work practice.

What social workers always need is the fullest possible understanding of the problems they and their clients face and the most robust conceptual tools for approaching these problems. Understanding human behavior in the social environment is essential if social workers are to grasp the nature of and effectively address clients' and social problems.

This understanding would be woefully incomplete if it did not include an examination of the relevance of values and value theories, and how they influence human behavior, the social environment, and the complex interaction between them.

REFERENCES

Abbott, A. A. (1988). *Professional choices: Values at work.* Silver Spring, MD: National Association of Social Workers.

Council on Social Work Education. (1994). *Curriculum policy statement.* Alexandria, VA: Author.

Frankena, W. K. (1973). *Ethics* (2nd ed.). Englewood Cliffs, NJ: Prentice-Hall.

Gewirth, A. (1978). *Reason and morality.* Chicago: University of Chicago Press.

Levy, C. (1973). The value base of social work. *Journal of Education for Social Work,* 9: 34–52.

Levy, C. (1984). Values and ethics. In S. Dillick (Ed.), *Value foundations of social work* (pp. 17–29). Detroit: School of Social Work, Wayne State University.

Pumphrey, M. W. (1959). *The teaching of values and ethics in social work.* New York: Council on Social Work Education.

Rawls, J. (1971). *A theory of justice.* Cambridge: Harvard University Press.

Reamer, F. G. (1990). *Ethical dilemmas in social service* (2nd ed.). New York: Columbia University Press.

Reamer, F. G. (1994). Social work values and ethics. In F. G. Reamer (Ed.), *The foundations of social work knowledge* (pp. 195–230). New York: Columbia University Press.

Reamer, F. G. (1995a). *Social work values and ethics.* New York: Columbia University Press.

Reamer, F. G. (1995b). Ethics and values. In *Encyclopedia of social work* (19th ed.) (pp. 893–902). Washington, DC: NASW.

Reamer, F. G. & Abramson, M. (1982). *The teaching of social work ethics.* Hastings-on-Hudson, NY: The Hastings Center.

Rokeach, M. (1973). *The nature of human values.* New York: Free Press.

Ross, W. D. (1930). *The right and the good.* Oxford: Clarendon.

Rejoinder to Dr. Reamer

KEVIN M. MARETT
W. EUGENE GIBBONS

Professor Reamer is correct in his assertion that the new CSWE Curriculum Policy Statement and its associated Accreditation Standards require that values be taught in the HBSE curriculum; however, it is important to reiterate that all curriculum content (sequence) areas are to include social work values. This clearly suggests that the treatment of values and ethics transcends any one curricular area and presupposes that a practicing social worker must ever be mindful of the impact values play in our day-to-day activities.

Dr. Reamer would appear to concur with our premise regarding the complexities associated with the concept of values and values clarification. Indeed, Rokeach (1968) did postulate that when we talk about one's values we are talking about "strong enduring beliefs" that are difficult to modify. In fact, Rokeach conceptualized values as a broader and more encompassing concept than either beliefs or attitudes. He viewed values as a dynamic concept with a strong motivational component as well as cognitive, affective, and behavioral components (p. 157). So what meaning does this have for social work? We suggest that values comprise such strength, magnitude, complexity, and "enduring" personal significance that we affect them very little in the social work educational process. We proffer that this is one of the major considerations for social work placing such high emphasis on the admissions process. Clearly, admissions must serve a major gatekeeping function for the profession. Frankly, we as colleagues have very little ability to *change* the basic values or "enduring beliefs" of our students. Thus, we attempt to enroll individuals who are not at odds with the mission and basic values/ethics of the profession. Social work educators spend a significant amount of their time in values clarification and teaching students how to interact with clients without imposing or superimposing their own personal values and beliefs on the client.

As suggested, the issue is not really one of teaching social work values and ethics. Students come to us with an intact and highly influential set of values that has developed over a lifetime. It thus becomes the responsibility of all social work faculty, in all social work classes and curriculum areas, to raise the level of awareness of each student to the potential impact of his or her personal values on the client. Although it might be nice and even appropriate at times to help clients understand the values behind their conflict (but not the causes), this very process begs the issue facing them. Although they need to live congruently with their personal values, they still need to attend to the problem at hand, and that is the successful resolution of the conflict.

It is obvious that social workers are not value free; thus, students need to be aware of and sensitive to the incongruence of certain personal values with those of their clients. Such awareness is just one critical attribute and dynamic that is needed as the practitioner seeks to free the client so that he or she can make a rational and responsible decision. Self-determination, free agency, diversity, client responsibility, and so forth are still central social work values that protect against the practitioner's prerogative or inclination to manipulate or control the decision-making processes of clients. It is not requisite that practitioners assure that their values/ethics match those of the client; rather the professional mandate is one of assuring that clients be taught effective problem-solving and conflict resolution processes without the imposition of our personal values on them. It is an understood principle that clients must feel sufficient ownership of the problem-solving process as to be able to live with the decisions they make.

It is often not easy to separate our own values and those of the profession with those of the client. For example, it appears quite likely that Professor Reamer knows the "right" answer regarding the relocation of low-income residents who are being displaced in favor of an "upscale" residential and shopping center. We would simply make the point that it is not the worker's decision to make—it is his or her responsibility to work with the low-income residents and to help them develop the knowledge and skills to act in *their own behalf and best interest according to their own values.*

Professor Reamer is correct in asserting that we should teach paradigms that assure we stay aware of and process our own personal values so as not to breach client trust. Professor Charles S. Levy (1993) has offered a paradigm that might serve as a model for those who have not yet identified a conceptual piece for awareness raising that could be integrated throughout the curriculum:

1. What principles of ethics are applicable in the practice situation, and to whom (or to what) are they applicable?
2. In relation to the social worker's primary responsibilities, how may priorities be justifiably ordered when ranking both the applicable principles of ethics and those (persons and interests) to whom they are applicable?
3. What are the risks and probable consequences to be taken into account by the social worker when making ethical judgments in a practice situation?
4. What considerations and values are sufficiently compelling to supersede the principles of ethics that might otherwise be suited to the practic situation?
5. What provisions and precautions will be required of the social worker to cope with the consequences of the social worker's ethical judgments and actions?
6. How can the contemplated decisions and actions be evaluated in the context of ethical and professional responsibility? (p. 53)

Although it may be a useful educational tool and experience to understand deontological and teleological philosophical views, it is even more important that we teach clients how to resolve their conflicts. Clients are not much into philosophizing about their pain and their dilemmas. They want relief from the pain, stress, and unbearable living situations. The applied nature of social work requires that we respect values and use those values to empower clients and help them in improving their quality of life, not analyze and evaluate and dissect their values. The emphasis of both teaching and practice needs to be on the practical realities of life, not on the ethereal theories of academia.

124 Debate 8

REFERENCES

Levy, C. S. (1993). *Social work ethics on the line.* Binghamton, NY: The Haworth Press.
Rokeach, M (1968). *A theory of organization and change.* San Francisco: Jossey-Bass Inc.

NO

Kevin M. Marett
W. Eugene Gibbons

For this debate to have any coherence, there needs to be clarification as to what is meant by the terms *values* and *ethics*. For the purposes of this paper, the definition of values employed by Loewenberg and Dolgoff (1992) will be used: "values are meant to serve as guides or criteria for selecting good and desirable behaviors" (p. 19). While accepting this definition, it is important to point out that, "A value determines what a person thinks he ought to do, which may not be the same as what he wants to do, or what it is in his interests to do, or what in fact he actually does" (Central Council for Education and Training in Social Work, 1976, p. 14).

Although ethics are similar to values, they are not identical. Ethics are concerned with the principles and criteria people use in deciding what is right and wrong. As Loewenberg and Dolgoff (1992) further point out, "values are concerned with what is good and desirable, while ethics deal with what is right and correct" (p. 21).

One of the core issues in this debate over whether values and ethics should be taught or emphasized as part of the HBSE curriculum is whether change is warranted. To implement change just for the sake of implementing change is questionable at best and foolhardy at worst. Any time change is being considered, two important questions arise. The first question simply asks if there is something wrong with the status quo that would benefit from a change (i.e., *is there a problem that needs to be fixed?*). The other question to be addressed when planning change asks if there is a better way of doing what is being done (i.e., *can the status quo be improved on?*).

Social work has been addressing the issue of values and ethics since its inception. The current guidelines for teaching values and ethics from the CSWE allow flexibility while concurrently offering structure. The status quo as mandated by the Council on Social Work Education (1994) in its *Curriculum Policy Statements* for both baccalaureate and master's degree programs identifies six value statements that are to be incorporated into every social work curriculum. Additionally, "Social Work Values and Ethics" are one of the nine specific content areas required for the professional foundation. These guidelines further state, in broad terms, where values fit in with the general purpose of social work education: "The purpose of professional social work education is to enable students to integrate the knowledge, values, and skills of the social work profession into competent practice" and "Both levels of social work education must provide a professional foundation curriculum that contains the common body of the profession's knowledge, values, and skills" (1994, pp. 98, 136). The guidelines then go on to specifically address the place of values and ethics in social work education: "All baccalaureate/master's social work programs must: *Infuse throughout the curriculum* the values and ethics that guide professional social workers in their practice" (1994, pp. 98, 136; emphasis added). Additional clarity on the teaching of values and ethics is subsequently provided in these guidelines: "Programs of social work education must provide specific knowledge about social work values and their ethical implications and must provide opportunities for students to demonstrate their application in professional practice. Students must be assisted to develop an awareness of their personal values and to clarify conflicting values and ethical dilemmas" (1994, pp. 100, 139).

The Council on Social Work Education clearly indicates the need for teaching values and recognizes the pervasive nature of values by infusing them across the curriculum. Nowhere, however, does CSWE indicate that values should be concentrated specifically in the Human Behavior and Social Environment (HBSE) content area. The fact that the Council has not recommended specific placement of values should be recognized for the statement it is making and not simply be dismissed or ignored. Having monitored the content and process of teaching values since its inception, the Council has seriously studied the placement of values and have formulated the current guidelines as a result. The current practice of teaching values and ethics in all areas is most practical and most warranted. Values cover all areas and, consequently, should be taught in all areas. It would seem highly incongruent that the profession would choose not to teach values that are "good and desirable" and ethics that are "right and correct" in policy, practice, or research courses.

The other question to be addressed, can the status quo be improved on (i.e., Is there a *better* way to teach values than the way they are now being taught?) is also a matter of conjecture. There is no evidence to suggest there is a better way of teaching values than the way they are being taught, that grounding the teaching of values and ethics in the HBSE content area is more effective (or even as effective) as the way the guidelines currently mandate.

Research on values does not provide convincing support for any specific method of teaching values. As Loewenberg and Dolgoff (1992) so aptly stated:

> Educators still do not know much more about value-and-ethics education than Socrates did more than two thousand years ago when he told Meno that he did not know how values were acquired and whether they could be taught at all. These questions still require answers. (pp. 12–13)

One of the underlying assumptions of CSWE's guidelines for teaching values and ethics as part of social work curriculum is that students who learn professional ethics will practice those professional ethics. Unfortunately, that assumption has not been well supported by research. Timms (1970) echoes this concern when he suggests that research on values needs to focus on what social workers actually do when faced with an ethical dilemma rather than focusing on what social workers say they would do. The complexity of these ethical dilemmas make these concerns even more problematic. Horne (1987) found that the values employed by social workers facing an ethical dilemma were affected not only by the social workers' personal values, but also by the context created by the agency or institution and the context created by the nature of the relationship with the client.

Given the importance placed on the teaching of values and ethics in the social work curriculum, the paucity of research is surprising, and the overall trend of that research is disturbing. Feldman and Newcomb (1970) examined more than 1500 empirical studies on values and ethics across the United States over a wide range of disciplines and concluded that, generally speaking, student values were influenced very little by curriculum. This finding is consistent with the results of a study by Gibbons (1974), who found that social work students' values did not change to any significant degree from the time they started college to the time they graduated. Only two studies examining value changes in social work have indicated any positive change (Moran, 1989; Sharwell, 1974), whereas the greater majority have reported either no change or a negative change (e.g., Horne, 1987; Judah, 1979; Varley, 1968).

Because values can be idiosyncratic and personal, they are not always amenable to accommodation. People choose social work as a profession because it fits their value system: they do not choose their value system because it fits social work. Some students select social work as a major because the corresponding professional values match their own, and other students select physics or business as a major because of the match with those professional values (Gibbons, 1974). In many respects it would seem as though the profession were simply teaching students to more consistently and systematically analyze the values that are already there rather than teaching new values per se.

To restrict the teaching of value theories and professional ethics to the HBSE concentration runs the risk of producing ethicists and philosophers rather than social workers with a pragmatic application of values and ethics. Students too often view HBSE theory as being overly ethereal and academic and not particularly useful. Social work education should not allow the teaching of values and ethics to become an excuse for turning out ethical philosophers or philosophical ethicists. Social work is an applied profession and, consequently, the emphasis of what is taught should be on application.

Reason would dictate a broad-based approach, as is currently being done, or, if for some reason there was a need to concentrate the teaching of values and ethics to a particular professional foundation area, practice would seem to be the most logical area because of the applied nature of the profession and the applied nature of values. Joseph (1991) states that, "ethical content should be infused throughout the curriculum, but opportunity should also be provided for the systematic analysis of ethical dilemmas confronted in practice" (p. 108).

Without demonstrating either a flaw in the current approach to infusing values throughout the entire social work curriculum or producing an improved method for concentrating the teaching of values and ethics in the HBSE content area, neither of these options being supported by research or compelling reason, the discussion at hand quickly loses merit. To mandate additional requirements to an already burgeoning social work curriculum is not appropriate at this time, particularly a requirement that is already being addressed as effectively as current knowledge permits. The old adage, "If it's not broke, don't fix it" may be the best social work education has to offer at this time.

REFERENCES

Central Council for Education and Training in Social Work (CCETSW). (1976). Paper 13: *Values in social work.* London: CCETSW.

Council on Social Work Education. (1994). *Curriculum policy statement.* Alexandria, VA: Author.

Feldman, K., & Newcomb, T. (1970). *The impact of college on students.* San Francisco: Jossey-Bass.

Gibbons, W. E. (1974). *Undergraduate social work: The influence on values of undergraduate social work education.* University of Utah Unpublished dissertation.

Horne, M. (1987). *Values in social work.* Aldershot, Hants, England: Wildwood House.

Joseph, M. V. (1991). Standing for values and ethical action: Teaching social work ethics. In *Teaching secrets: The technology in social work education.* Binghamton, NY: Haworth.

Judah, E. H. (1979). Values: The uncertain component of social work. *Journal of Education for Social Work, 15*(2), 79–86.

Loewenberg, F. M., & Dolgoff, R. (1992). *Ethical decisions for social work practice.* Itasca, IL: Peacock.

Moran, J. R. (1989). Social work education and students' humanistic attitudes. *Journal of Education for Social Work, 25*(1), 13–19.

Sharwell, G. R. (1974). Can values be taught? *Journal of Education for Social Work, 10*(Spring), 99–105.

Timms, N. (1970). *Social work: An outline for intending students.* London: Routledge & Kegan Paul.

Varley, B. K. (1968). Social work values: Changes in value commitment of students from admission to MSW graduation. *Journal of Education for Social Work, 4*, 67–76.

Rejoinder to Drs. Marett and Gibbons

Professors Marett and Gibbons have offered a number of thoughtful observations about the need for social work students to be exposed to and understand value theories and related ethical concepts. We seem to agree on at least one major point: it is essential for this content to be included in *various* courses in the social work curriculum.

This consensus aside, however, we seem to have approached the question from remarkably different angles. Marett and Gibbons apparently interpreted the question to mean that content on value theories should be taught *only* in the HBSE curriculum. I do not believe that was the question with which we were presented. In contrast, I interpreted the question to mean that this content should be *included* in the HBSE curriculum, although certainly this would not preclude presentation of this material elsewhere in the social work curriculum.

I would never argue that content on value theories should be taught *only* in the HBSE curriculum. What would that accomplish? To my knowledge, no one has ever argued that value theories should be taught exclusively in the HBSE curriculum, and that is not what the question we are debating here suggests. In fact, along with Marett and Gibbons, I argued in my original commentary that this content should be taught throughout the curriculum, and I stressed the importance of presenting this content in HBSE courses.

Contrary to Marett and Gibbons' claim ("the Council has not recommended specific placement of values" in the social work curriculum), CSWE states, quite clearly, that social work education programs *must* include values-related content in the HBSE curriculum (although certainly not only in the HBSE curriculum). To reiterate CSWE's standard in the curriculum policy statement: In the HBSE curriculum, "*content about values and ethical issues related to bio-psycho-social theories must be included*" (standards B6.7 and M6.9; emphasis added).

Marett and Gibbons assert at the conclusion of their commentary that the status quo ought to be maintained: "If it's not broke, don't fix it." I beg to differ; in my view, the machine is, indeed, broken. Relatively few social work education programs teach ethical theory in any kind of systematic way. Although the general subject of ethics is broached in many courses, instruction is usually limited to relatively superficial discussion of social work values and ethical problems that arise in the field. Very few courses include deliberate, in-depth, rigorous, and theory-based analysis of ethical issues. As Black et al. (1989) concluded from their extensive national survey of graduate social work education programs, there is a "serious question regarding the effectiveness of the predominant mode of ethics instruction in graduate schools of social work today.... Given the current interest and relevance of ethical issues in social work practice, it is incumbent upon the profession to meet the challenge of the pressing need for effective education in ethics. . . . In light of the importance of ethical tenets and ethical reasoning in social work practice, it is clear that educational parameters relating to ethical instruction, both in terms of content and structure, need further refinement" (pp. 147, 148). To embrace the status quo is to endorse superficiality, fragmentation, and mediocrity.

One other quibble: Marett and Gibbons believe that educators do not know much more about values and ethics education than Socrates did. Do they truly believe there has been no significant benefit from the ambitious efforts of such prominent and visible organizations as the Hastings Center, Georgetown University's Kennedy Institute of Ethics, the University of Chicago Center for Clinical Medical Ethics, the University of Minnesota Center for Biomedical Ethics, Case Western University's Center for Biomedical Ethics, the Park Ridge Center, the University of Nebraska's Center for the Teaching and Study of Applied Ethics, Dartmouth College's Institute for the Study of Applied and Professional Ethics, the Josephson Institute of Ethics, Harvard University's Program for Ethics and the Professions, the Association for Practical and Professional Ethics, and the Poynter Center, among others, that have had an enormous influence on the way values and ethics are taught in higher education and professional schools? Have the diverse workshops, symposia, conferences, institutes, research, and literature on the subject produced nothing of substantial value? Certainly we still have a long way to go, but I have observed firsthand dramatic improvement in the quality of values and ethics instruction in many social work education programs. I am confident that continual refinement of social work educators' approach to the task, consistent with CSWE's guidelines, will be fruitful.

Using Marett and Gibbons's own words, "Having monitored the content and process of teaching values since its inception, the Council [on Social Work Education] has seriously studied the placement of values and has formulated the current guidelines as a result." Hence, it behooves social work educators to comply with the current CSWE curriculum policy statement and include value theories and related ethics concepts in the HBSE curriculum.

REFERENCES

Black, P. N., Hartley, E. K., Whelley, J., & Kirk-Sharp, C. (1989). Ethics curricula: A national survey of graduate schools of social work. *Social Thought, 15* (3/4), 141–148.

Should the HBSE Core Curriculum Include Genetics and Sociobiology?

EDITOR'S NOTE: New content relevant to human behavior is aris-
ing rapidly from many disciplines, such as biology, urban studies, economics, behavioral medicine, ecology, epidemiology, public health—to
name just a few. That genetics and sociobiology have been given
special prominence by some raises this debate question.

Julia B. Rauch, Ph.D., is associate professor and Director, Maternal and
Child Health Social Work Leadership Training Project, School of Social Work,
University of Maryland, and writes extensively on genetics and social work.
Llewellyn Cornelius, Ph.D., is an associate professor at the School of
Social Work, University of Maryland—Baltimore. His current research interests
involve access to medical care for African and Hispanic Americans.

YES

JULIA B. RAUCH

The genetics revolution is promise and peril. Promise, giving hope of preventing,
effectively treating, and even curing genetic disorders. The peril, in an inequitable
society, is harmful eugenic use of genetic technology.
     Depending on the specific gene or genetic disorder, a variety of genetic
services are available: *prenatal, neonatal, or presymptomatic screening* for genes
potentially harmful to individuals or their offspring; *prenatal diagnosis; intrau-*

terine treatment; infant, child, and adult *diagnosis; treatment; genetic counseling.* Gene therapy, once the stuff of science fiction, is on the horizon. Reproductive options include (with genetic preselection already possible) *in vitro fertilization, artificial insemination, egg donation, embryo transplant,* and *surrogate mother-hood.* An array of psychosocial, legal, and ethical issues enfold genetic services (Andrews, 1987; Daniels, 1986; Reilly, 1977; Schild & Black, 1984; Yesley, 1992).

Social work must address both promise and peril. Genetics content must be included in the HBSE core to prepare students for practice in a world in which genetics knowledge and technology is rapidly proliferating (Rauch, 1988). HBSE students also must be able to assess genetic behavioral research because (1) it may bear on practice and (2) behavioral genetic concepts have been abused historically to justify eugenic policies and practices. Thus, the foundation HBSE curriculum must prepare students to support the promise and combat the peril. In this chapter, gene/environment interaction and the genetics of population diversity are reviewed. The rationale for using genetic knowledge in practice is presented. The history of eugenics in the United States and the risk of a new eugenics are sketched.

Human Genetics

Human genetics deals with those qualities that distinguish human beings from other species and that differentiate populations, families, and individuals. Genetic scientists study the causes of hereditary similarities and differences, ways in which they pass from generation to generation, and factors that affect gene expression. Medical genetics is concerned with the causes, prevention, diagnosis, and treatment of genetic disorders. All of these topics are relevant to social workers and belong in the HBSE foundation.

Gene/Environment Interaction

Human development, physical functioning, and behavior result from gene/environment interaction. That simple sentence is more complex than it seems. Environmental and genetic processes are complicated and difficult to untangle. Social workers understand that human environments encompass multiple, interacting systems. When intervening, they look at the physical environment (housing, neighborhood) and an array of social systems: family, friends, school and work settings, role models, indigenous helpers, etc. Macro systems are also considered, for example, racism and social policy.

Genetic complexity rivals environmental. The widely held belief that genes are deterministic, that is, that they have fixed outcomes, is incorrect. Look at the skin on the back of your hand. Each of its cells—and each of your other body cells—has the same constellation of genes (genome). Your hand demonstrates that not all genes are expressed in the same place at the same time; your hand is not undergoing prenatal development; you do not have eyes on your fingertips; your palms do not sweat neurotransmitters. In fact, most of the genes in your skin are inactive.

Gene Expression

Gene expression depends on a variety of factors: a gene's partner; the individual's other genes; the host cell and body system; the time of relevant biological cycles. Differential gene action in space and time is illustrated by prenatal development, sexual development during puberty, daily regulation of metabolism, the onset of aging, and the like.

No one-to-one relation exists between a gene and its outcome. One child may be born with cystic fibrosis (CF) so severe that he dies in infancy; another, even in the same family, may be so mildly ill that she is not diagnosed until adolescence and lives to adulthood.

The external environment can affect genetic processes. A positive example is the use of special diet, respiratory therapy, and antibiotics to extend the life expectancy and quality of life of people with CF. The psychosocial environment also plays a role, as indicated by Patterson, McCubbin, and Warwick's (1990) finding that, in children with CF, family stress correlates with worsened physiological functioning and symptoms.

The environment can also damage (mutate) genes, contributing to cancer, infertility, and other disorders. A new specialty, ecogenetics, has emerged (Vogel & Motulsky, 1986, p. 313). Ecogenetics looks at humans' responses to environmental agents. Cigarette smoke, low-level radiation, asbestos, dioxin, and Agent Orange are but a few of the agents (mutagens) known to hurt genes. Gene/environment interaction is exemplified in *multifactorial inheritance*. Multifactorial traits result from the interaction of multiple genes with environmental factors. Height is one example. The range of possible heights for an individual is genetically determined; diet and health influence the actual height achieved. Intelligence is another important multifactorial inherited trait.

Genetically, the nature/nurture controversy is absurd. First, the question is not whether a trait has genetic or environmental origins, but how nature and nurture interact to achieve their effects. Second, one consequence of the genetics revolution is that technology to change genes themselves is being developed. Potentially, individuals' genetic constitutions will be mutable, not immutable.

Genes and Race

Humans are more alike than different; two-thirds of all human genes are identical in all people. Diversity derives from the one-third of genes that have different forms (polymorphism). In general, all human populations have the same types of polymorphic genes, differing only in the percentages. For example, the gene for B-type blood is found in approximately 30 percent of the Eastern Asian population in India but in only approximately 5 percent of Western Europeans (Thompson, McInnis, & Willard, 1991, p. 161).

Genetically, race is not a useful concept. So-called races are identified by visible, external features, such as skin color. However, a population might be like another on one characteristic but different on another. For example, people from Africa and Asia both have black hair, but the texture differs. Similarly, the sickle cell gene is found in caucasian, Asian, and African populations native to malarial zones.

The Promise: Changing Social Work Practice Demands

Social workers are increasingly serving people with genetic disorders and concerns, in part because their numbers are expanding. Improved diagnosis and treatment is extending life expectancy of people with conditions that were once fatal in childhood. Because of deinstitutionalization, people with mental illness, mental retardation, and disabilities—conditions often of known or suspected genetic origin—are residing in communities. Medical research is discovering that conditions once believed to be entirely environmental in origin have genetic origins.

Social workers need to adapt their practice to help people cope with genetic concerns and disorders, for example, listening with the "genetic ear" to elicit unstated concerns (Bishop, 1993). Genetic family history-taking skills are needed. For example, a common presenting problem, depression, appears to be inherited in some families (McGuffin & Murray, 1991). Practitioners must know how to take family histories of affective disorders (Rauch, Sarno & Simpson, 1991) and make appropriate referrals for medication evaluation and psychiatric genetic counseling.

Ability to obtain genetic family histories (GFHs) is vital in child welfare. Child welfare workers are often the only professionals in contact with family members who can provide the information. GFHs are useful, even necessary, for optimal health care. To the extent obtainable, they should be available for children in out-of-home care, to prospective adoptive parents, and to adult adoptees (Rauch, 1990).

Any client in any setting, however, may have genetic concerns. GFHs, which are similar to genograms, should be integral to biopsychosocial assessment (Bernhardt & Rauch, 1993).

Awareness of the psychosocial aspects of genetic disorders, services, and decisions is important (Rauch & Black, 1995). Genetic disorders have much in common with other chronic health problems (Mailick, 1979). They are also distinctive (Schild, 1977; Schild & Black, 1984). They bear on sexuality and reproduction. Nuclear and extended family members are involved, even if at war with each other. They may be approached for health information. They may learn that they have a genetic disorder, or will have one, or might give birth to affected children. The process of obtaining a genetic diagnosis may uncover family secrets, such as incest or adultery. People may assume a negative genetic identity, carrier of "bad seed." Pregnancy termination for genetic reasons appears to be more difficult for women than voluntary termination and also appears to stress the couple and other children in the family (Black, 1993; Furlong & Black, 1984; Silvestre & Fresco, 1980).

Understanding of inheritance and gene expression is particularly important in mental health services. Social workers need to be able to evaluate and appropriately apply behavioral genetic research. Some psychiatric genetic researchers believe that schizophrenia, the affective disorders, and other major psychiatric disorders originate in multifactorial inheritance. Even if a single gene for a specific disorder is found, however, the environment will affect its expression, as discussed.

For the reasons identified, social workers should understand and use basic genetic concepts, know how to take genetic family histories, be aware of genetic services, be oriented to psychosocial issues of genetic disorders and services, and be able to evaluate genetic behavioral research. Of concern is that the naive social worker may buy into findings of methodologically weak behavioral reports, especially when they are widely publicized and accepted.

The Peril: A New Eugenics

Who will benefit from the promise? Genetic services are not universally available. They are most accessible to people who can pay out-of-pocket or whose health insurance covers them. Whether Medicaid will pay for genetic services, and which ones, varies from state to state. Other barriers also exist (Kavanagh & Kennedy, 1992). Genetic services are generally not available to people with no health insurance. Thus, class affects access to desired genetic services. People of middle and high socioeconomic status are more likely to benefit from the genetic revolution than people who are poor. Worse, a new eugenics may target poor people, native-born people of color, and immigrants from majority world countries.

Conclusion

We live in a genetic brave new world, one of promise and peril. Social workers must respond to both. The response to the promise is to apply genetics knowledge into practice and work to extend the benefits to the underserved. Social work's commitment to combat racism and to promote social justice demands a thoughtful and informed response to the peril.

References

Andrews, L. B. (1987). *Medical genetics: A legal frontier.* Chicago: American Bar Foundation.

Bernhardt, B., & Rauch, J. B. (1993). Genetic family histories: An aid to social work assessment. *Families in Society, 74,* 195–205.

Bishop, K. K. (1993). Psychosocial aspects of genetic disorders: Implications for practice. *Families in Society, 74,* 207–212.

Black, R. B. (1993). Psychosocial issues in reproductive genetic testing and pregnancy loss. *Fetal Diagnosis and Therapy, 8,* supplement 1.

Daniels, K. R. (1986). New birth technologies: Researching the psychosocial factors. *Social Work in Health Care, 11,* 49–60.

Furlong, R. M., & Black, R. B. (1984). Pregnancy termination for genetic indications: The impact on families. *Social Work in Health Care, 10,* 17–34.

Kavanagh, K., & Kennedy, B. (1992). *Promoting cultural diversity: Strategies for health care professionals.* Newbury Park, CA: Sage.

Mailick, M. (1979). The impact of severe illness on the individual and the family: An overview. *Social Work in Health Care, 5,* 117–128.

McGuffin, P., & Murray, R. (1991). *The new genetics of mental illness.* Boston: Oxford, Butterworth-Heinemann.

Patterson, J., McCubbin, H., & Warwick, W. (1990). The impact of family functioning on the health changes in children with cystic fibrosis. *Social Science and Medicine, 32*(2), 159–164.

Rauch, J. B. (1988). Social work and the genetics revolution: Genetic services. *Social Work, 33,* 389–397.

Rauch, J. B. (Ed.). (1990). *Genetics and adoption: Every child potentially a special needs child.* Proceedings of a Workshop, May 3–5, Washington, DC, Baltimore, MD: University of Maryland School of Social Work.

Rauch, J. B. & Black, R. B. (1995). *Encyclopedia of social work.* (19th ed.). Vol. 2. Silver Spring, MD: NASW.

Rauch, J. B., Sarno, C., & Simpson, S. (1991). Assessment of affective disorders. *Families in Society, 72*(18), 602–609.

Reilly, P. (1977). *Genetics, law and social policy.* Cambridge, MA: Harvard University Press.

Schild, S. (1977). Social work with genetic problems. *Health and Social Work, 2,* 58–77.

Schild, S., & Black, R. B. (1984). *Social work and genetics: A guide for practice.* New York: Haworth.

Silvestre, D., & Fresco, N. (1980). Reactions to prenatal diagnosis: An analysis of 87 interviews. *American Journal of Orthospychiatry, 50,* 610–617.

Thompson, M., McInnis, R., & Willard, H. (1991). *Genetics in medicine* (5th ed.). Philadelphia: W. B. Saunders.

Vogel, F., & Motulsky, A. (1986). *Human genetics* (2nd ed.). New York: Springer-Verlag.

Yesley, M. (1992). *Bibliography: Ethical, legal and social implications of the Human Genome Project.* Washington, DC: Department of Energy, Office of Energy Research.

Rejoinder to Dr. Rauch
LLEWELLYN CORNELIUS

I was pleased to see after reading Dr. Rauch's paper that we have more common-alties than differences. Like Dr. Rauch, I express some concerns about the potential problems in genetic research. In fact, I argue in my paper that we should not teach genetics courses precisely because there is a groundswell of scholars that promote the mythology that "genes are deterministic" and that a "one-to-one relation exists between a gene and its outcome."

The fact that Dr. Rauch has to correct these mythologies in her own paper supports my contention that we can not succeed in academic studies in this area by merely introducing the issues in the HBSE curriculum. If Dr. Rauch, as a scholar, has to counter the onslaught of popular opinion to inform her readers, what challenges would students face who are new to the area? How can we as social workers "evaluate and appropriately apply behavioral genetic research" if we have to wrestle with basic issues, such as correcting errors perpetrated by genetic scientists, as I contend in my paper? In the end, Dr. Rauch's essay is a laudable goal of what social work can do *if* only one can overcome the barriers posed by misinformation in this field. However, I still contend that we cannot achieve this complex goal within the context of the HBSE foundation.

NO
LLEWELLYN CORNELIUS

The thesis of this paper is that genetic theory and sociobiology should not be taught as part of the HBSE core. It will be argued that it is inappropriate to teach these concepts in the HBSE core because scholars, researchers, and practitioners fundamentally disagree about the ability to apply genetics theory to social situations. Three types of problems are discussed to support this thesis: (1) the lack of scientific integrity in notable examples of genetic research; (2) the misreporting of the findings by the media; and (3) the inability of the studies to draw the link between heredity and human behavior (the fallacy of social causation).

Introduction

At the foundation of human behavior genetics research and theorizing is the notion that there is a statistical relationship among IQ, personality traits, and heredity (Scarr & Kidd, 1983). Its strongest proponents believe that human behavior is in fact determined largely by heredity—not the environment. One of these propo-nents claims that "parental genes determine their [own] phenotypes, the child's genes determine his or her phenotype, and the child's environment is merely a reflection of the characteristics of both parents and child" (Scarr, 1992; p. 1).

Human behavioral geneticists typically rely on the findings of studies of twins to support their contention that it is heredity that determines human behavior. The most common method of establishing the relationship between heredity and the influence of the environment is through the study of twins. Twins are used because of their high degree of genetic similarity. It is believed that if one can control the environment in which twins grow up, then the remaining difference in human behavior would have to be a result of heredity. As such, researchers attempt to study twins as members of intact families or adopted families to determine whether there are differences in types of human behavior within pairs of twins. Recent studies have focused on comparing phenotypes (the observed manifestation of a given trait) such as intelligence test performance, sexual preference, schizophrenia, alcoholism, and Alzheimer's disease among pairs of twins. Critiques of the state of the art of genetics research have found these studies to be fraught with methodological problems, problems regarding the misinterpretation of the results, and problems in proving causality.

Lack of Scientific Integrity

One of the problems that makes it inappropriate to introduce this topic into the HBSE core is the lack of scientific integrity of studies in genetic theory. This problem is reflected in the types of methodological inconsistencies found in studies of genetics. For example, the Minnesota study of fifty pairs of twins led by Thomas Bouchard received worldwide attention. He claimed that factors such as religiosity, political orientation (i.e., conservative or liberal), job satisfaction, leisure time interests, and proneness to divorce were all tied to genetic characteristics (cited in Horgan, 1993). Yet, other researchers found that the study was filled with methodological problems such as selection bias (which occurred because the researchers used the media to recruit new twins). Next, Sir Cyril Burt, who was considered the foremost in his field through the 1970s, claimed that intelligence was inherited (cited in Horgan, 1993). Yet Kamin and Gillie could not find the twins that Burt used for his study and have reason to believe that his collaborators may have been fictitious (Gillie, 1976). Horgan suggests there were other problems with Burt's study, namely that "identical twins supposedly raised apart are often raised by members of their family or by unrelated families in the same neighborhood; some twins had extensive contact with each other while growing up" (Horgan, 1993; p. 125). When Kamin reported his findings that called into question the work of Cyril Burt, his

> competence was denigrated, his motives were questioned, and the errors he found were dismissed as the result of merely poor memory of an aging giant.

The extent of the scandal was finally acknowledged in professional circles three years later only after attention from the popular press, including The Sunday Times of London, Time, Newsweek, and the New York Times, made Kamins' thesis a fact too difficult any longer to ignore. (Hirsch, 1991; p. 333)

By pitting Kamin against Burt, the scientific community demonstrated that they were willing to set aside commonly held principles of scientific investigation to allow the promotion of this genetic theory.

Misreporting by the Media

A second problem in this area of inquiry that makes it inappropriate to introduce genetics theory and sociobiology to the HBSE core is the tendency of the media to distort genetics research findings. The problem here is the tendency of the media to focus on only a small portion of the issue, thus fostering the widespread discussion of information that is only partially true. This creates a social trap because students in HBSE classes become unwittingly involved in discussing the applications of genetic theory to human behavior, without having all of the correct information at their disposal. As a result, students run the risk of creating social policy or practice on the basis of fiction rather than fact.

A case in point is a recent study regarding the link between genetics and homosexuality. Hamer, Hu, Magnuson, Hu, and Pattatucci (1993) recently reported that there was a relationship between an identified X chromosome and the presence of homosexuality in thirty-three of forty pairs of brothers. Yet Maddox (1993) reports that media coverage in Great Britain after the study was less than delicate and solemn. Immediately after the publication of the study, three articles appeared in *The Sunday Telegraph* with the headlines "Born To Be Gay," "A Lot of Mothers Are Going to Feel Guilty," and "The Gene Genie Comes Out Fighting" (Maddox, 1993; p. 281). A more serious examination in the scholarly journals suggested that the Hamer et al. research should be interpreted cautiously because of the inconsistencies found in the results (Risch, Squires-Wheeler, & Keats, 1993).

The Fallacy of Social Causation

A third problem that makes it inappropriate to introduce genetic theory into the HBSE core curriculum is the generous overstatement of the relationship between heredity and human behavior. The belief that there is a causal relationship between genes and human behavior creates a situation in which students run the risk of assuming that findings in genetics and sociobiology have more profound implications than what is actually true. One of the important goals of genetic research is to prove that heredity causes human behavior. This requires that one sees a high proportion of twins exhibiting a particular behavior. However, longitudinal studies of adopted twins report that only 30 percent of the variation in traits such as IQ and neurosis can be accounted for by heredity. The same study found that the rate went up to 50 percent for the children in identical twin studies (Plomin, 1990). Other research by Wahlsten has suggested that only 35 to 70 percent of the variance is intelligence is inherited (Wahlsten, 1990). This throws out the window the issue of causality, because anywhere from 50 to 65 percent of human behavior is left unexplained.

However, what becomes problematic is not the findings themselves but the blind leap made from these studies to the making of unsupported inferences regarding the nature of human behavior, and the use of such findings by helping professionals as the basis of interventions with their clients. This is done by confusing correlation with causation. As noted by scholars in the field (Jackson, 1993), the modal type of study in genetics is based on the analysis of variance (ANOVA). ANOVA attempts to identify the correlations between a series of factors. However, *correlation is not causation.* As noted by Nachmias and Nachmias (1992), three things are needed to prove causation in science: One has to prove covariation—that two or more factors vary together; second, one has to prove nonspuriousness—that the relationship established between two factors cannot be explained by a third factor; and third, one has to prove there is a time order—that the factor you have identified as the "cause" occurs in time before the factor you call the "effect" (Nachmias & Nachmias, 1992). The problem here is that the environment is so complex that it is difficult, if not impossible, to measure all of the factors one believes account for the apparent relationship between heredity and the environment. At the same time it is possible that any one of a multitude of factors can serve as a viable and plausible explanation for the observed statistical relationships.

The saddest part of this dilemma is that the misapplication of genetic theory to human behavior is very old indeed. In 1866, the public first heard about this issue under the title of Social Darwinism. Social Darwinism represented the application of the biological principles of natural selection imbedded in Charles Darwin's *Origin of the Species* to human behavior. Social Darwinism, as advocated by Herbert Spencer, suggested that some humans were endowed with certain traits that accounted for their success in life, such as skill, intelligence, self-control, and the power to adapt through technological innovation—what he called "survival of the fittest." Herbert Spencer went so far as to oppose state aid to the poor, stating that they were unfit and should be eliminated (Hofstadter, 1944). Herbert Spencer's call for natural selection had set the stage for serious scholarly debate regarding the meaning of social Darwinism for ethics, politics, and social affairs for the rest of the nineteenth century (Hofstadter, 1944).

The principles of heredity embedded in Social Darwinism were not merely used for idle discussion among intellectuals; they became a "rational" justification for racist and unethical experiments with humans. One case in point is the

Tuskegee experiment in untreated latent syphilis. The Tuskegee experiment was a longitudinal experiment (1932–1972) that was designed to observe the long-term effects of untreated syphilis. The subjects were 600 African American men with latent untreated syphilis, living in Macon County, Alabama. To determine the outcome of "untreated" syphilis, the experimenters withheld medical treatment for syphilis from the African Americans. The "scientists" believed they were justified using this population because

> the Negro in America was doomed. Particularly prone to disease, vice and crime, black Americans could not be helped by education or philanthropy. Social Darwinists analyzed census data to predict the virtual extinction of the Negro, for they believed the Negro race in America was in the throes of a degenerative evolutionary process. (Brandt, 1978; p. 21)

In summarizing the prevailing medical opinion at the time, Brandt noted that, according to physicians, the Negro "possessed an excessive sexual desire, which threatened the very foundations of white society... According to these physicians, lust and immorality, unstable families and reversion to barbaric tendencies made blacks especially prone to venereal diseases" (Brandt, 1978; p. 22). Calling African Americans less than human gave them an excuse to start an unethical experiment. The experiment continued for forty years in spite of the clinical proof that syphilis can be cured.

Sad to say that this was not the only experiment conducted on humans, using "natural selection" as a justification. It is common knowledge that the Nazis experimented on the Jews in the death camps during World War II, using the notion of the "superior" Aryan race as a justification for medical experimentation. Aside from medical experimentation by the Nazis, there is also some evidence that the Japanese engaged in involuntary medical experimentation during World War II. Thus, as seen through the lenses of time, the principles of "heredity" and natural selection have been used as a justification to invoke inhumane treatment to the disadvantaged, the poor, the disabled, and ethnic minorities.

The reader must be warned not to fall into the social trap that is often created by looking into the past. We often fall into a trap by claiming that these things only happened in the past, and we are "more enlightened." Nevertheless, it is often said, "those who do not learn from history are doomed to repeat its mistakes." For example, the line of inquiry pursued by Social Darwinism in the nineteenth century has been revised and popularized more recently in the book *The Bell Curve* by Richard Herrnstein and Charles Murray (1994).

Herrnstein and Murray begin their book by stating that "measures of intelligence have reliable statistical relationships with important social phenomena, but they are a limited tool for deciding what to make of any given individual" (Herrnstein & Murray, 1994; p. 21). However, Herrnstein and Murray contradict themselves by stating that one of the central premises used as the basis for the book is that 40 to 80 percent of intelligence is inherited (Herrnstein & Murray, 1994; p. 21–23, 106). By accepting the notion that 40 to 80 percent of intelligence is inherited, they implicitly accept that there is a causal relationship between the intelligence of parents and their offspring.

After their discussion of the role of heredity in human behavior, Herrnstein and Murray provide extensive analyses of correlational data that show a negative statistical relation between intelligence tests scores and measures of poverty (Herrnstein & Murray, 1994; p. 20), dropping out of school (p. 154), the chances of pregnancy for unwed mothers (p. 179), the chances of long-term welfare dependency (pp. 193–194), crime rates (p. 247), and other types of social behavior. They conclude their treatise by suggesting that the reason these problems occur is that "the United States is run by rules that are congenial to people with high IQs and that makes life more difficult for everyone else" (Herrnstein & Murray, 1994; p. 541). The solution they offer is to make the rules of society simple for all to understand (Herrnstein & Murray, 1994; p. 541–546). In short, they assume that the problems in society are attributable to a lack of cognition on the part of individuals and not to society in and of itself.

References

Brandt, A. M. (1978). Racism and research: The case of the Tuskegee syphilis study. *The Hastings Center Report, 8*(6), 21–29.

Gillie, O. (1976, October 24). Crucial data was faked by eminent psychologist. London: *The Sunday Times,* pp. 1–2.

Hamer, D. H, Hu, S., Magnuson, V. L., Hu, N., Pattatucci, A. M. (1993). A linkage between DNA markers on the X chromosome and male sexual orientation. *Science, 261*(5119), 321–327.

Herrnstein, R. J., and Murray, C. (1994). *The bell curve: Intelligence and class structure in American life.* New York: The Free Press.

Hirsch, J. (1991). Race, genetics and scientific integrity. *Journal of Health Care for the Poor and Underserved, 2*(3), 331–334.

Hofstadter, R. (1944). *Social Darwinism in American thought.* Boston: Beacon Press.

Horgan, J. (1993). Eugenics revisited. *Scientific American, 268*(6), 122–131.

Jackson, J. F. (1993). Human behavioral genetics, Scarr's theory and her view on interventions: A critical review and commentary on their implications for African American children. *Child Development, 64*(5), 1318–1332.

Maddox, J. (1993). Wilful public misunderstanding of genetics. *Nature, 364*(6435), 281.

Nachmias, C. F., & Nachmias, D. (1992). *Research methods in the social sciences* (4th ed.). New York: St. Martin's Press.

Plomin, R. (1990). The role of inheritance in behavior. *Science, 248*(4952), 183–188.

Risch, N., Squires-Wheeler, E., & Keats, B. J. (1993). Male sexual orientation and genetic evidence. *Science, 262,* 2063–2065.

Scarr, S. (1992). Developmental theories for the 1990s: Development and individual differences. *Child Development, 63*(1), 1–19.

Scarr, S, & Kidd, K. K. (1983). Developmental behavior genetics. In M. M. Haith, J. J. Campos (Eds.), *Handbook of Child Psychology: Vol. 2. Infancy and Developmental Psychobiology* (pp. 343–433). New York: Wiley.

Wahlsten, D. (1990). Insensitivity of the analysis of variance to heredity-environment interactions. *Behavioral Brain Science, 13,* 109–161.

Rejoinder to Dr. Cornelius Julia B. Rauch

My thesis is that (1) the genetics revolution is both promise and peril and (2) social workers need to address both. For that reason, I advocate inclusion of human genetics content in the core HBSE curriculum. Social work educators must prepare students to become informed users of genetic concepts and to respond thoughtfully to the peril of a new eugenics.

I am flattered that Dr. Cornelius apparently finds my practice-based argument irrefutable, as he does not address that issue at all. Instead, he focuses on genetic behavioral research. He makes three central points: (1) lack of scientific integrity in notable examples of genetic research; (2) the misreporting of findings by the media; and (3) the inability of the studies to draw the link between heredity and human behavior. He documents his thesis with important examples of faulty "genetic" research and unwarranted inferential leaps.

Dr. Cornelius' argument does not rebut, but supports, my thesis. Historically, genetic science and the eugenics movement were closely allied; genetic claims were made then on the basis of unsound research. Genetic claims continue to be made on the basis of unsound research, such as a recent twin study of homosexuality that was widely publicized and believed by many. Unwarranted inferences about links between genes and behaviors are made. Thus, Dr. Cornelius pinpoints exactly why I believe social workers need to understand genetic complexity—so that they will not be taken in by bogus claims.

Dr. Cornelius's discussion illustrates a common error made by genetics critics: misunderstanding of *inherited.* How that word is interpreted is critical. What does it mean? I discussed gene expression, environmental impacts on genes, and multifactorial inheritance. I emphasized that no one-to-one relationship between a gene and its manifestation exists. Even genes that normally have "fixed" outcomes can be overridden by other genes, as in the case of genes for skin, eye and hair color and genes associated with albinoism or phenylketonuria (PKU). Contemporary genetic science does not support genetic determinism. Dr. Cornelius, misunderstanding the nature of inheritance, almost seems to fall into the trap of genetic determinism himself!

Dr. Cornelius also confuses the work of genetic scientists with the work of people who make genetic inferences on the basis of nongenetic research. Neither of the authors of *The Bell Curve,* for example, are geneticists; their claims betray their ignorance. Dr. Cornelius quotes Starr, a psychologist, that the "foundation of genetics research and theory is the notion that there is a statistical relationship between IQ, personality traits and heredity." This is absurd. Laboratory genetic scientists study genes and genetic processes directly; population geneticists use epidemiological methods to look at population diversity. Their interests are far broader than intelligence, a *multifactorial* trait.

Dr. Cornelius largely critiqued not contemporary genetic research, but inferences derived by nongeneticists from nongenetic data. He rightfully points out the abuse of genetic concepts. But this, too, reinforces my thesis, that social workers need to be equipped to distinguish between genuine genetic research and bogus genetic findings.

Should HBSE Concentrate on a Few Topics as Metaphor for the Whole, Rather Than Give a "Broad Brush" Perspective to Many Diverse Issues?

EDITOR'S NOTE: America is an extraordinarily diverse society. Individuals develop over time in many different possible types of family structures and forms, subcultural groupings, neighborhoods and communities, lifestyles and sexual orientations, and mental and physical abilities. This raises the perplexing question, is it possible to teach all of these forms of cultural pluralism in adequate depth to provide a working base of knowledge for social workers in the twenty-first century?

Neil Abell, Ph.D., L.C.S.W., is an associate professor at the School of Social Work, Florida State University. His most recent activities include validating the Willingness To Care scale examining personal capacities and attitudes toward caring for a person with AIDS, and course development of "Living with HIV/AIDS: Prevention, intervention, and care," for graduate and undergraduate students.

Karen Sowers-Hoag, Ph.D., is associate professor and Director of the School of Social Work, Florida International University. She is a member of the Board of Directors of the Council on Social Work Education and publishes in the areas of child welfare practice, culturally competent social work practice, and social work education.

YES

NEIL ABELL

Yes, HBSE should be developed around a clearly defined topic area, and human immunodeficiency virus/acquired immune deficiency syndrome (HIV/AIDS) provides an ideal universal metaphor. Although no one would argue that diversity issues should be minimized in social work education, the "broad brush" approach offered in many seminars accomplishes little more than a simplistic overview of topics. Developmental and systemic theories are cataloged in cradle-to-grave scenarios as instructors struggle to cover the high points of too many theorists addressing too many problems in too little time. Although such efforts are well intended, they often amount to uninspired "walk-throughs" of a host of subjects. Students are minimally informed about many things and left with no practical framework within which to apply their fragmented knowledge. It is little wonder that, for many, these courses are as unpopular to teach as they are frustrating to take.

CSWE's 1992 Curriculum Policy Statement specifies that social work curriculum should "prepare . . . professionals (for) services to the poor and oppressed" (p. 1). In particular, HBSE content should help students develop an appreciation for human diversity and for the influence of their personal values on assessment and intervention decisions. Additionally, students should understand the "patterns, dynamics, and consequences of discrimination, economic deprivation, and oppression" (p. 8) on populations at risk.

In responding to these charges, HBSE education must accomplish several broad goals, each of which serves the common aim of contextualizing students' understanding of assessment and intervention. First, students should be meaningfully exposed to a useful cross-section of mainstream theories. Second, they should be challenged to recognize that such theories are, at best, rough templates for understanding the uniqueness of individual experience. Third, they should be awakened to the ways in which their own reactions and biases may limit their capacities to see clients "as they are," and to work with them in respectful and effective ways. In the end, students should achieve a balanced appreciation for the guidance good theory can provide when tempered with an individualized understanding of needs and capacities.

Ideally, HBSE course work should introduce students to a meaningful core of mainstream theories in a manner encouraging "real-world" application to social work problems. This means that content should be carefully selected so that students are challenged to learn the diagnostic and interventive languages formulated by key thinkers across a variety of disciplines. The biopsychosocial and ecosystemic frameworks referred to so often in social work literature require exposure to a host of conceptual and professional orientations spanning biology, medicine, psychology, psychiatry, sociology, anthropology, political science, and organizational behavior (to name a few!). In addition, students are expected to develop critical thinking skills to assess these theories. This step requires an integrated understanding of the empirical support for each theory and the policy implications of making decisions based on them. Responding successfully to these ambitious objectives is, by itself, a Herculean task. Consideration of diversity comes next.

Social workers have historically argued that individual characteristics and circumstances must be carefully considered in assessment and intervention. This indispensable position has, nevertheless, created an enormous educational dilemma in which faculty are expected to cover a numbing array of specialized topics and interests. We are challenged, for starters, to address differences based on gender, age, physical or mental ability, race, ethnicity, religion, social class, and sexual orientation.

Although the inspiration for inclusiveness is unarguable, the difficulty comes when students, asked to digest too much in too little time, resort to shallow analyses dominated by reactivity to whatever is least familiar in their own experience. Theories whose (dated) assumptions fail to appreciate recently identified needs and wishes of particular groups are "thrown to the wolves" as useless artifacts, and respect for diversity becomes a superficial scanning for offensive terminology or concepts. The result is, at worst, a politically correct mishmash that students find irritatingly difficult to digest.

The trick for educators is to actively engage students with essential assessment and intervention theories, and to encourage them in the struggle of sorting out their own resulting frustrations. In response to our initial question, I suggest that this is best accomplished by giving depth to a single topic that encompasses nearly all diversity issues, triggers strong reactivity in virtually everyone, and poses one of the most frightening challenges to U.S. health and human service delivery in the late twentieth century.

HIV/AIDS

The human immunodeficiency virus and the condition it eventually fosters, AIDS, have generated a pandemic of epic proportions. Since first reported among gay men in the United States in 1981, the disease has mushroomed to an estimated 400,000 cases increasing by some 40,000 in 1994 alone. Whereas the illness in the United States was originally concentrated among gays, its contemporary range is indiscriminant: reported cases among women and children represent the most dramatic proportional increases in recent years.

Ironically, the broad spread and tragic consequences of HIV-related illness make it nearly perfect as an organizing frame for diversity curriculum in social work. Applications to CSWE's curricular goals are sketched below, with limited samplings from the constantly expanding literature.

Sexual Orientation

Early misconceptions regarding the origins and transmission of HIV led to strong, primary associations with sexual orientation. For many, reactions to the illness and its consequences led to an identification of male homosexuality with contagious, sinfully transmitted terminal disease. (Awareness of lesbian incidence rates and issues is only recently emerging.) Homophobic responses arguably delayed early dissemination of information regarding the growing epidemic and subsequently contributed to a cultural mindset focused on blaming the victims rather than vigorously pursuing education, prevention, and cure.

Many complications in prevention, treatment, and caregiving stem from the dual stigmas of "coming out" simultaneously as gay and HIV positive. Social responses to these characteristics can be overwhelming, even for those who are "tainted" only by association through their compassionate roles as caregivers. For social work students, confronting HIV/AIDS presents a direct challenge to one's fears regarding sexual orientation and related sexual behaviors. Mortality strikes a chord in everyone, and the common association of sexual orientation with death (however mistaken) provides a powerful opportunity for exploring underlying biases and tendencies toward reactive rather than carefully considered treatment and policy agendas.

Age

HIV/AIDS is increasingly prevalent among children and the elderly. Although AIDS-related illness is fast becoming a classic example of the unbiased spread of a virus across the life cycle, cultural assumptions regarding persons living with AIDS (PLWAs) vary widely with age differences. Children with the virus are generally held blameless, as are the aged, based primarily on assumptions regarding those groups' "innocent" acquisition of the virus (i.e., through gestation or transfusion). In between, attributions of responsibility vary from the casually ignorant or oblivious (adolescents) to the wantonly reckless or deserving (i.e., homosexual adults, sex workers and their customers, or injection drug users [IDUs]).

Interventions for children or the elderly tend to develop in less contentious atmospheres, largely because of more accepting social attributions. Children, however, are not immune to the irrational fears that can still lead to public policies fostering isolation or virtual quarantine, as in the case of the Ray family in Arcadia, Florida (Petrow, 1990). The elderly may (wrongly) be assumed to be immune to risks associated with sexuality. Mortality, however, remains the great leveler. Across the life cycle, social workers must confront the implications of untimely death almost universally associated with AIDS.

Gender

Women's issues in HIV illustrate a tendency to be underrepresented and underserved as patients. The CDC's decision in 1993 to include invasive cervical cancer as partial criteria for rendering AIDS diagnoses (USDHSS, 1994) led to a substantial increase in reporting women's incidence rates and, subsequently, to an increase in their eligibility for treatment trials and services. Prevention efforts focus on empowering women to more successfully negotiate their sexual relations, particularly through mastery of assertiveness skills in persuading partners to use condoms (Harrison et al., 1991).

Caregiving issues also present a potent educational opportunity, in that gender stereotypes are both confirmed and challenged in HIV-related illness (McDonell, Abell, & Miller, 1991). Although women still bear disproportionate responsibility for caregiving tasks, men are substantially involved as well. Perhaps in no other context are diverse definitions of "family" (i.e., of origin, procreation, blood, law, or choice) more extensively represented than in HIV/AIDS caregiving.

Linking the topics of gender and age, students may consider the implications of a woman with AIDS enduring not only the death of a heterosexual partner (for whom she may have been the primary caregiver), but also anticipating her own death while trying to survive the illness of her child, who acquired the virus through gestation.

Race, Ethnicity, and Social Class

Although each deserves separate consideration, race, ethnicity, and social class play crucial roles in understanding the personal and social implications of HIV/AIDS. Osmond et al. argue that these factors, further combined with gender, represent a "multiple jeopardy" in which "(affected members') access to resources in terms of public attention, popular concern, and political–economic power is critical in determining how well they fare in the AIDS epidemic"(1993, p.117).

Prevention programs are increasingly designed with respect for and attention to race, ethnicity, and class (House & Walker, 1993), and federally funded research virtually insists on inclusion matching reported population surveillance rates. Still, the persistent tendency to disempower poor persons of color, particularly those additionally stigmatized by a fear-inspiring illness, helps maintain a climate where those without influence are pushed aside and, if possible, out of view.

Access to health care, employment, education, and housing, already substantial civil rights concerns, are highlighted in the context of AIDS. Educators will find unparalleled opportunities for emphasizing social worker's roles as advocates, facilitators, and case managers, and for encouraging reflection on how one's own biases influence decisions on behalf of clients.

Physical or Mental Ability

These aspects of diversity seem, at first, self-evident in the face of devastating illness. An immense literature addresses the health-related complications of HIV/AIDS (Gil, Arranz, Lianes, & Briebart, 1995). From AIDS-related dementia to systems-ravaging opportunistic infections, the illnesses associated with HIV are staggering in their variety and effects.

Again, however, numerous stereotypes abound. Emergent publications (e.g., *POZ*) emphasize that, increasingly, HIV positive persons are surviving (and thriving) longer. As with other "differently abled" populations, many PLWAs wish to maintain their independence and autonomy as long as possible and resent unwanted intrusions into their privacy. However, the nature of their illness generates an exceptional double bind. PLWAs are pressured to disclose the nature of their illness, knowing that, if they do, the consequences may well be isolation, rejection, and the condemnation of their families, friends, or co-workers. Faculty will find many opportunities for raising opposing points of view on complex ethical dilemmas.

Religion

Never to be underestimated, religious views contribute hugely to understanding and managing HIV/AIDS in American culture. Moral debates over origins and transmission of the virus have shaped prevention and treatment efforts on the community, group, and individual levels. Whether high schools distribute condoms, injection drug users gain access to clean needles, or gay men of color find refuge in their home communities depends largely on the persuasive power of religious institutions. Other than abortion, it is hard to imagine a substantive focus for diversity studies with greater polarizing potential than HIV/AIDS.

Conclusion

I have argued here that structuring HBSE diversity studies around the unifying metaphor of HIV/AIDS has several strong advantages. First, it provides a format for illustrating many complex notions in one organizing frame. Given the scope of theoretical and empirical content to be addressed in HBSE foundation coursework, such a frame seems not only desirable but necessary if students are to integrate (not just memorize) a host of otherwise fragmented ideas. Second, use of HIV/AIDS pushes students' reactivity across topic areas as perhaps no other subject can. We have known since Freud that sexuality and death are hard to beat as compelling topics and, in this case, calling on them is not just an academic exercise. Finally, the prevalence rates of HIV/AIDS, particularly among populations traditionally served by social workers (i.e., diverse and disadvantaged) makes it seemingly mandatory to imbed (not just "infuse") this topic deeply into our curriculum. To argue otherwise risks wasting a unique and valuable opportunity.

REFERENCES

Council on Social Work Education. (1992). *Curriculum policy statement for baccalaureate degree programs in social work education.* Washington, DC: Author.

Gil, F., Arranz, P., Lianes, P., & Briebart, W. (1995). Physical symptoms and psychological distress among patients with HIV infection. *AIDS Patient Care,* November, 28–31.

Harrison, D. F., Wambach, K. G., Byers, J. B., Imershein, A. W., Levine, P., Maddox, K., Quadagno, D. M., Fordyce, M. L., & Jones, M. (1991). AIDS knowledge and risk behaviors among culturally diverse women. *AIDS Education and Prevention, 3*(2), 79–89.

House, R. M., & Walker, C. M. (1993). Preventing AIDS via education. *Journal of Counseling & Development, 71,* 282–289.

McDonell, J. R., Abell, N., & Miller, J. (1991). Family members' willingness to care for people with AIDS: A psychosocial assessment model. *Social Work, 36*(1), 43–53.

Osmond, M. W., Wambach, K. G., Harrison, D. F., Byers, J., Levine, P., Imershein, A., & Quadagno, D. M. (1993). The multiple jeopardy of race, class, and gender for AIDS risk among women. *Gender & Society, 7*(1), 99–120.

Petrow, S. (1990). *Dancing against darkness: A journey through America in the age of AIDS.* Lexington, MA: Lexington Books.

U.S. Department of Health and Human Services. (1994). *HIV/AIDS surveillance report, 6*(1). Atlanta, GA: Centers for Disease Control and Prevention.

Rejoinder to Dr. Abell KAREN SOWERS-HOAG

The debate on whether HBSE should be concentrated on one or a small number of elements of diversity in depth, rather than giving a "broad brush" to the range of diversity in America and the world, has been ongoing for too many years. It is time to put this debate to rest! As global distances between peoples continue to shrink and immigration patterns and cultural diversity in the United States increase, social work educators can no longer afford the luxury of debating this crucial issue. We *must* prepare our students to be culturally competent practitioners—and the HBSE curriculum content must provide the prerequisite foundation based on a multicultural world perspective.

Dr. Neil Abel, my friend and respected colleague, suggests that social work educators consider that HIV/AIDS serve as the universal metaphor for HBSE content in social work education, rather than giving a "broad brush" to the range of diversity issues in American culture. Within this context, he presents an innovative and intriguing framework for organizing the diversity curriculum. And he provides a compelling argument for this narrow approach to diversity content.

Probably none among us would debate the importance of HIV/AIDS content in the social work curriculum. In fact, in recognition of the growing importance of this relatively new practice arena, many departments and schools of social work have incorporated HIV/AIDS content into their curriculum. Consistent with Abel's proposal, it would seem plausible to consider several other variables as possible unifying frameworks for presenting diversity content in the HBSE curriculum. Cancer, heart disease, poverty, or oppression—all which have far-reaching and devastating effects and consequences—could serve as an overarching framework in which to present diversity content. This approach, however, has some major limitations.

I am in agreement with Abell that the HBSE curriculum is already too heavily burdened with curricular expectations and goals. In his discussion, Abell points out the importance of making certain that our emphasis on diversity not become "a superficial scanning for offensive terminology or concepts," thus indicating a clear and specific need for attention specific to diversity in both scope and depth. Abell's suggested framework for presenting diversity content has the potential danger of placing emphasis on HIV/AIDS content *at the expense of* providing students with a sufficiently broad perspective across cultures. Also, placing HIV/AIDS content as the overarching theme might allow students to analyze various groups specific to that content but would not provide a knowledge base sufficiently broad for comparative analysis across a broad spectrum of variables. This partialized perspective focusing primarily on a relationship specific to one variable with a limited time in history will not prepare our students for the complexity of cross-cultural practice in the future. Now more than ever, we must remain diligent in our efforts to educate social workers prepared to serve multicultural populations through a broad examination of historical and contemporary sociocultural influences.

NO

KAREN SOWERS-HOAG

Cultural pluralism, the recognition of and regard for the existence of different ethnic groups who vary in color, physical characteristics, language, country of origin, or religious practice, has long been a value associated with the practice and education of professional social workers. Racial and ethnic content has been required in the curricula of accredited schools of social work since 1971. Students who are representative of the cultural mix of the larger society have been recruited into schools of social work on the basis of such a value commitment. However, despite our best efforts to recruit minorities, most professional social workers and social work students continue to be from the majority culture. Often referred to as "unhyphenated whites," these students represent the second or third generation of immigrants who lack any clearcut identification with, or knowledge of, specific European origins. They are usually aware that they may be different from other ethnic groups, whose race, recent immigration, or marginalization are omnipresent reminders of their ethnic identification.

The United States is once again experiencing a period of historic immigration. At the same time, recent advances in technologies are shrinking the global distances between peoples. Given the nature of our profession, which brings us into constant contact with people different from ourselves, the pursuit of knowledge of people's variability and differentness becomes a fundamental concern. Today as never before, social work, like no other profession, involves itself actively and intimately with the boundless variability of human beings (Masuda, 1984). As the cultural diversity of the population continues to increase, the need for social workers prepared to serve multicultural populations becomes increasingly important. The growth of ethnicity and multiculturalism as a social force has posed a vigorous challenge for social work education to prepare students to deal effectively with human and cultural diversity. In the past ten years it has also provided an impetus for social work to conceptualize interpersonal helping for cross-cultural contexts. Recently, educational models (Chau, 1990; Latting, 1990; Nakanishi & Rittner, 1992; Sowers-Hoag & Sandau-Beckler, in press) and models of social work practice with racial and ethnic groups (Devore & Schlesinger, 1991) have been developed.

It is impossible for any social work student or practitioner to be thoroughly knowledgeable about all of the cultural groups they are likely to encounter. It is therefore imperative that we adopt an educational model that incorporates a cultural competence approach to social work practice (Sowers-Hoag & Sandau-Beckler, in press). The following five elements of culturally competent practice adapted from the work done at Portland State University and others (Devore & Schlesinger, 1987) have been identified as essential elements for becoming a culturally competent helping professional: (1) awareness and acceptance of difference; (2) self-awareness; (3) dynamics of difference; (4) knowledge of the client's culture; and (5) adaptation of skills to compensate for cultural difference.

The Human Behavior Sequence (HBSE)

The first and most critical step in the development of culturally competent practitioners is the awareness of the importance of being culturally competent. The social worker should value diversity through the use of conceptual constructs that view cultural, ethnic, and the unique aspects of varying backgrounds as strengths and resources that can be fostered and supported for their benefit. The content in the human behavior sequence should focus on broadening students' awareness and acceptance of diverse racial, ethnic, and cultural heritages and instill in students the need to develop and maintain the attitude that learning about cultures and cross-cultural practice is an essential ongoing process synonymous with professionalism. To help students learn how to work effectively with racial and ethnic groups, the model of interpersonal practice we teach must itself be culturally responsive and able to give unbiased attention to concerns of the larger society and those unique to racial and ethnic groups (Chau, 1990). Within this context, the human behavior sequence should help students become aware of their own culture and recognize and accept personal responsibility for value judgments, fostering in students an ability to act among *all* people, an ability that often includes a major change in outlook and attitude. If we really believe that knowledge and values affect behavior, the values and knowledge taught in the human behavior sequence must include concepts and ideas that embrace *diversity* and reinforce a sensitivity to the importance of diversity in the behavior and thinking of our students (Chau, 1990). HBSE should provide a theoretical framework that embraces a global perspective, providing utility to our current and future students well into the twenty-first century.

The human behavior sequence should be designed to allow students the opportunity to acquire the first four essential elements to becoming a culturally competent practitioner: awareness and acceptance of difference; self-awareness; dynamics of difference; and knowledge of the client's culture. Several conceptual frameworks for studying cultural diversity have been suggested in the literature. These range from the studying of ethnocultures as separate entities, the studying of the points of interaction of subcultures, and the need to focus study on the oppression and discrimination that may be directed at ethnic minorities, rather than on ethnic groups themselves. Although each provides a valuable perspective, it must be noted that important aspects of individual human behavior can only be understood through the examination of sociocultural influences—historic and contemporary—and that all human behavior is an emergent quality not traceable to a single influence. Diversity may best be understood when an ethnoculture is examined in its own context and then even better appreciated when it is compared and contrasted with other ethnocultures.

The study of culture as it applies to practice is best undertaken in a comparative and global context. Social work students are a mixed group, from a range of cultures and backgrounds. Clients are also varied and disproportionately from black and Hispanic groups. A substantial number of social work transactions are intergroup, and it is within the comparative context that they are best appreciated (Jenkins, 1988). Using the comparative approach, one of the main tasks is the discovery of generalizations that transcend the boundaries of single societies—what the debate question terms "a broad brush approach." This approach examines the social context of ethnic relations, asking such questions as "are the same phenomena operating in black–white relations as in black–Puerto Rican relations? In Italian–Polish relations as in Sephardi Jewish–Ashkenazi Jewish relations? What differences can be attributed to class? To national origins? To time of migration?" The goal is not to build an encyclopedia of customs and habits but to study ethnic issues to differentiate similarities from differences (Jenkins, 1988). Ethnicity informs consciousness and influences behavior. Yet, ethnic differences are not etched in stone but are themselves the product of history, class, place, and time (Steinberg, 1982). The comparative approach, involving more than the study of specific groups or the interaction among groups, sets interaction within its social context.

Because of the complex nature of human behavior, the tremendous and rich diversity that exists among the various subgroups of minority populations in this country and the world, and the enormous role that culture plays in the lives of all human beings, it is important that the human behavior sequence adopt an inclusive philosophical framework that promotes the understanding that people think differently and make different choices based on cultural traditions and experiences. At the same time, extreme caution must be taken to avoid the dangers of stereotyping of any group of people. Although all people share common basic needs, there are vast differences in how people of various cultures go about meeting those needs. These differences are as important as the similarities. The inclusive comparative framework allows for acceptance of the fact that each culture finds some behaviors, interactions, or values more important or desirable than others. This can help the service provider interact more successfully with differing cultures. Awareness and acceptance of differences in communication, life view, and definition of health and family are critical to the successful delivery of services. This approach leads to a more accurate reflection of the cultural, ethnic, and philosophical diversity in the world.

Conclusion

When a department or school of social work confers a degree on a graduate, the faculty of that school are attesting to a minimal level of knowledge and skills attained by that graduate. All graduates of CSWE-accredited departments and schools of social work are expected to have mastered foundation content necessary for generalist practice. The social work degree from a CSWE-accredited program does not restrict the student geographically or in working with certain populations. And even the place-bound students will find themselves increasingly engaged in cross-cultural practice and confronted with the complex challenge of relating to various diverse groups of clients. As such, the human behavior sequence must prepare our graduates in knowledge of the culture (history, traditions, values, family systems, artistic expressions) of ethnic minority clients, knowledge of the impact of class and ethnicity on behavior, attitudes, and values, knowledge of the role of language, speech patterns, and communication styles in ethnically distinct communities, and knowledge of the help-seeking behaviors of ethnic minority clients. A narrow, in-depth study of one or two groups does not necessarily develop sensitivities and knowledge that will generalize to other groups. Nor does it provide a knowledge base sufficiently broad for comparative analysis.

Providing a narrow, in-depth educational focus in the human behavior sequence that is primarily reflective of the cultural groups within the region of the social work program may not provide a sufficiently broad knowledge base for the graduate who moves out of the region or finds himself or herself working with other cultural populations. Additionally, such an approach reinforces a "regional-centrism." A partialized perspective concerned with only one set of relationships, a limited combination of groups, or one time in history does not prepare the student for the complexity of cross-cultural practice. Instead, human behavior content should present a multicultural world perspective—and a broad brush approach. Becoming culturally competent is a developmental process for the individual. It is not something that happens because one reads a book, studies one group or problem, attends a workshop, or happens to be a member of a minority group. It is a process born of a commitment to provide quality services to all and a willingness to risk. The human behavior sequence must, then, prepare students for lifelong self-examination and learning. Providing students with a broad perspective across cultures helps students understand the concept of "cultural relativity"—the recognition that different cultures provide different behavioral options for satisfying the universal physical and psychological needs of human beings. This understanding lays the foundation for a kind of cultural literacy, the acceptance of people as cultural beings. It is this content that is a critical prerequisite for the development of a culturally competent social work practitioner. Without this foundation, knowledge and skills presented in the subsequent curricular areas will be irrelevant.

REFERENCES

Chau, K. L. (1990). A model for teaching cross-cultural practice in social work. *Journal of Social Work Education, 26*(2), 124–133.

Devore, W., & Schlesinger, E. G. (1991). *Ethnic-sensitive social work practice.* New York: Merrill/Macmillan.

Jenkins, S. (1988). Ethnicity: Theory base and practice link. In C. Jacobs & D. D. Bowles (Eds.), *Ethnicity and race: Critical concepts in social work.* New York: National Association of Social Work.

Latting, J. (1990). Identifying the "isms": Enabling social work students to confront their biases. *Journal of Social Work Education, 26*(1), 55–68.

Masuda, R. (1984). Human differentness: A critical variable for international practicum in social work. In D. S. Sanders & P. Pederson (Eds.), *Education for International Social Welfare.* Council on Social Work Education.

Nakanishi, M., & Rittner, B. (1992). The inclusionary cultural model. *Journal of Social Work Education, 28*(1), 27–35.

Steinberg, S. (1982). *The ethnic myth: Race, ethnicity, and class in America.* Boston: Beacon Press.

Sowers-Hoag, K. M., & Sandau-Beckler, P. (in press). Educating for cultural competence in the generalist curriculum. *Journal of Multicultural Social Work.*

Rejoinder to Dr. Sowers-Hoag NEIL ABELL

No one (not even debate-driven colleagues like Dr. Sowers-Hoag and myself) could argue the necessity of emphasizing diversity and cultural competence in social work education. The questions are "for whom" and "how"?

First, Dr. Sowers-Hoag is correct in noticing that social work remains a profession nominally dominated by "unhyphenated whites." I doubt, however, that she really means to imply that education for diversity should be focused exclusively (or even mainly) on bringing this group "up to speed" with characteristics attributed to "minorities."

In fact, many schools of social work *have* succeeded in attracting students in ethnic/racial proportions comparable to the communities from which they are drawn, and the memberships (and leaderships) of NASW and CSWE reflect a strong measure of success in achieving diversity. The issue is whether we are prepared to educate *all* students for the cultural competence she correctly supports. Blindness, indifference, and antipathy toward the values of others are, sadly, more universal than is implied by attributing them solely to the "majority."

Next, in considering the means toward this end, we share several points. We agree, first, that becoming thoroughly knowledgeable about all cultural groups is probably impossible and that educating for self-awareness and a more general knowledge of others are essential goals. In limiting her illustrations to culture and ethnicity, however, Dr. Sowers-Hoag unintentionally omits reference to the many other ways in which we (as educators, workers, and clients) differ from one another. Overlooking gender, age, sexual orientation, and ability, for instance, precludes fully appreciating the more subtle and complex ways we may dismiss each other *within* ethnic and cultural boundaries.

Dr. Sowers-Hoag argues for HBSE curriculum embracing a global perspective and emphasizing the impacts of oppression and discrimination. These are fine goals that, we agree, cannot be overrated. However, the question is how to bring all of this *alive* for our students.

In an era witnessing a backlash against "politically correct" thinking and a resurgence of conservative "blame the victim" policies, we cannot take for granted that students will truly embrace the very difficult challenges proposed here just because, as faculty, we think we are right. The "broad brush" approach, however admirable in principle, remains, for most, a survey of abstractions. It simply cannot be counted on to shake students out of their complacency. Answering the "how" question demands that faculty apply a truly comprehensive perspective on diversity (i.e., moving beyond just cultural or ethnic identities) to urgent problems students are likely to encounter and need answers to *today*. HIV/AIDS provides the perfect (not merely convenient) metaphor for HBSE education.

Should the HBSE Core Curriculum Include Developmental Disabilities Content?

EDITOR'S NOTE: People differ in their abilities in part because of their genetic inheritance, in part because of their life experiences, and in part because of the interaction of nature and nurture. Social workers need to be aware of all of these factors because they are likely to be working with people presenting a full range of abilities. The question arises as to whether the study of developmental abilities and disabilities should be incorporated as part of the general curriculum, or whether it should be limited to a specialized course.

Audrey L. Begun, Ph.D., is an associate professor at the University of Wisconsin—Milwaukee, where she teaches courses in lifespan development, family development, and developmental disabilities. She has recently been involved in developing training materials related to early intervention with children with disabilities and their families.

Martin Bloom, Ph.D., is a professor at the School of Social Work, University of Connecticut, where he teaches HBSE classes. His book, *Evaluating Practice: Guidelines for the Accountable Professional* (2nd ed.) (with Joel Fischer and John Orme), was published in 1995.

Waldo C. Klein, Ph.D., is an associate professor at the School of Social Work, University of Connecticut, where he has taught gerontology, HBSE, and research methods. His research interests include long-term caregiving systems, with current projects studying the use of alcohol in nursing homes and the experience of nursing homes in providing services to residents with AIDS.

YES

AUDREY L. BEGUN

Over the years, Human Behavior and the Social Environment (HBSE) education has completed several evolutions, if not revolutions. The greatest advantage of these evolutions has been the educational system's capacity to respond adaptively to changes in society, social issues, theoretical positions, and the profession's knowledge base. In this spirit, it is argued here that content about developmental disabilities, and the full spectrum of human abilities, should be incorporated into the core of HBSE curriculum, as opposed to limiting this content to specialized courses. The 1992 Council on Social Work Education (CSWE) Curriculum Policy Statement serves as an organizing structure for the initial arguments. Arguments include issues related to the bio-psycho-social development approach in HBSE education, as well as teaching human diversity, populations at risk, systems of oppression, promoting social justice, and ethics across the curriculum. Practical concerns are also addressed.

Bio-Psycho-Social Development

The CSWE Curriculum Policy Statement recommends that HBSE education provide content about theories and knowledge of human bio-psycho-social development; that students should understand the interactions between and among human biological, social, psychological, and cultural systems as they affect and are affected by human behavior. One relatively recent evolution of HBSE education is reflected in an emphasis on presenting systemic approaches to understanding the human experience (Chess & Norlin, 1988; Martin & O'Connor, 1989).

Developmental disabilities, as a field of study, is replete with examples and models that implicate both systemic models (e.g., Crnic, Friedrich, & Greenberg, 1983; Minuchin, 1978; Seligman & Darling, 1989) and bio-psycho-social models of influence on development, as well as models that illustrate the interactive nature of effects. Therefore, social work educators have a rich array of materials available from the field of developmental disabilities for demonstrating these critical components of the core HBSE education experience.

For example, the lifelong impact of prenatal exposure to teratogenic agents such as certain viruses (e.g., rubella and acquired immune deficiency syndrome [AIDS]), alcohol, or prescription and illicit drugs clearly demonstrate the biological forces implicit in the bio-psycho-social model. More specifically, their roles in the causes, incidence/prevalence rates, and prevention of developmental disabilities are demonstrated, such as in fetal alcohol effects (FAE) and fetal alcohol syndrome (FAS), visual and auditory impairments, communication disorders, learning and cognitive deficits, motor and mobility impairments, and so forth.

Similarly, the study of developmental disabilities exemplifies those psychological, social, and cultural factors that produce diverse developmental courses.

The developmental impact of severe maternal depression or stress and distress, as well as the multigenerational impact of malnutrition associated with extreme poverty, serve as powerful examples representing these forces—and the fact that these forces are as salient as the biological when discussing the human experience. Furthermore, culturally based beliefs, along with social class, ethnicity, and religious variation, have been discussed as having an impact on the ways in which family and community systems adapt to a child's disabilities (Seligman & Darling, 1989). The field examines the impact of social support systems and the characteristics of support networks as mediating factors in the lives of people with developmental disabilities and their families, as well as addressing the individuals' impact on social systems (Seligman & Darling, 1989).

Examination of the families' similar and different experiences conveys several key concepts: (1) the risks inherent in relying on stereotypes about such a heterogeneous population either in professional practices or policy positions; (2) the similar and dissimilar nature of experiences between families with and without disabled members; and (3) the ways in which discrimination, oppression, and other facets of diversity, such as gender, socioeconomic status, religion and religiosity, race, and ethnicity interact in significant ways with disability (e.g., Cushner, McClelland, & Safford, 1992; Gropper, 1983; Kalyanpur & Rao, 1991; Seligman & Darling, 1989).

This content integration also lends support to the HBSE mission of educating students about complex interaction patterns among the full range of biological, psychological, social, and cultural factors, thus moving them beyond reliance on simple, linear, cause-and-effect models. Again, in preparing social work students to use HBSE content, the study of developmental disabilities provides opportunities to develop these complex, bio-psycho-social conceptualizations. However, developmental disabilities content serves more HBSE education functions beyond that of providing a rich array of examples for key concepts.

Human Diversity

The social work curriculum, in general, must prepare students to understand and appreciate human diversity. In many social work programs, much of this preparation occurs through core and advanced HBSE education. The curriculum must provide content about differences and similarities in the experiences, needs, and beliefs of people. Among the standards of the Curriculum Policy Statement regarding human diversity and populations at risk, groups distinguished by physical or mental ability are specifically referenced; therefore, including people with developmental disabilities throughout the curriculum is clearly of relevance.

Diversity and developmental disabilities intersect in a commanding manner, because they are all about the effects of lifestyles and life chances on the ways that people live (Berger & Federico, 1985). They are also about stereotypes, prejudice, and oppression in the lives of people on both sides of the equation. It is valuable for social work students to be exposed to the similarities and differences in needs and experiences of people with developmental disabilities as part of diversity education. For example, Cushner et al. (1992) discuss disabilities as a significant aspect of their analysis of human diversity content in education.

The "developmental delays versus differences" debate addresses core HBSE issues concerning how people are similar and how they are different. Do people with developmental disabilities have the same thoughts, feelings, and needs as other people but express them differently? Or, do they have different thoughts, feelings, needs, and experiences? And, how can we know? What students learn in response to these critical analyses leads the educator to address another recommendation presented in the Curriculum Policy Statement: How to use communication skills differentially with a variety of client populations, and also, the issue of preparing social workers to deliver their interventions to populations that exhibit a wide range of abilities and disabilities (e.g., McDaniel, 1989; Whitman, Graves & Accardo, 1989).

In sum, integration of content on developmental disabilities (as part of the full range of abilities) into the HBSE core curriculum greatly enhances training about human diversity. Students can be better prepared to understand the ways in which their assessments and interventions must be modified to create a "good fit" for differing populations.

Systems of Oppression, Populations at Risk

An important aspect of HBSE education is to develop students' understanding of the ways in which the societal contexts affect the lives of individuals, families, and other social institutions. According to the CSWE standards regarding HBSE education, the curriculum must provide content about the ways in which systems promote or deter people in the maintenance or attainment of optimal health and well-being. Students are expected to develop an understanding of the forms and mechanisms of oppression and discrimination; the patterns, dynamics, and consequences of discrimination, economic deprivation, and oppression; and the strategies and skills of change that work toward the achievement of social and economic justice.

Many lessons may be gleaned about society's overt and covert stereotyping, discriminatory practices, violence, and oppression from reviewing the history of American people with developmental disabilities (e.g., Scheerenberger, 1983; Sobsey, 1994). A review of historical and contemporary trends in societal responses to people with developmental disabilities further extends the HBSE curriculum content (e.g., Safilios-Rothschild, 1970; Tomaszewski, 1992). In educating students about family and community violence, it is important to highlight the increased vulnerabilities of people with disabilities to violence and abuse

(Sobsey, 1994; Waxman, 1991). This also applies to child welfare concerns: children with developmental disabilities are at a disproportionately high risk of maltreatment and of having their special needs going unmet.

As a means of educating a diversely prepared student body, it may be helpful to introduce concepts of oppression and discrimination in the context of people with developmental disabilities as a population of "blameless victims." Students then may be more receptive and less defensive about discussing the very same (emotionally provocative) processes in reference to populations where their own personal stereotypes and prejudices might be challenged (e.g., race, ethnicity, gender, religion, and sexual orientation).

From a positive perspective, there are numerous examples in the developmental disabilities field of empowering responses and efforts to help individuals in achieving their greatest potential. Normalization principles and numerous policies have emerged during the past two or three decades that are strong representations of an HBSE relevant "strengths perspective" approach (Saleeby, 1992). Students can analyze approaches designed to foster, stimulate, and support the growth and development of individuals with developmental disabilities and to minimize, reduce, and remove barriers to that optimal growth. Great strides toward reducing barriers have been made since advocates and people with disabilities entered the sociopolitical realm (Hahn, 1985). For example, PL 94-142 guarantees nondiscriminatory evaluation, appropriate education in the least restrictive environment, and procedural due process; early intervention and family-centered care are aspects of PL 99-457; protection from discrimination is promised through the Americans with Disabilities Act, etc. Increasingly, educational resources concerning empowerment and advocacy related to individuals with developmental disabilities are available (e.g., Goldman, 1991). Furthermore, many of the materials take into consideration the ways that the groups themselves define and cope with the problems. According to Garvin and Tropman (1992), appropriate understanding is best fostered through learning to recognize the communications, habitats, social structures, socialization, economy, beliefs, and sentiments of the population engaged. Although they refer primarily to ethnic diversity, this observation applies to the disability "culture," too. These models all supply the HBSE educator with materials to demonstrate general principles of advocacy, empowerment, social change, and prevention.

In sum, the field of developmental disabilities presents many powerful demonstrations of the ways in which the processes of discrimination and oppression operate in American society, and of the impact of these destructive processes on individuals, families, and communities. Conversely, the field also offers significant demonstrations of the ways in which individuals and groups have effected change in the systems that failed them. Students can learn how to enter into collaborative partnerships with these individuals—an evolving, highly significant social work role.

Practical Concerns

In the social work profession, a relatively small percentage of students will assume employment in jobs that are "pure" developmental disabilities positions (Martin & O'Connor, 1989). They are more likely to have jobs in which they incidentally come into contact with people who have developmental disabilities. Developmental disabilities content spans multiple fields of practice (schools, hospital, family and child, child welfare, poverty and employment, criminal justice, etc.). Furthermore, social workers are likely to move in and out of job arrangements over the course of their careers. For these reasons, to ensure that the needs of people with developmental disabilities will be adequately met, students need exposure to developmental disabilities content integrated with all aspects of their professional training.

This is not to say that the development of specialized courses in developmental disabilities should not be encouraged. However, social work programs should not rely on this as the primary method of integrating the content into the curriculum. Many institutions do not have access to professionals who can effectively teach these specialized courses; many do not have a critical mass of interested students to sufficiently enroll in specialized courses. In an era of reduced resources for higher education, it is a more adaptive strategy to integrate the content throughout the curriculum. This strategy of general exposure to the content may serve also to increase the number of students who are exposed to the content and eventually choose to work in the specialized field of developmental disabilities.

Finally, we need to consider the future nature of the student body. As the Americans with Disabilities Act (ADA) effects change, social work programs increasingly will be educating students with all types of disabilities. Having been exposed to the issues in the core HBSE curriculum, students will have skills and knowledge that help them to interact more appropriately with their colleagues who have disabilities. Integration of the content relevant to these students and their families represents a significant step toward facilitating their professional development. It also facilitates the emergence of a learning environment that encompasses the values, ethics, and regard for individual dignity that facilitate mutual participation.

In sum, considering the practical aspects of social work education, the mission of social work education, and the philosophical foundations of HBSE education, it is important for developmental disabilities content to be integrated throughout the core HBSE curriculum.

References

Berger, R., & Federico, R. (1985). *Human behavior: A perspective for the helping professions* (2nd ed.). New York: Longman.

Chess, W. A., & Norlin, J. M. (1988). *Human behavior and the social environment: A social systems model.* Boston: Allyn and Bacon.

Council on Social Work Education. (1992). *Curriculum policy statement for baccalaureate degree programs in social work education.* Washington, DC: Author.

Crnic, K. A., Friedrich, W. N., & Greenberg, M. T. (1983). Adaptation of families with mentally retarded children: A model of stress, coping and family ecology. *American Journal of Mental Deficiency, 88,* 125–138.

Cushner, K., McClelland, A., & Safford, P. (1992). *Human diversity in education: An integrative approach.* New York: McGraw-Hill.

Garvin, C. & Tropman, J. (1992). *Social work in contemporary society.* Engelwood Cliffs, NJ: Prentice-Hall.

Goldman, C. D. (1991). *Disability rights guide: Practical solutions to problems affecting people with disabilities.* Lincoln, NE: Media.

Gropper, N. (1983). Access to equality: The first national conference on educational equity for disabled women and girls. *Children Today, 12*(1), 24–25.

Hahn, H. (1985). Toward a politics of disability: Definitions, disciplines, and policies. *The Social Science Journal, 22,* 87–105.

Kalyanpur, M., & Rao, S. S. (1991). Empowering low-income black families of handicapped children. *American Journal of Orthopsychiatry, 61*(4), 523–532.

Martin, P. Y. & O'Connor, G. G. (1989). *The social environment: Open systems applications.* New York: Longman.

McDaniel, B. (1989). A group work experience with mentally retarded adults on the issues of death and dying. *Journal of Gerontological Social Work, 13*(4), 187–191.

Minuchin, S. (1978). *Psychosomatic families.* Cambridge, MA: Harvard University Press.

Safilios-Rothschild, C. (1970). *The sociology and social psychology of disability and rehabilitation.* New York: Random House.

Saleebey. D. (Ed.). (1992). *The strengths perspective in social work practice.* New York: Longman.

Scheerenberger, R. (1983). *A history of mental retardation.* Baltimore: Paul H. Brookes.

Seligman, M., & Darling, R. B. (1989). *Ordinary families, special children: A systems approach to childhood disability.* New York: Guilford.

Sobsey, D. (1994). *Violence and abuse in the lives of people with disabilities: The end of silent acceptance?* Baltimore: Brookes.

Tomaszewski, E. P. (1992). *Disability awareness curriculum for graduate schools of social work.* Washington, DC: National Center for Social Policy and Practice/NASW.

Waxman, B. F. (1991). Hatred: The unacknowledged dimension in violence against disabled people. *Sexuality and Disability, 9*(3), 185–200.

Whitman, B., Graves, B., & Accardo, P. (1989). Training in parenting skills for adults with mental retardation. *Social Work, 34,* 431–434.

Rejoinder to Dr. Begun

MARTIN BLOOM
WALDO C. KLEIN

We are pleased to have a colleague as articulate as Professor Begun arguing the case for increased attention to the needs of people with developmental disabilities, and the responsibility of professional social work to address those needs. However, we believe that her argument favoring specialized content on developmental disabilities in the core HBSE curriculum leads educators in an ill-fated direction.

First, she presents her position by arguing that developmental disabilities content be included "in spirit." "In spirit" we have no difference; however, as educators we are called on to develop and implement curricula *in reality*. In reality, developmental disabilities represents only one of a great many equally worthy areas of practice. We contend that to incorporate specialized developmental disability content into the *core* of HBSE is to require inclusion of *all* equally deserving target populations, thus so minimizing "specialized content" on any individual one to the point of triviality and meaningfulness. Fortunately, social work education offers students opportunities to specialize as a part of their advanced training. To prepare for that training, it is imperative that students receive a firm grounding in the foundation knowledge of theory and practice. Thus, it is essential that we consider the factors that mitigate against the inclusion of specialized developmental disabilities content in the core of HBSE. We have outlined the most important of these pragmatic realities in stating our own position.

Professor Begun argues that the area of developmental disabilities "is replete with examples and models" to achieve the goals of the HBSE. That ample material exists within the realm of developmental disability is not at question. Rather, the question being debated is whether such a singular focus should be allowed to dominate a core HBSE curriculum. We welcome the use of examples drawn from the developmental disability literature to illustrate various topics and themes of the HBSE curriculum. However, we believe that other areas of practice might serve *equally well* to provide such examples.

It is not surprising that Professor Begun sees people with developmental disabilities as less threatening than others about whom students might hold stereotypes. However, social work education needs to attack all stereotypes; holding people with developmental disabilities up as "blameless victims" implicitly "blames" other groups, even when done in support of some positive teaching goal.

Professor Begun argues that "to ensure that the needs of people with developmental disabilities will be adequately met" developmental disabilities content needs to be integrated with all aspects of student training. We are not at all clear what she is suggesting by integration. If, by integration, she is proposing that developmental disabilities literature be used to provide examples of larger learning concepts, we agree. However, such a practice would not seem to "ensure" that needs be adequately met. Doing so would seem to require specialized content. Yet, her model of "integration" becomes more confusing with her apparent proposal to "integrate the content" as a strategy in response to a shortage of "professionals who can effectively teach" specialized developmental disability courses. We are gravely concerned that "content integration" may be seen as a solution to a lack of expertise. Although we have high regard for Professor Begun's own expertise, the practice proposed here seems to attempt to hide ignorance behind superficiality.

Professor Begun is correct in anticipating that social work programs will increasingly need to confront the challenges presented by a student body (and practice community) with all types of disabilities—as well as all other types of diversity. We rejoice in this challenge! To the degree that effective social work with people with developmental disabilities (or who represent any other unique segment of a diverse human population) requires specialized knowledge and skill, it should be addressed in specialized classes. To the degree that it does not require such specialized attention, it may be addressed through a solid and well-planned HBSE curriculum—with appropriate use of balanced examples and illustrations of human behavior in all of its diverse dimensions.

NO

MARTIN BLOOM

WALDO KLEIN

Human behavior and the social environment content (HBSE) is fundamental to social work as its knowledge base. HBSE serves as a primary source of information on which practice is conceptually enlightened ("This is the way the world most likely works"); through which practice is guided to make specific action hypotheses ("If I do X, the client and context are most likely to respond by doing or changing in Y ways"); and by which practice is sustained in its value judgments ("This action is most likely to help and least likely to do harm"). Thus, the tasks assigned to HBSE are enormous; they challenge even the most dedicated of educators. It is with regret that we argue that HBSE ought not to incorporate a full-formed developmental disabilities content into its core curriculum. We certainly recognize that the area of developmental disabilities presents important information, and all social workers ought to know something about it. But this should not be done through a superficial survey of this topic along with a dozen others in a required course. Not only is this the wrong way to deliver the content, but there are better alternatives, ones that would in the long run accrue positively to this field.

We argue that developmental disabilities ought not to be taught in the basic HBSE class for several general reasons: (1) There is not enough time nor space for particular topics when there are so many facets of information that have to be taught. (2) The claim to HBSE time is equally great from many other important special topics, and the educational domain of developmental disabilities has no special claim to extensive time in a required foundation course. (3) HBSE instructors cannot be reasonably expected to provide expert content in every diverse area of human experience, such as developmental disabilities. (4) Developmental disabilities are a complex topic in their own right, and are best taught in a separate class, to self-selected students who show interest and talent in this topic.

First, some basic definitions and clarifications. The term *developmental disabilities* is itself a political creation that changed over time as the implications of including or excluding certain disabilities became clear. DeWeaver (1995) details this history as he summarizes the current definition of the term in the Developmental Disabilities Assistance and Bill of Rights Act of 1990 (P.L.101-496):

Developmental disability means a severe, chronic disability of a person 5 *years or older* that:

A. Is attributable to a mental or physical impairment or combination of mental and physical impairments
B. Is manifested before the person attains age twenty-two
C. Is likely to continue indefinitely
D. Results in substantial functional limitations in three or more of the following areas of major life activity: (i) self-care, (ii) receptive and expressive language, (iii) learning, (iv) mobility, (v) self-direction, (vi) capacity for independent living, and (vii) economic self-sufficiency
E. Reflects the person's need for a combination and sequence of special, interdisciplinary, or generic care, treatment, or other services that are of lifelong or extended duration and are individually planned and coordinated. . . . [with some exceptions]

This functional or performance definition is exceedingly complex and involves mental retardation, cerebral palsy, epilepsy, and autism—each a complex topic requiring interdisciplinary expertise. Also, the fact that this term has been defined within a political process means that financial and other support hangs in the balance of expert judgment. This is not a topic for survey-type knowledge, lest the student with a little knowledge presumes to go a long way, to the detriment of the client.

Now, we turn to our arguments against including a large, self-contained unit on developmental disabilities in the core HBSE class. We certainly do not object to the mention of developmental disabilities in their various forms, as examples of challenges in human development and adaptation. Indeed, this is the function of an introductory HBSE course and may provide the interested student with further readings and references. The instructor should know where the student might talk with professionals in this field, as a way of furthering interest and field practicum opportunities. But this is far from presenting the depth of coverage that could be done in a single-topic course.

Not Enough Time or Space for Special Topics

The core HBSE curriculum is mandated by CSWE to include a number of topics on general development in general contexts. There is no directive to teach developmental disabilities mentioned in the most recent CSWE curriculum policy statement. The HBSE mandate itself is so enormous that teachers dispair of ever covering anything like a comprehensive portion of the material and have to make agonizing selections as it is to honor the spirit of the mandate. Consider: there is the vast territory of information on ordinary growth and development over the life course. This content (or, actually, a survey of this information) is presented so that students will understand the frame of reference against which specific experiences may be set—such as how developmental disabilities, mental illness, social upheavals, economic downturns, or even accidents might produce diverse changes in these developments. There are also many theories of personality that purport to guide practice, along with relevant empirical research and critical reviews. There are theories of the social environment that offer a larger picture of the developmental contexts. These too have a large research base and a critical literature. Ethical and value issues, as well as discussions of prejudice and discrimination, are often included in the basic HBSE course. Also mandated are considerations of the special developmental experiences of persons according to their gender, ethnicity, social class, religion, sexual orientation, urban/rural status, and other factors including differential mental and physical abilities.

It is not a matter of being able to sample this broad range of topics—we can do this by fiat, by deciding what areas to read and what topics to discuss, as listed under broad mandated categories. The underlying issue that must be faced is how much students can profitably learn in such a crash survey class, with all the bits and snippets from everywhere—each seemingly important to those who advocate for it. We would submit that students are shortchanged when they are exposed to large numbers of small pieces of specialized information on which they are supposed to gain an adequate degree of competence as the basis of their practice.

Claimants to HBSE Time

If the topic of developmental disabilities is introduced in the foundation HBSE content, then we should probably expect that soon many other important specialties would seek their place in the HBSE sun as a required experience for all students. At minimum, this would include topics regarding persons with visual or auditory disabilities, with mental illnesses, with special medical conditions (such as AIDS or cancer), with environmental pollution, with war and violence at all levels, with the world of particular risks and hazards of modern life. All would rightly claim that it is important to know some of the basics about x, y, and z, because all students will no doubt meet with clients with these conditions over the course of their career. A small introduction will enable students to get a sense of the literature and to know where to begin their intensive search for knowledge pertinent to their client. All of this is true, but the implications of many special areas all being taught as part of the foundation course would paralyze the course and make a mockery of this general content. Students need to know some current factual and conceptual information, but the introductory course should teach more of the strategies of obtaining information on any needed topic, and fitting that new information with an existing body of knowledge and experience.

Expertise of HBSE Instructors

We believe that one of the values of the mandated HBSE curriculum is that it does provide students with the critical skills both to use acquired information on theories of human behavior to guide practice, and to seek additional information to address newly experienced practice situations. It is through the solid grounding of HBSE instruction in the general theories, research, and values/ethics literature that these achievements are attained in schools of social work around the nation.

Yet, it is the reality for most HBSE educators (and indeed most social work educators and practitioners in general) that they bring specialized expertise in one or perhaps several areas of knowledge (such as experiences with specialized theories, problems, or populations) to the classroom. The inclusion of content on developmental disabilities (along with the other special topic content areas that would undoubtedly also be competing for HBSE time) would require instructors to acquire new expert knowledge in all of these special topics. This is probably an unlikely event to transpire, and it would appear to be a pedagogically unsound overload. Given the complexity of any one of the subtopics in developmental disabilities, it would be asking too much of nonspecialist teachers to devote the time required to master the language and the content as part of understanding the broader picture of human growth and development. Moreover, because developmental disability specialists are relatively few in social work, this would impose some additional stresses on the teaching of HBSE on top of the already existing overload.

Developmental Disabilities Belongs to a Specialized Course

The major argument to be made against teaching a sampling of developmental disabilities in the foundation HBSE course is that this is the wrong place to teach such important materials. The general thrust of the major types of developmental disabilities might better be taken up in specialized classes or on the job with persons exhibiting these conditions. Let us explore these options.

We could foresee a foundation HBSE course discussing normative and non-normative growth and development, the former being a frame of reference for the latter. We could foresee the discussion of some basic terms, including developmental disabilities and the specific components currently viewed under this rubric. But this introduction would merely be a point of departure for a variety of topics and would supply students with the skills to think critically about any issue and to know how to retrieve information effectively on any topic. Then, when the situation called for it, students would have a professional orientation toward any topic of practice, including the area of developmental disabilities.

This taste of the topic may whet the appetite for some students who had no contact before with developmental disabilities, as well as to confirm a career choice of students whose personal or professional experiences had already brought them into contact with this population. Then, these self-selected students would be most likely to take elective courses on developmental disabilities (theories, research, practice, policy, value issues), bringing to these classes the enthusiasm and possibly the life experiences that provide solid grounds for new generations of workers in these areas.

Specialized courses could devote the time needed to the many subjects that form the conceptual, empirical, and practical base for work with people challenged by developmental disabilities. Many schools of social work have one or more specialized classes on developmental disabilities in their existing curricula. No argument is needed that these are fully appropriate and useful courses. Indeed, one might argue that we probably need an advanced seminar that would focus on the commonalities across different developmental disabilities, and what information and practices in one area might offer ideas useful in the other areas.

Yet another avenue toward specialized knowledge of developmental disabilities is through field training. What introductory survey classes cannot convey well is the experience of working with people with various developmental challenges. There is need for a distinctive kind of creative adaptations in helping people face these challenges that may be honed through close working relationships. Thus, we would argue that all students, in addition to regular client experiences, might profitably have some introductory or prefield experience with those who adapt effectively to their developmental challenges—as clients, colleagues, or supervisors. This is not the exclusive property of HBSE classes, but rather belongs to the more general type of course that often goes under the name "Introduction to Social Work." This could be done by field visits, or a well-chosen set of videotapes and films, with follow-up discussions led by experienced people in this field. This would provide an exciting window of opportunity to a broad range of students, some of whom might follow through with specialized class experiences. Frankly, we would prefer to have this kind of self-selection take place than try to force all students to have more than many would want on this topic area. In the long run, we believe that this approach would contribute more to professional services with those who face developmental challenges than any segment in an introductory HBSE course.

There is another reason that we think the area of developmental disabilities should be briefly introduced in HBSE and in an introduction to social work course: We must face stereotypes or aversions that some students have about persons who may be different from themselves, including persons with developmental disabilities with physical manifestations, but also with regard to the many forms of "isms"—racism, sexism, ageism, among others. We believe that it is more important to face the general issue of individual and group differences than to address specific manifestations of aversions and stereotypes. Our focus should be on respect for individual and group differences, as illustrated in the many ways people may differ, and the use of strengths of the people as a fundamental point of departure for assessment and practice. To do this requires a different way of putting together teaching materials than simply adding one important topic like developmental disabilities in one foundation course. We need both specialized courses in developmental disabilities and very brief surveys in HBSE and introduction to social work courses to address the similarities across these special topics. And thus, we say "No" to a full-formed introduction of content on developmental disabilities in the foundation HBSE curriculum.

REFERENCE

DeWeaver, K. L. (1995). Developmental disabilities: Definitions and policies. In R. L. Edwards and others (Eds.), *Encyclopedia of Social Work* (19th ed.). Washington, DC: NASW.

Rejoinder to Drs. Bloom and Klein
Audrey L. Begun

In general, it appears that the differences of opinion expressed in the two positions (YES versus NO) are actually differences in degree rather than in basic perspective. In arguing that developmental disabilities content belongs in the core HBSE curriculum, I concluded that advanced "specialization" courses related to developmental disabilities should also be available to social work students. However, I also argue that students require more than "mention" of developmental disabilities content in the HBSE curriculum, as suggested by Drs. Bloom and Klein. Students deserve more than a mere "taste" of the content; they deserve at least a full meal.

The following are my arguments:

1. Although I agree with Drs. Bloom's and Klein's argument that "HBSE instructors cannot be reasonably expected to provide expert content in every diverse area of human experience," it is equally true that not every social work program is fortunate enough to have instructors expert on developmental disabilities issues available for launching a specialized course for self-selected students. Curricular materials are easily accessible (as are community leaders for guest speaking engagements) for insertion into a variety of HBSE courses.

2. I do not envision the HBSE core as a course, which is the implication underlying much of Drs. Bloom & Klein's argument. The HBSE core is best envisioned as a series of courses that explore models of human behavior and its relationship to varied social environmental contexts. Hence, HBSE content should not appear once in a student's career, but should be integrated throughout the training period. This allows for greater depth of exploration and exposure to special topics, such as developmental disabilities content.

3. Drs. Bloom and Klein submit that "students are shortchanged when they are exposed to large numbers of small pieces of specialized information." There is a cogent rationale for making space for specialized information related to developmental disabilities as opposed to some of the other pieces of small change that might otherwise be offered. This field of study offers a rich array of content that is vitally relevant to the core of what the social work profession is all about: confronting oppression, stereotyping, and empowerment needs; intervening through the integration of multiple, complex social systems, at multiple levels; understanding the interplay between biological, social, and psychological systems in development; adapting interventions and research techniques/strategies for diverse populations; and so forth. Thus, there is some rationale for prioritizing this content over some others in the core HBSE curriculum.

In sum, in a perfect world, social work students would be exposed to developmental disabilities content throughout the curriculum, including across the core of the HBSE curriculum. They would also have available to them specialized coursework (with sufficient enrollments and adequately trained educators) in this content area. However, given the current realities, it is perhaps a "best compromise" solution to ensure that the content is integrated into the core HBSE curriculum.

Does Religion and Spirituality Have a Significant Place in the Core HBSE Curriculum?

EDITOR'S NOTE: Few topics generate as much heat or light as the discussion of religion in everyday society. In the educational context for the helping professions, we find a somewhat different problem, whether these feelings about the sacred and about ultimate sources of meaning should have a part in problem solving. Few deny the importance of religion in everyday life. However, there are sharp differences of opinion as to the place of religion and spirituality in the education of social workers.

Edward R. Canda, Ph.D., is an associate professor and chairperson of the HBSE curriculum component at the School of Social Welfare, the University of Kansas. He is also founder and chairperson of the advisory board for the Society for Spirituality and Social Work. He recently guest-edited a special issue of the journal, *Reflections: Narratives of Professional Helping,* on the spirituality of helping.

Daniel Weisman, Ph.D., is Chair of the B.S.W. program and professor at the School of Social Work, Rhode Island College. In 1992, he won a U.S. Supreme Court decision (Lee *v.* Weisman) banning organized prayer at public school graduations. His article on "Double jeopardy: Poverty and civil liberties violations," will appear in the *Journal of Progressive Human Services.*

YES

EDWARD R. CANDA

It is crucial to study religion and spirituality to understand human behavior in all levels of social systems, from the individual to family, group, organization, community, nation, and world. As an aspect of personhood, spirituality involves the quest for meaning, purpose, and morally fulfilling relations with self, other people, the encompassing universe, and ultimate reality, whatever a person understands that to be. On a more profound level, spirituality is the irreducible wholeness of what it is to be a person, with inherent dignity; it is the integrity of full humanity that gives context and completeness to the bio-psycho-social-spiritual aspects. Religion involves the patterning of spiritual beliefs and practices into social institutions, with community support and traditions maintained over time (Canda, 1988, 1989). Although everyone has spirituality, not everyone has religion.

For individuals, religion and spirituality provide ways of coping with life challenges and death. For families, they affect values and patterns of communication and discipline, and they determine life cycle rituals, such as marriage and funerals. Many therapeutic and support groups draw on spiritual principles, such as "reliance on a Higher Power"; and all helping groups address fundamental spiritual issues of empathy, caring, and resolution of suffering. Many social service organizations are religious in nature, such as Lutheran Social Services, the Salvation Army, Jewish communal services, and Buddhist temple–based mutual assistance associations. Furthermore, the fundamental values of all organizational cultures reflect spiritual concerns, such as the risk of alienation and dehumanization in bureaucracies. On an international level, religiously based wars contribute to massive destruction and refugee flight, whereas religiously based relief organizations try to help the victims. The global crises of environmental degradation and pollution challenge all people to reconsider the spiritual principles governing how we relate to the earth and to each other.

Therefore, religion and spirituality should be given significant attention in the HBSE core curriculum. The familiar social work phrase that distinguishes interrelated human aspects, "bio-psycho-social," presents an incomplete picture of what it is to be human. Spirituality, and its expressions in religious forms, are central to the personal and social construction of meaning, to the ways people make sense of the joys and agonies of life, and the ways we define and respond to issues of personal satisfaction and social justice. Thus it would be better to use the phrase "bio-psycho-social-spiritual," as implied by Charlotte Towle (1965) earlier in our professional history.

To exclude spirituality and religion from HBSE content, or to render them peripheral, is simply absurd. As I shall discuss, there are legitimate concerns about mixing religion and spirituality with social work, but to cut off the topic entirely because of such concerns is like "cutting off your nose to spite your face." Cutting spirituality out of the human being is to dehumanize and to oversimplify.

Unfortunately, the social work profession, and education in particular, have often excluded religion and spirituality from consideration. First, I reflect on how the profession came to "cut off its nose" earlier in its history. Then, I consider the recent trend and controversy about reincluding spiritual and religious aspects of human behavior. Finally, I suggest guidelines for how such content can be included appropriately in the core HBSE curriculum.

Historical Concerns

It is well known that professional social work in the United States developed under the influence of Christian and Jewish religious values, theological accounts of human behavior, and sectarian institutions and support systems (Canda, 1988; Loewenberg, 1988). Although charitable efforts to assist the poor and distressed may be praiseworthy, the biblical concept of charity (unconditional love) has been too often distorted into condescending pity and love "with strings attached." Service would sometimes be delivered with a sermon and pressures to convert, and the threat to remove help if the client did not conform. The poor were distinguished as worthy and unworthy, thus "blaming the victim." People suffering from substance abuse might be judged as moral reprobates to be punished or converted, rather than helped to overcome an addiction. Rival sectarian groups sometimes fought over who was right and legitimate and who should control resources and strategies for helping. Sometimes, religious social service zealots supported the destruction of spiritual traditions and practices different from their own, as in the efforts of missionary schools and religious adoption programs to separate First Nations (Native American) children from their families and to assimilate them to Christian, Euro-American standards. In the larger society, sometimes religionists have used religious rationalizations for torturous discipline of children, attacking so-called heretics and deviants, and pressuring members into self-destructive and suicidal acts. Unfortunately, contemporary news reports and social work case records show that such problems still abound.

Despite our profession's religious roots (or maybe because of them), these religious abuses made many social workers suspicious or even hostile toward mixing spirituality and religion with social work education. Also, in the effort to move toward nonsectarian and scientific models for understanding human behavior, theological and metaphysical views were dropped from education. Some educators have feared that discussion of the topic will violate the Constitutional separation between church and state. Apparently, they have somehow missed the fact that American state universities have supported nonsectarian educational programs and content in religious studies and anthropology of religions since their inception without a problem.

This shift in educational attitude is reflected in the history of the CSWE Curriculum Policy Statements concerning human behavior theory content. In the first and second statements (1953 and 1962), "spiritual influences and attributes" were considered important for understanding "the essential wholeness of the human being" (Marshall, 1991). However, the 1970 and 1984 statements omitted any reference to this. As we shall discuss, this neglect is now being redressed.

Reconsidering Spirituality and Continued Controversy

Actually, the fact that religion may be misused supports the need for teaching and learning about religion and spirituality in social work education. To the extent that religious ideologies and institutions play a role in causing personal affliction and social injustice, we must understand them to respond to them. "Know your enemy" for self-defense is good advice in a situation of conflict. Likewise, the religious injunction to "love your enemy" is also good advice in this situation. How can we learn to understand and respond in a compassionate way to the suffering, confusion, and turmoil within the hearts and minds of people who cause harm in the name of religion, unless we get to know them? As Mahatma Gandhi and Reverend Martin Luther King emphasized, the only kind of social action that can bring about an end to injustice and oppression for all is the kind that encourages understanding of everyone's perspectives, upholds the inherent dignity of everyone, and seeks the mutual benefit of everyone.

The "bad news" about spirituality and religion offers negative reasons why social workers need to learn about them. But there is also "good news" to motivate study. Spirituality and religion provide many personal strengths and community resources for people. For example, in hospice work, social workers find that spiritual beliefs and practices of dying individuals and their loved ones may help them to deal with grief and prepare for death. In work with refugees, the partnership between governmental resettlement programs, sponsoring Christian churches, Jewish family services, and Buddhist temples, and ethnic mutual assistance associations is key to success. In psychotherapy that supports development of full human potential, growthful religious and spiritually based insights and altered states of consciousness are often fostered by client-centered prayer, meditation, ritual, and retreats. Many oppressed communities have drawn on religious ideologies and institutions to preserve themselves and to resist oppression. The development of the antislavery movement, the underground railroad, the civil rights movement, and daily community-based mutual support among African Americans and their supporters has been deeply entwined with Christian faith, for example.

Whether one believes that religious and spiritual factors are more or less positive, their prevalence in human experience cannot be denied. In general, surveys of the United States population show that most people believe that God or other divine powers are affecting their lives, that miracles are possible, and that they have experienced extrasensory perception. In the publishing industry, books on religion and spirituality make up one of the fastest-growing sectors of the market. Politicians and policy makers frequently appeal to religious values and interest groups to mobilize support. So social work educators must present information about religion and spirituality as well as theoretical frameworks for understanding them, because they are woven into the fabric of our clients' (and our own) lives.

However, for many faculty, it still seems easier to avoid the topics of religion and spirituality. Based on conversations with colleagues, I suspect that the hypocrisy, judgmentalism, and coerciveness of some religious groups, which faculty may have experienced in their own lives, have led many to distance themselves from spirituality and religion in education. Recent surveys of practitioners and educators indicate that some practitioners and educators who recognize the positive potential of spirituality and religion in their own personal lives choose to avoid the topic when teaching or practicing because of the concerns about the possible negative results I have summarized. They also may avoid them because they feel unprepared by their own education (Dudley & Helfgott, 1990; Sheridan, Bullis, Adcock, Berlin, & Miller, 1992). This causes fragmentation of the conception of the person in terms of human behavior theory. It also splits the educator into pieces, public and private, and makes for an incomplete and misleading presentation of self in the classroom. Avoidance only perpetuates a cycle of silence and professional incompetence.

Such pedagogy, whether well intentioned or not, is a poor example to students. They quickly get the message that they must also fragment themselves in the classroom and in the field, perhaps even hiding some of their most precious and satisfying sources of meaning and motivation to help clients. Even worse, many times students have told me of being ostracized by educators and field instructors for trying to integrate spirituality into their practice. Spiritual perspectives may be dismissed as "unscientific." Religious convictions may be derided as "right-wing." Spiritually based support systems, such as twelve step programs, in which many social work students participate, may be mocked. Religious practices unfamiliar to the educator, such as charismatic prayer, meditation, and shamanic rituals, may be derided or ignored when a student mentions them. When educators behave in this intolerant and discriminatory manner, they perpetuate the very dogmatism, judgmentalism, and oppressiveness to which they object.

Fortunately, there is a growing consensus in our field that these topics are indeed crucial and that we must find ways to deal with them that are in keeping with professional ethics and educational standards. In recognition of this, the current Council on Social Work Education Curriculum Policy Statement identifies religion and spirituality to be relevant educational subjects in relation to human diversity and social work practice, thus making it imperative to provide a theoretical understanding of them in HBSE. Finally, after more than two decades of avoidance, spiritual and religious aspects of human behavior are being given their due.

Surely, there are legitimate reasons for caution about how these topics are addressed. But the topics must be addressed. So the only realistic question is, "What is the appropriate way to address spirituality and religion in social work education?" In keeping with the CSWE Curriculum Policy, the NASW Code of Ethics, and an emerging consensus among social work scholars, four principles should guide teaching about religion and spirituality in HBSE core curriculum (Canda, 1989, 1991; Furman, 1994). First, the person must be addressed as a whole, including the biological, psychological, social, and spiritual aspects. For example, human development theories need to take into account the potential for creativity and transpersonal experience (Canda, 1991; Cowley & Derezotes, 1994). Secondly, diverse and contrasting spiritual and religious views need to be included in a respectful manner. Thirdly, theories should be used to encourage critical reflection on similarities and differences, helpful and harmful impacts, and historical and cultural variations within and between spiritual perspectives. Finally, because spirituality and religion are relevant to all aspects of human behavior, pertinent content should be infused throughout the core HBSE curriculum as well as elective courses. In conclusion, the HBSE core curriculum should include significant content on spirituality and religion, not only because they are ubiquitous aspects of our clients' and our own lives, but also because to do otherwise would be to neglect the very basis of what it is to be human.

REFERENCES

Canda, E. R. (1988). Conceptualizing spirituality for social work: Insights from diverse perspectives. *Social Thought, 14*(1), 30–46.

Canda, E. R. (1989). Religious content in social work education: A comparative approach. *Journal of Social Work Education, 25*(1), 36–45.

Canda, E. R. (1991). East/West philosophical synthesis in trans-personal theory. *Journal of Sociology and Social Welfare, 18*(4), 137–152.

Cowley, A. S., & Derezotes, D. (1994). Transpersonal psychology and social work education. *Journal of Social Work Education, 30*(1), 32–41.

Dudley, J. R., & Helfgott, J. P. (1990). *Journal of Social Work, 26*(3), 287–294.

Furman, L. E. (1994). Religion and spirituality in social work education: Preparing the culturally-sensitive practitioner for the future. *Social Work and Christianity, 21*(2), 103–117.

Loewenberg, F. M. (1988). *Religion and social work practice in contemporary American society.* New York: Columbia University Press.

Marshall, J. (1991). The spiritual dimension in social work education. *Spirituality and Social Work Communicator, 2*(1), 12–15.

Sheridan, M. J., Bullis, R. K., Adcock, C. R., Berlin, S. D., & Miller, P. C. (1992). Practitioners' personal and professional attitudes toward religion and spirituality: Issues for education and practice. *Journal of Social Work Education, 28*(2), 190–203.

Towle, C. (1965). *Common human needs* (rev. ed.). Washington, DC: National Association of Social Workers.

Rejoinder to Dr. Canda   DANIEL WEISMAN

Inclusionism is based on the following (true but irrelevant) premises: The vast majority of American people are believers; religion is a powerful societal force, serving both positive and negative ends (from social work's perspective); the profession has significant religious roots and organizations. But the majority embraces many beliefs, including Proposition 187, the death penalty, and "welfare reform" that punishes poor women and children for being poor. Ironically, if First Amendment protections for religious minorities were dependent on public approval, they likely would be defeated.

Besides religion, a multitude of societal forces influence clients' lives: fashion trends, professional sports, and advertising, to name three. Each may be said to have good and bad sides, but these are not compelling enough reasons for HBSE inclusion. Social work has religious roots. True. But our roots are diverse and also include pacifism, anarchism, trade unionism, socialism, elitism, secularism, and nonsectarian, nonreligious philanthropy, to name a few. No one root characterizes social work, and we cannot be reduced to one antecedent.

If we were to teach about all the major societal beliefs or systems, or roots of the profession, we would need to expand HBSE beyond the scope of either degree. And instead of educating social workers to think through situations they face in practice, we would be turning out automatons imbued with encyclopedic information banks but no assessment or discernment skills.

There is one fundamental basis for conceptualizing HBSE: what do social workers need to know to practice effectively and appropriately? Inclusionists' writings suggest that they would teach about religion in HBSE to teach (in methods classes and practicum) how to practice religion with clients. They appear to view religion as an appropriate component of practice, and they would have social workers intervening in clients' religious practices. I have documented how this combination of roles (religion and social work) is inappropriate and unethical from both professions' perspectives. Nothing in the proffered inclusion argument challenges my analysis.

Inclusionists need to propose precisely what religious/spiritual material they would include in HBSE, and for what application in practice. They should acknowledge and address the practice and pedagogical dangers inherent in their proposal. They have made the valid point that psycho-social assessments should not ignore religion. They have a lot more homework to do.

Church–state issues are far more complex and less clearcut than presented in my opponent's paper. I refer the reader to my original discussion of the topic. Also, the notion of "freedom to unrestricted practice" is simplistic and requires more space than is allotted here. See the literature on separation and religious liberty (e.g., Glasser, 1991; Levy, 1986).

REFERENCES

Glasser, I. (1991). *Visions of liberty: The Bill of Rights for all Americans.* New York: Arcade.

Levy, L. W. (1986). *The Establishment Clause: Religion and the First Amendment.* New York: Macmillian.

NO

DANIEL WEISMAN

"Discounting the impact of spirituality as a dimension that shapes human behavior would be like ignoring magnetism as a force in the physical world because we cannot see it" (Berger, Federico, & McBreen, 1991, p. 31).

This is as good a starting point as any for arguing against spiritualism as content in core HBSE curricula because it eloquently captures the specious premise behind that proposal: we all have it, so social workers need to practice with it.

We do not need to understand or intervene in magnetism to be affected by it. We can even measure it precisely without knowing exactly why (e.g., geological and magnetic north are considerably divergent, but who cares besides pilots and boaters?). Nor are social workers compelled to practice in a wide range of human experiences, merely because they are common (e.g., medical procedures, home plumbing problems, income tax preparation). Also, assertions aside, there is no empirical evidence that "we all have it."

The teaching of spiritualism in HBSE, for the purpose of preparing students to intervene in clients' religious beliefs or practices (hereafter, inclusion), does not belong in core curricula. This is not because spiritualism cannot be seen or measured (which is not true), or because it does not exist (also untrue), or even because it contradicts our commitment to scientific-based practice (which is debatable), but because it is inconsistent with generalist practice, as a framework for intervention. Prospiritualist social work educators (inclusionists) tacitly acknowledge this point by focusing on advanced M.S.W. curricula as the place for inclusion, but even this is wrong.

Why Spiritualism Does Not Belong in Core HBSE Curricula

Arguments in favor of inclusion fall into two general categories: it is required to accommodate our commitment to multicultural diversity, and it is essential to our understanding of human behavior. I review these closely related points in order.

Diversity

Inclusionists argue that various ethnic, national, religious, racial, and cultural minorities tend to adopt spiritual views that are notably different from those of the white, Judeo-Christian majority (Lum, 1992, pp. 43–45). To be appropriate with those minority groups, we must be able to recognize the importance of the role of spirituality in their identities, behaviors, and experiences. Thus, social workers cannot be effective if they have not been taught spiritualism.

Human Behavior

Similarly, inclusionists propose that the ecological model of person-in-environment, as a basis for assessment of problems and formulation of intervention strategies, requires us to understand all salient factors related to individuals and their environments, including spirituality (Canda, 1988; Prest & Keller, 1993; Sheridan, Wilmer, & Atcheson, 1994). This requires social workers to be cognzant of spiritual components of clients' identities and communities, as well as knowledgeable and comfortable with their own spirituality (Canda, 1988, 1989).

At question is where these discussions leave us. When working with clients who are different from the practitioner, it is essential that the worker use culturally and ethnically sensitive techniques to understand what is being experienced, how it is interpreted, what the various response options are (including their meanings to the client system), what resources are available (including client system strengths), and what kinds of collaboration with other helping resources are appropriate. A component of these imperatives is the need for awareness of the meaning of difference, so to assess situations accurately and to avoid imposing one's own realities on others.

Similar points apply to utilization of the ecosystems framework in generalist practice. To unravel the myriad of presenting issues, practitioners should be able to explore a range of personal, family, community, and organizational factors that may contribute to problems and solutions. Spiritual issues are no different from a wide range of topics to be assessed.

In actuality, both directives (diversity and ecosystems) are basic practice principles with direct implications for HBSE: provide the requisite knowledge base. But good practice does not require practitioners to provide all of the services, resources, or interventions that clients require. When appropriate, we coordinate our efforts with those of others who are either specialists in particular aspects of practice or professionals in corollary disciplines.

Thus, it is entirely reasonable for a competent and sensitive social worker to assess a situation as having a spiritual component, and to refer the client to an appropriate source for religious or spiritual guidance. When these issues are inherently intertwined with social work interventions, the two practitioners can work collaboratively, so long as they have the client's consent.

To recapitulate, there is considerable empirical and theoretical support for the view that religion and spiritualism are important to many, perhaps most, people, and should be a component of assessment. But the evidence does not support social workers practicing religion or religious rituals with clients, or educating students to be spiritual advisors, practitioners, or leaders. These roles should be separate.

Why not teach spirituality in HBSE as a basis for teaching it as a social work intervention? In brief, the dangers far outweigh the advantages, and there is no need: there are ample religious professionals, in every community, to whom social workers can refer clients for spiritual guidance. Also, several knotty pedagogical challenges remain unresolved, including how to teach spiritualism competently and how to avoid coercing clients, students, and faculty into practicing religions other than their own.

Prest and Keller (1993) identified some possible negative consequences of combining social work and spiritual practice: the two may contradict each other; one may mask the other; sometimes they cannot be addressed separately because they are intertwined. Rotz, Russell, and Wright (1993) advocated for integrating spirituality and practice but argued for keeping spiritual and social work roles separate: "religious correctness" could become the clients' focus, with social workers acting as spiritual mediators; multimember client systems could experience internal competition for the social workers' allegiance on religious grounds, along lines of "more spiritual" versus "less spiritual" members; role confusion could result in clients interpreting social workers' views as God's will or endorsing particular concepts of religious practice.

The inherent risk in combining religious practice and social work practice is the potential to compromise clients' self-determination, regardless of whether clients and workers are of the same faith. There is reason to be concerned that workers can impose their interpretations, practices, and priorities on clients, whose defenses may be relaxed because of their trust of the practitioner.

In the case of a sectarian agency, it can be argued that clients may know what they are getting into, but even this assumption is questionable. Sometimes, referrals are made on rotating bases among cooperating agencies, for example, and clients may not be aware of the organization's sponsor or mission. Or clients may find their way to an agency as the result of a convenience or informal recommendation, and not know the agency's agenda. Perhaps the client has no options. Or the trust clients develop in their social workers may lead to the relaxing of defenses.

Other threats emanating from combining roles include compromising neutrality and nonjudgmental attitudes, sacrificing one or the other's values, (unconsciously) manipulating and coercing clients, and failing to inform or empower clients to pursue all their options (Popple & Leighninger, 1993, pp. 115–117).

The issue of church–state separation has been raised as an argument against inclusion, at least in public colleges and universities (Sheridan et al., 1994). In fact, the Establishment Clause of the First Amendment prohibits government from endorsing religious practice or any one religion. But Federal courts have interpreted the Establishment Clause rather loosely, especially at the postsecondary level, viewing college and graduate students as adults who are sophisticated enough to resist religious imposition by professors and administrators. Thus, official religious prayers are legal, albeit inappropriate, at public colleges, but unconstitutional at the public high school level.

The courts have been reluctant to restrict the religious activities of publicly subsidized sectarian agencies, such as the Salvation Army or Y's. Yet virtually every dollar that finances human service work, even in for-profit private agencies, has some inherent publicness, emanating from government subsidies, tax status, or other allowances. At a conceptual level, at least, practicing spirituality with clients does place the social worker in the position of promoting religion with some degree of public sponsorship, albeit indirect at times. Although this may pass judicial review, it still places social workers in the delicate position of violating the concept of separation, as inclusionists have found (Sheridan et al., 1994).

But what about religious colleges and universities with social work departments, sectarian social agencies, and clergy who also hold social work degrees? Social work's emphasis on client primacy directs me to suggest that social work and its imperatives must take precedence over religion's demands. Any compromise with social work values, regardless of the setting, can be harmful to clients who place their trust in social workers.

The social worker/clergy person should select one of the two roles and refer the client to another source for the second role. Social workers in religion-sponsored social agencies should work within their systems to ensure that they can provide their clients with services that are consistent with social work's commitment to self-determination, empowerment, and full awareness of all their options.

For B.S.W. and M.S.W. programs in church-sponsored institutions, I believe that limiting spiritualism to assessment, and keeping it separate from practice, combined with teaching students to keep roles separate and distinct, is sufficient. Faculty should model these values in their own practice; field placements should also implement this approach. Adult learners can separate the identity of their university's sponsor from the subject matter they study, but they will integrate what they see, hear, and experience into their definitions of practice.

What do students need to know? If they are going to be competent practitioners, they need to understand the role of spiritualism in assessment of social problems at micro, mezzo, and macro levels. If they want to be sectarian social workers, intervene in clients' spiritual systems, or maintain dual identities, social workers need close colleagues in one or the other field, so they can keep religious and social work practice separate, protecting the imperatives of both professions, as well as their clients.

REFERENCES

Berger, R., Federico, R., & McBreen, J. (1991). *Human behavior: A perspective for the helping professions* (3rd ed.). New York: Longman.

Canda, E. R. (1988). Spirituality, religious diversity, and social work practice. *Social Casework, 69,* 238–247.

Canda, E. R. (1989). Religious content in social work education: A comparative approach. *Journal of Social Work Education, 25*(1), 36–45.

Lum, D. (1992). *Social work practice & people of color: A process-stage approach* (2nd ed.). Pacific Grove, CA: Brooks/Cole.

Popple, P. R., & Leighninger, L. (1993). *Social work, social welfare and American society.* (2nd ed.). Boston: Allyn & Bacon.

Prest, L. A., & Keller, J. F. (1993). Spirituality and family therapy: Spiritual beliefs, myths and metaphors. *Journal of Marriage and Family Therapy, 19*(2), 137–148.

Rotz, E., Russell, C. S., & Wright, D. W. (1993). The therapist who is perceived as "spiritually correct": Strategies for avoiding collusion with the "spiritually one-up" spouse. *Journal of Marriage and Family Therapy, 19*(4), 369–375.

Sheridan, M. J., Wilmer, C. M., & Atcheson, L. (1994). Inclusion of content on religion and spirituality in the social work curriculum: A study of faculty views. *Journal of Social Work Education, 30*(3), 363–376.

Rejoinder to Dr. Weisman   Edward R. Canda

Professor Weisman accepts that "religion and spiritualism are important to many, perhaps most, people, and should be a component of assessment." He also recognizes that religion and spirituality are relevant to culturally competent practice and to forming a person-in-environment understanding of clients. To this point we agree. However, his misunderstanding of the nature of religion and spirituality leads him to fracture them off from the person in both education and practice.

The first major problem is that Professor Weisman does not define his key terms, so it is very difficult to know what he is talking about. For example, the vagueness and interchanging of the terms *spiritualism, religious,* and *spirituality* make it impossible to evaluate some of his assertions, such as that spiritualism can be seen and measured. The word *spiritualism* means a belief in communication with spirits, as by seances for contacting the souls of the dead. Certainly whether a person holds such a belief could be observed, but this does not seem to be what Professor Weisman means. Perhaps he refers to what social survey researchers often call religiosity, which means the degree of belief and participation in formal religious activities (such as church-going or prayer). This could be measured, but that would not tell much about the person's spirituality. Such confusion about terms, and resulting confusion in theory and research, is not uncommon in social work—a further indicator of the need to educate students about this in HBSE courses.

A second major error is Professor Weisman's assumption that it is possible and desirable to split off spirituality and religious issues and to divorce a spiritual or religious role from social work. As I explained, spirituality involves the search for meaning and moral relationship; further, it is the wholeness of personhood. It is not possible to dissect spirituality out without violating the integrity and humanity of the client, the worker, and the helping relationship. It may be easier to bracket religious issues, but there are practical problems. For example, Professor Weisman recommends that the worker learn how to assess if there is a religious issue and to refer the client to a religious professional. But to do this, the worker needs to have HBSE education about types and dynamics of religious support systems as well as spiritual aspects of life span development. How else to know to whom to refer, the potential benefits and risks of referral, or how to collaborate with diverse religious helpers ranging from Christian clergy to Buddhist monks and indigenous healers? Furthermore, we cannot rely on religious specialists to do social work–related assessment and treatment. DSM-IV diagnosis requires us to be able to assess and respond to spiritual and religious issues (a V-Code) and to distinguish between hallucinations and religiously meaningful visions. Social workers in hospice care, substance abuse treatment, and hospital work are required by accreditation standards to address spiritual and religious-issues. Furthermore, what if the client wants nothing to do with religion, but wants to deal with spiritual development issues in the context of the social work relationship? Do we just cast the client out the office door?

Professor Weisman rightly points out the dangers of incompetent or unethical social work practice regarding spiritual and religious issues. However, we cannot escape these dangers by maintaining ignorance or "passing the buck" to other professionals. Thorough education in knowledge, theory, and practice pertaining to spirituality and religion is the only safeguard, and the foundation must be laid in the core HBSE curriculum.

Should the HBSE Core Curriculum Include International Theories, Research, and Practice?

EDITOR'S NOTE: World societies are having increasingly close contact with and influence on one another. Events taking place this minute in the Middle East, Europe, Africa, Asia, and the Americas will likely have pronounced effects on us, if not immediately, then in a brief time. For social workers, this presents problems and opportunities: International stresses may have powerful effects on our clients, but also the social experiments in different lands may teach us to understand and to serve our clients more effectively.

Pranab Chatterjee, Ph.D., is a professor at the Mandel School of Applied Social Sciences, Case Western Reserve University. He is currently the editor of the *Journal of Applied Social Sciences.*

M. C. "Terry" Hokenstad, Ph.D., is the Ralph S. and Dorothy P. Schmitt Professor and Professor of International Health, Mandel School of Applied Social Sciences, Case Western Reserve University.

Paul R. Raffoul, Ph.D., is an associate professor, at the Graduate School of Social Work, University of Houston, where he teaches research and HBSE. His current position as Director, Office of Planning and Information Analysis, combines his interest in technology with both of his teaching areas and his new book, *Future Issues for Social Work Practice* (with C. Aaron McNeece).

Susan P. Robbins, D. S. W., is an associate professor at the Graduate School of Social Work, University of Houston, where she has chaired and coordinated the HBSE curricular area for the past thirteen years. She teaches courses in HBSE, substance abuse, and mediation. Her publications include a wide range of social work topics and she is currently co-authoring an HBSE textbook (with Pranab Chatterjee and Edward R. Canda), under contract with Allyn and Bacon.

YES

PRANAB CHATTERJEE
M. C. HOKENSTAD

Human behavior can only be understood from an international perspective. Without such a perspective, the study of human behavior becomes limited, provincial, and isolationistic. In this essay, we argue that the study of HBSE from the international perspective is the only perspective with contemporary academic and practice integrity.

Full appreciation and understanding of human behavior in the context of the social environment requires inclusion of an international and comparative dimension in course content. The globalization of contemporary society influences all aspects of human life. A world economy increasingly impacts on the social and psychological well-being of individuals in every country. Worldwide problems such as environmental pollution and global warming affect everyone's biological well-being. Mass migration of people coupled with increasingly unequal distribution of wealth among nations have a direct impact on the quality of life for most if not all Americans. Social work students who do not comprehend this global environment in which each person develops and functions operate at an enormous handicap in the practice domain.

Seminal thinkers in the social and behavioral sciences have long recognized that cross-national studies are an essential dimension for full understanding of social phenomena. For example, Emile Durkheim's classic study of suicide draws much of its data and resulting conclusions from a cross-national examination of suicide rates. Without evidence of dramatic differences in cross-national patterns of suicide, Durkheim's conceptual argument would have been much more limited, and the modern science of sociology that grew out of his research would have been weaker. Explanations of behavior continue to be illuminated by international comparisons.

Consideration of cross-national research also enriches the understanding of human behavior by enabling students to distinguish the general from the specific. Durkheim's (1951, p. 41) dictum that "only comparison affords explanation" argues that only a comparative mode of analysis can provide full understanding of how people function in different social environments. Comparative studies add a dimension to HBSE by differentiating between culturally specific and cross-culturally generalizable outcomes. The cross-national branch of comparative research helps students to identify culturally specific behaviors, for example, what certain groups take to be the "right" way for performing basic human tasks such as disciplining children or toilet training. Comparative research also helps students to gain an appreciation of similarities in behaviors across cultures and nations, such as how different cultures construct their views of the sacred.

Many components of the HBSE curriculum benefit from an international perspective. It is not possible in the space available to cover all aspects of the curriculum. Thus, we provide examples of the critical contribution of the international dimension to the student's understanding of human development, social stratification, and cultural diversity.

Human Development

The biological human is born and goes through a life cycle punctuated by transition rituals. These transitions rituals, such as graduation, initiation ceremonies, marriage, baby showers, divorce, retirement, and funerals, are culture specific. However, these rituals reflect how a given culture punctuates the stages of human development.

In a famous debate between anthropologist Bronislaw Malinowski and psychoanalyst Ernest Jones (Freud's biographer), the central issue was whether certain human developmental phases are universal (cf. Parsons, 1967). Malinowski argued that the concept of the Oedipal phase in human development is not universal and is perhaps a phenomenon found only in patriarchal Eurocentric societies. Jones responded that the phase was indeed universal, and Malinowski's example of a New Guinea culture without the Oedipal phase in child development was not thoroughly studied. Jones, on detailed examination of Malinowski's exemplar, argued that the Oedipal phase was indeed present in the New Guinea culture, with the mother's brother serving the same Oedipal role as the father did in Freud's Europe.

Whichever side of the debate one chooses to be on, it remains a good example of why the study of human behavior is incomplete when seen from the perspective of only one culture. Observations from one culture only create provincial, limited, and often inaccurate knowledge. On this subject, Berger and Luckman (1967, p. 137) observed:

> The age at which, in one society, it may be deemed proper for a child to be able to drive an automobile may, in another, be the age at which he is expected to have killed his first enemy. An upper class child may learn the "facts of life" at an age when a lower class child has mastered the rudiments of abortion technique. Or, an upper class child may experience his first stirring of patriotic emotion about the time that his lower class contemporary first experiences hatred of the police and everything they stand for.

In this passage, Berger and Luckman provide support for learning human behavior as it varies within national groups (variation of child behavior by social class at a certain developmental phase) as well as between national groups (variation of child behavior by macro-level cultures). The study of human behavior as it varies between national groups provides an international dimension to the education. Both dimensions are important for a comprehensive understanding of how the social environment shapes human development.

Social Stratification

The study of social stratification is common in all of the social sciences. Depending on the disciplinary origin, it becomes stratification and economic behavior, stratification and political behavior, stratification and temporal orientation, or stratification and interpersonal style (cf. Banfield, 1971).

At its essence, stratification refers to social hierarchies. It is usually part of what is known as "human diversity" in social work education. The study of class stratification and its impact on human behavior and the quality of life is less common than the study of racial/ethnic stratification in HBSE courses. Consequently, social work students often lack sufficient knowledge about class as one key determinant of human development. An international perspective can help to overcome this deficit.

Figure 13.1 depicts a model for analyzing both class and racial ethnic stratification in the United States. Here we see five major types of ethnic stratification: white (a mixture of ethnic groups from Europe); African American (a mixture of ethnic groups from Africa and other locations); Asian American (groups from various parts of Asia); Hispanic (Spanish-speaking groups of various origin); and Native American (American Indian groups of various origin). These five groups, shown at the top part of Figure 13.1, represent five vertical strata that are very important to the understanding of subcultural behavior patterns and cross-cultural discrimination and inequality in the United States. The bottom part of Figure 13.1 depicts social class as a second form of horizontal stratification that also must be given attention to understand both opportunity structures and human behavior.

		White American	African American	Asian American	Hispanic American	Native American
Social Class Groups in the United States	Upper Class					
	Middle Class					
	Working Class					
	Poor					

FIGURE 13.1
ETHNORACIAL GROUPS IN THE UNITED STATES

Viewing human diversity (social stratification) from the perspective of the matrix presented in Figure 13.1 has several advantages. First, it creates well-conceptualized and measurable independent variables and can be studied in relation to a series of dependent variables, such as life expectancy, utilization of social goods and services, health, and mental health conditions (Hollingshead & Redlich, 1958), and so on. Second, the argument put forward by some scholars that in industrial societies social class is a more dominant form of inequality than racial or ethnic stratification (Wilson, 1979) can be seriously studied. Finally, such a framework makes possible the cross-national study of inequality.

Cross-national comparisons add an additional dimension to the understanding of social stratification. Class stratification may play a more dominant role in the social environment in countries that have less ethnic diversity in their population. For example, in the Scandinavian countries, social class has historically been the dominant factor in politics and consequently social policy. This one key factor that has led to a very different social welfare system than that in the United States. Thus, comparative studies can illuminate the differential impact of ethnoracial and social class stratification on the social environment.

Cultural Diversity

The concept of social stratification helps us understand some problems around cultural diversity. It teaches us that diversity of cultures in the United States exists in a hierarchical and not in a parallel fashion. Hierarchical refers to the condition in which one culture is dominant, and all other cultures are tacitly labeled as inferior. Parallel refers to the existence in which no one culture is dominant. In America, white Anglo-Saxon Protestant culture is dominant, and all other cultures are not dominant. Social workers have been trying to teach respect for all cultures as if they are parallel, and bicultural socialization (cf. de Anda, 1984) is promoted as a way to promote parallel cultural diversity. However, the reality of hierarchy of cultures in America makes members of nondominant cultures live in a hostile environment (Chestang, 1972). Growing up in a minority culture thus calls for one of the three following styles of adaptation: *assimilation* or angloconformity; *biculturalism* or *pluralism;* and *separatism* (Farley, 1988).

Promoting pluralism in an American setting can happen more readily if one examines the cultural backgrounds in other nations. An international orientation that makes systematic comparisons of cultural and subcultural adaptations in their native habitat (rather than in their transplanted habitat), compares opportunity structures and the impact of various forms of stratification on these opportunity structures, and facilitates insights into how different cultural groups fit into American society. The relationship between majority and minority cultures in the United States can be better explained through an awareness of the cultural roots of different ethnic groups. This also will help the practitioner to better distinguish between culturally normal behavior and behavior produced by conflict with the dominant culture. Because immigration continually changes the ethnic mix of American society, the international roots of culture have current as well as historical significance.

These then are a few examples of how an international dimension adds depth and richness of knowledge to the HBSE curriculum. Cross-national examples and content provide increased understanding about how the social environment shapes human behavior. Cultural diversity and inequality can both be better understood in an international context. Finally, comparative research provides information and insights about human development beyond those available studies within one nation. These are all important reasons an international perspective is essential.

REFERENCES

Banfield, E. (1971). *The unheavenly city.* Boston: Little, Brown.

Berger, P., & Luckman, T. (1967). *The social construction of reality.* Garden City, NY: Doubleday Anchor.

Chestang, L. (1972). *Character development in a hostile environment.* Chicago: University of Chicago.

de Anda, D. (1984). Bicultural socialization: Factors affecting the minority experience. *Social Work, 29,*(2), 101–107.

Durkheim, E. (1951). *Suicide* (J. A. Spaulding & G. Simpson, Trans.). New York: Free Press.

Farley, J. (1988). *Majority-minority relations.* Englewood Cliffs, NJ: PrenticeHall.

Hollingshead, A. B. & Redlich, F. C. (1958). *Social class and mental illness: A community study.* New York: Wiley.

Parsons, A. (1967). Is the Oedipus complex universal? In R. Hung (Ed.), *Personalities and cultures* (pp. 252–299). Garden City, NY: Natural History Press.

Wilson, W. J. (1979). *The declining significance of race.* Chicago: University of Chicago.

Rejoinder to Drs. Chatterjee and Hokenstad

PAUL R. RAFFOUL

SUSAN P. ROBBINS

The term *international* is at the heart of the question being debated. Unfortunately, in their affirmative position, Drs. Chatterjee and Hokenstad use inconsistent terms and meanings throughout. In their attempt to argue for the inclusion of a broad international content base for HBSE courses, they continuously switch terminology and appear to loosely equate "international perspective" with "comparative dimension," "comparative studies," "cross-national studies," "cross-culturally generalizable outcomes," and "cultural diversity." Thus, their failure to clarify exactly what they mean by the term *international* further obfuscates the issue with their use of different (and not necessarily equivalent) words to mean similar things.

For example, in arguing for the inclusion of international content, they write that "the study of human behavior as it varies between national groups provides an international dimension to the education." This ignores the national diversity that exists within the United States and implies that one cannot gain an international perspective or comparative understanding of cultural and ethnic variation by studying the myriad nationalities and cultural groups that live within our boundaries. Given that most students will be practicing social work in the United States, we believe that it makes more sense to provide core curriculum content that will assist students in working with the diverse groups with which they will have the most contact.

Also problematic is their failure to address the issue of *core* curriculum content; thus, their response may easily be interpreted to include advanced HBSE courses and electives. If this is the case, then we are in agreement with their position that international content (once it is sufficiently defined) may well be a desirable addition. This, however, sidesteps the issue of core content to be required of *all* students.

Furthermore, their position that cross-national studies will, in and of themselves, provide us with an understanding and appreciation of national and cultural differences has been widely debated by postmodern theorists and scholars in the fields of feminist, ethnic, cultural, and gay and lesbian studies. There is an increasing awareness that claims of universal knowledge about human behavior are, at the very least, culturally and historically specific and are infused with the ideology and rhetoric of the group(s) in power. The logical–positivist paradigm that underlies, until recently, most of our research endeavors has been criticized for its distinctly masculine, Eurocentric, heterocentric, middle-class biases that portray differences as deficiencies. Cross-national studies that are embedded with these biases are not likely to further our understanding of people from other nations or cultures. To the contrary, they will most likely promote negative stereotypes that emphasize intergroup differences and ignore intragroup variability.

In underscoring the importance of an international perspective, the authors cite, as an example, the debate between Malinowski and Jones regarding the universality of Freud's Oedipal phase. It is interesting to note that this debate was about the existence or absence of a specific phase of development in a given culture rather than a broader attempt to question the validity of the theory itself or to provide a critique of its underlying premises! This is an important consideration because it makes little sense to debate the universality or cross-cultural application of a theory that cannot be verified or falsified.

We fully concur with the authors on the importance of adding explicit content on social class to the core HBSE curriculum. This is a critical dimension of human development that has received, at best, minimal coverage in most HBSE and practice textbooks. We do not agree, however, with the notion that an international perspective on class stratification is necessary to teach students about ethnoracial oppression in the United States. There is sufficient content related to our uniquely American history of class structure, race relations, genocide, prejudice, discrimination, and the oppression of marginalized groups (ethnoracial and others) to fill an entire foundation HBSE course. Although cross-national data might provide a good framework for international comparisons in the study of policy and politics, they are not likely to increase our understanding of the way in which social class impacts people in their day-to-day lives in American society. Furthermore, many of our disenfranchised immigrant groups come from largely agricultural societies, where social class, as we define it, has little meaning. Although stratifications of different types exist in all cultures, *class* divisions are uniquely a product of industrialization.

Finally, despite the seeming differences in our positions about the inclusion of "international" content in core HBSE curriculum, we note that it is the terminology rather than the requisite content that is at the core of our disagreement with the authors' position. As we have previously noted, the cross-fertilization of ideas that already exist within social work theory, research, and practice combined with the rapid "shrinking" of the global world because of technological advances that have made instant cross-national communication a reality make it clear that *all* information is quickly becoming *international* knowledge.

NO

PAUL RAFFOUL
SUSAN ROBBINS

What is meant by "international" content in the HBSE curriculum? Does that term refer to knowledge and theories from other nations, nationalities, cultures, or ethnic groups? Does it refer primarily to knowledge and theories developed in nonwestern societies? Or does it refer to a broader understanding of human behavior than that derived from theory and research based on mainstream American norms?

If it means the former, one could easily argue that even the most traditional HBSE courses have typically included international content as embodied in the works of Sigmund Freud, Carl Jung, Erik Erikson, Jean Piaget, and other theorists from a variety of western European countries. More current international theorists might also include those from the British school of object relations, such as Melanie Klein, or feminist psychoanalytic authors such as Alice Miller. If, however, international content reflects primarily nonwestern thought, would it include the work of Pavlov, Vygotsky, or other Soviet theorists? If so, this might be a problematic distinction because many of their ideas have also been incorporated into the American mainstream. Or, if it means the inclusion of a broader perspective, we can already find contemporary paradigms of human behavior in a recent text by Schriver (1995). Schriver's introductory HBSE text challenges our overreliance on traditional paradigms (positivistic, hierarchical, Eurocentric, and patriarchal) and contrasts these with alternative ones (interpretive, intuitive, diverse, feminist, and integrative) to arrive at a more holistic understanding of human behavior and the social environment. But even this text does not use the term *international* in describing this alternative world view.

There are no currently published HBSE texts that explicitly include "international" theories, research, or practice. This is not surprising, given the difficulty in definition. Unlike curricular areas such as social policy or social work practice, where international content is more clearly defined by models used in other countries, it is more difficult to determine the parameters of international content for inclusion in human behavior courses. Because the literal meaning of international HBSE content is vague and unclear, it is difficult, on the face of it, to support the position that such content be a core part of the human behavior curriculum.

Secondly, we must ask ourselves what we are trying to accomplish with the inclusion of international content. Is it an expanded knowledge about other nations, cultures, or ethnic groups? Or are we in search of overarching theories developed elsewhere? Are we looking for commonalities among people and their environments? Or are we looking for differences? It seems that we are putting the cart before the horse if we are not clear about what we hope to gain.

Some might argue that international content is necessary to expand our knowledge of cultural diversity in a shrinking world. Clearly, theories and research that generate knowledge about racial, ethnic, and cultural diversity are essential content for HBSE courses. Fortunately, the United States provides enough cultural and ethnic diversity within its geographic borders that we need not look elsewhere to find it. The historically popular conception of the United States as a "melting pot" has been replaced by the reality of a "potpourri," as successive waves of immigration have shaped our country into a myriad of cultures (Ramakrishnan & Balgopal, 1995). Surely one would not suggest that we ignore the cultural diversity around us in favor of that found in other nations.

Despite repeated attempts to force assimilation into mainstream American culture, most immigrant groups, as well as Native Americans, have maintained their unique identity and traditions (Howard & Scott, 1981; Ramakrishnan & Balgopal, 1995). The changing demographics and increasing diversity within the United States have led social scientists to the recognition that assimilation is only one of several modes of cultural adaptation (Jenkins, 1988). Other modes identified include marginal adaptation, traditional adaptation, acculturation, and bicultural socialization (de Anda, 1984; Galan & Robbins; Ho, 1987; Huang, 1995). If the intent in adding international content is to gain a broader and more relevant understanding of the cultural diversity that typifies our clients, we would be better served to include content about racism, ethnic identity, cultural personality, and patterns of acculturation that will aid us in the accurate assessment of racial, ethnic, and cultural minorities in the United States. To avoid stereotyping based on assimilation ideology, we also need to develop a transactional and multidimensional understanding of the way in which minorities adapt to the dominant culture (Galan & Robbins; Green, 1982).

Little of this content is featured prominently in either HBSE texts or our major professional journals (McMahon & Allen-Meares, 1992; Schlesinger & Devore, 1995). This is not surprising, because the profession has responded to the call for knowledge about cultural diversity by adopting an "add and stir" approach. Under the pressure to comply with CSWE accreditation guidelines, we have added new content about African Americans, Hispanics, Asians, and Native Americans to already existing curricula. The result, as portrayed in contemporary social work literature, has been simplistic and stereotyped views of minorities (McMahon & Allen-Meares, 1992). Simply adding international content to core HBSE curriculum will not alter these stereotypes; more likely, it will exacerbate them. We would caution those who chose to include theories and methods developed in other countries or cultures that they also need to recognize the reality of immigrants and native people who not only filter their experience through their culture of origin, but through the American context as well (Norton, 1978; 1983). To do otherwise will lead to continued stereotyping.

Thirdly, we must ask what we can realistically include, given the voluminous content that is necessary for a holistic view of people and their environments. Perhaps more than any other curricular area, core content in HBSE calls for an extremely broad base of knowledge. Brooks (1986, p. 18) observed that: "If you are expected to be an expert on the biological, psychological, social, economic, and cultural dimensions of behavior... you are undoubtedly a teacher of Human Behavior and the Social Environment." The task of teaching such diverse content is a formidable one at best. It requires mastery of a substantial and quickly expanding knowledge base derived from multidisciplinary theory and research. It also requires the ability to address linkages between the person and the environment to make this content relevant for social work practice.

In the last decade, several studies have found that the HBSE curriculum continues to be dominated by an overriding psychological, life-span orientation along with a systems or ecological perspective (see Brooks, 1987; Fiene, 1987). These findings clearly suggest that we must expand our knowledge base if we are to foster a fuller understanding of the spiritual, biological, social, cultural, economic, and political dimensions of behavior. To achieve this objective, *it seems more prudent to argue for explicit inclusion of a multidisciplinary knowledge base rather than an international one.* These, of course, are not necessarily mutually exclusive, as knowledge from the fields of cross-cultural psychiatry, cross-cultural psychology, and cultural anthropology, all of which are based on international research, is essential to our understanding of cultural variation.

Students enter social work from an ever-widening background of undergraduate experience. Preparing them to understand human behavior in its broadest sense is sufficiently demanding of the HBSE curriculum so as to preclude any meaningful coverage of the international scene. The new CSWE Curriculum Policy Statement now emphasizes the need to address issues of oppression, poverty, and religious and spiritual diversity, which content has historically received little attention in most HBSE texts and courses. Quite simply, it is impossible to cover everything, and priorities for core curriculum have to be based on what students MUST be taught rather than what we might PREFER. We are faced, as always, with a question of choice: breadth versus depth in content coverage. It is a decision based on values, both personal and professional, as to what has to be taught in the foundation course(s) versus what one might like to teach in an unrestricted and unlimited set of courses. It is not realistic, however, to think that we can successfully do it all.

Finally, the world in the 1990s is becoming a very small place, with technology helping us to communicate through the Internet with almost anyone, anywhere, at anytime. International trade, multinational corporations, and shared technology, for example, are all contributing to the blurring of what were once national boundaries. In a very real sense, all information is quickly becoming "international." Or, to state this in the form of a question: When does national information known to us become international information known to others? The question asked in this chapter would seem to be better phrased as one of cultural diversity rather than that of geographic boundaries.

Conclusion

Content on human diversity is a critical component of the HBSE curriculum. This content should be infused throughout both foundation and advanced HBSE courses. New CSWE guidelines that have expanded the requisite content in HBSE courses should serve to make students more sensitive to issues involving diversity. Likewise, cultural sensitivity is an integral component of social work practice; this is especially true given the client populations that social workers are called upon to work with. Excluding or minimizing content on cultural diversity would be unconscionable and inappropriate for any HBSE course, whether in foundation or advanced curricula. In addition, we must be especially cautious about the use of simplistic stereotypes in presenting content about different races, ethnicities, and cultures. Another important goal is to teach students to treat all clients in a nonjudgmental manner through a broad understanding of normative behavior within both the cultural and societal contexts. Curriculum should be designed to meet these goals.

Human behavior theory development in the United States has always relied on the cross-fertilization of ideas among theory, research, and practice from an international arena. It is likely that this not only will continue but also will be enhanced by modern telecommunication. However, simply labeling specific content as "international" and thereby deciding, on that merit alone, as to its inclusion, does not address the larger question of its utility. We cannot assume that all international content is equally relevant to the HBSE curriculum because it is assigned an international label. Nor can we allow ourselves to assume that augmentation of core curriculum can be undertaken arbitrarily with respect to the national origin of the content, in exclusion of an evaluation of the individual merits of that content. As already discussed, the "add and stir" approach to HBSE curriculum has not served us well. Given the overriding need for a multidisciplinary knowledge base in HBSE, we do not believe that it is advisable to explicitly incorporate "international" content into an already strained HBSE curriculum.

REFERENCES

Brooks, W. K. (1986, winter). Human behavior/social environment: Past and present, future or folly? *Journal of Social Work Education, 1,* 18–23.

de Anda, D. (1984). Bicultural socialization: Factors affecting the minority experience. *Social Work, 29,*(2), 101–107.

Fiene, J. I. (1987). *Evolution of human behavior and social environment curriculum: 1950 to present.* Paper presented at the Annual Meeting of the Council on Social Work Education, St. Louis, MO.

Galan, F. J., and Robbins, S. P. Assimilation, acculturation and bicultural socialization. (unpublished manuscript).

Green, J. W. (1982). *Cultural awareness in the human services.* Englewood Cliffs, NJ: Prentice Hall.

Ho, M. K. (1987). *Family therapy with ethnic minorities.* Newbury Park, CA: Sage.

Howard, A., & Scott, R. A. (1981). The study of minority groups in complex societies. In R. H. Munroe, R. L. Munroe, & B. B. Whiting (Eds.), *Handbook of cross-cultural development* (pp. 113–149). New York: Garland Press.

Huang, K. (1995). Tripartite cultural personality and ethclass assessment. *Journal of Sociology and Social Welfare, 22,*(1), 99–120.

Jenkins, D. (1988). Ethnicity: Theory base and practice link. In Jacobs & Bowles (Eds.), *Ethnicity and race: Critical concepts in social work* (pp. 140–151). Washington, DC: NASW.

McMahon, A., & Allen-Meares, P. (1992). Is social work racist? A content analysis of recent literature. *Social Work, 37*(6), 533–539.

Norton, D. (1978). *The dual perspective: Inclusion of ethnic minority content in the social work curriculum.* Washington, DC: Council on Social Work Education.

Norton, D. (1983). Diversity, early socialization, and temporal development: The dual perspective revisited. *Social Work, 38*(1), 82–90.

Ramakrishnan, K. R., & Balgopal, P. R. (1995). Role of social institutions in a multicultural society. *Journal of Sociology and Social Welfare, 22*(1), 11–28.

Schlesinger, E. G., & Devore, W. (1995). Ethnic sensitive social work practice: The state of the art. *Journal of Sociology and Social Welfare, 22*(1), 29–58.

Schriver, J. (1995). *Human behavior and the social environment: Shifting paradigms in essential knowledge for social work practice.* Boston, MA: Allyn & Bacon.

Rejoinder to Drs. Raffoul and Robbins

PRANAB CHATTERJEE
M. C. "TERRY" HOKENSTAD

At one time, there was room for only psychological theory—primarily that of Sigmund Freud and occasionally that of Otto Rank—in the human behavior courses of the social work curriculum. In the 1960s, content illuminating the importance of culture on human behavior had to be wedged into what is now the HBSE curriculum. Arguments against including cultural content as a major component in HBSE courses centered on the lack of space for additional bodies of knowledge in a crowded curriculum.

Now similar arguments are made about incorporating international content into the social work curriculum. Raffoul and Robbins rightly point out that it is a major challenge to cover expanding knowledge from many disciplines, which contributes to social work students' understanding of human behavior in the social environment. However, curriculum building should never simply involve adding additional content to already crowded courses. Rather, it must make selective and creative use of added dimensions of knowledge to increase understanding of the interaction between the environment and the individual. As we have shown, an international dimension does exactly that by differentiating between culturally specific and cross-culturally generalizable behaviors, by providing comparisons between class-based and culturally based stratification systems and by offering a fuller explanation of how people function in differing social environments.

Raffoul and Robbins recognize that a multidisciplinary knowledge base and an international knowledge base "are not necessarily mutually exclusive" and that knowledge from disciplinary fields based on international research "is essential to our understanding of cultural variation." These points support our basic position that human diversity cannot be fully understood without knowledge of the cultural roots of different ethnoracial groups. Unfortunately they still argue for "inclusion of a multidisciplinary knowledge base rather than an international one." In fact, these are mutually reinforcing rather than mutually exclusive dimensions of knowledge development, and both are needed to shed full light on interaction between the environmental context and human behavior (Easton, 1991). The pitfalls of specialization are in fact exacerbated by national myopia in knowledge building and dissemination.

Our fellow debaters conclude by stating that "we cannot assume that all international content is equally relevant to the HBSE curriculum because it is assigned an international label." We have no quarrel with that position. Of course, there must be guidelines for determining what content should be included in the curriculum. Relevancy to social work practice is an essential criterion for any theory or body of research to become part of required social work knowledge. International knowledge, like other bodies of knowledge, should be judged by its contribution to and illumination of the context for practice.

Our basic position can be summarized as follows: that there are two interrelated foundations of human behavior. One of them is more or less universal, whereas the other is guided by local cultures. The universal foundation is the realm of human biological functioning, whereas the culturally guided foundation is human social functioning. The understanding of social functioning, in turn, can be divided into either culturally appropriate or deviant. In the United States, despite efforts to promote cultural pluralism, almost all non–Anglo-Saxon cultures are accorded a deviant status. Members from non–Anglo-Saxon cultures are made to feel that their culture is something of which they should be ashamed. When a whole culture assumes a deviant status, it is not possible to understand the behavior of its members in the same way as it would be when that culture operates as a dominant culture. Internationalizing studies of human behavior permits the study of culture where it is dominant and where it is marginal or deviant.

We argue that to fully understand human behavior in a social context, it is necessary to use knowledge derived from cross-national studies. Such comparisons illuminate differential environmental impact on behavior. They help to explain the effect of both culture and cultural conflict. Also, a social worker cannot fully understand the social context without some appreciation of the global environment. Human behavior is both directly and indirectly influenced by the globalization of the economy, the polity, and the social structure. Thus, international content is both relevant and necessary in the HBSE curriculum.

REFERENCES

Easton, D. (1991). The division, integration, and transfer of knowledge. In D. Easton & C. S. Schelling (Ed.), Divided knowledge: *Across disciplines, across cultures* (pp. 7–36). Newbury Park, CA: Sage.

Should HBSE Continue to Be Taught as a Separate Course?

EDITOR'S NOTE: HBSE is one of the mandated content areas established by the Council on Social Work Education. Yet, it is only by convention that micro and macro emphasis of this topic are taught in separate classes rather than being blended throughout the social work curriculum. Is this the best way to teach human behavior?

Elizabeth D. Hutchison, Ph.D., an associate professor at the School of Social Work, Virginia Commonwealth University, teaches HBSE at the baccalaureate, master's, and doctoral levels. Her primary research interests include issues of family and child welfare. Dr. Hutchison's new book, *Human Behavior in the Changing Environment: A Multidimensional Approach for Social Work* (Pine Forge Press, with J. Forte), will be released in 1996.

Sophie Freud, MSW, Ph.D., professor emerita, School of Social Work, Simmons College, is currently applying postmodern ideas to social work theory and practice. She is widely published and has given national and international workshops in this area.

YES

ELIZABETH D. HUTCHISON

For several decades, social work education has used an organizational framework that divides the knowledge base for education of social workers into five components, presented in alphabetical order: field, human behavior and the social environment (HBSE), policy, research, and social work practice. This framework for curricular design, like any other, has both strengths and limitations, and it is long overdue for a rigorous evaluation. I applaud the Council on Social Work Education's (CSWE) Commission on Educational Policy for initiating the Milennium Project to take stock of societal transformations that provide the changing context of social work practice and to "develop new conceptualizations of and approaches to social work education and practice" (Council on Social Work Education, 1995, p. 3). Current attempts to dismantle the welfare state accentuate the urgency of this Project.

As social work curricula are currently organized, there is a need to have a distinct HBSE subject matter. The purpose of this subject matter should be to assist students to scan widely for, and think critically about, the factors involved in contemporary problems of living, to form the basis for creative and discriminating strategies for prevention and amelioration. Whatever innovations are developed for the organizational framework for social work education, it seems likely that we will continue to need a distinct HBSE subject matter to serve this purpose.

A few years ago, as a minor piece of my dissertation research, I asked child welfare workers whether current child protective services are overly intrusive, underprotective, or strike the proper balance between child protection and family privacy. One thoughtful social worker responded, "We tend to provide the same services to both high- and low-risk cases. Therefore, we are underprotective to the high-risk family and overly intrusive to the low-risk cases" (Hutchison, 1988, p. 119). This observation, that social service delivery is often standardized rather than individualized, is consistent with analyses presented in recent years by both Carol Meyer (1987, 1993) and Eileen Gambrill (1990). I suggest that the most potent corrective to the narrowly focused, standardized intervention is coursework that builds a base of knowledge for understanding the multidimensionality of human behavior and the complex biopsychosocial interactions involved in contemporary problems of living (Hutchison & Forte, forthcoming).

Meyer (1987, 1993) suggests that social work curricula are long on processes of intervention and short on content about populations and problems, marked by an emphasis on "doing" rather than on "thinking about what the matter is" (1993, p. 6). She suggests that our narrow, routinized interventions become increasingly inadequate in the face of complex social problems that are developed and maintained by a "confluence of economic, political, sociocultural, and psychological factors" (1993, p. 6). I would suggest that she should have also included biological factors. Meyer (1993, pp. 6–7) identifies three forces that are driving social workers to think narrowly about practice situations. First, social workers are responding to the complexity of social problems that appear increasingly insoluble by maintaining a narrow focus on private and internal aspects of client situations. This narrow focus, which neglects the impact of environment, avoids many frustrations and contributes to a greater, even if false, sense of mastery. Second, the explosion of theories and empirical data about human behavior presents a formidable knowledge base for social workers. One solution is to retreat to one way of thinking about human behavior with the rationale that it is better to know one way of thinking well than to get overwhelmed by a proliferation of ways of thinking about a situation. Third, the increased demand for accountability and evaluation has contributed to a search for single interventions with quantifiable outcomes, a situation that is incompatible with the multilevel interventions needed for complex problems.

Gambrill (1990) also notes the tendency for contemporary social workers to think narrowly about practice situations, but she cites personal biases of the social worker as the primary factor interfering with interventions individualized to the client's situation. Gambrill provides convincing evidence that social workers often act on first impressions, based on personal biases, while claiming to individualize to the unique situation of the client. She suggests that drawing on general knowledge from a variety of sources will encourage social workers to pay more attention to the multiple dimensions of behavior, particularly environmental dimensions, and assist them to overcome personal biases.

I would agree with Meyer (1987) that social work is at risk of becoming an irrelevant profession, one doomed to ineffectiveness as well as alienation from its institutional roots, if we continue with the current focus on "doing" within a narrow psychotherapeutic band. We can regain our relevance only if social work education becomes reinvigorated with more emphasis on "thinking about what the matter is," thereby providing better balance in the curriculum between thinking and doing. Social workers are people of action, but social work action must be based on the purposes and values of the profession as well as on knowledge of the people, situations, and problems that are encountered, and not simply on the techniques that have been mastered. An overemphasis on "doing" leads us to "understand" client situations from the perspective of what we know how to do rather than to base our actions on our understanding of client situations. This directs us to the "same solution for all situations" described by the child welfare worker earlier. It also inhibits the serious questioning of the effectiveness of existing methods for the problems at hand.

It could be argued that maintaining a distinct HBSE subject matter contributes to the false dichotomy that many social workers create, a dichotomy between knowing and doing. Indeed, it has been my observation that many social work students think of the HBSE courses as "academic" courses and practice courses as the "real" social work courses. This idea is often carried forward into professional life, and knowledge about methodology is the only respected knowledge. Thinking about human situations becomes alienated from doing. This is a compelling argument, one that would seem to call for the integration of course content on knowing (HBSE) and doing (practice).

Saleebey (1989) has noted that this dilemma is not a minor problem for social work education or for the social work profession. The answer does not lie, however, at least not at the current juncture, in the total curricular integration of content about HBSE with practice methods. There is a need for better integration of all of the existing curricular components, but there is also a need for distinct HBSE content. What social workers need to know about human behavior should not be defined by existing methods, and I am using "methods" here in the comprehensive sense to include methods of direct practice, methods of policy practice, and research methods.

What social workers need to know and do should flow from the mission of the profession. Unfortunately, there is deep division among social workers about the professional mission (Reamer, 1993). Meyer (1987) reminds us, however, that social work is more than a profession; it is also a societal institution. Although the social work profession has struggled with recurrent issues about its societal mission, history suggests that as an institution social work is intended to be a communal force to correct for the injustices that occur with the exaggerated individualism of a modern, industrial, capitalist state (Wakefield, 1988). Therefore, when social workers "think about what the matter is," they should begin by attempting to understand the structures and cultures of contemporary society and the differential impact of these on various societal groups. They also should attempt to understand the nature of human interactions at multiple levels and the ways in which these interactions privilege some groups and not others. Finally, they should attempt to understand the ways in which human biological processes in constant interaction with the multidimensional environment influence critical aspects of human behavior. With some understanding of these issues, they can begin to think about possible points of intervention to strengthen the life chances for vulnerable groups. Thinking social workers recognize that this information serves only as general context for understanding the unique situations of the people they encounter, but they recognize that no intervention can be effective if the social context, and the meanings clients make of it, are ignored.

Societal structures and cultures are continually changing; in addition, we live in an era when the theoretical and empirical knowledge about human behavior is rapidly expanding. Social workers need to stay updated about changes in societal structures and cultures and their impacts on various societal groups. They also need to keep abreast of knowledge advances that add to, correct, or challenge our understanding of contemporary problems of living. It is the incorporation of new knowledge about human behavior that should drive innovations in methodology, and not existing methods that should drive the choice of content on human behavior. The HBSE curriculum should assist students to see the practice implications of theory and research, but it also should present theories and research about human behavior that are divergent, as well as new knowledge for which the practice implications are not yet clear. Exposure to divergent theory and research can help students understand that more than one method may reach the same outcome, therefore providing them with backup strategies when a favored strategy fails, suggesting multiple interventions to increase the likelihood of success, and, most importantly, assisting them to respect the client's ideas about what will work. New knowledge may challenge existing methods or open possibilities that are not yet well articulated. The content for the HBSE curriculum should not have to meet the criterion of having direct and clear methodological application. It needs, instead, to meet the criterion of being particularly useful in "thinking about what the matter is."

Social work, as well as the social sciences, seems to be beginning to transcend the positivist–antipositivist debate to recognize that both traditional positivistic theories and research as well as the newer postpositivist approaches are useful in understanding human behavior. The well-conceived HBSE curriculum will assist students to understand both the possibilities and the limitations of multiple ways of knowing about human behavior. Therefore, students will come to recognize that objectivist theories and research cannot predict individual human behavior in anything more than a probabilistic manner, but they will appreciate the way in which these theories and research direct their attention to possibilities they might not have considered otherwise. By studying subjectivist theories that understand reality as either personally or socially constructed, students will come to appreciate the importance of the meaning that clients make of their situations. By studying interpersonal theories, students will come to recognize that their visceral, emotional, and cognitive reactions to clients are important data about themselves, their clients, and situations. By studying critical theories, students will learn to recognize whose voices are not being heard in traditional theories and research. By juxtaposing personal stories with social and behavioral science theories and research, students come to recognize the need to carefully evaluate client situations against existing theories and research. In this way, the HBSE curriculum is helping students learn to integrate behavioral science evidence that is multifaceted, and oftentimes divergent, with the details of a client's story, which is oftentimes ambiguous.

I suggested earlier that there is a need for better integration across existing curricular components, as well as for a distinct HBSE content. Efforts to assist students to minimize the "estrangement of knowing and doing" (Saleebey, 1989) and to value both knowing and doing need to occur in all curricular areas. The HBSE curriculum can contribute to these efforts by assisting students to recognize both the possibilities and limitations of existing theories and research for helping social workers to "think about what the matter is," by assisting students to move from behavioral propositions to principles of action, and by presenting knowledge that reflects the "confluence of economic, political, sociocultural,...psychological" (Meyer, 1993. p. 6), and biological factors involved in human behavior. To prevent students from retreating into a narrow focus on private and internal aspects of client situations, direct practice teachers will need to assist students to cope with the feelings of helplessness that are generated when they acknowledge structural injustices as well as to value the provision of concrete and linking services. The research curriculum needs to be rethought. We certainly need practice effectiveness research and program evaluation research, but the methods of research should reflect the complexities of the situations encountered within the context of the mission of the profession. We are approaching a situation in which existing research methods drive both choice of situations we will tackle and practice methods we will use. We are discouraged from multilevel interventions or from tackling tough problems because our repertoire of research techniques cannot track these attempts as well as single interventions with easily measured outcomes. Students are discouraged from thinking multidimensionally when such thinking gets them in trouble in the research class. We should also question if we have sufficient emphasis in our research curricula on nonapplied research, basic research about human behavior. The current downplaying of such research reinforces the idea that social workers are doers but not thinkers. Students in my HBSE courses have sometimes interpreted this to imply that we can count on the social and behavioral sciences to do all of our thinking for us, and to wonder if that means these other academic disciplines and professions take our mission as seriously as we do.

Understanding human behavior in the social environment for the purposes of promoting social justice is not a small job. It is, however, the assignment that the social work profession has accepted historically. It was never a small assignment, and it could easily be argued that the demands have steadily increased since the Progressive Era. Some scholars have tentatively proposed that such a knowledge base may be beyond the profession's grasp (Meyer, 1987), but we clearly cannot continue to accept a societal mission for which the knowledge base is beyond either our grasp or our motivation. I suggest that the profession should put its best heads to deliberating the question of mission and the implications of mission for the required human behavior knowledge base.

When I was a student in an M. S. W. program in the late 1960s, the prototypes of our current HBSE courses were taught largely by social and behavioral scientists, not by social work practitioner–scholars. That practice was heavily curtailed as doctoral programs in social work expanded during the 1970s. I would not suggest that we return to such an approach, because no existing academic discipline is sufficiently broad to capture the multiple dimensions of human behavior that social workers need to understand. It may well be, however, that schools of social work could benefit by collaborating more with colleagues in other disciplines for development of the HBSE curriculum. Social work was interdisciplinary long before interdisciplinary approaches became the vogue in higher education. Unfortunately, by the time interdisciplinary efforts became highly valued, we had almost abandoned such an approach to pursue the monetary and reputational rewards that we perceived to be attached to the psychotherapeutic role narrowly defined. The latest version of that side trip has soundly disconnected us from our institutional roots and robbed vulnerable populations of our strong presence in perilous times. A stronger HBSE curriculum is one strategy for reinvigorating the social work profession and preparing it to face the challenges of the twenty-first century.

REFERENCES

Council on Social Work Education. (1995). Commission on educational policy outlines millennium project work plan. *Social Work Education Reporter, 43*(1), 3–6.

Gambrill, E. (1990). *Critical thinking in clinical practice.* San Francisco, CA: Jossey-Bass.

Hutchison, E., & Forte, J. (forthcoming). Human behavior in a changing context: A multidimensional perspective for social work practice. Thousand Oaks, CA: Pine Forge Press.

Hutchison, E. (1988). *Factors which influence child protective screening decisions.* Unpublished doctoral dissertation, State University of New York at Albany.

Meyer, C. (1987). Content and process in social work practice: A new look at old issues. *Social Work, 32,* 401–404.

Meyer, C. (1993). *Assessment in social work practice.* New York: Columbia University Press.

Reamer, F. (1993). *The philosophical foundations of social work.* New York: Columbia University.

Saleebey, D. (1989). The estrangement of knowing and doing: Professions in crisis. *Social Casework: The Journal of Contemporary Social Work, 70,* 556–563.

Wakefield, J. (1988). Psychotherapy, distributive justice, and social work. Parts 1 & 2. *Social Service Review, 62*(2–3), 187–210, 353–382.

Rejoinder to Dr. Hutchison   SOPHIE FREUD

Dr. Hutchison makes this an easy debate for me, because we both agree that our profession needs to be devoted to promoting social justice, have an interdisciplinary approach, and that it needs to be redirected toward outer space and context, rather than emphasize a narrow therapeutic inner space perspective. In many ways my debater even agrees with me on the means toward these goals.

Dr. Hutchison joins me, for example, in the thought that our current "framework for curricular design . . . is long overdue for a rigorous evaluation." My proposal precisely addresses this very need. My suggested teaching approach also addresses my debater's concern regarding "standardized interventions." Indeed, the problem-centered approach proceeds from the individual situation with its unique complexity to seeking answers in broader theoretical frameworks, assuring the individualized approach Dr. Hutchison advocates. Such teaching is in contrast to the traditional Procrustean methods, where each case has to somehow fit into the general theories students might have been exposed to.

Again, Dr. Hutchison and I both want to emphasize the socio-economic-political context in which each client system is embedded. Students are therefore directed, in my proposal, to the policy, institutional, financial, and cultural implications of a situation before focusing on the inner psyche of their clients. Dr. Hutchison herself concedes that the dichotomy between "knowing and doing," (i.e., theory and practice) is dysfunctional and finds "a need for... integration of all the existing curricular components."

A problem-centered approach does not interfere with seeking out tried and perhaps true as well as emerging theories, and I specifically suggest that students, working in small groups, will come up with several avenues on how to help the client system, and that these avenues may lead the case into different directions. I hope that students will learn to recognize in this self-directed learning process that there is divergent thinking in the field, that certain interventions might be more suitable than others for a particular situation, or even that alternate interventions could be considered for the same situation. I emphasize that there is no attempt to eliminate or cut short understanding about the intricacies of human behavior, but simply a new method of acquiring that knowledge. Like my debater, I also believe that social work should turn to several different disciplines, from anthropology to biology and economics, to understand a situation. I knew Dr. Hutchison would applaud the effort to expose students to multiple possibilities rather than the one and only truth, because she would like students to learn to recognize "both the limitations and possibilities of existing theories."

I, in turn, join my debater most heartily and even go further than she does, when she calls for a revision of our traditional research approach. Research necessarily undergirds explicitly or implicitly much of the rest of the curriculum, and my proposal emphasizes that research cannot remain in its own pristine domain. It think it will be useful to assign research articles with contradictory outcomes, demonstrating to students that not only theories, but even research findings, can be influenced by the values and bias of the researcher in terms of questions posed, type of methodology used, sampling procedures, and the like. It is of course to be hoped that outcome research might give students a guidance as to what approach to adopt, but students might also have to learn that research findings can substitute neither for ethical values nor for the uncertainty of life decisions.

Dr. Hutchison mentions repeatedly that the essence of social work practice is to "think about what the matter is." She and I are, once again, on the same wavelength. Problem-focused teaching trains students to follow this very same principle.

NO

SOPHIE FREUD

During the twenty-five years that I was in charge of designing and teaching the basic year-long HBSE course, I constantly had to negotiate domain disputes with our practice teachers. They accused me, perhaps rightly so, of overstepping the boundaries between theory and practice. I tended to be attentive to my colleagues' complaints, but I compromised as little as possible in this particular matter. Reasons for my intransigence were both the students' appreciation of the *combination* of theory and practice that we evolved, and my own pedagogic convictions regarding *professional* training. At the same time, my colleagues, who taught social policy in this clinical school, constantly and not always successfully wrestled with the task of showing the relevance of their material to these future social work clinicians. When our school started a doctoral program, some ten years ago, I had hoped that we would transcend the traditional, yet, in my eyes, dysfunctional, sequence boundaries, but tradition prevailed and domain disputes continue.

Let me thus take this space to suggest a first-year curriculum organization for a school that trains clinical social workers that would radically abolish sequence boundaries, yet keep much of the important material that is taught during the first introductory year. Indeed, it is my contention that the problem is not with content, but with the segmental out-of-context way in which teaching proceeds. My approach not only will help students to integrate theory, practice, policy, and research, showing the relevance of each to actual client situations, but also would be extremely effective in integrating academic and field work, something we have done poorly since time immemorial.

I am proposing that the first year of social work school curriculum be taught by the case method. The use of *canned cases* has long been a favorite method of teaching in the practice course, but I propose to expand and modify this approach to integrate the whole curriculum. Such a new approach shifts emphasis from teaching to learning, with teachers acting mainly as guides, facilitators, and consultants, whereas students take a great deal more responsibility for their own learning than in a more traditional curriculum. I use the rest of this discussion to outline some of the steps that need to be taken to achieve such a goal.

I foresee that a faculty committee, carefully mindful of several criteria, will select the approximately four or five cases to be discussed during the year. These cases will need to present a variety of problems occurring to people from different cultures, racial backgrounds, and ethnicities, at different stages of the life cycle, needing interventions at different levels—individual, family, advocacy, with regard to social systems—that can be done from different theoretical perspectives and in different timeframes.

It is hoped that a combination of cases could be found that would cover most traditional aspects of the social work curriculum. It might be convenient to take the life cycle as an organizing frame. I could imagine including a pregnant mother, a marital conflict case, a situation dealing with divorce, custody, and merged families, an AIDS situation, and perhaps end with an elderly couple in which the man suffers from Alzheimer's disease, although these are of course only arbitrary suggestions. I am also not clear whether four to five cases is too ambitious a goal; thus both the number of cases and the kind of cases will go through a trial-and-error phase. Ideally, each case should lean on a real and frequent intake situation, albeit modified for teaching purposes. It is also possible that existing movies could introduce a problem situation, or videos could be constructed in which a client (or clients) tell of a presenting problem.

Let us take the case of an impoverished, pregnant fifteen-year-old teenager at risk, and let her be a Puerto Rican girl who had come to the city at age ten. She was perhaps referred by the hospital to the social work department, because she is viewed as "at risk." The case could go from the fourth month of pregnancy through the first six months of the infant's life. The class receives the referral and is asked what they would best need to know *before* they meet this young woman.

The instructor would keep track of the list generated by students and perhaps add to it through expanding questions. Apart from the task of learning what goes into a basic assessment, there will be many questions pertaining to this particular case. For example, *who* is to be seen, the girl alone, with her family, including or not including her potential boyfriend? Who might be an optimal worker for such a case? Knowledge will be needed about her ethnic background, including the differences between the culture of her homeland and the immigration culture into which she moved. The case introduces several developmental levels, such as the physical, mental, and emotional issues and needs of an adolescent, a pregnant woman, and an infant. Knowledge about the mother–child unit and attachment theory will be very important. What are the girl's options while pregnant, and what will be her options if she chooses to become a mother? The instructor will assign small groups of students to every question generated in this process, to be reported on in the next few sessions before the actual work with the case is continued. It is thus expected that task forces will be formed around issues of adolescence, adolescent pregnancy as similar or different from later pregnancies, options of abortion, adoption, teenage marriage, integrating baby into family and going to school, living with baby on Aid to Families with Dependent Children (AFDC), infant development and developmental needs, attachment theories, Puerto Rican culture, Puerto Rican family lifestyles, the effects of poverty, the effects of migration, housing policies, maternal and infant health maintenance, to mention only the most obvious ones. Because all of this is anticipated, a syllabus will guide the various task forces so as to not overwhelm the students. Any first case will generate the most questions, and later cases can then build on knowledge acquired earlier. For example, health policies will come up around the teenager's pregnancy and potentially well-baby care, and reviewed and expanded if an acquired immune deficiency syndrome (AIDS) case and an Alzheimer's case were to be chosen. A first case will thus need to be especially carefully chosen and could even be developed for as long as three months of the full academic year.

Students might be given several weeks for only library research, during which time no classes would be held, but instead, faculty would serve as guides and consultants in their various areas of specialty. Much of the material will come from "the middle" of some subject matter that is usually discussed in a more systematic fashion. Thus, as students return to the classroom to report on their readings, instructors will give didactic introductory orienting lectures, which also will be reinforced by readings from the syllabus. In the above example, I foresee that a lecture will be needed on the concept of human development, which will contextualize the students' new knowledge on adolescence and infant development. Another lecture will introduce the concept of culture and ethnicity and the importance of sensitivity to clients' values, beliefs, and lifestyles—then to be illustrated by the example of this Puerto Rican family. (The woman's partner could be an Italian young man, introducing the theme of different cultural expectations within a couple). Reports on AFDC will be introduced with the concept of entitlement programs and even touch on their history, because we would never want to shortchange learning about the Elizabethan Poor Laws. Students will thus be assigned a few articles on their own specific subject matter, along with readings on the general larger conceptual background from which it is drawn, which will be assigned to the whole class. For example, while a student would concentrate on adolescent cognitive development, she and her classmates would also have to read an overview of Piaget's cognitive developmental theory.

Much of this preparation has focused on the client's *outer space,* problems of sheer survival in a complicated society. It is pedagogically useful that each case should be approached first of all from this societal perspective—the impact of social forces, poverty, immigration, social policies on the individual. This introduction, which might last at least one month (the first introduction being necessarily the longest, with the most orientation) will also help students with the necessary bio-psycho-social assessment, because they now have a beginning knowledge of what aspects might be important to know about a client. A full appreciation of what an assessment might usefully consist of, including potential personal and social resources and knowledge of the family system, will only come at the end of the case. This initial preparation will also incline students toward exploring issues with a client that they might not have considered initially.

The second month will be devoted to practice—how do we proceed with the case—and the theories that would stand as rationales behind different sorts of interventions, making the link between practice and theory clearer than in more traditional teaching. The example on hand might lend itself to two somewhat contrasting approaches. One approach would be an individual approach to the young person, understanding her ego strengths and potential ego deficits with focus on her developmental history. An attempt might be made to *work through* possible traumas or abuse experiences, with the hope that they will thus not need to be passed on to the next generation. The relationship of the worker to the young person will be seen as instrumental in encouraging further developmental maturation. Here we can see how psychodynamic theory (of ego psychology, object relations, perhaps self-psychology) could proceed hand in hand with a psychodynamic intervention approach, establishing a relationship, exploring the developmental history, exploring feelings about the situation, personal hopes, fears, and expectations about the future.

The other approach could be a family systems approach with emphasis on how the young pregnant woman and her potential future baby fit into the family system and how they will both get good enough care for their development within that system, while being mindful and respectful of the varying needs of other family members. Both approaches, which could well be used in combination, will be leaning again on general introductions by the instructor and general as well as individual-focused readings by students. Length of contact has become a very important factor in all fields of social services. Students might need to read about brief and extended clinical contacts and their potential outcome and differential application to cases, and develop an understanding of the crucial effect of finances on client care.

I visualize that the prepared case *starts* with a particular problem but will then take different trajectories depending on directions taken. I thus do not propose that we should be faced with a finished case, but merely with a presenting problem. It will be very fruitful to role-play the development of the case with different decisions reached by the client that may or may not be influenced by the worker's approach (for example, does the worker favor or oppose abortion); interventions based on different theoretical approaches that may or may not influence the course of events; different lengths of contact, possibly with a referral at the end of the case. At the end we may have at least four potential developments of the initial "presenting problem." It is in this phase of meeting the actual client, albeit through role plays, that the complexity of an individual case that often contradicts expectations from the readings might emerge and pose new challenges.

Students thus should be guided by the syllabus to available research on these subjects. Students might need to know, for example, what the research indicates about long-term effects of abortion versus giving a child up for adoption, or what is the long-term effect of bringing an infant home, versus living alone on AFDC. Students will thus experience first hand the utility and limitations of research findings.

There are those who will object that "students cannot possibly learn so many things all at once" but that is precisely what they *have to* achieve in the field, cases do not present themselves in an organized lock-step fashion. As students recognize at least *partial similarity* between a case of their own with the classroom case, they will be expected to use them as examples in classroom discussions. In this way, we will be ensuring that live material from the field enters the classroom. It will be important that students take on rotating assignments, so that students who may have researched a social policy issue in one case may be assigned some practice issue in the next case, and perhaps a theoretical piece for the third case.

It is suggested that students will have a more traditional curriculum during their second year of specialization, where some of the lacunae that *might* occur during the first year will then be filled. This should reassure those faculties and students who prefer a most structured learning/teaching approach, partly out of anxiety that some important content area might not be fully covered, which is especially worrisome in the fields of professional education.

I think that in this proposed system, students should come to the second year with more intellectual maturity and lively questions than they currently do, and the second year could thus be taught in greater conceptual depth. Moreover, the first year of social work school is seen by many students as predominantly a "survival year," and I have some conviction that such a case approach will have such similarity to the student's field experience and that the whole course of study would add so much instant coherence, relevance, and immediate application that it would decrease the pain of learning so much new material.

I visualize that each faculty member would guide a group of students at least through one entire case, with a possible change of instructor for the next case. Faculty could continue to use and expand their special knowledge in one area, because they will be acting as consultants in their specialty, but this case method teaching would require that all faculty become acquainted with all aspects of social work practice, which is a challenging but achievable and worthwhile goal.

I have the deep conviction that once general fear of change, the students' anxiety about being poorly prepared to enter the competitive market, and the natural opposition by the faculty to engage in additional work is conquered, this problem-centered case approach will generate a great deal of enthusiasm. It will resolve most of the HBSE dilemmas discussed in this book. It will revitalize our traditional social work curriculum and prepare social work education for the twenty-first century.

REFERENCE

Council on Social Work Education Curriculum Policy Statement. (1995). *Encyclopedia of social work* (19th ed., pp. 2649–2659). Washington, DC: NASW Press.

Rejoinder to Dr. Freud
ELIZABETH D. HUTCHISON

Sophie Freud's proposal for an integrated social work curriculum, organized on the case method, in the first year of a program "that trains clinical social workers" has strong merits and could serve to enliven discourse about how to organize social work education. It addresses the critical issue of how to weave together the unique situations of individual clients with a universalist-oriented behavioral science knowledge base, but it also raises issues that go to the quick of social work's identity in the late twentieth century and to the core of curriculum design for social work education.

The major strength of the proposal is the use of the case method to organize teaching and learning. As Freud reminds us, most students usually respond positively to the use of the case method because it is consistent with their experience in the field, where they are called on to think about the unique and multifaceted situations of specific client systems. Freud demonstrates well how one case can be used to explore the multidimensionality of human behavior and to do so in some depth. She reminds us that the case method can be used to assist students to be more active learners and to think more critically about behavioral science theory and research. I would strongly agree that the case method is not just for practice classes.

Some issues would need to be elaborated and some assumptions clarified before this reader could give a sufficiently critical evaluation of Freud's proposal. The reader is confronted by the first unsettling issue in the first two paragraphs. Freud assumes that the social work practice for which we are educating students is "clinical social work." No definition is provided for "clinical social work," but the designation of *clinical* seems to indicate a special class of social work. The reader is left to ponder why "clinical social work" rather than "social work" was chosen as the focus of Freud's proposal. The choice may be based, simply, on her own practice and academic experience. Or, is she expressing a bias toward "clinical social work" as a superior class of social work? This question goes to the quick of contemporary social work's professional identity and is, of course, inextricably tied to the larger question of professional mission. Regardless of the reason for the specification of "clinical social work," the reader is still left to ponder whether Freud would have proposed the same curriculum model if she were addressing social work education more broadly. More specifically, does she think that the same first-year curriculum can serve the needs of all social work students, or is she implying a need, or the possibility of a need, for a different curriculum model for social work students who are something other than "clinical"? Put another way, is there a common base to social work? This question goes to the core of the CSWE's efforts to provide leadership on curriculum design.

Another issue core to curriculum design for social work education is the issue of depth versus breadth. When I was a second-year student in an M.S.W. program in the late 1960s, the Dean of my school called off classes for one day to allow faculty and students to engage in organized discourse about significant issues related to social work education. I met with a group that was assigned the task of answering the following question: should social work education emphasize depth or breadth of knowledge? At the time, I thought that the question could only be answered "yes." Almost thirty years later, I humbly appreciate the enormity of the challenge if we answer "yes" to that question, but I still think there is no other answer. So, what are the implications for curriculum design? The operative Curriculum Policy Statement proposes breadth in the first-year curriculum and depth in the second year. Unless I misunderstand her, Freud recommends a reversal of this for students of "clinical social work"; she appears to recommend depth in the first year and breadth in the second. In my affirmative answer to the question, "Should HBSE continue to be taught as a separate course?" I did not attempt to delineate between first-year and second-year content, and, frankly, I doubt seriously that there is a one best way to make such distinctions. I hope that the depth–breadth issue is one that will receive serious attention in CSWE's Milennium Project, but, at the risk of becoming redundant, I would suggest that discourse on this issue is inextricably tied to the issue of professional mission.

Freud begins by protesting the segmenting of content into "domains" or curriculum components, that is, HBSE, practice, policy, research. Her proposal appears to continue the segmental tradition, however, with knowing and doing to be introduced linearly rather than contemporaneously as in the current model. In the first month, students focus on what they "need to know" and "the second month will be devoted to practice." Content in the first month appears to be an integration of current HBSE, research, and policy contents: very long on HBSE, short on policy, and shorter on research. Content in the second month looks very similar to content in existing direct practice courses. Freud's linear model of knowing then doing is reminiscent of "study, diagnosis, and treatment" and will be a comfortable fit for many linearly and analytically oriented faculty and students. It does not appear to have advantages over existing curricular models, however, for assisting students to reconcile a multidimensional perspective for understanding human behavior with the narrowly focused repertoire of interventions that are typically taught in courses on direct practice.

Can HBSE Classes Discuss Socially Sensitive Topics without Being Labeled "Politically Incorrect"?

EDITOR'S NOTE: The human behavior courses inevitably discuss sensitive topics, including those dealing with many different aspects of ethnicity and gender. The facts involving these topics are often unpleasant and discouraging—which groups are disproportionately represented in statistics on poverty and welfare, crime, unemployment, illegitimacy, mental illness, physical and sexual abuse, and so forth. But talk about these topics we must!

Kathryn G. Wambach, Ph.D., A.C.S.W., is an assistant professor at the School of Social Work, University of Texas at Austin. Her teaching has focused on HBSE, research, cultural diversity, and psychopathology. She has published in the areas of AIDS prevention, substance abuse, and cultural diversity.

Darlene Grant, Ph.D., L.M.S.W.-A.C.P., is an assistant professor at the School of Social Work, University of Texas at Austin. Her current teaching and research interests include chemical dependency and psychiatric services. She has published in the areas of maternal perinatal drug addiction, culturally competent social work practice, and the impact of maternal incarceration on children.

Pranab Chatterjee, Ph.D., is a professor at the Mandel School of Applied Social Sciences, Case Western Reserve University. He is currently the editor of the *Journal of Applied Social Sciences.*

YES

Kathryn G. Wambach
Darlene Grant

Social work students have been expected to integrate knowledge, values, and skills to become effective practitioners. The need for this integration has created the emphasis on critical thinking implicit in the question: Is it possible for students or teachers to analyze critically racial and gender issues, without being labeled as racist, sexist, or more generally, without being politically incorrect? Careful consideration of the processes involved in critical thinking and the concept of political correctness will lead to the conclusion that it is necessary to discuss controversial issues in HBSE classes and that using guidelines of critical thinking allows open and honest discussions without risk of the negative label, political incorrectness, being applied.

Critical Thinking

Although discussions of critical thinking have rarely provided clear, simple definitions, a recent special issue of the journal, *Long Term View,* was devoted to the application of the concept in education. In that issue, several key characteristics emerged. Halpern (1994) concentrated on the process involved in critical thinking, which includes systematic questioning of facts and ideas including consideration of alternate explanations. Paul (1994) described critical thinking as a self-assessment process aimed at improving one's own intellectual standards. Lipman (1994) stressed the practical application of such thinking: ". . . it is not just a process—it seeks to develop a product" (p. 41), noting specifically that critical thinking is necessary to resist effectively bias, stereotyping, and prejudice.

More explicitly, critical thinking can best be understood as a process for evaluating information. Any argument must be dissected to discern clearly the premises, conclusions, and underlying assumptions. Facts must be examined in terms of their source(s) and significance to the argument. Alternative conclusions must be enumerated and examined as well. Any argument should be examined for fallacies (i.e., errors in thinking). Individuals must be familiar with their prejudices and fixed habits of thought to accomplish the process faithfully. Finally, opinions or courses of action must be formed based on this thorough, objective analysis.

Within the social work profession, Eileen Gambrill has placed critical thinking center-stage. Her 1990 text, *Critical Thinking in Clinical Practice,* focused on the application of these processes in practice situations, and she has founded the controversial issues series of which this book is a part. These texts have provided models for the processes (i.e., critical thinking) in which students, practitioners, and educators are forced to engage in attempting to understand and to intervene in human affairs.

Political Correctness

The term *political correctness* has its origins in the multicultural debates on campuses across the nation. The range of definitions of political correctness have reflected the parameters of the turmoil. In an article summarizing the issue in *Time* magazine, Paul Gray (1991) suggested that political correctness is a movement seeking to suppress statements and thinking that have been deemed offensive to women or various racial and ethnic groups. In contrast, Ann Hartman (1994) described it as ". . . a derisive term for a range of 'liberal' attitudes concerning expanded rights and protections for minorities, women and other oppressed groups" (p. 37), a more accurate definition, in the view of these authors.

The debate about political correctness has usually depicted the central issue as a conflict between freedom of speech and protection from verbal harassment or threat. That analysis, however, assumes that language is essentially neutral, a contention called into question by postmodernists, who insist that words shape (and, perhaps, constrain) one's view of the world (Hartman, 1994).

Mimi Abramovitz (1991), although not focusing on political correctness per se, has offered a glossary of examples of the power of language. To mention only one, the term *feminization of poverty* obscures the historical overrepresentation of women among the poor. Further, the term has clear implications regarding causality; specifically, the rising numbers of families headed by women are emphasized, rather than economic conditions systematically disadvantaging women in terms of opportunities and wages. Abramovitz (1991) suggested *the povertization of women* as the more accurate depiction of the phenomenon in question.

From the postmodernist viewpoint, then, the heart of the debate about political correctness concerns who has the right to determine/define acceptable language. It was from that perspective that Ann Hartman (1994) argued that social workers should support the efforts labeled political correctness because of the profession's historic commitment to empowering poor, disenfranchised groups whose voices have most frequently been disallowed in public discourse.

Unaddressed in this conclusion, however, has been the status that the traditional censors of public discourse, white males, may retain in determining/defining public language. It can be argued that this oversight has been the real culprit in fanning the flames of this debate. Without insuring that everyone has some right to label language offensive, political correctness simply shifts the right of censorship from one group to another. Whatever the appeal of such a shift among members of historically disenfranchised groups, vindictiveness is unlikely to help accomplish equity or achieve social justice.

Human Behavior in the Social Environment

The study of human behavior in the social environment (HBSE) in social work has traditionally focused on the interplay of individual development (the micro) and the dynamics of the social environment (the macro), producing the profession's unique perspective of the "person-in-environment." Recent Curriculum Policy Statements (CPS; CSWE, 1992) for both baccalaureate and master's-level programs stressed the need to address (1) the impact of social and economic forces on systems (both micro and macro) and (2) the value and ethical issues related to theories examined. Also, at both levels of education, "students must be taught to evaluate theory and apply theory to client situations" (BSW: p. 7; MSW: p. 8).

Clearly, to meet these standards, HBSE classes will have to address the issues in the midst of the political correctness turmoil: race, class, gender, age, ability, and sexual orientation. In looking at various theories of individual human development (the micro level), the most common challenges/criticisms of particular theories involve the exclusion of certain population groups from consideration in the process of forming the theories and the consequent concerns regarding the applicability of those theories to those population groups. For example, feminists have harshly criticized many traditional psychological approaches. It can certainly be argued that the rich sexual fantasy life of children posited in Freudian theory as a crucial stage in personality formation grew directly from his refusal to believe that the widespread client reports (particularly from women) of childhood sexual abuse could be true.

Similarly, many traditional psychological theories have received criticism because of insensitivity to differing social environments based on racial/ethnic groupings. Erikson's stage theory implicitly assumes equal opportunity for social success, a situation not realistic for many people of color. This point emphasizes the need to consider macro theories. Any judgments about an individual's behavior (either within or outside a particular theoretical framework) must take into account the limitations imposed by that individual's situation in his or her society. Without such considerations, students will be prone to blaming the victim or constructing interventions doomed to failure.

When examining macro theories (i.e., those that attempt to explain the behavior of large groups or societies), however, the same tensions are not only present, but codified. Sociological theories can be characterized as ranging along a continuum from functionalist perspectives to conflict perspectives. The functionalists generally view societies as systems within which there is general agreement on common values and norms, which has led to organization of its parts to pursue agreed-on ends. Any problems are viewed as temporary imbalances that will be solved by returning to a state of equilibrium. In contrast, conflict theories view societies as arenas of struggle for power (and associated scarce resources) among various social groups. From this viewpoint, any commonalities in values and norms among various social groups are generally seen as relevant only in setting the parameters within which these inevitable conflicts are enacted and in ensuring continuation of conflict (i.e., all groups are seeking the same ends).

Again, clearly, discussions regarding human behavior in the social environment may not be structured to avoid the kind of sensitive issues that lie at the heart of debates about political correctness. Indeed, hiding behind the specter of political correctness as an excuse to avoid these kind of discussions negates the intent of social work education.

Critical Thinking in HBSE

The crux of the question remains: Is it possible for students or teachers to analyze critically racial and gender issues without being labeled as racist, sexist, or more generally, without being politically incorrect? We assert that the answer lies in the manner in which such discussions are conducted and that the concept of critical thinking provides the guidelines for discussing sensitive topics and remaining politically correct.

More specifically, discussions of controversial issues in HBSE should involve careful acknowledgment of underlying assumptions. Facts should be subject to analysis regarding their sources, potential bias, reliability, and validity. Alternative conclusions must be examined. Furthermore, these discussions must include a willingness to identify and acknowledge fallacies in thinking from all parties.

Teachers in HBSE classes must take responsibility for modeling and monitoring the tone of such discussions. The use of any pejorative language in the course of this kind of public discourse is entirely inappropriate and should be stopped. By explicitly setting common sense boundaries of good taste in preparing classes for discussion, teachers can avoid most potential problems. At the same time, the parameters set must allow *any* party to the discussion to object when discussion has become offensive to him or her. When this occurs (and inevitably it will), the teacher must acknowledge the validity of the objection and help the class find acceptable language with which to proceed.

It is particularly important that the most basic intent of critical thinking, the goal of self-assessment and the formation of individual opinion, be supported. Although the social work profession has clearly articulated values and even policy stances, the tenets of critical thinking do *not* support creating a hierarchy of acceptable conclusions. Indeed, most (if not all) social workers find themselves at odds with at least one particular policy statement promulgated by one of our professional organizations. Consequently, presentation of the profession's views on any subject must be included as part of the material subject to examination and discussion, not as the necessary (or correct) decision.

What remains is to acknowledge just how difficult and important a task conducting discourse with intellectual integrity is when the foci are (or can be) controversial and, frequently, emotionally laden. Teaching or studying human behavior in the social environment is arguably appropriate preparation for another monumental task, promoting social and economic justice in an increasingly polarized society. In conclusion, we submit that the real danger in this endeavor is not political incorrectness but retreat from our purposes and goals. Failing to engage in difficult discussion or constraining that process with foregone conclusions will certainly not prepare students to be effective practitioners.

REFERENCES

Abramovitz, M. (1991). Putting an end to doublespeak about race, gender, and poverty: An annotated glossary for social workers. *Social Work, 36*(5), 380–384.

Council on Social Work Education. (1992). *Curriculum policy statement for baccalaureate degree programs in social work education.* Washington, DC: Author.

Council on Social Work Education. (1992). *Curriculum policy statement for master's degree programs in social work education.* Washington, DC: Author.

Gambrill, E. (1990). *Critical thinking in clinical practice.* San Francisco, CA: Jossey-Bass.

Gray, P. (1991, July 8). Whose America? *Time,* pp. 12–17, 19–20.

Halpern, D. F. (1994). Critical thinking: The 21st century imperative for higher-education. *The Long Term View* (Special issue on Critical Thinking), *2,* 12–16.

Hartman, A. (1994). *Reflection & controversy: Essays on social work.* Washington, DC: NASW.

Lipman, M. (1994). Some generic features of critical thinking. *The Long Term View* (Special issue on Critical Thinking), *2,* 39–43.

Paul, R. (1994). What is critical thinking and why is it essential to education? *The Long Term View* (Special issue on Critical Thinking), *2,* 22–26.

Rejoinder to Drs. Wambach and Grant

PRANAB CHATTERJEE

Drs. Wambach and Grant make us aware of the importance of critical thinking in social work, and it is hard to debate with the importance of the points they make: (1) that it is important to teach critical thinking in professional socialization; (2) that language is seldom neutral; and (3) that who gets to select the language that defines groups may be an important issue. We could not agree more.

However, Drs. Wambach and Grant do not speak to the core of our point: *the subculture of inner-city black populations is a dysfunctional subculture,* and it is this subculture that needs to be the target of intervention. It is this subculture that allows adolescents to have babies, prevents young adults from building labor force attachment, creates a sense of false security that gangs are a safe haven from life's responsibilities, and prevents the building of enduring relationships between men and women leading to family stability. To say that postmodernists teach us that all of this needs deconstruction is a stylish response but avoids the core point. Our core point is that inner-city black culture is dysfunctional, does not need linguistic deconstruction, but does need cultural reconstruction. To hide behind the postmodernists means bypassing the need to define a major target of intervention: the subculture of inner-city black America.

Having said that inner-city black subculture should be the target of intervention, we go further. We suggest what aspects of this subculture need to be changed, and how leadership development is needed to make this change proposal realistic. After our itemized traits of this subculture, the following items specifically need attention: (1) family instability; (2) illegitimacy; (3) developing and supporting appropriate role models; (4) valuing education (education is the only legitimate route to upward mobility for those without capital); (5) reducing adolescents' groups from delinquent and deviant subcultures to friendship and peer groups; and (6) promoting respect for women and education in the music, artifacts, and other means of communication of this subculture.

Who should give leadership to these needed changes? The profession of social work, for the most part, cannot provide these leaders but can only support such change-oriented leadership when and where it is available. At this point, such leadership seems to be coming from such community groups within the inner-city black community as the Nation of Islam. However uncomfortable the white media may be with such leadership groups, it is the leadership of Nation of Islam that has supported respect for family, for women, for education, and for work. Social work programs need to support such community groups when they teach community self-respect and pride and not when they foster hate toward any outgroups.

NO

PRANAB CHATTERJEE

Examining Issues of Race

The basic argument developed in this essay is that there is often a "right" or "wrong" position in social work education, and that, despite efforts to be "scientific," these right or wrong ideological positions, much like party lines in political parties, are taught at "truth" to social work student. During the B.S.W.-M.S.W.-level education, students are trained (not educated) to internalize the "right" party lines. A prime example of such a party line in social work education (in social policy curricula) is: increased spending by the state in social programs, administered by social workers, is desirable and can eventually solve all social problems. In other parts of social work education (in the human behavior sequences, for example), another such party line is: the use of the concept of "dysfunctional culture" (also know as the deficit culture thesis) applied to certain community groups (especially to inner-city black populations) is wrong. Those who dare to use it as a concept to explain human behavior in the inner city commit heresy and should be punished immediately. It is our position that having such a party line, or a politically correct answer to controversial issues, is not good education.

The party line in social work education is not against the use of the concept of culture itself. It is an important and a basic concept applied to the explanation of group behavior and organizational behavior (Whyte, 1981; Schein, 1992). Given that it is applicable to the larger set called "group" (with organizations seen as a particular form of groups), it is therefore applicable to any subset of that, and one such subset of the larger set is low-income, inner-city, black community groups.

The party line in social work education is not against the use of the concept of dysfunctional culture, either. In fact, the concept of dysfunctional culture is used as a minor premise here, and the syllogism can be stated as follows:

- All human groups interacting together over time form a culture of their own.
- A culture can be either functional or dysfunctional for adaptation in its larger environment.

However, when it comes to following position,

- Inner-city low-income black groups have formed a culture, and this culture is dysfunctional for adaptation in the larger, postindustrial American environment,

the social work party line is that this is a racist statement!

The origins of this party line can be traced to the publication of *The Negro Family* by the Office of Policy Planning and Research, United States Department of Labor (1965). This small monograph, authored by Daniel P. Moynihan, became known as the Moynihan report. Its preamble read as follows:

The United States is approaching a new crisis in race relations.... There are two reasons. First, the racist virus.... Second, three centuries of sometimes unimaginable treatment have taken their toll.... [The] circumstances of the Negro American community in recent years has probably been getting worse, *not better.* [Italics original.]

Moynihan went on the further document the conditions in the inner-city black communities: the unstable matriarchy, the increasing welfare dependency, illegitimate births, low educational accomplishment, absence of fathering (and mentoring), high delinquency, and alienation.

The Moynihan report was followed by several scholarly works. Billingsly (1968) argued that the black family and low-income black culture have spent more time in surviving than in thriving, and that explained why the scenarios were the way they were. Wilson (1979; 1989) argued that social class division since the 1960s has created two groups within the black community: a new middle class, which is relatively privileged; and an underclass, which is truly disadvantaged. The latter outnumber the former category by vast numbers. And in 1990, Shelby Steele (a black scholar himself) wrote:

> By many measures, the majority of blacks—those not yet in the middle class—are further behind whites today than before the victories of the civil rights movement. But there is a reluctance among blacks to examine this paradox, I think, because it suggests that racial victimization is not our real problem. If conditions have worsened for most of us as racism had receded, then much of the problem must be of our own making. To admit this fully would cause us to lose the innocence we derive from our victimization. And we would jeopardize the entitlement we've always had to challenge society.... So we have a hidden investment in victimization and poverty. (p. 15)

My basic argument thus is not just that the culture of inner-city black America is dysfunctional for adaptation in a postindustrial society, but that it is becoming more dysfunctional every day. By the middle 1990s, the indicators of such an increasingly dysfunctional culture can be listed below.

Family Instability

Almost all cultures develop and enforce social control of sexual behavior and offer templates of care and custody of children born out of sexual behavior. In the inner-city black culture, such templates are seemingly absent. Men do not and cannot take responsibility for their involvements and form "approach–avoidance" relationships with women. It is an approach dictated by biology, and avoidance formed by a dysfunctional culture.

Illegitimacy

A culture of family instability leads to increased live births of illegitimate children. Removal of stigma on illegitimacy condones and sanctions having children where there will be little long-term involvement of fathers in family life. In fact, it contributes to the development of large numbers of female-headed single-parent families about which Moynihan was concerned (1965).

Condoning Deviance

A culture of family instability also leads to the inability of single mothers to enforce discipline. This lack of discipline is further complicated when the inner-city culture supports the wrong role models for its youth. At times, such role models are adulterers, drug addicts, and convicted felons who are put in leadership roles (as was done in Washington, D.C., in 1994).

Devaluing Education

The Moynihan report documented that education was not valued among inner-city black males, that females often were better students than males, and that this contributed to the inability of males to get jobs or support families or achieve stable life stations. The culture of family instability contributes to this phenomenon more, where resorting to violence is the only way a male can prove his manhood.

Gang Socialization

All-male gangs develop in most cultures (Tiger, 1969), and these gangs are known as clubs, priesthoods, athletic teams, or the military. These gangs provide male solidarity and sanctuary from females and help retain control over key resources, such as knowledge, information, and instruments of violence. In lower-class inner-city black communities, male gangs also reinforce the use of violence. However, they do not help develop and control such key resources as knowledge or information. Instead, they allow devaluing of education and permit the development of delinquent or deviant subcultures. Adolescents are attracted to gangs because they promise to provide more safety and security than the unstable family.

Artifacts and Aesthetics

A culture of family instability, like any other culture, creates its own artifacts and aesthetics. One example of such creativity is rap music. The lyrics of much rap music, however, often give legitimacy to devaluing women and education, promote violence, and set up deviant figures as heroes.

Thus outlined are some of the attributes of a dysfunctional culture that has become increasingly more so since the publication of the Moynihan report. Practitioners in the social work profession are aware of this culture and have to deal with it. However, it is considered impolite and politically incorrect to talk about it in the human behavior curricula. Acknowledging the presence of a dysfunctional culture, in social work education, means risking being called a racist.

Examining Issues of Gender

The pioneering paper on women's position in the stratification system is perhaps the work of French author Simone de Beauvoir. She demonstrates how women have been subjected to "a second status" since the dawn of history, and how perhaps this subjection started in the stone-age technology of hunter-gatherer societies (de Beauvoir, 1949). This view corroborated a similar view taken earlier by the English philosophers Mill and Mill (1970).

American author Betty Friedan argues for gender role equality, somewhat within the existing patriarchal and capitalist system (Friedan, 1963). Nes and Iadicola (1989) have classified her work as a "liberal feminist" position.

In radical feminism, patriarchy is viewed as the main source of oppression of women (Al-Hebrew, 1981; Dickered, 1979; Firestone, 1970). Abolishing gender role and values, work roles, and other stereotypes is the goal of radical feminism, as is removal of patriarchy, participatory democracy, and assertion of sexual freedom (Nes & Iadicola, 1989, p. 14).

Class and gender oppression are interlinked in socialist feminism (Nes & Iadicola, 1989, p. 14). It is argued that class oppression is "rooted in production of things," whereas gender oppression is "rooted in production of people" (Nes & Iadicola, 1989, p. 14).

There are, however, position papers on gender stratification in the social science literature that seem opposed to the above views. Although Gerde Lerner (1986) argues that patriarchy is socially constructed and socially maintained, Symons (1979) and Goldberg (1973) argue that patriarchy is universal in all technologically developed societies and is inevitable. They further argue that human sexuality evolved during the ice ages (Pleistocene Age), and that the position of most feminists reflects what ought to be rather than what is predetermined by natural selection.

Psychoanalyst–author Marie Robinson (1959) wrote that the best way for women to be happy is to take a posture of "sexual surrender" toward their men. This posture reassures men, and in the process of reassuring men of their masculinity obstructs the path of empowerment for women. Although this view is not very popular in the 1980s, it was a result of serious scholarship emanating from psychodynamic theory. The work of Chodorow (1978; 1989; 1994) included a review of this position.

In social work education, however, the works of Symons and Goldberg are censored. Feminist-oriented social workers deny them not only equal time, but any time at all. Robinson's work does not seem to do any better because it too is against the party line of social work. Only the work of Chodorow is used, perhaps because she succeeds in taking a neutral line in the battle of the sexes.

REFERENCES

Al-Hebrew, A. (1981). Capitalism in an advanced state of patriarchy: But Marxism is not feminism. In L. Sargent (Ed.), *Women and revolution: A discussion of the unhappy marriage of Marxism and feminism* (pp. 165–193). Boston: South End.

Billingsley, A. (1968). *Black families in white America.* Englewood Cliffs, NJ: Prentice Hall.

Chodorow, N. (1978). *The reproduction of mothering: Psychoanalysis and the sociology of gender.* Berkeley: University of California Press.

Chodorow, N. (1989). *Feminism and psychoanalytic theory.* New Haven: Yale University Press.

Chodorow, N. (1994). *Femininities, masculinities, sexualities.* Lexington, KY: University of Kentucky.

de Beauvoir, S. (1949). *Le Duxieme Sexe.* Paris: Gallimard.

Dickered, B. S. (1979). *The women's movement: Political socioeconomic and psychological issues.* New York: Harper and Row.

Firestone, S. (1970). *The dialectic of sex.* New York: Bantam Books.

Friedan, B. (1963). *The feminine mystique.* New York: Dell.

Goldberg, S. (1973). *The inevitability of patriarchy.* New York: Morrow.

Lerner, G. (1986). *The creation of patriarchy.* New York: Oxford University Press.

Mill, J. S., & Mill, H. (1970). *Essays in sex equality.* Chicago: University of Chicago Press.

Moynihan, D. P. (1964). *The Negro family: A case for national action.* Washington, DC: U.S. Government Publication.

Nes, J. A., & Iadicola, P. (1989). Toward a definition of feminist social work: A comparison of liberal, radical, and socialist models. *Social Work, 34*(1), 12–21.

Robinson, M. N. (1959). *The power of sexual surrender.* London: Allen.

Schein, E. H. (1992). *Organizational structure and leadership.* (2nd ed.) San Francisco: Jossey-Bass.

Steele, S. (1990). *The content of our character.* New York: St. Martin's.

Symons, D. (1979). *The evolution of human sexuality.* New York: Oxford University Press.

Tiger, L. (1969). *Men in groups.* New York: Random House.

Whyte, W. F. (1981). Street corner society: The social structure of an Italian slum. Chicago: University of Chicago Press.

Wilson, W. J. (1979). *The declining significance of race.* Chicago: University of Chicago.

Wilson, W. J. (1989). *The truly disadvantaged.* Chicago: University of Chicago Press.

Rejoinder to Dr. Chatterjee

Kathryn G. Wambach
Darlene Grant

In replying to Dr. Chatterjee's argument, we must first acknowledge that the term *political correctness* was defined quite differently by our colleague. Although we focused our discussion on the *conduct* of discourse, his presentation clearly is focused on its *content.* As indicated in our original argument, we disagree with his definition. Furthermore, we view focusing on content (with an underlying suggestion of suppressing information or viewpoints) as little more than a ploy to dismiss or avoid the important issue of how to engage in critical examination of controversial issues without offense and polarization.

The second point we wish to address involves Dr. Chatterjee's implication that the social work profession should not have ideological stances. No occupation may be considered a profession without an ideological basis from which to organize a systematic body of knowledge, to claim autonomous authority or achieve societal sanction, to guide ethical behavior, or to delineate common values and norms. To assert either that social work should not have ideological stances or that such stances should not be shared with students in professional education is simply ludicrous.

A more serious assertion by Dr. Chatterjee centers on his statement that social work ". . . students are trained (not educated) to internalize the 'right' party lines." This claim was supported by allegations that certain references or concepts have been banned from social work classrooms under threat of punishment. No such a blacklist has ever been shared with these writers, nor would such an approach be acceptable under the current Curriculum Policy Statements, which emphasize critical thinking (particularly in the evaluation of theory and its application to individual client situations).

Finally, we would like to address some of the content of Dr. Chatterjee's discussion and thereby provide examples of appropriate theory analysis (see Fischer, 1973, for further guidelines). The problem with the dysfunctional culture concept/theory is, in fact, primarily ideological. No one can argue the reality of disintegration occurring in inner-city populations (although to characterize this as an exclusively black phenomenon is certainly problematic). However, the dysfunctional culture argument focuses blame quite narrowly, ignoring broader societal trends that sustain this disintegration (e.g., job migration, loss of nontechnical jobs, welfare disincentives, etc.). Fixing blame at a relatively micro level supports continuation of these broader social trends, insuring continued disintegration regardless of individual response. Similarly, arguing that patriarchal systems are inevitable or predetermined obviously blocks critical examination, thereby insuring its continuation. Furthermore, to assert that "sexual surrender" is the path to empowerment for women is frankly offensive and clearly imposes a hierarchical interpretation of social and economic justice.

In closing, we wish to make note of one area of agreement with Dr. Chatterjee. To ignore controversy, ban certain ideas, or demand narrow adherence to any ideological stance without careful examination would certainly not constitute good education. Controversial issues must be examined and to accomplish this, intellectual honesty and civility (i.e., critical thinking and political correctness) must be maintained in the classroom.

REFERENCE

Fischer, J. (1973). A framework for the analysis and comparison of clinical theories of induced change. In J. Fischer, *Interpersonal helping* (pp. 110–130). Chicago: Charles C. Thomas.

Should Students Bring Significant Amounts of Their Own Life Experiences into HBSE Class Discussions/Papers?

EDITOR'S NOTE: Every student in the classroom was born, went to school, faced numerous life challenges, and now comes to the HBSE class with a wide range of human experiences that might greatly enrich class discussions. Yet, all such reports are personal, idiosyncratic, and limited as instances of behavioral science knowledge. What is the optimal relationship between personal experiences and scientific knowledge in HBSE?

Marcia Abramson, Ph.D., associate professor, School of Social Work, Rutgers, the State University of New Jersey, is currently involved in work concerning multicultural approaches to ethics and spirituality.

David E. Cournoyer, Ph.D., associate professor, School of Social Work, University of Connecticut, teaches in the areas of HBSE and research methods. His primary research interests include parent–child interaction and patient–professional collaboration in treatment of mental and emotional disorders of children.

YES

MARCIA ABRAMSON

This debate is really about epistemology—the nature and origin of knowledge. It concerns how we know and what counts for knowledge, because it is our understanding of epistemology that provides the foundation for what and how we teach.

In a stunning editorial in *Social Work* entitled "In Search of Subjugated Knowledge," Hartman (1992) discussed Foucault's (1980) notion that knowledge is power, and that knowledge and thus power have been monopolized by a few claiming the privileges of the methods of science and formal global unitary knowledge. This has led to the subjugation of local, popular, indigenous knowledge of disenfranchised, oppressed, devalued groups located at the margins of society. Hartman calls on social workers to participate with their clients in the "insurrection of subjugated knowledge." To do this, she suggests that social workers have to be open to local knowledge, to the narratives and truths of our clients; to be able to listen to, honor, and validate our clients' expertise; and to learn to bracket our knowledge so that it does not get in the way of our questioning, listening, and understanding information from our clients that would challenge our views (Hartman, 1992). In my opinion, there is no better place to learn this skill than in the classroom on human behavior in the social environment. And the best way to start is for the instructor to validate the knowledge claims of students as she or he would have the students learn to validate the knowledge claims of their clients. Therefore, teachers have to be open to the students' stories and experiences; be able to listen to, honor, and validate their students' knowledge claims, including those that come from life experience; and learn to bracket their own knowledge so that it does not get in the way of hearing what the students have to say about what they already know from their own living.

With that in mind, I give the Hartman editorial to my students the first day of class in HBSE and ask them to answer one of the following questions for their first journal assignment: (1) Comment on the relationship between knowledge and power in your own experience; (2) Comment on Hartman's assertion that social workers may disempower our clients through our role as experts; or (3) Comment on your own personal/professional experience with what Foucault called the "insurrection of subjugated knowledge."

My goal is to engage the students according to the principles articulated by Congress (1993) and others for reaching adult learners in social work: (1) to use what students already know and can do, by moving from the familiar to the unfamiliar; (2) to teach material that is interesting and relevant to the students; and (3) to actively involve students in their learning and provide opportunities for them to discuss, question, and debate presented material.

Social work students invariably enter the classroom with their own theories of human behavior in the social environment (Dean & Fleck-Henderson, 1992). These theories may be more or less explicit and conscious. More often they are implicit and tacit, and they have to be drawn out and examined before new learning can take place. As a result, the course on human behavior is as much about helping students to become aware of their own assumptions, biases, and world views as it is about teaching formal theories. As Levy (1973) said in an early paper on social work ethics, we all make assumptions about the nature of human behavior and how it is manifest. The learning demands in HBSE call forth those assumptions as students experience and reexperience past and current developmental issues in their own lives as they read and think about theories and research (Germain, 1991b). If these assumptions and biases are not explored, they remain powerful in their secrecy and can interfere with new learning. Conversely, if they are articulated, the student is given the opportunity to hear other students' reactions and perspectives as well as place his or her own beliefs in some kind of context. Part of learning to be self-aware about one's own attitudes and values is to articulate them in an atmosphere where theoretical perspectives can be applied to illuminate them.

The Importance of Self-Knowledge

Socrates was the first to be given credit for articulating the tenet that the central task of life was the acquisition of self-knowledge, and conversely, that the unexamined life was not worth living. He was talking about all of us, not just students who are learning how to help others. Nonetheless, his wisdom suggests that if we do not know ourselves, we cannot possibly know others.

In this modern day, it is feminists and most particularly feminists with an Afrocentric world view who have developed the notion of the importance of self-knowledge to the greatest degree. Writers such as Mary Field Belenky (1986), Patricia Collins (1991), and Linda James Myers (1993) have most clearly articulated the belief that self-knowledge is the basis of all knowledge. The key epistemological concern is the question of what constitutes adequate justifications that a given knowledge claim, whether it be a fact or theory, is true (Collins, 1991). In contrast to positivist approaches to knowledge that seek to create scientific descriptions of reality by producing objective generalizations through distancing oneself from values, vested interests, and emotions generated by class, race, sex, or unique situation, Afrocentric feminists and feminists in general see knowledge as coming from experience. That experience is concrete lived experience that is shared in dialogue with others and is based on an ethic of caring that appreciates the uniqueness and expressiveness of each individual, encourages the expression of emotion in dialogue, and calls on the listeners to respond in empathy. The knowledge claim and validation process is then grounded in an ethic of personal accountability.

What does this mean in the classroom? This means that a student sharing her own experience of a family ritual as an example of how rituals help or hinder family processes would be encouraged to describe the concrete experience and engage in dialogue with her classmates about its meaning. Her unique and expressive contribution, the emotional overtones with which it was presented, and her classmates' capacity for empathy would be grounded in the personal accountability of all concerned to treat this sharing as a valid knowledge claim, one that merits respect and from which one could gain a richer understanding of the role of rituals in families. Then the particular lived experience can once again be connected to the theoretical and research materials on rituals in families.

Instructor's Role

This kind of teaching/learning situation requires a community of trust, one in which the instructor participates as a full person with his or her own personal experiences. Teachers educate in part by modeling the behavior they expect of students. What is "caught" by students may be more important than what is "taught" (Lewis, 1987), so that the instructor's ability to incorporate his or her own life experiences as relevant is crucial in the modeling process.

Germain talks about sharing her own experience of naming as a catalyst for students to respond with stories of how they were named and what effects their names had on their identity formation (Germain, 1991b). She also comments on how Elaine Pinderhughes's (1982) story of her search for her family history back to the time of slavery sparks a beginning examination and deepened awareness of the impact of racism on all racial and ethnic minorities in our society. The sharing of relevant personal experiences by the instructor can often help to strengthen the student–teacher relationship as well as help the class as a whole move toward a more interconnected process.

Since my husband was killed in an automobile accident in May 1991, I have included that information in what I tell my students about myself in the first class of the semester. After introducing myself professionally—what kind of work I have done, what schools I have taught in, what subjects I have taught, and what my research interests are—I tell them about Max and what impact his sudden and unexpected death has had on me and my family. I use it as an example of a second-order change in a family (Germain, 1991a), one that shattered my family's meaning system irrevocably and required rebuilding meaning in life. I tell them that if I did not share this event and its meaning with them, then I could not really be there with them when we talked about such issues as death and dying, loss, and grief because emotionally I would be trying to contain my feelings. I tell them that they too may have issues that course material may tap, and that they will have to use their own judgment about sharing and in what context, whether it be the journal, small group, or the class as a whole. I truly believe that I cannot ask students to even consider risking sharing their own stories unless I am willing and able to take that risk myself.

Diversity in the Classroom

Life experience can be a wonderful way of building on the strengths of diversity in the classroom. Older students often teach younger students through sharing their life experiences, and younger students, particularly those fresh from an undergraduate program, can integrate that knowledge into what they have been learning in the classroom. They in turn help anchor the older students' learning through life experience into what the books and their undergraduate professors had to say. A cohort exercise, one in which students explore the context in which they grew up and from which they have been imprinted with all kinds of messages about human behavior, helps to solidify some of that cross-learning, both intellectually and affectively.

Actually, diversity is one of the most important topics in HBSE that lends itself well to teaching through personal experience. For example, there is no better way to learn about the pervasiveness of institutional racism in the United States than to hear an African American classmate talk about her experience of being followed in what she believed was a suspicious manner by the floor clerk in a local store. Or to learn about the meaning of homophobia and heterosexism through hearing about the experience of "coming out" from a classmate whose family rejected him when they learned he was gay.

One of the ways to develop cross-cultural sensitivity through analogy and metaphor described by Rodwell and Blankebaker (1992) lends itself well to the use of personal experience. Students are offered an understanding of the wounding that occurs when a culture or an individual within that culture is oppressed, devalued, or stigmatized. Through comparing the forms, consequences, survival strategies, and treatment possibilities, students are helped to examine the intersecting continuums of overt and covert physical and psychological wounding as they occur to individuals in child abuse and minority groups through ethnocentrism. Because of their own experience or the experience of family members, friends, or clients, students can identify with the overt and covert physical and psychological forms of child abuse, from physical battering to invasive hygiene to terrorizing and psychological shaming. Others, because of their own group membership, relate to lynching and gay bashing, physical constraints on expression, pejorative labels, and stereotyping. The sharing of experiences in the development of the analogies helps those students who tend to focus on the individual to expand their perspectives to include sociocultural and sociostructural elements, while it encourages the students who tend to see issues as public rather than private to an understanding of wounding as experienced by a vulnerable individual. The metaphors lend themselves to grasping theoretical principles having to do with such issues as learned helplessness, internalized oppression, endemic stress, post-traumatic stress syndrome, and the effect of power differentials in relationships.

Conclusion

There are many ways of knowing, and there are many ways of helping others, such as students, to know. Life experience is one way of knowing that is an important part of being able to learn to know about how other people perceive and behave in their social environments. Rather than encouraging substitution of the idiosyncratic for the general knowledge on which science is based, it permits and encourages people who know themselves through their own experience to use that experience and to know others.

REFERENCES

Belenky, M. F., Clinchy, B. M., Goldberger, N. R., & Tarula, J. (1986). *Women's ways of knowing: The development of self, voice, and mind.* New York: Basic Books.

Collins, P. H. (1991). *Black feminist thought: Knowledge, consciousness and the politics of empowerment,* London: Harper Collins.

Congress, E. P. (1993). Teaching ethical decision-making to a diverse community of students: Bringing practice into the classroom. *Journal of Teaching in Social Work, 7,* 23–36.

Dean, R. G., & Fleck-Henderson, A. (1992).Teaching clinical theory and practice through a constructivist lens. *Journal of Teaching in Social Work, 6,* 3–20.

Foucault, M. (1980). *Power/knowledge: Selected interviews and other writings.* New York: Pantheon.

Germain, C. B. (1991a). *Human behavior in the social environment: An ecological perspective.* New York: Columbia University Press.

Germain, C. B. (1991b). *Instructor's manual for human behavior in the social environment, an ecological view.* New York: Columbia University Press.

Hartman, A. (1992). In search of subjugated knowledge. *Social Work, 37,* 483–484.

Levy, C. (1973). The value base of social work. *Journal of Education for Social Work,* 34–52.

Lewis, H. (1987). Teaching ethics through ethical teaching. *Journal of Teaching in Social Work, 1,* 3–14.

Myers, L. J. (1993). *Understanding an Afrocentric world view: Introduction to an optimal psychology.* Dubuque, IA: Kendall/Hunt Publishing Co.

Pinderhughes, E. (1982). Black genealogy: Self liberator and therapeutic tool. *Smith Studies in Social Work, 59,* 232–251.

Rodwell, M. K., & Blankebaker, A. (1992). Strategies for developing cross-cultural sensitivity: Wounding as metaphor. *Journal of Social Work Education, 28,* 153–165.

Rejoinder to Dr. Abramson
DAVID E. COURNOYER

There is much to like in Professor Abrahamson's ideas about social work education. Her emphasis on application of the principles of adult learning, creating a respectful learning environment, and using theory to facilitate self-awareness are all fine goals (although I tend to be somewhat less concerned with self-awareness in my HBSE classes.) However, I do have several concerns about Professor Abrahamson's characterizations of science, teaching, and the HBSE curriculum.

First, I am concerned about Professor Abrahamson's thoughts on the subject matter of HBSE. Much of her essay is dedicated to preaching the gospel of social constructionism as a corrective for something called "positivist approaches to knowledge," which I presume to mean science. This poses a major problem for me in the context of the HBSE curriculum because the political positions associated with social constructionism, postmodernism, and at least some of the Feminist and Afrocentric political ideologies are blatantly anti-science (Gross & Levitt, 1994). Social constructionists and persons embracing related approaches appear intent on the replacement of the application of reason and careful observation with political correctness or just plain silliness. Approaches to knowledge that privilege personal experience naively ignore substantial demonstrations of the fallibility of unstructured observation. Social scientists both here and abroad have amassed significant demonstrations of logical errors and systematic distortions common in accounts of personal experience (Gilovich, 1991, Reich, 1983). It is silliness to assume that all personal statements about human behavior are equally valid. The antiscience bias in social constructivism amounts to a rejection of the very idea of the HBSE curriculum, to produce a professional who is knowledgeable and appropriately critical about the scientifically derived knowledge on which the profession is based. Approaches to the teaching of human behavior that privilege personal knowledge are invitations for malpractice, not education for a profession. The reader who sees this comment as merely inflammatory would do well to look at the recent research concerning repressed memory, especially false memory syndrome, to see the harm that can be caused by a therapist who is unaware of or unconcerned with the difference between products of the imagination and events that are verifiable (Loftus, 1995).

I also suggest a cautious approach to Professor Abrahamson's advice concerning the instructor's use of his or her own personal experience in teaching HBSE classes. The reciprocal roles of "teacher" and "student" typically contain boundaries and restrictions that are culturally prescribed and professionally codified at least partially to protect the interests of the parties with less power (the students). Creating and maintaining a respectful and sensitive climate for learning clearly is an important part of the teacher's role. However, in the context of the HBSE curriculum, I do not view myself as potentially a therapist or peer. Sharing personal troubles and crises with students moves the teacher close to the boundary of exploitation (that is, using a class to meet personal needs at the expense of students). Likewise, I am immensely fond of many of my students but resist close personal friendships until that time when our relationships are more power balanced. The boundaries on interpersonal relationships between students and instructors are not artificial symbols of our power as teachers or masks to hide our real selves. Rather they are respectful and responsible ways of protecting students from abuse of the very real power that we wield. Our role in the context of the HBSE curriculum is to help students learn what social science is and begin their exploration of how the products of science relate to the helping process. This is the goal toward which our efforts should be directed.

References

Gilovich, T. (1991). *How we know what isn't so: The fallibility of human reasoning in everyday life.* New York: Free Press.

Gross, P. R., & Levitt, N.(1994). *Higher superstition: The academic left and its quarrels with science.* Baltimore: Johns Hopkins University Press.

Loftus, E. (1995). Remembering dangerously. *Skeptical Inquirer, 19*(2), 20–29.

Reich, R. (1983). *The next American frontier.* New York: Times Books.

NO

David E. Cournoyer

In framing a position with regard to the use of personal experience in the HBSE curriculum, I am reminded of a fable that instructional development expert Robert F. Mager (1984) tells at the beginning of his classic *Preparing Instructional Objectives.* The story involves a hapless seahorse who is lured to an early demise by being poorly focused. In the fable the tragic character is sold one redirection after another because his goals were unclear. The final redirection included a turn into the jaws of a shark. In my response to the question regarding use of personal experience in the HBSE curriculum, I urge you to consider the goals and objectives of this instructional intervention and ask if the use of personal experiences facilitates achievement of instructional objectives or redirects energy away from those goals.

Mindful that many debates within the social sciences have been launched around imaginary differences between ill-defined entities (e.g., quantitative versus quantitative, emic versus etic, relativistic versus universal), a good place to start is with some definitions. For the purpose of this essay, the use of personal experience in the HBSE curriculum refers to assignments and class exercises that invite students to apply the subject matter of the course to their lives, past, present, or future. Some examples might include analyzing one's own personality, support networks, culture, or socialization experience. These exercises and assignments may be shared in class or submitted in writing or kept in a required private journal. By "extensive use of personal experience," I mean class exercises that occupy more than one half of one lecture, or assignments representing one week of study focused primarily in the application of course materials to personal experience or belief.

Council on Social Work Education standards make it clear that the overall goal of the HBSE curriculum is to acquaint students with the empirical and intellectual basis of social work through exposure to social science theory and research. Textbook writers for this area of the curriculum are basically in agreement on the general principle and the enormity of the task. Taking an admittedly convenience sample of HBSE texts on my bookshelf, this impression seems shared by several of our esteemed colleagues. For example, Ralph Anderson and Irl Carter (1990) note that the goal of their HBSE text is to "introduce students in the human services to ideas and theories that are fundamental to understanding human behavior." Anderson and Carter further note how vast the body of relevant knowledge is and the impossibility of presenting enough information in one book. Similar concerns are evident in other texts on my shelf (Longres, 1990; Specht & Craig, 1987; Zastrow & Kirst-Ashman, 1990). I offer these examples to make the point that a curriculum intended to introduce social work students to those portions of cultural anthropology, economics, education, human biology, psychology, and sociology that are relevant to social work has an enormous task. The enormity of that task should lead us to guard instructional time jealously and strongly resist time-wasters and diversions. Although the use of activities that include sharing of personal experiences can make the experience more enjoyable, the likelihood that these activities will needlessly divert class time from content seems significant.

In light of research evidence that human memory and reason are facilitated by connecting new ideas to prior experience, it is seductive to consider extensive use of personal experience in teaching human behavior content in social work education. We all were children, experienced frustration, learned, have social supports, and live in communities. Besides, are not social workers supposed to "feel" their profession, not just experience it rationally? So would not our goals be advanced by having students participate in class exercises that include life histories, introspection, genograms, or just general testimony of life's way?

In the context of the HBSE curriculum, I would settle for more of the rational, if you please. My objections to extensive use of personal experience in the teaching of HBSE are that such techniques (1) are inefficient, (2) miss the point of HBSE in the curriculum, (3) are demeaning to our students, and (4) encourage the continuation of egocentric conceptions of people and their lives. I will expand on each of these objections below.

Excessive Use of Personal Experience in Teaching HBSE Is Inefficient

Extensive use of personal experience in the HBSE curriculum is an inefficient way to learn concepts that can be mastered symbolically. Personal experience is a powerful aid to learning and memory, but to argue that valuable class and study time should be taken up immersed in personal stories is equivalent to arguing that the best way to learn traffic safety is to be hit by a bus. Both techniques have the very real risk of cutting off the possibility for additional learning. Experiential activities are time intensive. Not only is time involved in the generation and sharing of the personal experience material, a responsible instructor must respond to the strong affect that may accompany such revelation. Helping students work through their own limitations is an important part of social work education, but should this be attempted in the HBSE curriculum? More on this later. The current point is that while students are participating in activities such as discussions of their personal helping networks, it is important to recognize what are we *not* talking about—the empirical evidence concerning what helping networks do and do not do for the people who will be our students' clients.

One might argue that the HBSE ability to learn symbolically is the principle tool that extracted at least a large portion of the human species from the periphery of death by starvation, exposure, or predation. Although social work takes strong responsibility for correcting wrongs brought about by the limitations of human culture, overall we have worked out a fairly good life for our species as lives of medium-sized predators go. This is in part because we can integrate the experience of countless lives and experiences into our own without the necessity of living and experiencing everything directly. This results in a fantastic buildup of experience and technology that is passed on to successive generations. In fact, the emergence of social work education can be taken, in part, as a response to the buildup of knowledge and the need for efficient means of transmission. The profession and the craft that it plies has simply become too complex for the simple apprentice approach to education, where direct experience is the primary mode of instruction. Although teaching methods that involve personal experience are entertaining, they do not meet the need for more efficient means of dealing with a truly enormous body of information that is relevant to the practice of social work. It is simply foolish to worry that students will not integrate symbolic knowledge with their day-to-day lives—humans have been doing that for thousands of years. However, what in our culture except our HBSE curriculum will motivate students to pick up an article critiquing the empirical support for age/stage theories of human development? For a curriculum segment that is intended as both graduate and as advanced undergraduate training, an enormous amount of learning must be accomplished by the student in an HBSE course. Efficiency in the transmission of that content must be a major concern.

Extensive Use of Personal Experience Misses the Point of the HBSE Curriculum

This brings up the second objection to excessive use of personal experience in HBSE courses—that it misses the point of this portion of the curriculum. Although the exact function of the HBSE portion of the curriculum, like nearly everything in the profession, is subject to a wide range of specifications, most major texts seem to converge on a few points. Essentially, the HBSE curriculum is intended to acquaint students with a wide range of social science theories that inform social work practice and foster critical thinking about how the theories connect to practice. It is true that the HBSE curriculum is also intended to reinforce certain humanistic values of the profession, but the major point of the HBSE curriculum is to provide the student with the abstract and symbolic scientific base of social work practice and foster the ability to think about that base critically. These are largely intellectual, symbolic tasks. The students and I do not need to recite personal stories about domestic violence to critically evaluate the evidence that violence against women, children, animals, and outgroups are expressions of certain sociocultural processes. However, to do justice to this important topic, we may need to read several hundred pages of very demanding empirical and theoretical writings and develop the skills necessary to sort out the good from the bad. The twenty-minute description of the personal experiences of a student who was sexually abused may be a moving experience, but it contributes significantly less to the students' professional competencies that an equal-length treatment of the methodological problems in obtaining evidence of child maltreatment. Even when the intent of such sharing is to bring life to the research and theory regarding the human condition, we may send the wrong message to students. Do we wish to teach that congruence between personal experience and social science theories is the measure of a true and useful theory? If teaching critical thinking about research and theory is an important aspect of the HBSE curriculum, we can ill afford to reinforce student perceptions that personal fit is a valid theory evaluation device.

Excessive Use of Personal Experience in the HBSE Curriculum Is Demeaning to Students

This objection to the excessive use of personal experience is the result of feedback from many students. Students with the liberal arts and social science backgrounds (that social work programs seem to value) consistently complain about the lack of intellectual challenge in the HBSE curriculum. While we admit an appalling number of students who would never, if they could avoid it, crack a book where numbers are used for anything but page identification, a large portion are quite skilled intellectually and in particular in the empirical study of human behavior. These students look to social work educators to help them arrive at a critical synthesis of this knowledge and to fathom how this applies to their chosen profession. These students are capable of functioning intellectually as equals with master's students in any profession, if we but train them. Instead we offer them the instructional equivalent of fingerpaint. Frustration with the infantalization of the HBSE curriculum is particularly intense in students in dual-degree programs that study human behavior and social science theories in other disciplines. Students who go on to doctoral work are also especially critical about the way their time was often wasted telling stories in HBSE classes. These students are no less personally committed than less intellectually gifted students; they just want us to stop the preaching to the choir and get on with the learning.

Excessive Use of Personal Experience in the HBSE Curriculum Reinforces an Egocentric View of the World

Just as legitimizing personal experience as the measure of a good theory poses problems, so does limiting application of the content to the range of cultural diversity at hand. If the implicit instructional message is that the only ideas worth learning are those that apply to the personal situation, how will students understand persons whose life experiences are radically different from their own? Perhaps we intend to use the diversity in our student population to remedy this. Personal stories from women, blacks, Latinos, Asians, and others should broaden our students views of human experience, one might think. However, the reality is that this technique broadens our students very little. What will the reliance on the testimony of one or two (generally middle-class women) minority students about their socialization experiences do to help students with different backgrounds understand the role of ethnicity, social class, and gender as determinants of the human experience? Some measure of the futility in this strategy is found in the numerous comments from minority students about their frustration with the assigned role as spokesperson for persons within their ethnic group. This is attributable in part to the fact that diversity *within* ethnic groups may often be greater than that *across* ethnic groups. Few of us have a complete understanding of the complexity of our own ethnic groups, differences related to gender, social class, urban versus rural socialization, and many others. The observation that "she" is different from "me" is too easily translated into yet another stereotype of what "they" are like. Although a skilled educator undoubtedly can and does point out the fallacy of this translation, why not forgo the entire problem by not inviting the personal testimonies in the first place? Then the time could be better spent examining the diversity within human populations and how this is related to social work practice. In my HBSE courses, I use readings from *Human Behavior in Global Perspective* (Segal, Dasen, Berry, & Portinga, 1990) to study intergroup conflict and ethnocentrism precisely because most of the sociocultural groups mentioned there are not represented in the United States. I do not want students to think that they know what to expect from "those people," but rather to be comfortable with the idea of greatly different world views and customs. If students truly understand and accept the idea of cultural diversity, they will be open to clients' efforts to educate them about their cultural realities.

In summary, none of this is intended to say that connecting readings and lectures with personal experience is not helpful. Clearly, memory, attention, and motivation are all facilitated by the personal salience of the presentation. Likewise, examination of personal experience is also instrumental at achieving the kinds of self-awareness that we desire in a social worker. However, the primary goals of the HBSE curriculum are academic, not therapeutic. HBSE is about internalizing massive amounts of useful fact and theory and fostering a critical, balanced view of the value of those facts and theories. Our students do not need structured activities to help them connect social science theories to their personal lives. They could not stop the process of making such connections if they tried—the human mind just works that way. What we can and do subvert by excessive use of personal experience testimonials in the HBSE class is the acquisition of enough symbolic knowledge and critical thinking ability to facilitate a professional approach to social work.

Instructional styles that emphasize sharing of personal experience are often experienced positively by both students and faculty. In addition to the value of such techniques in maintaining interest, sharing of personal experience is likely to contribute positively toward forming a sense of community and personal commitment to the profession. These are real and positive outcomes. However, in social work education I have often observed so much attention to the issues of identification and sense of community that the "craft" side of social work, the part that requires serious mental effort, seems to get lost in all the hugging.

REFERENCES

Anderson, R. E., & Carter, I. (1990). *Human behavior in the social environment: A social systems approach* (4th ed.). Hawthorne, NY: Aldine de Gruyter.

Longres, J. F. (1990). *Human behavior in the social environment.* Itasca, IL: Peacock.

Mager, R. F. (1984). *Preparing instructional objectives* (2nd ed.). Belmont, CA: Lake.

Segal, M., Dasen, P., Berry, H., & Portinga, Y. (1990). *Human behavior in global perspective.* New York: Pergamon.

Specht, R., & Craig, G. J. (1987). *Human development: A social work perspective.* Englewood Cliffs, NJ: Prentice-Hall.

Zastrow, C., & Kirst-Ashman, K. (1990). *Understanding human behavior and the social environment.* Chicago: Nelson-Hall.

Rejoinder to Dr. Cournoyer
MARCIA ABRAMSON

I certainly agree with Professor Cournoyer that there should not be "excessive" use of personal experience in teaching HBSE. Excessive use is not the question. Exclusive use of any way of gaining knowledge is the issue for debate. Students need to be able to receive information such as facts and theories from authoritative sources as well as listen to and learn from their own and other's experience and feelings. Both are important ways of knowing and learning, because truth or knowledge is not an "either/or" proposition. Because it is the instructor's responsibility to help students integrate theory with practice, so it is his or her job to help them incorporate the different ways of knowing into how they approach and understand the world.

Professor Cournoyer suggests that use of personal experience is an inefficient way to teach and likens it to the simple apprentice approach to education. To the contrary, if the teachable moment is captured by someone's story, then the instructor can use that story very efficiently to generalize from the specific to the universals that undergird the particular, using personal experience to get there much faster than with abstract intellectual theory.

Professor Cournoyer then suggests that use of personal experience misses the point of HBSE. Personal experience integrated with the abstract and symbolic scientific base of social work practice helps students to think critically about what they learn from lived experience as well as what they learn from texts and abstract discussions. Congruence between personal experience and social science theories is certainly one way that we test both the validity of the theory and the applicability of the lived experience to other situations.

Thirdly, Professor Cournoyer indicates that personal experience in the HBSE curriculum is demeaning to students, especially the more intellectually gifted. Calling the use of personal experience ". . . the instructional equivalent of fingerpaint," he suggests that use of personal experience results in lack of intellectual challenge, frustration, and infantalization. All students, including the intellectually gifted, need to connect with the material they are learning about HBSE not only intellectually but emotionally and imaginatively. Social work is both an art and a science, and the art is often expressed in very personal ways.

Finally, Professor Cournoyer believes that use of personal experience reinforces an egocentric view of the world because using personal experience as a form of knowledge building suggests ". . . that the only ideas worth learning are those that apply to the personal situation . . ." That need not be the case if the instructor is careful to make it clear that personal experience is only one way of knowing. Just as one student should not be assigned to be the spokesperson for an entire group, and diversity within groups should be articulated as clearly as diversity amongst groups, so learning about groups not represented in the United States needs to be integrated with learning about the student sitting in the next chair. It is all part of learning about how to learn about ourselves in society.

Should HBSE Favor Social Environment Theories over Theories of Individual Behavior?

EDITOR'S NOTE: The very name of this field, human behavior and the social environment, leads us to another debate. Should we emphasize the (individual) human behavior portion of this name, or should we emphasize the (collective) social environment side? Mary Richmond wrote nearly eighty years ago of the distinctive retail and wholesale aspects of social work practice. Can we teach them separately? Can they be combined in one course? Or should one portion take precedence over the other?

Deborah Siegel, Ph.D., professor at the School of Social Work, Rhode Island College, where she teaches advanced clinical practice with families and children, is a research and evaluation practitioner. Her research on the long-term effects of "open adoption of infants" was reported, in part, in *Social Work* (1993, *38,* 15–23).

Nina Rovinelli Heller, Ph.D., is an assistant professor at the School of Social Work, University of Connecticut. Her academic and research interests are in the areas of women's mental health and the connections between social work practice and theory. Dr. Heller's current work (with Terry T. Northcut), on the use of cognitive–behavioral techniques in psychodynamic practice with clients diagnosed as borderline is forthcoming in the *Clinical Social Work Journal.*

YES

DEBORAH SIEGEL

Absolutely! The social work profession, including its educators, has drifted away from a simultaneous dual focus on person-and-environment. The person-in-environment perspective has long distinguished social work from other human service professions and has been the foundation of social work's unique contributions in helping people and society. But of late, we have focused so much on theories of individual, family, and small group dynamics that we have come to pay insufficient attention, in comparison, to the societal dynamics that create, sustain, and exacerbate peoples' miseries (Specht, 1990).

Although today's social workers may acknowledge the idea that public issues create and sustain private troubles, the typical practitioner's daily work is to assess and intervene in private troubles, not the public issues that spawn and feed them ("Membership Survey," 1983; Goleman, 1985). This is like trying to halt a tidal wave with a stop sign. The typical HBSE course unwittingly reinforces this futility, by paying more attention to "HB" than to "SE," and by paying lip service to the interactions between these two arenas.

One indication of many B.S.W.s' and M.S.W.s' lack of professional commitment to pursuing social justice may be the fact that many do not join the National Association of Social Workers (NASW), the organized arm of the profession whose mission is to influence public policy and do advocacy with and on behalf of oppressed and vulnerable populations (Gibelman & Schervish, 1993). They may believe that NASW's investments in political agendas divert the organization's attention away from supporting clinical practice. Perhaps they do not think that membership in NASW offers them enough benefits to merit their annual dues (Lawrence-Leiter, 1991). Clearly, some do not believe that NASW's political action committee or legislative lobbying efforts merit their financial support. Splinter groups of clinical social workers form their own professional organizations because they think that NASW does not adequately represent their interests.

In my view, these folks separate "case" and "cause." They see psychotherapy and social action as separate agendas and believe that we can attend to one only at the expense of the other. I argue that the minute we engage in this sort of dichotomous thinking we blunder into simplistic reductionism. Person and environment are inseparably intertwined with intricate complexity. Attending to one and not the other dooms us to fail in our efforts to understand the causes of peoples' misfortunes and intervene to alleviate suffering.

It is perfectly reasonable to argue that social work education should emphasize *both* theories of individual behavior *and* those addressing the influence of the social environment. For purposes of this paper, however, I argue that we should favor the latter, because our boat is tipping overboard in one direction already. My hope is that in arguing the antithesis of current practices, some synthesis can ultimately be found.

Why do I think our professional boat is tipping overboard in the direction of excessive attention to assessment and intervention with individuals and families? For one thing, the content included in the typical HBSE course does this. The course generally focuses on topics such as theories of personality and related concepts such as the defense mechanisms; id, ego, and superego; behaviorism;

cognition; adaptation and coping; motivation, capacity, and opportunity; the stages of human development and of the family's life cycle; and psychopathology nomenclature.

The typical course pays scant attention, however, to the factors in the social environment that inextricably interact with those issues, shaping them immeasurably; for example, lack of economic, political, educational, and social opportunity because of discrimination and oppression shapes personality as much as—or more than—one's stage in the lifespan. Or, a person's vulnerability to succumb to a mental disorder listed in the DSM can be exacerbated by environmental conditions such as poverty, community violence, and unavailable or inaccessible preventive or emergency mental health services.

Although HBSE courses may acknowledge from time to time that these environmental forces matter, most of the readings and assignments require students to master material related to how human beings function, rather than details about how society's political and human service institutions function and fail to respond to human needs, often maintaining their prerogatives at the expense of the client; running roughshod over clients' needs by ignoring differences of race, culture, class, ethnicity, religion, sexual orientation, mental and physical ability, and so on. The typical HBSE course does not dwell on different theories of how political, economic, and human service organizations and institutions operate; or on theories that describe and explain the dynamics of oppression. Hence, the course implies that if we can understand what makes the individual tick, we can begin to fashion effective interventions that target the individual. The course content suggests that the client system, target system, and action system ought to be the individual, family, or small group, not the human service organization itself, an oppressed community or group in society, legislatures, or other large systems.

Often environmental forces are more powerful and compelling influences on human behavior than are intrapsychic and familial dynamics. To illustrate this, let us examine a perplexing social problem often addressed in HBSE—escalating numbers of unmarried teenage parents. Much of the literature and HBSE coursework on this topic reflect society's tendency to focus on intrapsychic and familial, rather than social, political, and economic causes, and to think linearly rather than systematically. As a result, social workers' interventions tend to focus on unmarried pregnant and parenting teens and their families, rather than on the larger systems issues that produce unmarried teenage parenthood.

The typical HBSE course notes that the rate of teenage parenthood is exploding; 29.8 percent of births to unmarried women in 1992 were to teenagers. Between 1982 and 1992, births to unmarried females ages fifteen to nineteen increased by 55.4 percent (Center on Hunger, Poverty and Nutrition Policy, 1995). The course might also acknowledge some of the adverse consequences of unmarried teenage parenthood, such as a higher maternal death rate; short- and long-term medical, developmental, and educational risks for the child; increased risk of poverty and social isolation for both mother and child; and increased risk of child abuse (Armstrong, 1991).

The course then typically explores explanations for why teenagers become pregnant, focusing on psychological, developmental, and family of origin characteristics of female adolescents. Teenagers from dysfunctional families of origin, the thinking goes, become pregnant out of a need to be loved and to have someone to love because these needs have never been adequately met. By becoming parents themselves, they hope to create the family they crave and gain attention from friends and family. Developmentally, adolescence is a time of egocentrism, impulsivity, feelings of invulnerability, lack of ability to anticipate realistically the future long-term effects of one's actions, and susceptibility to peer pressures. Physical maturity exceeds intellectual, emotional, and social maturity, leading to unprotected sexual behavior, denial of pregnancy, and delay in acquiring prenatal care (Armstrong, 1991).

This line of thinking might suggest to HBSE students that the "cure" for teenage parenthood lies in individual and family therapy. However, when one examines the larger social, political, and economic circumstances surrounding the issue, one begins to see that the psychological and developmental causes of teenage parenthood are themselves created by, or at least exacerbated by, other more potent and compelling forces. Hence, HBSE courses should forego their traditional emphases in favor of in-depth exploration of how the social environment produces human behavior.

Specifically, studies show that the growth in the number of families headed by a single teenage mother is caused by declining economic prospects. When young people have reasons to view their economic futures optimistically, they are less likely to become teenage parents (Center on Hunger, Poverty, and Nutrition Policy, Tufts University, 1995; Duncan & Hoffman, 1990; Friedman, Hechter, & Kanazawa, 1994; Hernandez & Myers, 1993; Jargowsky, 1994; Jones et al., 1985; Lawson & Rhodes, 1993; Massey & Shibuya, 1994; Wilson, 1993 and 1986). When teenagers face poor prospects for future employment and educational advancement, they are less likely to postpone pregnancy and parenthood. "Research examining the determinants of teenage pregnancy in thirty-seven developed countries found that the higher extent of poverty in the U.S., and the more uneven distribution of U.S. household incomes, are determinants of higher teenage and out-of-wedlock birthrates in the U.S." (Jones et al., 1985; Friedman et al., 1994, cited in Tufts report, p. 11).

These economic and political factors interact with other aspects of the prevailing culture in the United States. The media (in print, movies, television, videos, music) are saturated with sexually explicit stimuli, with little if any attention to contraception or safer sex practices. Schools may provide sex education ambivalently and inadequately, if at all (Armstrong, 1991). There is a prevailing belief that explicit discussions with adolescents about birth control and safer sex invite teens to engage in sexual activity, although research indicates that this is not the case (Jones et al., 1985). Two-career or single-parent families, by economic necessity, often leave adolescents without adult supervision during after-school hours, because school-based and other after-school programs are unavailable or unaffordable.

These devastatingly potent macro issues envelop and assault the teenagers of America. These macro issues provide the context for and interact with the developmental and family of origin issues facing adolescents. HBSE courses must address in depth these large systems issues if social workers are to tackle meaningfully the increase in unmarried teenage parenthood. Our inclination to focus on the intrapsychic dynamics of one vulnerable teenager at a time, or on the family systems dynamics of one dysfunctional family at a time, instead of on the social, economic, and political forces bearing down on whole populations of vulnerable teens and their families, is pathetically ineffective.

The social work profession is embedded in the values and perspectives of the culture into which it was born. It is only natural that social workers harbor some of the same beliefs, points of view, myths, and biases that we have lived with all of our lives. Understanding this fact, and addressing it with courage in HBSE courses that have a radically different emphasis, offers new avenues for effective social work practice in the future.

REFERENCES

Armstrong, B. (1991). Adolescent pregnancy. In Gitterman, A. (Ed.), *Handbook of social work practice with vulnerable populations.* New York: Columbia.

Center on Hunger, Poverty and Nutrition Policy. (1995). *Statement on key welfare reform issues: The empirical evidence.* Boston: Tufts University (unpublished manuscript).

Duncan, G. J., & Hoffman, S. D. (1990, November). Welfare benefits, economic opportunities, and out-of-wedlock births among black teenage girls. *Demography, 27*(4).

Friedman, D., Hechter, M., & Kanazawa, S. (1994, August). A theory of the value of children. *Demography, 31*(3), 375–401.

Gibelman, M., & Schervish, P. H. (1993). *Who we are: The social work labor force as reflected in the NASW membership.* Silver Spring, MD: NASW.

Goleman, D. (1985, April 30). Social workers vault into a leading role in psychotherapy. *New York Times,* pp. C-1, C-9.

Hernandez, D. J., & Myers, D. E. (1993). *America's children: Resources from family, government and economy.* National Committee for Research on the 1980 Census. New York: Russell Sage Foundation.

Jargowsky, P. A. (1994). Ghetto poverty among blacks in the 1980s. *Journal of Policy Analysis and Management, 13*(2): 288–310.

Jones, E., Forrest, J., Goldman, N., Henshaw, S., Lincoln, R., Rosoff, J., Westoff, C., & Wulf, D. (1985). Teenage pregnancies in developed countries: Determinants and policy implications. *Family Planning Perspectives, 17,* 53–62.

Lawrence-Leiter & Co. (1991, March). *Membership survey.* Unpublished manuscript. Silver Spring, MD: NASW.

Lawson, A., & Rhodes, D. L. (Eds.). (1993). *The politics of pregnancy: Adolescent sexuality and public policy.* New Haven, CT: Yale University Press.

Massey, D. S., & Shibuya, K. (1994). *The effects of neighborhood context on teenage childbearing and welfare dependency.* Paper written for presentation at the Annual Meeting of the Population Association of America, Miami, FL, May 5–7, 1994.

Membership Survey Shows Practice Shifts. (1983). *NASW News, 28,* 6.

Specht, H. (1990). Social work and popular therapies. *Social Service Review, 64,* 345–357.

Wilson, W. J. (Ed.). (1993). *The ghetto underclass: Social science perspectives* (updated edition). Newbury Park, CA: Sage.

Rejoinder to Dr. Siegel

Professor Siegel argues her point persuasively and has chosen a pertinent example—that of teenage pregnancy—to support her position favoring an emphasis on theories of the social environment in the HBSE curriculum content. Implicit in her discussion is the larger question of the mission of social work and what professional roles we should be preparing our students to assume. Assuming that HBSE courses provide the knowledge base for sound social work practice, whether this practice is micro or macro, it is imperative that we ask the question of what we want professional social workers to be able to do with the knowledge we provide and encourage them to discover.

I agree with Professor Siegel's appraisal of the significant economic, social, and political factors that converge to increase the likelihood of an "explosion" in the rate of teenage parenthood. As a profession, we cannot ignore this context or the many factors that will maintain or exacerbate this trend. However, the young mothers, fathers, and their children who come to the attention of social workers in a variety of settings frequently do so with very immediate, personal, human needs that require empathic and skilled intervention on a micro level. Intervention on this scale requires a solid understanding on the part of the worker of the very areas of human behavior curriculum content that Dr. Siegel believes are overemphasized in current HBSE courses. This content is vital if social workers are to provide support, treatment, services, and advocacy for these clients. An "in-depth exploration of how the social environment produces human behavior" is necessary but insufficient for preparing social workers to carry out many direct practice functions. Knowledge of human behavior, however, must be both balanced by and enhanced by an evolving understanding of pertinent social environment theory. In a sense, this requires the social worker who works in direct practice to employ a number of lenses simultaneously. This synthesized view then, can enhance direct practice skills as well as social advocacy work.

For the social worker whose primary job responsibilities are carried out in the macro level, who develops policy, for example, an understanding of individual theories can illuminate the impact that a harsh social environment has on human development. In the case of teenage parenthood, this may result in increased attention to the importance of developing programs that make good educational and vocational opportunities accessible to young parents.

Social work is a complex field with various points of intervention and increasing numbers of practice arenas. This makes content demands on HBSE curriculum both daunting and exciting. Unfortunately, faced with competing needs, we are tempted to polarize positions. What is needed is a thoughtful and ongoing synthesis of theories of both human behavior and the social environment. Clients present to us with varying degrees of socially and environmentally induced and maintained problems. It is necessary that the social worker has a means of assessing the degree to which social and environmental factors influence a particular client. This maximizes the likelihood that a worker will selectively use a balance of appropriate theories in both assessment and intervention phases of the work.

Finally, I agree with Professor Siegel about the importance of the profession's commitment to pursue social justice issues. The HBSE curriculum is one avenue for teaching our students about the very complex and vital connections between human behavior and the social environment. This knowledge is equally important at both micro and macro levels of practice. As educators, we need to make these connections explicit both through examination of theory and in discussion of practice examples. This may help strengthen students' understanding of the imperative role of social justice in the practice of social work.

NO

NINA ROVINELLI HELLER

NO! Emphatically, no. In fact, it both concerns and encourages me that as a profession we continue to struggle with this question. It concerns me because the result of these discussions is often an unproductive polarization of people and their perspectives. It encourages me because it demonstrates a continuing effort to understand what we do as social workers, what we need to know as practitioners, and what we believe about how people and their worlds interact. Additionally, it indicates a continued struggle to assimilate and accommodate new knowledge about both individuals and their environments as it becomes available through research, clinical observation, and emerging theories. Eliminating an emphasis on theories of individual behavior in favor of those addressing the influence of the social environment will not correct for the admitted errors of the past of relying predominantly or exclusively on them, giving short shrift to the social environment. As social workers, it is vital that we continue to develop ways of understanding the person in relation to his or her environment. This is what numerous theorists and practitioners before us have struggled with, whether they have referred to the resultant concept or theory as person-in-situation, ecological life model (Germain and Gitterman, 1980), or psychosocial casework.

It is tempting in the face of what appears to be a current course of political backlash against many of the groups who have made some gains in the last decades to shift our attention solely to the very real and damaging oppressive social environment. Direct practice workers daily see the effects of these factors on clients and client groups. Phenomena such as increasing poverty; the dwindling resources and priority given to the needs of children; continuing racism, sexism, and domestic violence; and unemployment and ensuing homelessness have complex causes in our socioeconomic structures. If theories of individual behavior are used in place of those concerned with the influence of the social environment, we as a profession and as individual practitioners risk "blaming the victim" of these social and economic inequities. We also risk using limited resources to "cure" these victims, while leaving social, political, and economic structures that sustain or promote these inequities untouched. However, if we use theories of individual development to understand the common and the differential ways in which any of these societal factors influence specific individuals and families, we can provide needed services as well. This is not in place of social action. It is in addition to it. The provision of these necessary services also may result in the empowerment of individual clients to work toward their own definitions of social action on their own behalf.

What Do Theories Do for Social Workers?

Theory aids practitioners to organize data, anticipate outcomes, and recognize, understand and explain new situations. It should guide our practice and suggest appropriate interventions. It also should help us explain our work to others, to translate and transfer our skills. It also will help us to recognize when we have a situation that indicates a specific lack or gap in knowledge (Turner, 1986). This gap in knowledge may be specific to a particular worker or to our professional body of knowledge (Goldstein, 1980). Theory building is not static; we have made significant gains in the last decade in understanding the influence of gender and race, for example, on individual, family, and societal functioning. We also have made significant gains in identifying and understanding the importance of biological factors and vulnerabilities in development. In the face of rapid knowledge development in social work and allied fields (i.e., economics, medicine, psychology, sociology), it is tempting to handle this onslaught of material by isolating these areas of study. However, one of the historical strengths of the field and practice of social work has been our focus on biopsychosocial understandings of people and their environments. Reaching for understanding of diverse and complex points of view is both challenging and frustrating, and is imperative to good social work practice, whether one focuses primary professional activity in the areas of direct service or macro practice.

As noted earlier, sound theories should guide sound practice. In social work education, the human behavior sequence content provides these necessary underpinnings for the various practice sequences. Several contemporary practice situations underscore the need for understandings of theories of individual functioning in tandem with understandings of the multiple influences of the social environment.

Workers in inner-city agencies that serve the needs of children and families are seeing increasing numbers of children who are dealing with the daily and cumulative effects of poverty, violence, racism, and many forms of abuse. There can be no question of the persistent and negative effects of the social environment on these children. Any intervention with the child and his or her family requires an active understanding by the worker of the reality of these aversive factors. However, I strongly maintain that without a concomitant understanding of theories of individual behavior, we have no means of responding to the wide variance of effects this environment imposes on individual children. In other words, the impact of these factors is different for different children at different stages of development. By ignoring theories of individual behavior, we risk losing sight of the client as an individual, which may further reinforce the sense of isolation that adverse social conditions have introduced.

Consider the case of John, a fourteen-year-old African American boy who lives in the inner city, witnesses random violence on a daily basis, and is marginalized and discriminated against in nearly every realm of his life. I maintain that an awareness of psychological development, affective, social, biological, and cognitive development is essential to understanding the myriad effects that an adverse social environment has on this particular youth. For example, if John is constitutionally unable to screen out external stimuli, the sounds of gunshot fire are not apt to become background noise to him. Nor will he be able to concentrate and attend to tasks in a way that will allow him to achieve skills that will mitigate against the effects of the negative environment. Likewise, I maintain that John's ability to form close attachments, as well as the availability of people with whom to form them, will be crucial variables in understanding the impact of the environment. Additionally, an understanding of the particular developmental needs of a young adolescent in the biological and social realms are important in developing appropriate interventions and preventions for him. We need to know how this particular child incorporates and internalizes, at a particular point in his development, what he has been dealt.

Next, consider Eric, a twenty-year-old caucasian hospitalized for a psychotic break halfway into his academically successful sophomore year in college.

By all accounts, he is said to be privileged; he has had access to the privileges afforded by a middle-class white status—access to good education, sufficient financial resources, and membership in dominant groups. Here, knowledge of theories of the social environment are not sufficient to either explain his difficulty or to develop interventions with Eric and his family. Therefore, attention must be focused on other possible contributing factors. In interviews with the client and his family, the inpatient social worker finds that Eric has a maternal grandfather who had several psychotic episodes and a maternal uncle who is described as "eccentric." She also learns that Eric was the driver in an automobile accident six months earlier that left his best friend paralyzed. In this case, if the social worker is to focus primarily on the social environment, the factors of biology, impact of loss, and concept of survivor guilt, likely strong contributors here, go unexplored.

Resiliency—A Perfect Example of Needing Both Personal and Environmental Factors

Perhaps one of the most promising and convincing areas of inquiry that support my contention of the importance of adequate attention to individual theories of behavior is the area of resiliency theory. For example, in a recent review of studies of children with attention deficit hyperactive and attention deficit disorders (Brooks, 1994), resiliency is said to be influenced by three interrelated domains: the child, the family, and the larger social environment. Several authors, including Hechtman (1991), find that children with "easy temperaments" from birth have advantages over other children in the areas of problem-solving skills as well as cognitive, coping, and social skills. Careful attention to the assessment of individual functioning (both in terms of competency and deficit) in these areas will further the understanding of the complex interaction between the social environment and the individual. This understanding, in turn, should lead toward interventions that are specific to the needs of the child.

Here, I have focused on the needs of the social worker in direct practice for theories of individual behavior. I contend that this is also an important knowledge base for social workers who administer programs, develop policy, and organize communities. If we want to foster resiliency in all clients, we need to identify clear means of individual assessment and identify individual and community strengths. This will lead to the development of prevention services, such as mentoring programs, that are designed to provide individuals with "compensatory" figures in their lives, a variable associated with the development of resiliency. Also closely associated with the determination of resiliency is self-esteem. People in marginalized groups suffer repeated assaults to their self-esteem by the dominant group. Programs that foster pride in one's gender or racial background or sexual preference are apt to raise the self-esteem of both individuals and the collective communities to which they belong. Certainly, this is not something that can be "given" to clients, but agency policies, legislation, and community interventions can maximize the possibilities of the development of self-esteem.

The need for understanding of individual theories of development was recently expressed by a group of first-year social work graduate students who reflected on their completion of the first year of study. One of the students with a strong background in a public child protection agency raised her concerns about need for this knowledge. She spoke eloquently about the social work skills involved in working with children and families who are poor, overstressed, and living in communities of violence. A minority student, she is particularly knowledgeable about the impact of racism on individuals and families, and she sensitively incorporates that understanding in her work with clients. However, she also identified her appreciation of her developing familiarity with theory, which allows her to increasingly understand the dynamics of attachment theory, for example, the effects of which are particularly important in child protective work. To know something about the psychological, cognitive, and affective effects of removal of a child from his or her biological parents is essential in the provision of sensitive, client-centered services. As the discussion continued, other students began to identify what theoretical concepts of behavior had guided their interventions. In some instances, the students had not been aware at the time of what assumptions about human behavior they brought to the client situation. We all have personal assumptions about what guides behavior, whether we acknowledge this or not. We would do better to make these assumptions explicit, examine and test them, and discard what is irrelevant, outdated, or simply incorrect. Likewise, agency policies and legislation that reflect a contemporary understanding of individual behavior and the social environment are essential in supporting the work of workers on behalf of clients.

Having proposed that the inclusion of theories of individual development is essential in the human behavior curriculum, I leave the hotly debated and contentious question of *which* theories of behavior should be considered and taught for another time and forum. There, too, we must avoid the polarization that occurs among us, in favor of an openness to diverse points of view and a willingness to assimilate and accommodate new information as it becomes available to us. One of the weaknesses ascribed to many of our theories of individual behavior is their sometimes exclusive reliance on "practice wisdom" without the utilization of appropriate and diverse research techniques. Research, like practice, must begin to further our understandings of the complex interplay between the individual and the social environment. This will point the way to further our understandings about how to intervene in both arenas, that is, the individual and the broader social environment (Mailick & Vigilante, 1987). This presents a challenge of the best kind for the social work profession and allows for the use of a biopsychosocial lens. Human suffering and oppression, as well as resiliency and growth, are multidetermined. Our understandings and our interventions must be multidetermined as well and reflect a utilization of the broad array of social work skills available to us in the tradition of solid social work practice.

Paradoxically, perhaps, the utilization of individual theory to inform our practice can empower the very clients who are compromised by the deficits in a harsh social environment. We can at once work to change oppressive factors in society while intervening on an individual basis to help clients identify and mobilize the inherent and acquired strengths that they bring as individual, families, and communities to a less than optimally responsive environment.

REFERENCES

Brooks, R. (1994). Children at risk: Fostering resilience and hope. *American Journal of Orthopsychiatry, 64*(4), 545–553.

Germain C., & Gitterman, A. (1980). *The life model of social work practice.* New York: Columbia University Press.

Goldstein, E. (1980). Knowledge base of clinical social work. *Social Work, 25,* 173–178.

Hechtman, L. (1991). Resilience and vulnerability in long term outcome of attention deficit hyperactivity disorder. *Canadian Journal of Psychiatry, 36,* 415–421.

Mailick, M., & Vigilante, F. (1987). Human behavior and the social environment: A sequence providing the theoretical base for teaching assessment. *Journal of Teaching in Social Work, 1*(2), 33–47.

Turner, F. J. (1986). *Social work treatment: Interlocking theoretical approaches* (3rd ed.). New York: Free Press.

Rejoinder to Dr. Heller

DEBORAH SIEGEL

Obviously, Professor Heller and I agree, as do most social workers, that the concept of person-in-environment, known these days as the ecological systems perspective, should guide social work education and practice. Our papers both maintain that when we attend only to person, or environment, rather than to the complex interactions between the two, our efforts to understand human woes are myopic and less than optimally effective.

It seems that Professor Heller interpreted the question, "Should HBSE *favor* social environment theories over theories of individual behavior?" to mean "Should social work education *ignore* theories of individual behavior in favor of those addressing the influence of the social environment?" That interpretation of the original question, I think, feeds into the "unproductive polarization" that Professor Heller decries. Neither Professor Heller nor I advocates dichotomizing person and environment. Her paper suggests that she shares my view that when social workers think in terms of therapy *versus* social action we abandon our professional identity, roots, and mission. Social workers must maintain a simultaneous dual focus on "case" and "cause."

The ecological systems perspective has emerged as the prevailing frame-work that guides the processes of assessment and intervention with both small and large systems. The ecological systems perspective requires that both person and environment receive adequate attention. Only an ideologue on the fringes of the profession would argue that we ought to *ignore* theories of human behavior in social work education.

That is why I maintain that until the mainstream clinical social worker incorporates into her or his daily clinical practice some activities directed toward changing large systems (whether through organizing communities or groups of disenfranchised clients, seeking to change oppressive agency policies, lobbying legislators, or participating in marches, demonstrations, and press conferences), HBSE courses must *emphasize* theories about the influence of the social environ-ment. Currently, the typical social work student gets insufficient exposure to ways of understanding, and methods for changing, oppressive social conditions. We need to swing our educational pendulum in the other direction, in the hope of even-tually fulfilling the simultaneous dual focus that honors the profession's mission.

United States culture stresses the individual rather than the social whole. Our national heritage is rooted in rugged individualism, including the myth that people with enough moral fiber and willpower can pull themselves up by the bootstraps. We are a society that blames victims—we deem the poor accountable for their own misery, the rape survivor responsible for her victimization, the inner-city high school dropout a personal failure, rather than a failure of an unre-sponsive social institution. These beliefs help explain why the United States lags so desperately far behind all other western industrialized democracies in provid-ing cradle-to-grave human services.

Hence, a macro perspective does not come easily to the typical social work student. It is a relatively unfamiliar, uncongenial point of view that makes stu-dents, and faculty, uneasy because it challenges the world view that permeates our understandings of what causes human woes and how to help. We naturally tend to find material on narrowly defined clinical issues more "interesting" and "useful" than complex, counterintuitive analyses of macro forces. When HBSE faculty take the position that we must emphasize both micro *and* macro, they unwittingly emphasize micro in the minds of most students. Because our tendency is to lose sight of macro issues, we must give them special emphasis or they whither in our awareness. The movement of the social work profession toward therapy and away from social action in pursuit of social justice is tragic testimony to this fact.

Should HBSE Content on People of Color or Other Minorities Be Presented Only by Instructors of Minority Status?

EDITOR'S NOTE: The context of social work teaching, like that of practice, is a "real world," and may be filled with similar ranges of personal, cultural, and institutional prejudice, of which the persons involved—teachers and students—may or may not be aware. Some people question whether teachers can free themselves sufficiently from their upbringing to teach these sensitive materials they themselves have not directly experienced.

Paul R. Keys, Ph.D., professor and Dean, College of Health and Human Services, Southeast Missouri State University, is founding editor, *The Journal of Multicultural Social Work,* and author of the *Encyclopedia of Social Work* (19th ed.) chapter on "managing for quality."

Carla M. Curtis, D.S.W., is assistant professor, College of Social Work, The Ohio State University. Her professional interests and research focus on policy-relevant knowledge about programs and services for poor children and their families, particularly children of color.

Darlene Grant, Ph.D., L.M.S.W.-A.C.P., is an assistant professor at the School of Social Work, University of Texas at Austin. Her current teaching and research interests include chemical dependency and psychiatric services. She has published in the areas of maternal perinatal drug addiction, culturally competent social work practice, and the impact of maternal incarceration on children.

Kathryn G. Wambach, Ph.D., A.C.S.W., is an assistant professor at the School of Social Work, University of Texas at Austin. Her teaching has focused on HBSE, research, cultural diversity, and psychopathology. She has published in the areas of AIDS prevention, substance abuse, and cultural diversity.

YES

Paul R. Keys
Carla M. Curtis

If controversy is a desired outcome, to suggest that only instructors of color should teach content on people of color in the human behavior and social environment (HBSE) course sequence will certainly elicit a polemically impassioned response. The challenges that confront society today are the challenges that should prompt social work intervention. These politically contentious, economically uncertain, and socially debilitating times require societal responses that depart from traditional ways of conceptualizing problems and addressing complicated issues. Like society, social work practitioners and those responsible for training or educating students to practice social work must confront the most troublesome challenges with creativity and conviction.

Bludgeoned with growing demands on the economy, structural unemployment, limited employment opportunity, and a population preoccupied by "modern individualist desires" (Wolfe, 1990, p. 29), the American welfare state has not responded effectively to the social ills of the times. These include poverty, unemployment, inadequate or nonexistent health care, homelessness, and hunger.

Additionally, the unique experiences of people of color in this country magnify and make attending to basic survival needs more complex. Racial oppression requires that societal responses to basic needs of individuals be viewed with sensitivity to exclusionary practices, reinforced by the "isms" of the times—racism, classism, elitism, etc. Similar arguments can be made about other issues of oppression such as anti-Semitism, homophobia and heterosexism, ageism, etc.

As a profession, social work is charged with empowering individuals, groups, and communities, particularly oppressed groups, to participate in decision making and engage in effective problem solving over matters that influence day-to-day functioning. Social workers are expected to challenge and reconstruct, as necessary, the knowledge on which a world view evolves. This then becomes the basis for interpreting behavior, which is central to problem solving.

Social work educators are therefore central to the construction and interpretation of knowledge to students about client systems and their culturally determined values, beliefs, attitudes, and behaviors, which are reflected in HBSE theory and content. Knowledge typically emphasized in the history of the development of American culture excludes many groups whose experiences have played critical roles in the formation of society and culture. To reflect the contribution of oppressed and exclusionary groups, knowledge must be reconstructed (Andersen & Hill-Collins, 1995). The reconstructing of knowledge requires, however, an unquestioning belief in the value and importance of inclusivity. It also requires a recognition of the deprecating experiences associated with exclusionary practices and behaviors. Therefore, the authors respond affirmatively to the debate. HBSE content on people of color should be taught by people of color. The question that must then be responded to is "why?"

Interpreting HBSE Content for People of Color

To appropriately assess the cause of an individual or family problem in social functioning, a practitioner requires a knowledge of the psychosocial factors that influence human development. These are largely a function of culture. Effective intervention is dependent on adequate knowledge of social systems and of their cultural origin and dynamics (Solomon, 1987). These distinctive cultural patterns must be reflected in HBSE theory and content because practitioners learn how, in practice, to work with various cultures and subcultures through HBSE knowledge. The knowledge base for social work curricula, however, is based on the life experiences and stages of development associated with the majority or "civic culture" (Fuchs, 1990). Do the experiences of people of color require special analysis and consideration in a sociocultural context? The authors assert that HBSE content on people of color must consider the unique experiences of racism and oppression directed toward people of color because of skin color. How can majority group instructors interpret and portray the importance of racial identity and ethnic group affiliation among minorities of color in this country?

African Americans

People of color in this country, but particularly African Americans, because of forced migration and economic exploitation, have experienced an insidious kind of oppression and discrimination caused by racism. Racism, defined as a system of advantage based on race (Wellman, 1977), is pervasive. It is virtually impossible to live in the United States today and not be exposed to some aspect of the institutional, cultural, or personal manifestations of racism.

Racism is so provocative and all encompassing as to influence racial identity development among African Americans and whites (Helms, 1993). Racism, as manifested in the dominant/subordinate relationship between whites and African Americans in this society, influences the development of racial identity in different ways. The pattern of racial identity development for African Americans has been conceptualized as evolving and reevolving based on experiences in a hostile environment. This process includes self-devaluation, self-valuation, ethnocentric emphases, and the evolution of recognizable and achievable courses of action to promote both individual and collective interests (Cross, 1991). Though not mentioned specifically, there is evidence that suggests that identity development for other oppressed groups (Asians, Native Americans) is similar to that of African Americans (Tatum, 1992).

In spite of the frustrated aspirations of people of color caused by racism, positive self-valuation can and does prevail even when dissatisfaction with social and economic conditions is a factor (Foster & Perry, 1982). The African American family is critical to promoting values and beliefs that support and promote a positive racial identify (Spencer, Brookins, & Allen, 1985). African American families have of necessity mastered certain coping skills and survival techniques that may not be recognized or understood among majority group members. Included are the use of humor to release repressed feelings and alleviate suffering (Bowles, 1994) and the withholding of information to influence decision making, particularly when information may serve to reward or penalize applicants or recipients of public services (Chipungu & Everett, 1994). Other coping mechanisms are employed by people of color that can perpetuate painful circumstances. Some African Americans, for example, believe it is at times appropriate or beneficial to deny or ignore racial identity to cope with the realities of racism. Parents may avoid discussing with their children how dangerous the white world can be for people of color (Pinderhughes, 1989). African American children may grow up not knowing the possible recriminations that can occur to a young black male who whistles at a white female, or how walking through a shopping mall can result in unwarranted and inappropriate surveillance because of one's skin color.

Hispanics

When assessing the experiences of the Hispanic population for inclusion and discussion in courses emphasizing HBSE content, if the instructor is not very knowledgeable of pertinent history and facts, the issue of race may not be addressed, as if to suggest that Hispanics form a separate racial category. The criterion of definition is language, not race (Pinderghughes, 1989). When using the term *Hispanic,* the authors make reference to Mexican Americans (Chicanos), Puerto Ricans, Cubans, and people from other Spanish-speaking countries in Latin America and Spain. In fact, Hispanics can be of any race and yet we are constantly exposed, by the news media, to references of Hispanics as a race.

With the invasion of Latin America in the seventeenth century by Spaniards, a land previously inhabited by Indians was conquered by whites. Latin America, like the United States, imported slaves for economic exploitation and also underwent a period of immigration from Europe and Asia in the 1800s. Unlike the United States, intermarriage among Latin Americans has been more prevalent among distinct cultural groups. Thus today, in the United States, as well as in Latin America, many Hispanics are the products of racially mixed marriages.

As people from Latin America began to immigrate en masse to the United States about twenty-five years ago, they defied the traditional categorizations of race. Hispanics' skin color ranges from white to black and numerous shades in between. If by color alone some Hispanics can be viewed as white, differences in culture, and particularly language, have resulted in widespread discrimination and racism.

One of the current major issues for Hispanics and other new immigrants relates to language. There is growing sentiment to limit or virtually eliminate linguistic diversity. It has been suggested that efforts to make English the official language of the United States represent a movement that would prevent immigrants from speaking their own language at home (Portes & Rumbaut, 1990). Although this prediction may seem extreme, so too is the suggestion that language barriers are a "rite of passage that makes a new identity worth having" (Wolfe, 1990, p. 31).

Hispanics represent a socioculturally diverse group whose cultural experiences and adaptations are in a continuous state of flux and change. Cultural group membership can be viewed along a continuum where at one end an individual may have limited knowledge of a new cultural environment and the behavioral, social, and cognitive dimensions of the milieu; at the opposite end of the spectrum is the individual who has become totally acculturated or immersed into the cultural scenario. Midpoint between these extremes is the person who enjoys a "bicultural adaptation" (Delgado, 1992).

Implications for Teaching HBSE Content on People of Color

The experiences of people of color in this society must be viewed through a lens of oppression and racism. Racism and prejudice, or preconceived judgments or opinions about people based on limited information (Tatum, 1992), define in large part the sociocultural experiences of minority groups. One's values, beliefs, attitudes, and behavior are created and reinforced in a cultural context; social modes of adaptation are influenced by racial identity, which, in this society, evolves in a hostile environment and is manifest in dominant/subordinate relationships between whites and people of color (Tatum, 1992).

The prominence of racism in American society requires that people of color and oppressed minorities be addressed in HBSE course content in social work courses by instructors who can effectively manage racism. Pla-Richard (1991) refers to the technique of managing racism, defined by Dickens and Dickens (1982) as those behaviors developed by African Americans to counteract and neutralize those offensive, demeaning, and discriminatory behaviors directed to them by persons of other races or ethnic groups.

Managing racism is distinguished from managing conflict, which may arise when addressing race or other sensitive topics in a classroom setting. Managing racism requires firsthand experience in identifying prejudice and discrimination based on one's skin color. Though a sad commentary on the quality of life experiences for people of color, this experiential knowledge is necessary to effectively and accurately assess sociocultural variables or factors that may influence individual and group behavior and development.

Gitterman (1991) suggests that white instructors may manage conflict based on controversial course content but also may suppress it if the instructors are not comfortable with their own class, race, or sexual orientation. Singleton (1994) documents the personal discomfort and avoidance of discussion of oppression by social work faculty. People of color are more likely to risk confronting the difficult and even taboo topics of race and racism in ways that can diminish student resistance to talking and learning about racism (Tatum, 1992).

Social work educators must challenge the institutional, cultural, and societal forces that allow racism to thrive. If the literature is a reflection of practice, social work is arguably promoting the status quo regarding the status of people of color and other oppressed minorities versus promoting interventions that can effectively mitigate the experiences of racism, poverty, and other forms of oppression.

A content analysis of articles published in four major social work journals (*Social Work, Social Casework, Social Service Review,* and *Child Welfare*) between 1980 and 1989 found that social workers do not emphasize institutional, organizational, or societal change as a means of restructuring the sociocultural context in which we live and that serve to oppress people of color and other minorities (McMahon & Allen-Meares, 1992). McMahon and Allen-Meares (1992) found that less than 6 percent (117 articles) of the journal entries reviewed (1,965) proposed some intervention with or on behalf of minorities; the articles almost exclusively emphasized individual intervention aimed at enabling minority clients to adjust to their social circumstances, or sensitizing social workers to the cultural values and beliefs of minorities. This limited perspective on intervention strategies does not adequately or completely acknowledge the social context in which minority group members live (McMahon & Allen-Meares, 1992).

The profession becomes vulnerable to charges of being racist by demonstrating "a reluctance to undertake social action within a macrocontext" (McMahon & Allen-Meares, 1992, p. 537). Although the race or ethnic group affiliation of the authors whose work is included in the content analysis is not mentioned, one can speculate that most of the contributing authors are white males. Women and minorities of color do not publish proportionate to their numbers in the profession, at rates comparable to white males (Berger, 1990).

Conclusion

Social work education must place greater emphasis on societal and institutional change essential to minimizing the negative effects of poverty and racism that continue to oppress people of color and other minorities in this country. One of the ways to begin addressing this concern is to require that:

- Minorities of color teach HBSE content on people of color
- Social work education programs support faculty of color by encouraging academic exploration of difficult subject matter such as racism and racial and ethnic identity, and by making such content a mandatory component of HBSE course content in social work curricula

- Social work education programs must identify and provide those supports and research aids to enable faculty of color to publish in HBSE areas, thereby adding to the knowledge that influences society's world view of minority group issues and concerns.

REFERENCES

Andersen, A. L., & Hill-Collins, P. (Eds.) (1995). *Race, class, and gender: An anthology.* Belmont, CA: Wadsworth Publishing.

Berger, R. (1990). Getting published: A mentoring program for social work faculty. *Social Work, 35,* 69–71.

Bowles, D. D. (1994). Black humor as self-affirmation. *Journal of Multicultural Social Work, 3*(2), 1–10.

Chipungu, S., & Everett, J. (1994). The power of information: Exchange patterns between African-American parents and child welfare workers. *Journal of Multicultural Social Work, 3*(3), 17–34.

Cross, W. E., Jr. (1991). *Shades of black: Diversity in African-American identity.* Philadelphia: Temple University Press.

Delgado, R. (1992). Generalist child welfare and Hispanic families. In N. A. Cohen (Ed.), *Child welfare: A multicultural focus* (pp. 130–156).

Dickens, F., & Dickens, J. (1982). *The Black manager: Making it in the corporate world.* New York: Amacom.

Foster, M., & Perry, L. R. (1982). Self-valuation among blacks. *Social Work, 27,* 60–64.

Fuchs, L. H. (1990). *The American kaleidoscope: Race, ethnicity, and the civic culture.* Middletown, CT: Wesleyan University Press.

Gitterman, A. (1991). Working with differences: White teacher and African-American students. *Journal of Teaching in Social Work, 5*(2), 65–79.

Helms, J. E. (Ed.) (1993). *Black and white racial identity: Theory, research, and practice.* Westport, CT: Praeger Publishers.

McMahon, A., & Allen-Meares, P. (1992). Is social work racist? A content analysis of recent literature. *Social Work, 37*(6), 533–539.

Pinderhughes, E. (1989). *Understanding race, ethnicity, and power.* New York: The Free Press.

Pla-Richard, M. (1991). Connecting with difference: Black teacher–white students. *Journal of Teaching in Social Work, 5*(2), 53–64.

Portes, A., & Rumbaut, R. G. (1990). *Immigrant America: A portrait.* Berkeley, CA: University of California Press.

Singleton, S. M. (1994). Faculty personal comfort and the teaching of content on racial oppression. In Paul R. Keys (Ed.), *School social workers in the multicultural environment: New roles and responsibilities, and educational enrichment.* New York: Haworth Press.

Solomon, B. B. (1987). Human development: Sociocultural perspective. *Encyclopedia of Social Work, 1,* 856–866. Washington, DC: NASW.

Spencer, M. B., Brookins, G. K., & Allen, W. R. (Eds.). (1985). *Beginnings: The social and effective development of black children.* New Jersey: Lawrence Erlbaum Associates.

Tatum, B. D. (1992). Talking about race, learning about racism: The application of racial identity development theory in the classroom. *Harvard Educational Review, 62*(1), 1–24.

Wellman, D. (1977). *Portraits of white racism.* New York: Cambridge University Press.

Wolfe, A. (1990, December 31). The return of the melting pot. *The New Republic* pp. 27–34.

Rejoinder to Drs. Keys and Curtis

Darlene Grant

Kathryn G. Wambach

We do not endorse general and uncritical prejudgment or ability stereotyping of anyone. Arguments automatically judging all white instructors as incapable of the sensitivity and knowledge, respect, and value reconstruction necessary to join their colleagues of color and other oppressed minorities in adequately and effectively presenting HBSE content on people of color and other minorities are ludicrous. Similarly, we do not endorse the assumption that all colleagues of color and other oppressed minorities by virtue of their race or situation ground their teaching in the ideal of inclusivity or can sensitively discuss HBSE content on people of color without prejudice or bias. Furthermore, and the primary reason for responding negatively in this debate, is the reality that instructors of color and other minorities would end up teaching courses within a circumscribed range because of historical underrepresentation on social work faculties.

The inherent message in using only minority instructors is making multiculturalism synonymous with a "minority perspective." That white instructors are taken "off the hook" in terms of self-evaluation and enhancement and learning about and developing proficiency in teaching multicultural content seems significantly incongruent with social work values. We decry the development of an academy that supports and physically models an approach that suggests to students that their white colleagues cannot become proficient enough to understand or negotiate sensitive topics in the classroom or accurately assess sociocultural variables influencing client behavior and development.

The argument presented by Drs. Keys and Curtis uses as a premise the idea that people of color and other minorities are uniquely equipped to manage racism effectively, whereas white instructors, lacking experiential knowledge, cannot. They argue, rather, that white instructors tend to deny accurate history and contributions and capabilities of people of color and other oppressed groups. Taken to its logical end, this argument suggests the polarization of faculty based on race, sexual orientation, or physical ability, that nonminority instructors are not self-aware, lack the ability to be aware of and responsible for their beliefs, values, and emotions in reference to cultural difference, and may be ineffective in their own work with minority students and clients. Again, we disagree.

We recognize that instructors are likely to be reared, educated, and inculcated in U.S. culture and subcultures that continue to struggle with issues around racial discrimination and oppression, gender bias, ethnic cleansing, gay and lesbian bashing, and disability stereotyping. We also recognize the social work value base that suggests that we do not have to put up with a professional membership (be it practice or academic) that is reluctant to undertake social action within micro or macro contexts. To counter institutional indolence in the area of cultural competence and proficiency, we recommend the institutionalization of safeguards for all instructors, minority and nonminority, teaching HBSE content on people of color and other minorities. The academy should support inclusion, in terms not just of content but also presentation. All instructors, regardless of race, orientation, or ability, can and should be held accountable for becoming experientially knowledgeable, self-aware, and sensitive to cultural issues, oppression, and economic and social justice. The following safeguards are suggested as faculties assess instructor assignment and begin to formulate their conceptualization of HBSE content on people of color and other minorities:

- Development and dissemination of instructional tools and assignments that avoid superficial and abstract exposure to diversity content issues
- Development and dissemination of content-specific evaluation protocols for tracking student and instructor learning growth and development over time
- Development of assignments, including panel and other discussions that encourage meaningful personal interactions
- Use of cross-cultural teaching teams to (1) model cross-cultural interaction, debate, problem solving, and resolution and (2) provide nonminority and minority instructors experiential opportunities for processing and personal growth

In sum, it is incumbent on the academy to pull in as many minority and nonminority instructors as possible to wrestle with the issues and for the instruction and discussion of HBSE curriculum on people of color and other minorities. The payoff will be heightened awareness and more accurate perceptions, knowledge reconstruction, attitude, and value adjustments for nonminority and minority instructors alike. We recommend that this interaction and exchange take place on the broadest scale possible with a primary goal of producing practitioners who are culturally aware and proficient. We suggest that it is crucial to model meaningful cross-cultural interaction and that multicultural team teaching is the ideal toward which we should all strive.

NO

DARLENE GRANT
KATHRYN G. WAMBACH

This discussion places the decades-old "indigenous worker" controversy in the perspective of teaching human behavior in the social environment (HBSE). The indigenous worker assertion is that only persons of color or other minorities, by virtue of group membership or similarity in some key characteristic, can be experts on people of color and other minorities (Anderson, 1975; Brammer, 1985). The argument follows, then, that experts (i.e., indigenous instructors) are the only persons who should be used to teach HBSE content on people of color and other minorities (e.g., persons with disabilities, women, gay and lesbian people). Historically, the indigenous worker argument has been espoused in a number of social service contexts: only recovering alcoholics can effectively work with alcoholics (Handler, 1975); only disabled persons can understand what it is like to be invisible to fully abled persons (Asher, 1975); only blacks can fully understand and help other blacks survive the black experience in America (Devore & Schlesinger, 1991); and so forth.

The flip side of exclusive use of indigenous instructors for presenting HBSE content on people of color and other minorities involves inclusion of white instructors in the exchange. An inevitable outcome, on either side, is the mismatch of an unaware/unenlightened instructor who is disdainful of culturally relevant course content. There is no easy answer to this complex debate. We are committed, however, to the position that the ability to view all perspectives and to instruct without bias is open to most if not all instructors, minority and nonminority alike. We (those of us in the social work academy) cannot expect our students to believe in the importance and legitimacy of content on people of color and other minorities until that content is handled visibly, intimately, and responsibly by all faculty members. The social work ideal of valuing racial, ethnic, cultural, and other diversity will remain illusive until everyone is included in teaching diversity content, in enriching and expanding learning experience, and in wrestling with this course content individually and in discourse with students and colleagues.

The Indigenous Worker Argument

Dependence on indigenous workers by social service agencies reached its zenith during the War on Poverty and Community Organization movements, which were in process during the later part of the Civil Rights movement. In this same period, for example, the Black Panthers and leaders in the Muslim movements were developing social services for blacks that were staffed exclusively by indigenous workers. Community drug rehabilitation centers only wanted recovering drug addicts as service providers. Agencies that provided services to gay and lesbian clients were becoming more common, and their staffs were composed almost exclusively of gay and lesbian workers.

Frequently given the titles of "outreach worker" or "neighborhood aides," indigenous workers were used because they were members of or had similar characteristics to the client group. It was believed that the workers' personal knowledge of group characteristics and dynamics, intelligence, life experience, credibility with the client group, and ability to work with agency workers were necessary for optimal effectiveness (Anderson, 1975; Brammer, 1985).

Even within this historical context, exclusive reliance on indigenous workers produced some negative consequences. During the War on Poverty, indigenous workers became instruments of social control, expected to maintain the calm within their client groups by espousing and facilitating change through dominant society channels and protocol. The debate on whether this was inadvertent or purposeful and unethical use of these workers is beyond the scope of this discussion. However, adherence to rules and expectations of the agency worker resulted in the indigenous workers becoming co-opted, losing credibility within their groups, and losing their identification with agency workers (Anderson, 1975).

While they were socialized into the agency mentality, indigenous workers were also limited in areas in which they could perform for the agency. "Regardless of the level of performance, they [found] themselves in dead-end jobs" (Anderson, 1975, p. 392). Whatever their level of competence, indigenous workers found themselves frustrated, unable to advance, and ability-stereotyped by agency workers they had begun to perceive as their colleagues.

The Indigenous Instructor Argument

Turning attention to the application of these concepts to the educational arena, we see two main points supporting use of indigenous instructors: First, we must deal with evidence of historical discrimination in social services. Second, minority and nonminority students have doubts about the qualifications of white instructors to teach minority content; specifically, students were suspicious about the validity of their interpretation and presentation of ethnic and other minority content (Axelson, 1993; Lum, 1992). One specific example was the fact that past white and other nonminority instructors used a text that perpetuated black stereotypes, Liebow's (1967) *Talley's Corner,* to teach HBSE content on blacks. Today, however, this book may be viewed as an interesting example of field research with all of its threats to internal and external validity, while it is simultaneously considered obsolete in terms of its use with HBSE content on people of color.

The perception that only indigenous instructors can teach HBSE content on people of color is based in the belief that such a person will be more knowledgeable, supportive, and understanding of minority issues. It is presumed that the indigenous instructor is potentially free from dissonance raised during cross-cultural interaction and shares the same value and knowledge base as the individual client/client group under study. This approach can result in students categorizing instructors in terms of those who can versus those who cannot or should not teach it. The risk is that this perception and subsequent categorization can be generalized to other areas of social work performance, including practice and policy development.

Furthermore, it is unrealistic to think that students will not generalize what they see in the school context to how they should proceed in the world of practice. Would not disparate cultural values be communicated to students as they were taught diversity content only by people of color or other minorities?

If we follow the indigenous person as instructor argument further, the assertion is that whites and other nonminority persons cannot develop the nonbiased and credible knowledge, values, and skills needed to teach HBSE content on people of color and other minorities. The question arises, then why should white and other nonminority social workers in academic, practice, training, and other settings even bother to study or prepare to teach this content? Because there is evidence that practitioners rarely enter cross-cultural client–worker relationships sufficiently knowledgeable about the specific minority groups in the communities in which they work (Devore & Schlesinger, 1991), why should we even expect white and other nonminority students to commit time to course content and discussions on people of color and other minorities? Why do most current social work practice texts recommend that all students strive to understand their own motives, biases, values, and assumptions about human behavior to be good practitioners (Sue & Sue, 1990)?

An indigenous instructor assertion produces seriously undesirable consequences. It distances white and other nonminorities from intimate involvement with the content and issues, and it provides our faculties and students a framework of assumptions that reduces the legitimacy and importance of diversity content and issues. What about responsibility for letting our realities bump up against each others' so our individual and collective knowledge, understanding, and ability for accurate empathy, understanding, and values can expand (Gilligan, 1982)? What about offering white and other nonminority colleagues and students the opportunity to grow beyond the bounds of their group of membership?

We cannot decide to exclude white instructors from teaching HBSE cultural diversity content when confronted with statistics on the membership of mental health professions that estimate that anywhere from 84 to 90 percent of workers are white, (Axelson, 1993; Dana, 1993). Juxtaposed with 10 to 16 percent of minority graduate students, faculty, and practitioners, white faculty members and practitioners who depend on minority faculty to teach diversity content could place the faculty, students, and practitioners at a disadvantage by perpetuating ideas that result in continued mistrust and underutilization of services by minority students and clients (Dana, 1993).

Following the original assertion through to a logical end, then, it is likely that a large percentage of white mental health professionals can end their training experiences and move into work arenas where odds are against their interacting, to any significant degree, with persons of color or any other minority counselor. This scenario holds serious implications for white and other nonminority workers entering disparate workforces with the idea that only people of color or other minority persons can be experts in providing enlightenment on casework with people of color and other minorities.

Alternative Approaches

An understanding of and respect for different racial and ethnic backgrounds, different cultures, physical and intellectual handicaps, gender, sexual orientation, and age are just two out of a number of basic principles that guide social work practice and instructor selection (Devore & Schlesinger, 1991; Sheafor, Horejsi, & Horejsi, 1991). These principles demand that all instructors, regardless of their individual group membership, be present in examining the consequences of imbalance in power and devaluation and mistreatment of people of color and other minorities (Lum, 1992). In fact, numerous authors suggest use of teams of culturally and ethnically diverse, including white and other nonminority, teachers/trainers as one approach to creating optimum learning environments for trainees (Carney & Kahn, 1984; Pendersen, 1986).

The ideal culture of learning and social work practice would demonstrate that faculty, regardless of their ethnicity, gender, sexual orientation, or physical ability, should be part of the HBSE discussion on people of color and other minorities. It models for all students that nonminority persons need not be distant from this content and the issues, but must be close to and responsible in struggling with it inside and outside of the classroom setting. The potential disadvantage in the argument for indigenous instructors is that white and other nonminority students may report that their minority instructors fail to recognize or appreciate their nonminority "culture" (Nadelson & Zimmerman, 1993), while at the same time assessing their faculty's commitment to the value of diversity, noticing that it involves mere lip service because only minorities teach diversity content. Too many students will walk away from these types of learning experiences devaluing diversity.

If we argue against the indigenous person as expert and teacher idea, then what should we do? First, we must recognize that no one approach to teaching HBSE content is appropriate for all students and situations, nor are individuals from any one group (people of color or other minorities) singularly competent as instructors for HBSE content (Dana, 1993; Sue & Sue, 1990). The argument presented also suggests that the social work collective must strive to recognize the influence of historical and current oppression, eliminate discrimination in social services, increase and support attention to minority practice in practice texts, journals, and conferences, in the university, and in the classroom. Furthermore, we must provide the opportunity for white and other nonminority instructors to build and demonstrate that they are qualified to teach in this area and that they strive for cultural validity in their writing, research, and course content.

We risk alienating enlightened nonminorities and subsequently losing the wealth of knowledge they bring to the table having themselves evolved beyond ethnocentrism to understanding and practicing effectively with diverse populations. Subsequently, the ideal learning environment involves the minority and nonminority instructor as an instructor team that models healthy cross-cultural exchange and interaction for students. White or other instructors can reach outside of the classroom in collaboration with practitioners who are persons of color or members of other minority groups as a team to provide the broadest possible perspective and learning experience.

REFERENCES

Anderson, R. J. (1975). Volunteers and paraprofessionals. In D. Brieland, L. B. Costin, & C. R. Atherton (Eds.), *Contemporary social work: An introduction to social work and social welfare* (pp. 379–394). New York: McGraw-Hill.

Asher, N. W. (1975). The handicapped. In D. Brieland, L. B. Costin, & C. R. Atherton (Eds.), *Contemporary social work: An introduction to social work and social welfare* (pp. 321–335). New York: McGraw-Hill.

Axelson, J. A. (1993). *Counseling and development in a multicultural society.* Pacific Grove, CA: Brooks/Cole.

Brammer, L. M. (1985). *The helping relationship: Process and skills* (3rd ed.). Englewood Cliffs, NJ: Prentice-Hall.

Carney, C. G., & Kahn, K. B. (1984). Building competencies for effective cross-cultural counseling: A developmental view. *The Counseling Psychologist, 12*(1), 111–119.

Dana, R. H. (1993). *Multicultural assessment perspectives for professional psychology.* Boston: Allyn & Bacon.

Devore, W. & Schlesinger, E. G. (1991) *Ethnic-sensitive social work practice* (3rd ed.). New York: Merrill.

Gilligan, C. (1982). *In a different voice: Psychological theory and women's development.* Cambridge, MA: Harvard University Press.

Handler, E. (1975). The offender. In D. Brieland, L. B. Costin, & C. R. Atherton (Eds.), *Contemporary social work: An introduction to social work and social welfare* (pp. 336–353). New York: McGraw-Hill.

Liebow, E. (1967). *Tally's Corner: A study of Negro street corner men.* Boston: Little Brown.

Lum, D. (1992). *Social work practice & people of color: A process-stage approach* (2nd ed.). Pacific Grove, CA: Brooks/Cole.

Nadelson, C. C., & Zimmerman, V. (1993). Culture and psychiatric care of women. In A. C. Gaw (Ed.). *Culture, ethnicity, and mental illness* (pp. 501–516). Washington, DC: American Psychiatric Press.

Pendersen, P. B. (1986). Developing interculturally skilled counselors: A prototype for training. In H. P. Lefley & P. B. Pedersen (Eds.). *Cross-cultural training for mental health professionals* (pp. 73–88). Springfield, IL: Charles C. Thomas.

Sheafor, B. W., Horejsi, C. R., & Horejsi, G. A. (1991). *Techniques and guidelines for social work practice* (2nd ed.). Boston: Allyn & Bacon.

Sue, D. W., & Sue, D. (1990). *Counseling the culturally different: Theory & practice* (2nd ed.). New York: John Wiley & Sons.

Rejoinder to Drs. Grant and Wambach

PAUL R. KEYS
CARLA M. CURTIS

The authors suggest that the indigenous service workers argument is not an explanatory one for the case at hand of people of color presenting HBSE content. The issue here is one of imparting the best knowledge base to students for informed and aware practice. It is a question of expertise and knowledge. Students and graduates must work in an increasingly multicultural world of practice. They must be prepared to recognize and deal with the new multicultural realities. Current evidence shows that most white instructors do not have a sufficient knowledge base to adequately prepare students for this increased diversity in contemporary client loads (Matsushima, 1981; McMahon & Allen-Meares, 1992; Pla-Richard, 1991). The profession clearly needs to better prepare white instructors to teach the necessary HBSE content, but until then, instructors of color must model the appropriate knowledge, skills, and abilities in this area.

The field of philosophy advances the idea of *formal knowledge,* that is, to know what one knows and what one does not know. Literally, many white instructors, and obviously there are exceptions, currently do not know what they do not know. They do not, for example, know the life stages and experiences of persons of color sufficiently to interpret it appropriately in HBSE content. This leads to false assumptions, misinterpretations, gaps, and omissions. For example, some talk of "poor" as synonymous with "minorities"—"poor minorities," rather than "poor, minorities," showing that some minorities are poor, but that there is a decided minority middle class with different values from some poor. To the instructor of color, this shows the necessity of teaching HBSE from the strengths of successful minority families, recognizing the differences from the minority "underclass." It also may call for a recognition of traditional minority attitudes, for example, toward mental health services. Though it is rapidly changing, many persons of color still hold such services in low regard, believing them to be stigmatizing and demeaning.

There should be little question that *all* instructors must understand different cultures, and that teams of culturally diverse trainers may help create the optimal learning environment. Nor do we necessarily quarrel with the assertion that all faculty must be a part of the HBSE discussion of minorities. White instructors do need to "reduce their distance," grow, and increase their intimate involvement. Nevertheless, until the formal knowledge gap is closed in sufficient numbers, only minority HBSE instructors can be sufficiently qualified to teach the culturally relevant content.

This is clearly not to say that *no* whites are now qualified. Only a very few, by virtue of background, experiences, values, and predilection, come close to having this prerequisite formal knowledge. But these small numbers are not enough to sufficiently meet the current exigencies of the field and the profession. The very fact, as referenced by Grant and Wambach, that white students are disdainful of culturally relevant course content exemplifies this gap in formal knowledge. So does the fact, also cited, that students will not believe the content to be important unless taught by white instructors. The current composition of caseloads, 99 percent persons of color in some urban agencies, illustrates the relevance of the course content. Nevertheless, students (and faculty) are all too unaware of the subtle differences in practice required by this changed caseload.

We do need to create the team teaching advocated by the authors—modeled by instructors of color. Students will then see minority instructors in master teacher roles in relation to this content. This addresses the issue of respectfulness and of relevance of the content to the instructors, as mentioned by Grant and Wambach.

REFERENCES

Matsushima, J. (1981). Resistance in infusing minority content in social work education. *Smith College Studies in Social Work, 51*(3), 216–225.

McMahon, A., & Allen-Meares, P. (1992). Is social work racist? A content analysis of recent literature. *Social Work, 37*(6), 533–539.

Pla-Richard, M. (1991). Connecting with difference: Black teacher–white students. *Journal of Teaching in Social Work, 5*(2), 53–64.

Can a Feminist Perspective in HBSE Exist without "Blaming the Aggressor"?

Editor's Note: Feminists (women as well as men) are outraged by social inequality with regard to the status of women in this and other societies. These conditions have been analyzed in a wide range of feminist theories and research that have taken their place within the "canon" of HBSE. However, a sensitive issue emerges, because many causes of this inequality involve men, past and present, and the patriarchal society.

Nancy Humphreys, D.S.W., professor and former dean, School of Social Work, University of Connecticut, writes and teaches extensively in the area of women's studies. She also serves as the director of the Center for the Advancement of Political Social Work Practice.

Jo Nol, Ph.D., has a private clinical practice and recently completed her doctoral work at Smith College. She has taught at Smith College and the University of Connecticut and does workshops on clinical interventions with women.

Joan Laird, Ph.D., is professor of School of Social Work, Smith College. She has made many contributions to the social work literature, from the pivotal *Family-Centered Social Work Practice* (1983, Ann Hartman & Joan Laird), to her 1993 anthology, *Revisioning Social Work Education: A Social Constructionist approach.* She thanks Kathryn Basham, Assistant Professor, and Ann Hartman,

Professor Emerita, both from the Smith College School for Social Work, for their helpful comments.

YES

NANCY HUMPHREYS

JO NOL

It is fundamental to social work education that social work students learn to view people as complex beings in their social and cultural context. Rather than promoting a polarized and therefore simplified view of human motivation and behavior, new social workers are encouraged to develop a sophisticated, multifaceted understanding of their clients as well as of people in general. The Human Behavior and the Social Environment (HBSE) curriculum is the primary source for this perspective and information. Feminism and feminist analyses of the role gender plays have made essential contributions to the teaching and learning in this required foundation area of study. In teaching this material, educators must convey a nondichotomized perspective of female and male experience to be consistent with social work philosophy. Both social work and feminist views promote an understanding of human experience from a both/and perspective, this being a more accurate way to study any complex system.

To help students develop this more complex view, several strategies can be implemented and woven together throughout the courses. By clarifying that both men and women are harmed by the present sexist gender role expectations and institutionalized misogyny is one way of reducing the polarization. Furthermore, viewing the results of the dichotomization of the genders into demon and victim as symptoms of underlying forces, both individual and sociocultural, can be useful. To be effective social workers, students need to understand how oppression affects people. Thus, examining the purposes of maintaining these arrangements from several perspectives, political, sociological, economic, and psychological, using a feminist lens, can help diffuse the tendency to oversimplify female and male experience. In addition, a discussion of the limitations of generalizing about human experience is necessary. Finally, classroom experiences as well as readings and assignments should be designed to provide psychological safety for students so as to enable them to explore this often volatile material and to minimize the tendency toward polarization.

Theory and evidence from both the macro and micro practice views to support this endeavor are readily available. These include Ryan's (1976) work on the purpose and support for ongoing victim blaming as applied to male–female relationships. In addition, the feminist lens has been turned to the analysis of social policy (Abramovitz, 1988; Miller 1992) and the social definition of social problems (Davis, Hagen, & Early, 1994). New perspectives for understanding individual male and female development and interventions have been illuminated by the insights provided by a feminist perspective (Baker-Miller, 1976; Chodorow, 1978; Gilligan, 1982; Luepnitz, 1988).

Feminism

Contrary to the critics of feminism, especially the neo- or conservative feminists (an oxymoron?) such as Camille Paglia, feminism implies neither male-bashing nor an understanding of or promotion of woman-as-victim. Feminism in our view, and that of its most prolific architects, involves understanding how gender and gender role expectations influence, shape, and permeate all aspects of human functioning. Feminism brings a different light to the experiences of both women and men. This then is the central tenet of feminist analysis: that gender is an essential factor for accurately understanding all human interactions, and that a feminist analysis can be carried out without demonizing men or women, who are both products of gender role acculturation.

Feminism and Oppression Theory

A feminist perspective allows us to at least figuratively step outside our culture (as much as is possible, because we are after all members of the culture) and examine the world through a new and clarifying lens. What it shows to us is that we live in a society that is constructed around the requirements of patriarchal assumptions. Such arrangements place strict requirements, expectations, and limitations on both women and men. These patriarchal assumptions are expressed in sexism, an ideology of oppression.

Male domination and female subjugation are the two interlocking arrangements promoted by sexism. A sexist view suggests that gender is the most salient factor in determining the value of human beings; all that is associated with femaleness is devalued, and all that is associated with maleness is overvalued. Operationalization of sexism through the socialization of children is generally conducted along rigid gender-specific expectations and stereotyped characteristics so that adult behaviors are codified and segregated by gender. Chodorow (1978) offers interwoven sociological and psychological explanations for how this system is so tenaciously maintained even though both females and males pay enormous psychological prices for the sexist scripts.

Gender-based oppression is pervasive; it is expressed on the conscious intersubjective level and eventually becomes a part of the collective unconscious (Ryan, 1976). It is institutionalized in the policies and practices that govern all human commerce. Oppression is at the root of many of the problems for which clients seek services from social workers. The effects of oppression result in fewer options for both the object and subject of the oppressive script. Along with damaging a person's sense of well-being, it serves to limit coping tactics to those defined by the oppressive script, in this case gender role definitions. It may lead to increased distress and an embracing of the oppressive ideology, often expressed on an individual level as problems of self-esteem and competence. Internalization of oppression in the subordinate person may serve to reinforce the victim-blaming behavior by others as well.

Baker-Miller (1976) discusses the effects of this tragic system on those who belong to the dominant group as well as on those in the subordinate position. She identifies clearly the damage done to members of both groups, the least of which is that "mutually enhancing interaction is not probable between **un**equals. Indeed conflict is inevitable." (1976, p. 12, emphasis added).

A powerful result of oppression is that it can create a self-fulfilling prophecy; those who are oppressed come to believe and comply with the oppressive script and stereotypes that are held about them. Thus women can come to believe that they are inferior to men in ways set forth in the sexist script, and men can assume that they must carry the burden of being always in charge and maintaining a superior position.

Another effect of an oppressive ideology is that those who defy the script or stereotypes are punished, what might be thought of as a "catch 22": the harder an individual tries to step outside the gender role expectations or stereotypes, the more those who are invested in the ideology punish them. For example, women who act like they can manage organizations or exercise power and authority are commonly called "bitches" or are defined as failures because of some perceived management problem. Men who seek to do something traditionally done by women, such as serving as the primary caregiver for family members, often have to suffer torment and humiliation by others. Or they are responded to with exaggerated praise as if they are special (read deviant). "That really is wonderful of you, Tom, not to mind that Helen makes more money than you do!"

Victim-blaming is a pervasive force in modern American culture. The generic formula of victim-blaming involves "justifying inequality by finding defects in the victims of inequality" (Ryan, 1976, p. xiii). Victim-blaming is applied to almost every American problem. The purpose is "rooted in a class-based interest in maintaining the status quo" (p. 11) "by justifying a perverse form of social action to change, not society, as one might expect, but rather society's victims" (p. 8). Chodorow (1978) also suggests that the traditional male (dominant)–female (subordinate) relationship is promoted and supported by a capitalist economic system that benefits from it.

Psychological Purpose of Misogyny

There is a rich feminist literature that explores the psychological underpinnings of the fear and hatred of women and femaleness. These authors present an array of arguments and clinical data to show how both men and women use various psychological processes within a social context to protect themselves from both internal and external threats to self-integrity. Again, Chodorow (1978) offers an important foundation for understanding this process intrapsychically and interpersonally as well as sociologically. Others, such as Lerner (1988), Gilligan (1982), Baker-Miller (1976), Bernardez (1978), and The Stone Center papers, offer compelling discussions about how these processes meet individual psychological needs.

Impact of Generalizations

One must show that human behavior is far too complex for any generalized dichotomized explanation to be valid/accurate. Characterizing man as the aggressor and woman his victim (1) encourages polarization and a false dichotomy because we all have the potential for expressing both masculine and feminine characteristics; (2) reduces both women and men to two-dimensional caricatures; (3) overlooks the enormous variation within each group, such that, for example, women vary much more within group than women and men do, and (4) leaves the ubiquitous ideology of sexism untouched and unchanged.

Many feminist authors note that gender roles are socially constructed and as generally conceptualized encourage a false either/or view of maleness and femaleness rather than a more accurate and whole both/and perspective. Looking at explanations of male and female psychological and social developments using a feminist view can actually help diffuse the tendency to dichotomize the genders. Once there is an appreciation for the necessity of looking at people individually, their development, their experience, and how they construct their reality in response to social forces, it becomes more difficult to make someone fit into a preconceived idea of what it means to be female or male.

One of Chodorow's (1978) solutions is to encourage ongoing daily childcare by both women and men, because she understands mothering predominantly by women to be a major reason for the polarization of the sexes. Luepnitz (1988) says that "feminists know that it is subversive to patriarchy to bring fathers closer to the heart of child care and to bring children into the paternal heart" (p. 182). She suggests that understanding the family from a feminist viewpoint leads to a redefinition of gender roles and an appreciation of the pain involved for both in the old stereotypes. These views contrast sharply with the idea of male-bashing and the victimizing of women.

Although teachers may be able to teach from the position that both men and women suffer from the effects of sexism and that both share responsibility for the perpetuation of the oppressive ideology of sexism, it is often difficult for students to incorporate this idea. Often novice feminists or those exposed to it for the first time fuel their own changing ideological commitments by blaming the perceived oppressor. Other female students, acting on their own internalized sexist script, may, at the first sign of conflict, move to "protect" men in discussions of sexism and feminism. These positions are common to classroom discussions and take

considerable skill on the part of the teacher to move students from their initial position of male-bashing or protecting the male to a more mature and holistic position
of understanding the complexity of oppression and gendered experience.

Providing a safe environment wherein students may explore these issues
is essential. Using individual assignments such as journals as well as structured
small group activities to encourage students to address the most personal and
anxiety-provoking questions can be useful. Students can be encouraged to look
at oppressed groups who are removed from their own experience to use as a
point of discussion about how oppression operates.

Helping students understand that oppression is greater than the "oppressor"
serves the social work profession's interest in promoting social change. Male-
bashing, or holding any other "oppressor" responsible for the fact of sexism or
other oppressive ideology, triggers tremendous resistance from those who are
blamed. Not only is such a stance contrary to social work's view of human and social complexity but it discourages change as resistance is balkanized into opposition. Even more to the point, male-bashing lets the real source of oppression
flourish unchecked.

REFERENCES

Abramovitz, M. (1988). *Regulating the lives of women.* Boston: South End Press.
Baker-Miller, J. (1976). *Toward a new psychology of women.* Boston: Beacon
Press.
Bernardez, T. (1978). Women and anger: Conflicts with aggression in contempo-
rary women. *Journal of the American Medical Women's Association, 33*(4),
215–219.
Chodorow, N. (1978). *The reproduction of mothering: Psychoanalysis and the
sociology of gender.* Berkeley: University of California Press.
Davis, L., Hagen, J., & Early, T. J. (1994). Social Services for battered women:
Are they adequate, accessible and appropriate? *Social Work, 39*(6), 695–704.
Gilligan, C. (1982). *In a different voice: Psychological theory and women's de-
velopment.* Cambridge, MA: Harvard University Press.
Lerner, H. (1988). *Women in therapy.* Northvale, NJ: Jason Aronson Inc.
Luepnitz, D. (1988). *The family interpreted: Psychoanalysis, feminism, and fami-
ly therapy.* New York: Basic Books.
Miller, D. (1992). *Women and social welfare.* New York: Prager.
Ryan, W. (1976). *Blaming the victim.* New York: Vintage Press.

Rejoinder to Drs. Humphreys and Nol JOAN LAIRD

There are, not surprisingly, many points of agreement between my comments and
the arguments posed by my good and learned friends Professors Humphreys and

Nol. There are also some fundamental differences. We all seem to agree that, in taking a feminist stance in the classroom, teachers *should not* deliberately "blame the aggressor." It would be difficult for me to support that stance, even in play, even for the sake of provocative argument. But I do reiterate my own belief that right now it probably is not possible to meet the issues of gender head-on in the classroom without collision, without tension, without pain—a sense of injustice and a degree of defensiveness on the part of men, some anger, an equal sense of injustice, and considerable frustration on the part of women. It is (understandably) very difficult for teachers to find the delicate balance necessary to meet these issues squarely and fairly in the classroom. In fact, our students tell us that even though gender dialogue is promised on the syllabi and relevant readings are assigned, the content frequently is left undiscussed. Furthermore, when gender tensions do arise in the classroom, they are often overlooked or deliberately side-stepped. This suggests that many teachers, probably unconsciously, avoid the anxieties, outbursts, painful confrontations, mutual blaming, and stony silences that can accompany the introduction of gender, race, sexual orientation, and other "toxic" topics for our times.

Although I do not disagree with any of the specific points Professors Nol and Humphreys raise, particularly in their presentation of some of the major tenets of feminist thought, I find their discussion of patriarchy curiously disembodied, intellectualized, and depersonalized—theirs seems to be a patriarchy unattached to real people and particularly to men. They end their paper with the statement that "male-bashing lets the real source of oppression flourish unchecked." Although I am not in favor of male-bashing, I had to wonder who or what the "real" source was? In the Humphreys/Nol commentary, the "real" source seems to be some constellation of rather remote ideas—patriarchy, gender socialization, and the like. But who is, after all, "doing" patriarchy? Who is accountable for it? They seem to suggest that we all, men and women alike, participate equally in its genesis and its effects. Patriarchy is most overwhelmingly perpetuated by "real" people who are benefiting from its unequal rewards, people who are threatened by and who strike back at real or perceived challenges to it.

The overall argument put forth by Professors Humphreys and Nol suffers in two respects. First, their feminist stance stresses gender socialization and its psychological, equally harmful effects on both men and women. Although they acknowledge the issue of oppression, they emphasize patriarchy as an ideology, a psychology, in my view greatly underplaying the enormous differences in power and privilege between the dominated and subjugated and ignoring the unspeakable cruelties that have been inflicted on women, children, and less powerful males by more powerful males from the beginnings of recorded history. Second, they underestimate the very real and justifiable anger feminist women, including most of our students, carry, and nonfeminist women bury—often at enormous cost to themselves, an anger that can be threatening to male students and colleagues. Whether or not we like the idea of "victim," these are angers and injustices that must be acknowledged and confronted, in the classroom and in our practice. Avoiding generalization to all men or women and unpacking how both men and women are oppressed by patriarchal ideology helps establish a more fruitful context for discussion, but it will not resolve real inequities, real brutalities, and real feelings of outrage, confusion, and of blaming and feeling blamed.

Returning to the first point, their argument is basically a psychological and developmental one. They repeatedly cite Chodorow and her disciples and, although I do not wish to minimize the tremendous contribution of this wing of feminist theory, as Hare-Mustin (1987) has argued, one of the effects of this body of work has been to exaggerate the differences between men and women (what Hare-Mustin calls the "alpha error"). Whether Chodorow, Gilligan, and their followers so intended in their groundbreaking works, their emphasis on early socialization of males and females, on the social construction of a different self, and so on, at the expense of minimizing the issues of power and oppression, have the effect of essentializing gender differences and of contributing reductionistically to the psychologizing and individualizing of what is fundamentally a matter of differences between men and women in social, political, economic, and physical power.

This kind of argument, so seductive for mental health professionals who focus on private troubles, ignores the context of power that is so central in the construction of identity and in mediating human relationships. As Hare-Mustin (1987) points out, when women have real power over others, they do not necessarily use it in more benign ways than do men—witness the "Iron Lady" leadership of a Margaret Thatcher or the physical abuse of children by their mothers and other female caretakers. Or, as Blumstein and Schwartz (1983) discovered, in their massive study of opposite- and same-sex couples, it was money, not gender, that "talked" across variously gendered couples. What I am saying is that patriarchy is not just about gender differences in socialization or about ideology—it is also about the misuse of privilege and power, and destruction and damage. We cannot avoid that fact. Many if not most of our students are working with women and children who have been deeply hurt and in some cases permanently scarred by patriarchal practices. Many of our students themselves have traumatic histories or in other ways have suffered the consequences of patriarchy. These are realities that were in this century suppressed until the second wave of feminism opened up the possibility for women's long silences about their abuse and other forms of oppression to be spoken.

As men, including our male students, begin to hear women's stories, they face the same challenges that white people do in listening to the stories of people of color. It is easy enough, from a vantage point of psychological expertise, to diagnose the ills of the other and to devote oneself to helping "them" overcome the personal effects of oppression, as in counseling the "difficult" "borderline" woman. (What difference would it make if we were to overthrow DSM and name these women, or they could name themselves, "woman who was emotionally, physically, and sexually abused by _____ for most of her childhood," if we would publicly bear witness to their experiences, instead of colluding in blaming the victims?) In taking a "therapeutic" stance, we retain our vantage point of wisdom and expertise, of power and privilege, in relation to the unfortunate experiences of the other, usually women and children. It is far more difficult to refuse to participate in the silences and obfuscations of language, to dedicate oneself to dismantling coalitions of oppression, and perhaps most difficult to confront one's own privilege or to be willing to relinquish one's personal or social power in any area.

Furthermore, in the same way that whites, in studying racism, must face their privilege and become accountable for the ways they allow themselves to be advantaged by that privilege, to repeat a point I made in my original argument, men must become accountable for dismantling patriarchy, for refusing to allow themselves to be privileged by virtue of their sex, for refusing to tolerate the oppression of women. It will not do, then, to pretend that power and privilege are not at stake here, in the larger social world and in the classroom, or to ward off conflict at all costs. I do not advocate fostering mutual blame or personal guilt—it can be personally immobilizing as well as an excuse for inaction. But neither do I think we can avoid the tension and the passion that accompany the gender question. Face it. Men do not find it easy to notice or acknowledge, let along relinquish, the special privileges that patriarchy confers. They usually do not notice or easily give up the oratorical space in faculty meetings or in the classroom. And women do not find it easy to challenge gender inequality and gender oppression on their own behalf. What I hope will happen in social work education is that both male and female students will accept the moral imperative and the responsibility to examine themselves, their own privileges, behaviors, and practices, and will bring a lively feminist perspective to their personal and professional lives.

REFERENCES

Blumstein, P., & Schwartz, P. (1983). *American couples: Money, work, sex.* New York: William Morrow.

Hare-Mustin, R. (1987). The problem of gender in family therapy theory. *Family Process, 26,* 15–33.

NO

JOAN LAIRD

Two or three years ago, while teaching about the relationships between private troubles and public issues, I was showing a series of film clips to illustrate the social construction of gender and to foster discussion of gender beliefs and gender socialization. The film clip at hand was *Steel Magnolias,* which I was using to suggest that men and women in this society are differently socialized to handle loss and grieving. In the midst of our discussion, Doug, one of three male students in a class of eighteen, suddenly pounded his fist on the desk, startling everyone. "I've had it," he shouted, "that's enough! I've heard nothing but bullshit in this program for three years now about men and how unfeeling and oppressive they are!" Encouraged to say more, he went on to describe how his wife and he handled loss in exactly the same ways, and that he was sick of being discriminated against in this program. He was tired of being told how men had oppressed women; he believed that *he* had been oppressed in this female-dominated program. The female students were silent—they seemed fearful and angry. At the break, several of the women chastised me for not "coming down hard on him." I, in turn, challenged them to use their own voices, to confront their own silence. The class ended with everyone, including me, in a state of tension.

Afterwards, I struggled to understand what had happened, what I had done to encourage this outburst, and how we might use the incident for learning. From my point of view, the teaching content had been benign—part of a series of clips demonstrating how the larger social discourse prescribes different ways of thinking and behaving for men and women. Why, then, this angry tirade?

A year earlier, in a family-centered practice course, a female student whom I will call Helena, after some discussion and preparation with the class and with their permission, told her own story of childhood abuse. Sexually molested and even tortured by her father for many years, Helena recounted for the class how she had used fantasy and dissociation—made-up friends and a made-up other self—to survive childhood, how as an adult she had used treatment and her own writing to grow to reintegrate her fragmented self. The listening was difficult, the atmosphere tense. All of the students were clearly both empathic and pained themselves to hear her story, a story of failed and brutal parenting in an upper-middle-class family well-known and presumably respected in the community. But the reactions of the male and female students differed. The female students could identify with her experience and with the terrible oppression and violence she had suffered—they did not seem to think it an unusual experience for female children in this society. The male students—good men, caring men, men trying to understand—seemed to find her memories difficult to believe; they needed some explanation that would locate this as an isolated problem, an exception. Clearly distressed, they asked, "Was your father mentally ill? Was he abused as a child? Was he a drinker? Was your mother unavailable to him?"

Somewhat angrily, she replied: "I don't need to diagnose my father, I don't want or need to explain away his behavior. My father is a monster; he is an evil man and I wish to leave it at that!" After her comment, I suggested that individual, marital, or family diagnoses and explanations can obscure the identifying and naming of those social beliefs, those forces of gender oppression, that fail to punish, and indeed foster, this kind of violence. They label both the abuser and the abused as "sick," failing to identify the unequal power relationships that allow gender oppression and undermining Helena's need to name her oppressor and to re-author her life in a way that is self-empowering.

In retrospect, while I did some processing of student reactions to the presentation, I should have attended more carefully to the fact that people's thinking often becomes virtually paralyzed when dealing with emotional trauma, and some students may experience retraumatization or vicarious traumatization. In this situation, I did not ask how the gender of the students might be interfacing with their reactions to Helena's story, that is, how their responses themselves might be gendered. Such a discussion might have helped to unravel the sense I had that the men in the class were "warding off" the gender implications of her story.

Is it possible to take a feminist stance in HBSE teaching (or in any other sequence, for that matter) without "blaming the aggressor?" First, because I think it is always—or at least usually—irresponsible for a teacher to take a politically correct "blaming" stance, at least in terms of faulting individuals, I need to reframe the question to read, "Is it possible to take a feminist stance in HBSE teaching without male students *experiencing* a sense of blame?" Even if we try very hard not to locate blame in individual men? I do not think so. Otherwise, we probably are not doing a good job in deconstructing and dismantling gender politics and oppressive practices toward women.

To incorporate a feminist perspective in education, in my view, means to deconstruct the social discourse of gender, that is, to surface the gender narratives and the gender arrangements in the larger society and in one's own ethnic and family contexts that shape individual and family thought and behavior. However, this is not merely an intellectual endeavor. A feminist perspective also implies, in my view, a commitment to exposing and dismantling the hierarchies of gender privilege that strengthen certain voices and subjugate others. It means a commitment to helping both men and women free themselves from the constraints dictated by rigid gender expectations, to helping people widen the possibilities for pursuing more authentic and empowered paths.

In the second example, that of Helena, the teaching material was clearly painful and anxiety-provoking. I imagine that to be a male sitting in that class might feel a bit like being a young German listening to the atrocities perpetrated or at least tolerated by one's forebears in the Holocaust, or being the descendant of a slave-owning or Ku Klux Klan family that inflicted untold misery and violence on African Americans. You did not do it, you abhor what was done, you do not believe you are fascist or racist in your beliefs, you have even worked against white oppression, but you are forever linked to your heritage—guilt by association, tainted by being a member of an oppressor group.

But in the first example, that of Doug, why was it so difficult for a male student to consider that men and women are differently socialized, to examine gender beliefs as they are portrayed in popular culture and as they tend to influence and shape the behaviors of males and females? In that situation, I thought I was trying to help students examine how men, by virtue of gender restrictions, in this case the expression of certain kinds of emotional pain, can be denied helpful opportunities for resolution of loss. I was arguing that men, too, can be oppressed by rigid gender prescriptions.

The stories are similar in the sense that, in both cases, male students in particular found it painful to recognize gendered differences. To recognize difference means having to face one's own privilege or subjugation; to face one's own privilege means having to face the ways in which one's privilege is obtained at the expense of others. In the case of men, it means to recognize that male privilege is gained and maintained by the oppression of others. It means to recognize that male violence toward female strangers and their own wives, girlfriends, daughters, and sisters exists and is indeed most common. It is extraordinarily difficult and painful to face one's own privilege. It takes the same kind of courage and commitment we find among white allies, people who have begun to confront their own white privilege and their internalized racism, or among friends to lesbians and gays who have really confronted their own homophobia. It is even more difficult and challenging to move beyond the recognition of privilege to the acknowledgment of one's own participation in oppressing others, and beyond acknowledgment to accountability and responsibility for change.

In yet another example, this one extracurricular, after a panel on violence against women at a major family therapy conference, several of the alpha males in the family therapy field walked out of the conference. Apparently, they were deeply offended and believed that the papers, one of which reported startling and disturbing statistics concerning male violence against women, were divisive and male-blaming—this in a field that had been virtually silent on the entire issue in its major journals and conferences. It was material difficult for them to hear, and clearly they felt they, as men, were being blamed.

I do not think that feminism is about blaming men. But it will be virtually impossible for individual men *not* to feel blamed, if we are doing a good job bringing a feminist perspective to the classroom. And if we are not doing a good job bringing in the feminist perspective, perhaps we are silently sanctioning existing unequal arrangements of power and thus participating in perpetuating the oppression of women and, in some ways, men as well. If we make it too painless, too easy, too "balanced," we will, to paraphrase Tom Andersen, introduce too small a difference to make a difference.

There are, of course, ways we can help facilitate a feminist learning environment that will allow for debate and dialogue, that will encourage critical examination of the ways gender premises and gender biases are inherent in most of our "human behavior" assessments and diagnostic categories, that will allow for difference and even conflict to emerge. Teachers can strive to create learning contexts in which "blaming" is reframed as an issue of accountability and responsibility; that is, that men become responsible for acknowledging the ways that gendered power is misused and abused at the expense of women, in their own relationships and in the larger community. Men must become accountable for gender equity, and good men must become more active and accountable in not tolerating the behaviors of destructive men. These discussions can only occur and the potential conflicts tolerated and understood in an atmosphere of relative safety and mutual respect.

First, a teacher must always tack back and forth between the general and the particular, always being careful to suggest, for example, that gender behaviors and patterns are not by any means generalizable to all men. Certainly our own students will have had very different life experiences from each other. Some male students may have had exposure to and already been part of gender dialogues, and they may have already embraced feminist ideas, whereas these same ideas may be relatively new and threatening to others. Nor do we wish to either exaggerate or minimize the differences between men and women. We must examine what the differences may be, what accounts for them, and how they may work against full potential for either sex. What is important is that students' gender consciousness is sophisticated enough so that they can probe their own gender premises and also are sensitive to the ways gender is salient to each client's localized story and life experience, as well as to the professional contexts and communities in which they will be working.

In the class after the Doug incident, I asked students how they understood what had happened. Both the men and the women in this class, and particularly Doug, had thought about it a great deal in the interim. A lively conversation on how male and female students had experienced the gender issues and conflicts in their entire educational experience ensued. It was a dialogue that was heated at times, humorous at others, one that several students said was the best conversation on this issue they had ever participated in. Men described their experiences of being a minority (women were not very sympathetic on this one), and women talked about issues of women's "voice," of experiencing being silenced and discounted while men were more recognized in many classes and tended to occupy "talk space" far out of proportion to their numbers. Women argued that men did not deserve to be "protected" in the learning space, even though they were a minority—women had had to deal with similar "unsafe" issues all of their lives. Men talked about trying to be more sensitive, caring men, which seemed to stimulate anxiety among the women in their lives, who wanted them to be strong and aggressive—they felt the messages were mixed.

Meanwhile, Doug, interestingly, returned to the issue of loss, describing how he and his wife had dealt with the death of a close family member very differently and had had difficulty understanding each other; he wanted to move on, while she wanted to keep discussing it. He seemed to have forgotten his earlier stance of "no difference," acknowledging that facing his own issues of gender and his sense of masculinity were complicated by his family's criticism of his choice of social work, which they felt was no profession for a man. This experience taught me how important it is to move beyond the content to the learning context itself and to the "gendered" experiences of those in it, something I often forget in our rushed, content-laden theory classes. I think what worked here is what works in practice—opening up conversational space in a nonjudgmental and respectful way so that listening to the "other" is fostered, and alternative ideas and possibilities can emerge. One had the sense that Doug in particular already was changing—thinking more complexly about the ways stereotypical gender expectations were constraining his own life and choices.

Many of the teaching–learning strategies and exercises used in diversity or multicultural training focused on race and racism can be adapted for teaching gender and modeling a feminist perspective. In addition to fostering an atmosphere that is itself nonhierarchical, respectful, and freeing, I think it is also important to make gender and gender oppression, that is, the politics of gender, part of every class, sometimes at the center and sometimes at the periphery. Gender is *always* relevant, just as race, ethnicity, social class, and sexual orientation are always relevant to the discussion of every theory and of every case. To ignore gender is to separate the SE from the HB.

As I have said, it is extremely difficult to even acknowledge one's own power and privilege, let alone recognize how one has participated in a gendered world in which one's own privilege has come at great cost to others. Furthermore, it is extremely difficult to relinquish even a small share of this privilege. Many men ward off this kind of recognition by discrediting the feminist lens and feminists themselves, accusing them of blaming or even hating men.

One teaching stance that can neutralize some of the experience of blame on the part of men (women have been taught all of their lives that they *are* to blame!) and at the same time offer alternative stories for both men and women is to help students critically deconstruct the ways in which men themselves are oppressed by gendered scripts for human behavior. What, for example, are the costs to humanness and humaneness, to enjoying as full a human experience as possible, in measuring up to the myth of masculinity? What are the costs in physical and mental health to men when they are held fully responsible for the support of their families in a world of shrinking opportunity? How can men nurture and experience the joy of raising children or be emotionally available to their partners when they live in a society that raises them to leave others behind, that prepares them for the ruthlessness of both war and the corporate world, that tells them they dare not show any vulnerability? Or, in the case of many African American and other oppressed men, what does the myth of masculinity mean when all one can foresee is the despair of unemployment, poverty, and the violence of the inner city?

I have argued that it is difficult to do justice to the feminist perspective and, at the same time, to create a learning context in which men will feel unblamed. At the same time, I believe we must strive to move beyond blame. Blaming and self-blame are unproductive, whereas guilt is both paralyzing and even luxurious. To be mired in blame, denial, and guilt is to blind oneself to injustice and to excuse oneself from doing something about the social inequities that promote human suffering.

Rejoinder to Dr. Laird

NANCY HUMPHREYS
JO NOL

As we were writing our "yes" side of this debate, we struggled with the fact that as feminists we embrace and promote a both/and perspective in place of the more common but less accurate either/or position. Both sides of this argument contain some truth, and each position informs an important aspect of teaching about oppression. It is not surprising, then, that in the spirit of true feminism, we agreed with much of what Joan Laird has observed. We agree that blame and guilt do not promote the kind of learning and understanding of human functioning that is important for social work students to grasp. We also agree that feminism is not about blaming men. By rephrasing the question to ask how men may experience a feminist analysis, Laird has identified other important aspects of teaching about oppression and gender. Laird's examples drawn from her teaching provide strong evidence of the discomfort that students experience when they are asked to look directly into the face of oppression, especially at their roles and actions in accordance with the oppressive script. Often students, both women and men, experience the impact of learning about oppression and sexism, just as Pogo did when he observed "We have seen the enemy and it is us."

Facing oppression is difficult and painful for both the more and less privileged, the so-called oppressed and oppressor, the subordinate and dominant. In the case of sexism, both men and women will experience discomfort and guilt when examining their own participation in the oppression of self or other. Such discomfort is inevitable in teaching and learning; anxiety often gives rise to the most meaningful learning experiences.

Teachers face powerful challenges in how to present and facilitate the learning of emotionally charged content and to help students deal with painful realizations they may reach. Of course this experience must be respectfully shaped in as safe a learning environment as possible. However, what Laird discusses as the experience of guilt we would call the anxiety of the learning process. Thus, if the question is "can learning about oppression occur without some discomfort or guilt?" we would argue that it cannot. But at the same time we would note that some discomfort is an inevitable part of all learning and is particularly strong when the content to be learned challenges accepted ways of being in the world.

Does HBSE Teach Students to *Do* Anything?

EDITOR'S NOTE: Classes in social work practice methods teach students to practice; classes in policy and research teach students to be able to perform in these areas. Of HBSE, the fourth required social work curriculum area, a potentially embarrassing question arises as topic of this debate.

Charles Zastrow, Ph.D., professor in the Department of Social Work, University of Wisconsin at Whitewater, has written and edited a number of basic social work textbooks, including co-authoring the third edition of *Understanding Human Behavior and the Social Environment* (1994, Nelson-Hall).

William E. Powell, Ph.D., is associate professor and chairperson, Department of Social Work, University of Wisconsin at Whitewater. Recent research includes an evaluation of a multiyear Head Start demonstration grant. He has recently published in the areas of gerontological social work, and alienation and burnout in social work, and is book review editor of *Families in Society.*

YES

CHARLES ZASTROW

The "in-class" curriculum for undergraduate and graduate programs in social work has been classified into four different sequences: social welfare policy and services, social work practice, research, and human behavior and the social environment (HBSE). It is generally assumed that the practice sequence teaches students skills, knowledge, and values for social work practice; that the research sequence teaches students how to conduct research, and that the policy sequence teaches students how to make effective policy changes in various contexts. If these sequences are designed to teach students how to do specific things, the question then arises: Does HBSE teach students to *do* anything?

The HBSE Sequence Teaches Assessment

The Curriculum Policy Statement for both the Baccalaureate (1992a) and Master's (1992b) degree programs require the following in the HBSE sequence:

> Programs of social work education must provide content about theories and knowledge of human bio-psycho-social development, including theories and knowledge about the range of social systems in which individuals live (families, groups, organizations, institutions, and communities). The human behavior and social environment curriculum must provide an understanding of the interaction between and among human biological, social, psychological, and cultural systems as they affect and are affected by human behavior. The impact of social and economic forces on individuals and social systems must be presented. Content must be provided about the ways in which systems promote or deter people in the maintenance or attainment of optimal health and well-being. Content about values and ethical issues related to bio-psycho-social theories must be included. Students must be taught to evaluate theory and apply theory to client situations.

Quite a mouthful—isn't it? This is nearly everything about people that social workers need to know. However, what is all this HBSE content good for? Because the purpose of social work is to facilitate positive changes in individuals, groups, families, organizations, and communities (Pincus & Minahan, 1973), social workers must first *assess* these client systems. Barker (1991) provides this definition of assessment:

> The process of determining the nature, cause, progression, and prognosis of a problem and the personalities and situations involved therein; the social work function of acquiring an understanding of a problem, what causes it, and what can be changed to minimize or resolve it. (p. 17)

HBSE content is primarily designed to be used in this assessment process. And, after social workers apply interventions to client systems, they must assess the impact of the interventions—both during the time of the intervention process and after termination. These additional assessments are necessary to determine the degree of effectiveness of the interventions. For example, if an intervention is having a negative effect, the intervention in all probability should cease, and some other approach should probably be selected and applied. Again, the knowledge content that is used to do the assessment involves the HBSE content as just summarized.

Much of what social workers do involve assessments, from determining alleged child abuse to conducting a community needs assessment. Social workers need a base of knowledge to understand how various pressures affect their clients to know what kinds of information are important and what kinds of questions to ask. Consider this example: John R is referred to a psychiatric social worker to assess the potential for suicide. The psychiatric social worker has a variety of intervention options, including hospitalization or outpatient services, but needs to know a number of risk factors in this case to choose the best service option (Patterson et al., 1983):

- A greater danger exists if the person threatening suicide is male, because males are more apt to succeed in suicide attempts as compared with females.
- People who are age nineteen or younger and the elderly are in higher-risk groups, as statistically they have the highest rates of suicides.
- People who have tried to kill themselves before are at higher risk because they are more likely to succeed than people who are tying to commit suicide for the first time.
- People who are alcoholic or who are addicted to some illegal drug are more likely to commit suicide than those who are not addicted.
- People who suffer from depression or some other emotional disorder are at higher risk than those free from emotional disorders.
- People who feel no one cares about them may begin to feel useless and helpless, and are at higher risk.
- The more specific and organized an individual's plan regarding when and how the suicide will be undertaken, the greater the risk.
- The more lethal the plan for ending one's life, the greater the risk.
- Adults who have no spouse have a greater likelihood of committing suicide than people who are married.
- People who have long-term illnesses that place substantial limitations on their lives are at greater risk of suicide.
- People who display rapid changes in mood behavior, or general attitude, are at a higher risk of suicide.
- People who give away personal possessions that are especially important or meaningful to them are at a higher risk of suicide.

Such risk factors are part of the HBSE knowledge base. Knowing these kinds of facts, or where to find them when needed, is exactly what HBSE teaches students. Patterson et al. (1983) developed the Sad Person Scale based on these factors. Using this scale, a helping professional conducting an assessment with

John R could assign numerical scores for each risk factor that is present—with a very high total score indicating a need for hospitalization—and use this information as part of the basis for his or her practice decision.

The Importance of HBSE Theories in Assessment

Theories have crucially important functions in the HBSE sequence. Among other key functions, theories provide social workers with approaches for conducting assessments. For example, cognitive–behavior theory asserts that cognitions are the primary determinants of our behaviors and our emotions (Vondracek & Corneal, 1995). This theory asserts that assessing human behavior is largely a process of identifying the cognitions of clients that underlie unwanted emotions or dysfunctional behaviors. The theory further asserts that the determinants for any dysfunctional act (including crime) or any unwanted emotion can be identified by knowing what the client was telling himself or herself before and during the time when the act was being committed. Such theories provide theoretical frameworks for conducting assessments.

The ways in which theories in social work influence assessments can be illustrated in a historical perspective. From the 1920 to the 1960s, most social workers used a medical model approach (specifically, psychoanalytic theory) for assessing and changing human behavior. The "patient's" problems were viewed as being inside the patient. In the 1960s, social work began questioning the usefulness of the medical model. Environmental factors were shown to be at least as important, and research was demonstrating that psychoanalysis was probably ineffective in treating clients' problems (Stuart, 1970).

In the past few years, social work has increasingly focused on using an ecological approach, which integrates both internal and external factors and emphasizes the dysfunctional transactions between people and their physical and social environments. The ecological approach tries to improve the coping patterns of people and their environments so that a better match can be attained between an individual's needs and the characteristics of his or her environment. This person-in-environment conceptualization enables social workers to consider three separate areas: First, it can focus on the person and seek to develop his or her problem-solving, coping, and developmental capacities. Second, it can focus on the relationship between a person and the systems he or she interacts with and link the person with needed resources, services, and opportunities. Third, it can focus on the systems and seek to reform them so as to meet the needs of individuals more effectively.

The reader is probably wondering what difference it makes to do an assessment in terms of the medical model approach or the ecological model approach. Consider this illustration: in the 1940s and 1950s, the psychoanalytic approach (medical model) was generally used to explain why single women became pregnant in the United States. Pregnancy in those years was thought to be attributable to single women having an unresolved emotional disturbance, with the pregnancy being viewed as a symptom of emotional problems such as unresolved sexual conflicts, uncontrollable sexual fantasies that resulted from traumatic early childhood experiences, unconscious masochistic desires to harm oneself, or unconsciously wanting to get pregnant to inflict pain on their mothers, with whom they were in conflict.

In contrast, the ecological model directs helping professionals to look for causes not only internal to the person, but also in the environment, such as the glorification of unprotected sexual intercourse by the mass media, lack of quality sex educational programs in the school system or in the home, and socialization patterns for males that encourage them to be sexually active at a young age.

The forms of intervention that are used are based on the assessments that are conducted. If we want to reduce the rate of births outside of marriage, the psychoanalytic approach directs us to use a therapy that helps such disturbed young women relive and come to terms with their traumatic experiences from early childhood. In contrast, the ecological approach to the various internal and external factors contributing to unprotected sexual intercourse would be equally varied, such as the provision of quality sex education programs, education about the responsibilities associated with sexuality and parenthood, and increased access to contraceptives for young women and men who are sexually active.

In reviewing the psychoanalytic and the ecological approaches, which one appears to be most useful in assessing the reasons for births outside of marriage? And which approach then suggests the most effective intervention approach in reducing the rates of births outside of marriage?

Summary

I trust the above explanation, along with the examples, clearly documents that the primary focus of the HBSE sequence is to provide the knowledge for social workers to use in conducting assessments and providing effective services. To bring about effective changes in individuals, families, groups, organizations, and communities, social workers must first conduct an assessment, which involves determining the nature, cause, and prognosis of a problem and situation involved therein. The HBSE sequence provides the knowledge base to do exactly this.

When students study theories in HBSE, it is crucially important for them to be critical readers and consumers. For years, social work practitioners bought into the medical model (particularly the psychoanalytic approach) as the basis for assessment. As a result, important external assessment variables and significant intervention approaches were ignored. Fortunately, social work has moved recently to using an ecological approach to understanding and conceptualizing human behavior. Assessments, based on current HBSE theories and research, are the driving force that generates effective interventions, so that social workers can bring about positive changes in individuals, families, groups, organizations, and communities. The critical reader, I trust, will clearly see that the purpose and value of HBSE content is *assessment*.

REFERENCES

Barker, R. L. (1991). *The social work dictionary* (2nd ed.). Silver Spring, MD: NASW.

Council on Social Work Education. (1992a). *Curriculum policy statement for baccalaureate degree programs in social work education.* Washington, DC: Author.

Council on Social Work Education. (1992b). *Curriculum policy statement for master's degree programs in social work education.* Washington, DC: Author.

Patterson, W. M., Dohn, H. D., & Bird, J. A. (1983). Evaluation of suicidal patients: The Sad Persons Scale. *Psychosomatics, 24,* 343–349.

Pincus, A., & Minahan, A. (1973). *Social work practice: Model and method.* Itasca, IL.: Peacock.

Stuart, R. B. (1970). *Trick or treatment.* Champaign, IL: Research Press.

Vondracek, F. W., & Corneal, S. (1995). *Strategies for resolving individual and, family problems.* Pacific Grove, CA.: Brooks/Cole.

Rejoinder to Dr. Zastrow
WILLIAM E. POWELL

After reading my colleague's thesis, I am compelled to respectfully disagree. It would be a triumph of pedagogy to think that, in the course of taking one or two classes in the University, assessment could be learned. It is conceivable, however, to argue that students can be introduced to content matter used in assessments and to the process of assessment, but teaching the unfolding process of doing an assessment is another matter entirely.

Dr. Zastrow quotes Barker's (1991) definition of assessment from the *Social Work Dictionary* but only minimally notes a critical word in that definition: *process.* Process implies an activity done over the course of *time;* time (and interaction) is a critical element in learning to do assessments. I question whether in-class activities can adequately teach the ongoing process, over time, of assessing real clients' situations, can demonstrate the evolving and developmental nature of assessment, and teach the ongoing critical thinking that is necessary to the process.

Assessment can be described and illustrated in HBSE courses, but it is misleading to posit that exposure to a selected few theoretical frameworks, to some bits of information and knowledge, and to some selected ways of assembling facts can teach the process of assessing and understanding the circumstances and needs of clients. One danger in too quickly making an assessment is that clients and their situations can be judgmentally seen, can be stereotyped, and their circumstances can be reduced to simplistic cause-and-effect equations.

I think that my colleague is correct in suggesting that HBSE content can be used in the process of assessing clients' situations, but immediately after supplying the definition of assessment he muddies that same definition by also using *assessment* where *evaluation* would be more the more appropriate term. Generally, we *evaluate* the effect of interventions, and the *evaluation* of practice is, indeed, one of the bits of knowledge and skill that is expected to be in our curricula. If using Barker's definition, it would be best to remain within the parameters of that definition.

Dr. Zastrow correctly notes the importance of theories to assessment and focuses on two or three illustrative theoretical frameworks. In presenting his position, he discusses cognitive–behavioral and psychoanalytic theories and the ecological model. The brief discussion of these illustrative theoretical frameworks needs some response. In the section illustrating "the importance of HBSE theories in assessment," "*un*wanted emotions" is equated with "dysfunctional behaviors." I would assert that they are not necessarily synonymous and that only having "wanted emotions" may be little more than cognitive and emotional hedonism. Sometimes "unwanted" emotions and cognitions (e.g., grief or guilt) are perfectly appropriate to circumstances, however unpleasant. Also, psychoanalytic theory is incorrectly suggested as being synonymous with the medical model. These theories and others, when comprehensively presented, do establish frameworks for understanding the personal, interpersonal, and social situations of clients and bases for working with and for them. HBSE can teach theoretical frameworks and illustrations of the way that knowledge, facts, and perceptions can be organized and used. To do that important task, it is essential that information and theoretical frameworks be used for the development of students' own conceptual frameworks and conceptual skills. I believe that this is the critical importance of HBSE—the development of well-formed conceptual frameworks and critical thinking skills. These can be used in the learning of assessment and evaluative skills and, perhaps most importantly, the development of practice skills.

After positing that assessment is indeed taught in HBSE, my colleague asserts that "assessments, based on current HBSE theories and research, are the driving force that generates effective interventions, so that social workers can bring about positive changes in individuals, families, groups, organizations, and communities." I would agree that a well-done assessment is critical but instead suggest that assessment is a process rather than a summarized "thing." Furthermore, learning a process is not the intent of HBSE, but rather supplying knowledge—the theoretical framework and knowledge base—which supports that process is its intent. Finally, in responding to my colleague's argument and the quote above, I would note the absence of a critical element in learning to do a comprehensive and accurate assessment—the relationship with the client. A well-done assessment is more than a cerebral activity; it is greatly predicated on understanding gained from a productive working relationship. The importance of the relationship to effective work and connecting to others in assessing situations has long been noted (e.g., Buber, M., quoted in Kohn, 1990). HBSE best teaches students to think and to conceive situations and possibilities; these are foundations for the effective doing of social work.

REFERENCES

Barker, R. L. (1991). *The social work dictionary* (2nd ed.). Silver Spring, MD: NASW.

Kohn, A. (1990). *The brighter side of human nature.* New York: Basic Books.

NO

WILLIAM E. POWELL

In a literal reading of the question and after reviewing the 1992 Curriculum Policy Statement and its interpretive guidelines by the Council on Social Work Education, my answer to this question must be no. In responding negatively, it should be noted that the Curriculum Policy Statement does state that "Students must be taught to *evaluate* theory and *apply* theory to client situations." In one sense, this wording suggests that the closest this portion of the social work curriculum comes to expecting that students be taught "to do" is the cerebral processes of evaluating and applying theory. The Curriculum Policy Statement mentions nothing about learning skills and techniques in the HBSE portion of the curriculum. Because students are not explicitly required to be "in practice" at the time they take the HBSE course(s), "evaluation" and "applying" learned in HBSE may be primarily hypothetical exercises rather than the melding of knowledge and skill building. In any event, HBSE and the practice sequence have been reduced to distinct tracks rather than courses melded together in time.

Faculty who have considerable practice experience can effectively teach the required content in HBSE and are able to link that content and the evaluation of it, or apply theory, to the use of the professional self as is done in the conduct of social work practice. The ability to do that is, however, an example of quality instruction and course design rather than a logical or necessary result of content matter prescribed by the Curriculum Policy Statement. The content in the HBSE portion of the social work curriculum has much to do with the practice of social work and understanding how the role of the social worker is linked to the confluence of social circumstances and variations in human development. However, that content in texts is often primarily descriptive and, if well taught and its utility well modeled, is useful in helping students conceptualize the interplay of individual and social phenomena and to frame situations or circumstances that set the foundation for the effective use of self in the (future) doing of social work. Quality instruction can link topical matter and theories to the ongoing interplay of self and knowledge in learning the art of practice; HBSE is most effectively taught in that manner.

Too often, however, HBSE content is presented in texts as a "grab bag" of theories, sensational topics to pique students' interest, and poorly organized subject matter that lacks coherence, logical flow, and depth. Texts and courses thus organized are little more than brief compendiums of social problems, individual

failings and maladies, and discourses on the pathological vagaries of human existence. Indeed, a cynic might suggest that some HBSE texts are a litany of sensa-
tionalized human "ills" that pander to students' interest in the sensational but do
little to enhance students' organization of knowledge so that they can *evaluate*
and *apply* theory and knowledge. Such approaches to presenting HBSE content
do little to foster strengths perspectives in students' comprehensions. They also
render a jaded perspective on the totality of human behaviors and of the entirety of
the social environment within which people live and seek to improve their condition. Although we necessarily need to teach about problems in life and society, we
also need to teach about those things that constitute strengths and tools with which
successes can be achieved. To do otherwise is a failure to teach about hope and
possibility and what we are supposed to provide in HBSE—the intellectual tools
with which *evaluations* and *applications* of theory and knowledge can be made.

If we consider the notion that actual social work practice with clients is a
developmental and goal-directed *purposeful* process (with attendant interruptions
and unanticipated events), portraying HBSE topical matter as discrete topics not
linked to the context of practice and the realities of clients' lives misrepresents the
way that knowledge is employed in practice. As noted, we often find content in
HBSE presented as discrete and shallow topics that seek to satisfy the categorical
contents dictated by the Curriculum Policy Statement, but the content does not
always have coherence nor explicit linkage to its use in practice. This intellectual
reductionism is great for assembling a collage of sensational topics for texts or
courses and for accreditation purposes, but belies the intellectual processes needed
to grasp the totality of clients' situations and the purposeful activities needed to
change situations.

Often, too, the information contained in texts is inaccurate, biased, and dated.
In short, claims that HBSE teaches students to do some particular things are wrong
in the sense that such teaching must relate to the development of skills. That claim
may be stretched to have some minimal validity in particular instructors' classrooms if those instructors present learning to "do something" as being a discrete
technique such as the "doing" of an assessment, "doing" of a family history,
"doing" a genogram, or "doing" an eco-map. In such instances we may merely be
quibbling about the meaning and definition of "to do" as it is used in this debate.

Doing Minor Assessment Techniques

What passes as learning "to do" something in such instances as noted is often
merely a cursory exposure to such topics or techniques as those noted. In some
instances, however, such a cursory exposure to complex techniques may be misleading. For example, suggesting to students that doing the rudimentary mechan-
ics of developing and drawing a genogram is learning "to do" something may be
misleading. Without adequate attention paid to the very necessary thought processes and necessary knowledge connected with that minor assessment technique,
a genogram may be perceived as identifying very deterministic phenomena rather

than serving more correctly as a data collection instrument and interactive process in the service of professional thought and insight. Hartman (1995) provides a good overview of assessment techniques such as genograms and eco-maps and the complexity of the thought processes involved. These necessary skills should probably be addressed in practice methods classes rather than in passing fashion in HBSE courses. A poorly done assessment is not a particularly strong asset to productive work with clients.

My personal view remains that ". . . to do anything" refers to the use of self as a social worker rather than to the learning of isolated techniques. I doubt that learning how to do something related to the use of self occurs solely in response to mandated curricular content. When it does occur, as noted before, it is likely the result of good teaching rather than of the content dictated by the Curriculum Policy Statement per se or even by the use of some popular texts.

Students presented with discrete conglomerations of theory and the occasionally referenced technical process are, unfortunately, often left without the theoretical "glue," the context and comprehension needed for binding the bits and pieces of data and information into a coherent whole. The Curriculum Policy Statement section on HBSE is a listing of politically and professionally correct content with little reference made to the pedagogical need for linking that content to the act of doing social work. It is not necessarily integrated with the process of becoming a social worker who knows how to use knowledge, and himself or herself, to do social work with and for clients or for the purposes of advancing social justice.

By presenting purportedly objective information about problems rather than presenting information about those topics in the context-rich form of what "I" might think and do profoundly affects what students "learn to do." HBSE too often teaches students *about* things rather than teaching for the purposes of understanding how to link knowledge to the systematic and purposeful doing of something about those subjects. By focusing on discrete topics, it also tacitly implies that social work knowledge and knowing is predicated on a collection of "facts" and their manipulation. Experienced practitioners know that the artful interplay of knowledge (contained in the topical area addressed in HBSE), overlaid on one's ethics and sense of morality and compassion, and with thought and the artful use of self in interaction with others, is the way that "learning to do" is accomplished.

The Place of (HBSE) Ideas in the World of Practice

Perhaps the correct debate question could have been whether HBSE content (in textbooks and in course content) is explicitly linked to the practice of social work. That is the context within which students should learn HBSE content and make sense of why it is worth knowing. Unlinked to their own future careers and professional functioning, students may find the content to be a disjointed melange of topics only spuriously related to their needs. Taught thus, HBSE content may not transform the learner, influence the premises that shape the application of knowledge to "doing," nor help connect knowledge and experience and "doing" (Cranton, 1994). HBSE serves as a foundation for learning specific practice skills in other classes and in the field. It is where students learn to "do" for themselves and is a vehicle for the erection of their own professional knowledge base that also serves as a foundation that supports ongoing growth in skills and knowledge. HBSE should not be conceived of as an even larger "catch-all" in which it is presumed that students also learn token skills (the cursoriness of which misrepresents the intricate art of "doing" for and with clients).

Merriam and Caffarella (1991) suggest that the taking on of social roles (such as social work) differentiates adult learners from younger learners and that assumed roles serve as contexts for learning for adults and burgeoning adults (p. 303). Likewise, Brookfield (1986) suggests that adults like their learning activities to be problem-centered (the problem of their own development) and to be meaningful to their life situations. Belenky, Clinchy, Goldberger, and Tarula (1986) suggest that "educators can help women develop their own authentic voices if they emphasize connection (of ideas and knowledge) over separation, understanding and acceptance over assessment, and collaboration over debate" (p. 229). Each of these educators supports my contention that teaching persons to do something happens best in contexts meaningful to one's present and projected life situation, in contexts that emphasize the connections between disparate topics and theories, and when collaboration and understanding are goals rather than assessment and the debate of topics. HBSE does not automatically teach students to do anything. The employment of that required subject matter in the artful interplay of knowledge and the use of self by competent instructors can help students *learn* to do. Students are more likely to *learn to do* something if we teach for learning and understanding rather than teaching students to do noncontexted techniques. Hopefully, we comprehend the distinction.

REFERENCES

Belenky, M. F., Clinchy, B. M., Goldberger, N. R., and Tarula, J. (1986). *Women's ways of knowing: The development of self, voice, and mind.* New York: Basic Books.

Brookfield, S. D. (1986). *Understanding and facilitating adult learning.* San Francisco: Jossey Bass.

Council on Social Work Education. (1992). *Curriculum policy statement for master's degree programs in social work education.* Washington, DC: Author.

Cranton, P. (1994). *Understanding and promoting transformative learning.* San Francisco: Jossey Bass.

Hartman, A. (1995). Diagrammatic assessment of family relationships. *Families in Society, 76*(2), 111–122.

Merriam, S. B., & Caffarella, R. S. (1991). *Learning in adulthood: A comprehensive guide.* San Francisco: Jossey Bass.

Rejoinder to Dr. Powell
CHARLES ZASTROW

Dr. Powell's main points are curious. First, he finds that HBSE teaches students to do nothing—except "cerebral" processing with regard to evaluating and applying theory. That exception is vital. If we did not cerebrally process all of those conceptual materials from HBSE, we could not perform our professional social work practices because these actions require abstract thinking and decision making—that is, cerebral activities. Therefore, using his own criteria of what is important in social work—namely, a "developmental and goal-directed purposeful process"—then students absolutely need the conceptual knowledge base from HBSE (and elsewhere) to supply the cerebral processes necessary to plan a goal-directed effort.

Second, Dr. Powell is critical of HBSE texts and the failure to link HBSE content to practice. Having contributed to the numbers of HBSE texts, I agree all too fully that it is difficult to keep "inaccurate, biased, and dated" information out of these books. However, textbooks are a vital means of presenting large amounts of information that would be difficult to present in any other fashion. Textbook authors and classroom teachers should continually reiterate that every piece of information is dated and biased to some extent, and that the reader must beware. Yet, this is the best way to challenge students to read critically, to challenge standard textbook fare with current information from the journals and elsewhere— which, or course, might be equally inaccurate and biased. So, let us be clear that comprehensive textbooks in areas such as HBSE are probably inescapable, and that it is the duty of teachers and students to read carefully and critically, and to be alert to new information. We agree that practicing the connecting of HBSE information to case situations is important, and requires good teaching, but that is not exactly the topic under discussion.

Third, Dr. Powell speaks of "minor assessment techniques" such as genograms, eco-maps, and the like. He might also have mentioned other "minor assessment skills" like learning to read tables, understand epidemiological terms and statistical notations, or comprehend the intellectual background for some current topic. I would interpret all of these as assessment skills in the broadest sense, the very sense that HBSE seeks to instill in students. These and others like them are absolutely critical to a thinking social worker, and thus represent an important part of the business of HBSE.

However, assessment skills are exactly what HBSE is about, as I argue in my YES statement—providing the knowledge base for making an intelligent assessment in every social work case and situation. I conclude by emphasizing that HBSE-based assessment skills are the essence of social work and thus constitute an extraordinary contribution of this knowledge-building course.